Rebirth in Early Buddhism and Current Research

Rebirth in Early Buddhism & Current Research

Bhikkhu Anālayo

Forewords by

His Holiness the Dalai Lama

and

Bhante Gunaratana

Wisdom

Wisdom Publications
132 Perry Street
New York, NY 10014 USA
wisdom.org

Library of Congress Cataloging-in-Publication Data
Names: Anālayo, 1962– author.
Title: Rebirth in early Buddhism and current research / Anālayo.
Description: Somerville, MA: Wisdom Publications, 2018. | Includes bibliographical references and index. |
Identifiers: LCCN 2017037682 (print) | LCCN 2017041117 (ebook) | ISBN 9781614294627 (ebook) | ISBN 9781614294467 (hardcover)
Subjects: LCSH: Reincarnation—Buddhism. | BISAC: RELIGION / Buddhism / History. | RELIGION / Buddhism / Rituals & Practice. | BODY, MIND & SPIRIT / Reincarnation.
Classification: LCC BQ4485 (ebook) | LCC BQ4485 .A53 2018 (print) | DDC 294.3/4237—dc23
LC record available at https://lccn.loc.gov/2017037682

ISBN 978-1-61429-991-2 ebook ISBN 978-1-61429-462-7

29 28 27 26 25
5 4 3 2 1

Cover and interior design by Gopa & Ted2, Inc. Set in Diacritical Garamond Premier Pro 11.25/14.9. Cover image courtesy of Eric R. and John C. Huntington, The Huntington Archive at The Ohio State University. The index was not compiled by the author.

As an act of Dhammadāna, Anālayo has waived royalty payments for this book.

Printed on acid-free paper that meets the guidelines for permanence and durability of the Production Guidelines for Book Longevity of the Council on Library Resources.

Printed in Canada.

MIX
Paper | Supporting responsible forestry
FSC www.fsc.org FSC® C103567

Please visit fscus.org.

Contents

Foreword by His Holiness the Dalai Lama ix

Foreword by Bhante Gunaratana xiii

Acknowledgments xvi

Abbreviations xvii

Introduction 1

I. The Early Buddhist Doctrine of Rebirth 5

Introduction 5

1. Dependent Arising 6

The Twelve Links 7

Consciousness and Name-and-Form 9

Dependent Arising and Rebirth 12

Rebirth and the Underlying Tendencies 15

2. Recollection of Past Lives and the Intermediate Existence 18

The Buddha's Preawakening Recollection of Past Lives 18

The Buddha's Preawakening Witnessing of the Rebirth of Others 19

The Intermediate Existence 20

3. The Principle of Karma 22

Karma and Its Fruit 23

Karma and Right View 25

4. The Significance of Right View 27

The Denial of Rebirth 28

Different Types of Right View 30
Speculation and Direct Knowledge 32
Summary 34

II. Debates on Rebirth 37

Introduction 37

1. The Undeclared Questions 37
Right View and Speculative Views 37
The Poisoned Arrow of Speculative Views 39
The Reason for Setting Aside Speculative Views 41
The Destiny of an Awakened One after Death 42

2. Debating Rebirth in Ancient India 44
Misunderstandings of the Teaching on Rebirth 44
Experiments to Prove the Materialist Position 45
Continuity without an Unchanging Agent 48

3. Discussions on Rebirth in China during the Early Imperial Period 50
Arguments against Rebirth and Karma 51
Defending the Rebirth Doctrine 53
Near-Death Experiences in Ancient China 55

4. Debates on Rebirth in Modern Times 56
Misinterpretations of Karma and Rebirth 56
Confirmation Bias 60

Summary 62

III. Evidence Considered Supportive of Rebirth 65

Introduction 65

1. Near-Death Experiences 66
From Ancient to Contemporary Reports of Near-Death Experiences 67
The Case of Pam Reynolds 72

Verified Information Apparently Obtained During Near-Death Experiences 74
Children and the Blind 77
2. Past-Life Regression 80
The Workings of Memory 81
Therapeutic Benefits 83
Verified Information Apparently Obtained from Past-Life Regression 85
3. Children's Memories of a Past Life 89
Specific Information Recalled and Behavioral Continuities 91
Cases Documented Before Verification Attempts 99
Birthmarks and Birth Defects 108
4. Xenoglossy 113
Recitative Xenoglossy 113
Responsive Xenoglossy 114
Summary 116

IV. CASE STUDY IN PĀLI XENOGLOSSY 119
Introduction 119
1. The Case History 119
Personal Contacts 119
The Present-Life Story 120
The Past-Life Story and a Verification of the Recordings 122
2. The Chanted Texts and Their Background 125
The Transmission of the Pāli Canon 125
Textual Memory 126
The Chanted Texts 127
3. Errors and Variants 129
Memory Errors 130

Minor Variants 136
Major Variants 144
4. Omissions and Additions 148
Loss of Text 148
The Brain in the Listing of Anatomical Parts 151
The Devas' *Acclaim of the Buddha's First Sermon* 154
Summary 162
Conclusion 163
Transcriptions 167
Introduction 167
DN 15 *Mahānidāna-sutta* 168
DN 16 *Mahāparinibbāna-sutta* 174
DN 22 *Mahāsatipaṭṭhāna-sutta* 179
SN 22.59 *Anattalakkhaṇa-sutta* 209
SN 46.14 *Gilāna-sutta* (1) 213
SN 46.15 *Gilāna-sutta* (2) 214
SN 46.16 *Gilāna-sutta* (3) 215
SN 56.11 *Dhammacakkappavattana-sutta* 216
AN 10.60 *Girimānanda-sutta* 222
Khp 5 / Sn 258–69 *(Mahā-)maṅgala-sutta* 226
Khp 6 / Sn 222–38 *Ratana-sutta* 228
Khp 9 / Sn 143–52 *Metta-sutta* 232
Dhp *Dhammapada* 234
References 237
Index 273
About the Author 281

Foreword by His Holiness the Dalai Lama

I welcome the publication of this book examining the concept of rebirth, the idea accepted by most Buddhists that our lives have no beginning and that we move from one life to the next. Since Buddhists of all traditions accept that the scriptures preserved in Pāli are the earliest record of what the Buddha taught, Bhikkhu Anālayo's confirmation that rebirth is clearly explained there in the context of dependent arising and karma is valuable. He also highlights the commonly accepted accounts that recollection of his own previous lives and the lives of others had a vivid place in the Buddha's own experience of awakening.

Dignāga, the great Indian logician of the fifth–sixth century, examined the idea of rebirth extensively. He pointed out that when we talk about material things, we have to consider substantial causes and cooperative conditions. Our physical bodies, for example, are composed of particles. Each particle has a substantial cause, and we could theoretically trace these back to the Big Bang and even beyond that. Therefore we conclude that the particles that make up the material world have no beginning.

Just as there are no beginnings on a physical level, consciousness, too, is without a beginning. Dignāga argued that the substantial cause of consciousness must be of the same nature as consciousness. He asserted that, while matter can provide cooperative conditions in terms of our sense organs, brain, and nervous system, matter cannot be the substantial cause of consciousness. The substantial cause of consciousness must be of the same nature as consciousness. In other words, each moment of consciousness is preceded by an earlier moment of consciousness; therefore we say that consciousness has no beginning—and it is on that basis that we describe the theory of rebirth.

I share Bhikkhu Anālayo's goal of trying to understand things as they really are, so I am happy to see that he reviews here debates about rebirth before looking at other evidence. In discussions I have been holding with modern scientists for more than thirty years, I have noticed a shift from their earlier assumption that consciousness was no more than a function of the brain to an acknowledgment of neuroplasticity, and recognition that the relationship between mind and brain may be more interdependent than they thought. I have also asked whether, when a perfect sperm meets a perfect ovum in a perfect womb, the conception of a conscious being will automatically occur. Scientists concede that it will not but are unable to explain why. Buddhist science explains that the additional factor to consider is the presence of consciousness.

Bhikkhu Anālayo draws attention to reports of children who remember previous lives. I have come across several such children myself. In the early 1980s I met a couple of girls, one from Patiala and another from Kanpur in India, who had very clear memories of their past lives. They clearly and convincingly recognized their former parents, as well as where they had lived in their previous lives. More recently, I met a boy who was born in Lhasa, Tibet. Insisting that his birthplace was not his home, he urged his parents to take him to India. First they brought him to Dharamsala, where I live, but he continued to insist, "This is not where I'm from; my place is in South India." Eventually he led his parents to Gaden Monastery, found his previous house, and pointed out his former room. When they went in, he said, "If you look in this box you'll find my glasses," which indeed they did.

A similar story relates to the grandson of a Tibetan friend living in America. I recognized the boy as the reincarnation of a lama my friend had known. However, the boy's father did not want his son to be recognized and brought up as a reincarnate lama and sent him to school instead. The grandfather told me that eventually the boy spoke up of his own accord, saying, "This is not where I'm supposed to be. I should be in India at Drepung Loseling Monastery." In the end, the father accepted the situation and allowed him to join the monastery.

My mother used to tell me that when I was young I had clear memories of my past life. These faded as I got older, and now I can't even remember what happened yesterday. When I recently met the young boy who came from Lhasa to join his monastery, I asked him if he still remembered his past life, and he told me he did not. I was glad to know I am not the only one whose previous-life recollections have vanished.

The case Bhikkhu Anālayo cites, of a young boy able to recite Pāli from a bygone era that he is unlikely to have encountered in any other way, also corresponds to my experience. I have heard about people who can recite texts and verses that they have not knowingly memorized, and of course there are many who can memorize texts with unaccountable ease, as if they already knew them. That they have knowledge from previous lives seems an appropriate explanation. Such things happen, but so far science has no explanation for what is going on. However, I know several scientists who are interested in looking into this.

I agree with Bhikkhu Anālayo that the purpose of the exploration presented in these pages is not to impose a particular point of view, but to provide the opportunity for better understanding based on analysis and discussion. Many people predict that the twenty-first century will be a time when we really come to understand the way the brain works. If this is true, it will necessarily be a time when we develop a better understanding of the workings of the mind, too. I believe that such circumstances will throw light on the question of rebirth. Science may yet discover convincing evidence that rebirth is impossible. In the meantime, I recommend that interested readers take the Buddha's advice when he urged the monks who followed him to examine and investigate what he had said as a goldsmith tests gold by heating, cutting, and rubbing it. Read the evidence here, think about it, weigh it against your own experience, and make up your own minds.

Foreword by Bhante Gunaratana

THE BUDDHA GAINED DIRECT KNOWLEDGE of rebirth during the night he attained enlightenment. When he saw his own countless previous lives, and those of other living beings dying and taking rebirth according to their karma, he began to investigate the reason for this repetition of birth and death. Then he understood dependent arising (*paṭicca samuppāda*). He started with birth and receded until he discovered the ignorance that causes craving leading up to the committing of karma. The force that projects forward to the next birth is consciousness fully charged with karma, craving, and ignorance. Because craving links this life with the next, the Buddha called it a seamstress. Craving clings to objects—physical or mental. This is the driving force or the magnet that attracts a suitable place for rebirth to occur.

Feelings, perceptions, formations, and consciousness, together with craving, karma, and ignorance: these immaterial mental factors join the material factors to make a life. All of them are changing constantly and rapidly, which makes it impossible to ascertain experientially in what way exactly rebirth is taking place. Materialists, for this reason, unequivocally reject the teaching of rebirth. In societies where most people do not believe in rebirth, children who speak of their own previous-life experiences are discouraged and ignored. In societies where the majority of people believe in rebirth, adults pay special attention to children who say numerous things about their own previous-life experiences. The memories of young children with exceptional skills and capabilities—memories beyond what is possible at such a young age, such as those on a tape I heard over forty years ago—point to the spiritual reality of rebirth.

The hearing of that tape happened when I was living in the Washington Buddhist Vihāra between 1968 and 1988, the first Theravāda Buddhist temple in the United States. One day in the early 1970s, somebody gave me a cassette tape saying, "Please listen to this tape." I listened to it and found the very sweet voice of a little child chanting in Pāli. His Pāli pronunciation was very clear. His chanting style was unique—I had never heard such a chanting style before. I made copies of the tape and shared it with many people. Everyone who listened to his chanting was deeply touched. Finally, I decided to see this child.

In 1985, I stopped in Sri Lanka on my way to Australia. While in Sri Lanka, I contacted a friend of mine and mentioned that I had listened to this child's chanting and asked him where I could find this child. He himself did not know. But he took me to Bhikkhu Panadure Ariyadhamma, who was very popular at that time for his Bodhipūja chanting. After casual conversation, I asked him whether he knew this child's whereabouts. He gave me an address somewhere in Kandy. Since a friend offered to drive me there, I went to that address. I made three trips from Colombo to Kandy, looking for this child. Each time I was informed that nobody knew where he was.

Giving up on finding him, I went on to Australia, my next stop, to give some Dhamma talks and lead meditation retreats. Two ladies and a man drove me to a meditation center at Wiseman Ferry for the retreat. It was almost two hours' drive from Sydney. The driver was Elizabeth Gorski. On the way, I asked her whether she had heard a little Sri Lankan boy's chanting of Pāli *sutta*s. As her reply was affirmative, I asked her whether she had seen him.

"Yes," she said.

"I traveled to Sri Lanka and went three times to an address somebody gave me to meet him, without any success. Do you know where he is now?"

"Bhante, you are sitting with him right now in my car," was her reply.

The young man sitting with me on the back seat in her car was Dhammaruwan. I turned to him and asked why he had not spoken to me all that time. He said: "Since I did not have anything to say, I did not speak."

This young man provided me with his own personal experience of rebirth. Even though I have met several people who had past-life memories, this was the first time I had met someone who could give me a very vivid and detailed account of his own past-life experience. This was my first meeting with him. Since then, he has come to Australia each time I have been there to teach Dhamma. He has also been to the Bhāvanā Society Forest Monastery and Meditation Center in West Virginia several times. During a recent visit, he requested ordination. I ordained him on April 10, 2016, and named him Samādhikusala.

The Pāli chants by Dhammaruwan (now Bhikkhu Samādhikusala) have been studied in detail by Bhikkhu Anālayo. His indispensable book on rebirth has come at a timely moment, when the subject of rebirth has long been in discussion. Bhikkhu Anālayo's study makes an important contribution to understanding the theory of karma and rebirth in early Buddhist thought. His scholarly discussion of the subject is bound to draw the attention even of modern skeptics. Seldom can one find such a comprehensive analysis of rebirth as Bhikkhu Anālayo's profound presentation in this book. I am sure that, even though there are several publications on this subject, the discussion Bhikkhu Anālayo presents here offers an unparalleled perspective on karma and rebirth, both for believers and for nonbelievers.

Henepola Gunaratana Mahāthera
Bhāvanā Society, West Virginia, USA

Acknowledgments

I AM INDEBTED to Adam Clarke, Bhikkhunī Dhammadinnā, Linda Grace, Robert Grosch, Dhivan Thomas Jones, and Michael Running for comments on a draft version of this study.

Abbreviations

AN	*Aṅguttara-nikāya*
B^{e}	Burmese edition
Catubh	*Catubhāṇavārapāḷi*
CBETA	Chinese Buddhist Electronic Tripiṭaka Association
C^{e}	Ceylonese edition
D	Derge edition
DĀ	*Dīrgha-āgama* (T 1)
Dhp	*Dhammapada*
DN	*Dīgha-nikāya*
EĀ	*Ekottarika-āgama* (T 125)
E^{e}	PTS edition
Jā	*Jātaka*
Khp	*Khuddakapāṭha*
MĀ	*Madhyama-āgama* (T 26)
Mil	*Milindapañha*
MN	*Majjhima-nikāya*
Mp	*Manorathapūraṇī* (commentary on AN)
NDE	near-death experience
Paṭis	*Paṭisambhidāmagga*
Ps	*Papañcasūdanī* (commentary on MN)
PTS	Pali Text Society
Q	*Qian-long* (Peking) edition

SĀ	*Saṃyukta-āgama* (T 99)
SĀ[2]	*Saṃyukta-āgama* (T 100)
S[e]	Siamese edition
SHT	Sanskrithandschriften aus den Turfanfunden
SN	*Saṃyutta-nikāya*
Sn	*Sutta-nipāta*
Spk	*Sāratthappakāsinī* (commentary on SN)
Sv	*Sumaṅgalavilāsinī* (commentary on DN)
T	Taishō edition (CBETA digital version)
Ud	*Udāna*
Vibh	*Vibhaṅga*
Vin	*Vinayapiṭaka*
Vism	*Visuddhimagga*

Introduction

THE PRESENT INVESTIGATION has its starting point in the writing of an article at the request of friends for the purpose of clarifying the parameters of the early Buddhist doctrine of rebirth. While writing this article, it occurred to me to take a closer look at recordings of Pāli chants recited spontaneously and from memory by a small Sri Lankan child, whom I knew from the time I lived in Sri Lanka myself in the 1990s, by which time he had already become an adult. This brought to light support for his recollection of having learned these chants in the long-distant past, making it clear that they deserved a study more detailed than is possible within the confines of an article. In order to contextualize my findings, I also started to read up on various areas of research related to rebirth. This in turn made me realize that I had entered a minefield of at times firmly entrenched opinions regarding rebirth, leading me to investigate historical antecedents for the current debates on this topic. These four trajectories inform the four chapters of this book.

In the first chapter I study the early Buddhist doctrine of rebirth, in particular the teachings on dependent arising in relation to rebirth, recollection of past lives as an aspect of the Buddha's awakening, the law of karma held to be governing rebirth, and the importance accorded to the doctrine of rebirth as part of right view, the forerunner and foundation of the early Buddhist path to awakening.

With the second chapter I turn to debates on rebirth, starting with relevant instances from early Buddhist texts. I continue with snapshots of debating strategies from later sources in India, in China during the first centuries of its reception of Buddhism, and up to modern times. In relation to current debates, I also take up the issue of "confirmation bias" or "my-side bias," a recurrent tendency in discussions on rebirth to read data in such a way that it conforms to one's own preconceived notions.

The third chapter offers a survey of current research on rebirth. I begin with near-death experiences, with a particular focus on apparently verified perceptions during comatose conditions. Next I take up past-life regression, again with an emphasis on seemingly verified information obtained in this manner. Then I turn to reports of children who believe they are remembering past lives. The final topic in this survey is xenoglossy, an ability to speak languages that do not seem to have been learned previously in this life.

A study of a selection of Pāli chants recited spontaneously by a child in Sri Lanka forms the subject of the fourth chapter. After a survey of relevant background information, I compare the texts he recited with extant editions of the Pāli canon, showing the degree to which such comparison supports his remembrance that he learned these chants during a past life. An appendix at the end of the present volume has transcriptions of the Pāli chants studied in this chapter.

Although they stand in a thematic continuity, these four chapters cover different areas. This makes it quite possible that not all of my detailed presentations will be of equal interest to most readers. To help navigate the material presented in the following pages, I have provided summaries at the end of each chapter. Besides summarizing the main points covered, my intention is also to enable readers to consult first only the summary of a chapter whose topic does not naturally fall within their personal sphere of interest and then decide whether and to what extent they wish to follow up by reading the full discussion.

My interest throughout is to clarify and present information as truthfully as possible, not to campaign for acceptance of Buddhist doctrine. The early Buddhist scriptures contain passages that, at least on a literal reading, are not compatible with contemporary scientific knowledge. One example is the description of fish of a size that exceeds the depth of the ocean.[1] Another is a succession of kings of which the first lived for

1. AN 8.19 at AN IV 200,7 describes aquatic animals of the size of 500 *yojanas*, its parallels MĀ 35 at T 1.26.476b3 and EĀ 42.4 at T 2.125.753a11 even of the size of 700 *yojanas*. According to Skilling 1998, one *yojana* corresponds to about seven miles. Thus a single

more than 300,000 years.[2] Such instances make it impossible, in my view, to adopt a literal reading of such texts as definite and accurate reflections of reality. Instead, such descriptions are best understood as reflecting the symbolic function of numbers in an oral literature whose concerns are simply different from modern-day descriptions of scientific facts.

I would also like to mention that for me personally rebirth is not a crucial issue; in fact prior to being requested to write on this topic I had not given it much attention in my writings.[3] If I were to encounter strong compelling scientific evidence that rebirth is just impossible, I would certainly be very surprised, but this would not result in a major change in my personal lifestyle and practice. Although I do not depend on the results of the present research to confirm my personal beliefs, as a Buddhist monastic I am clearly sympathetic to the idea of rebirth.[4] My own sympathetic disposition in this respect has a counterbalance in my academic training as a university professor. I visualize my two roles as a meditating monastic and an academic researcher as having a converging point in an attempt to understand things as they really are, *yathābhūta*, in their conditionality and from the viewpoint of their historical development. This quest for understanding has informed all my other research and personal practice and, similarly, is my overarching concern in the present case.

---

yojana roughly equals the maximum depth of the ocean at the Mariana Trench (Vism 206,4 describes a mountain that reaches 84,000 *yojana*s into the sea, reflecting a notion of the depth of the ocean that would indeed be able to accommodate aquatic animals of the size mentioned in AN 8.19 and its parallels).

2. MN 83 at MN II 78,8 and its parallels MĀ 67 at T 1.26.514b5 and EĀ 50.4 at T 2.125.809a22 describe 84,000 generations of kings, the first of which lived four times 84,000 years (i.e., 336,000 years), the other kings being either implicitly or explicitly of a similar lifespan. Such a description can hardly be reconciled with the fossil evidence we have for the evolution of species and the coming into existence of *Homo erectus*.

3. Out of my over three hundred academic publications in the field of Buddhist studies, only a single article is concerned with the topic of rebirth, Anālayo 2008b, the compilation of which was motivated by the wish to investigate the significance of the term *gandhabba* (the text I study in Anālayo 2012b and 2013b relates to rebirth, but my studies focus on the debate character of the discourse).

4. It may be worth noting that well-known monks in the Thai tradition rejected the rebirth doctrine. On the skeptic attitude of King Mongkut, during the time when he was still a monk, regarding the existence of heaven and hell or any kind of future state of rebirth see, e.g., Bradley 1966, 39 and Reynolds 1976, 212; on Ajahn Buddhadasa's metaphorical reading of canonical references to rebirth see, e.g., Gabaude 1990, 214 and Seeger 2005, 111–15.

I. The Early Buddhist Doctrine of Rebirth

Introduction

In this chapter I survey selected passages from discourses spoken according to tradition by the Buddha or his contemporary disciples. These discourses are found in the Pāli *Nikāya*s and their parallels, preserved in the Chinese *Āgama*s as well as at times extant as Indic-language fragments or in Tibetan translation.[5] These reflect the earliest stage of the rebirth doctrine in the history of Buddhist thought that has been preserved in textual records and thereby take us as close to the time of the Buddha as possible within the limits of the textual witnesses still available to us. The position on rebirth reflected in these texts and its implications do not necessarily correspond to later expositions of this doctrine in various Buddhist traditions, so it would not be correct to assume that there is some sort of unified Buddhist doctrine of rebirth.

The discourses that are the mainstay of my exploration in this chapter are the final product of different lineages of oral transmission of the texts of early Buddhism, a term approximately reflecting the first two centuries in the history of Buddhism until the time of King Asoka. Comparative study of the final results of such transmission lineages enables reconstruction of the beginning stages of Buddhist doctrine, based on discerning the common core and identifying variations among these texts.[6]

In order to reflect the textual basis required for a reliable reconstruction of early Buddhist thought, in the footnotes to my discussion I list

5. On the Chinese *Āgama*s see in more detail Anālayo 2015.

6. In Anālayo 2012c I argue that material common to parallel versions can with considerable probability be reckoned as earlier than those parts that differ.

the parallel versions to a particular passage in question. Moreover, as part of my exploration I present translations of the Chinese *Āgama* version of a passage of particular interest in the main text, since for the most part these are not yet available in English translation. This is to enable the interested reader to follow up a particular passage and compare the Chinese version translated by me with the corresponding Pāli parallel, translations of which are more readily available.

In approaching the early discourses for information on any particular doctrine, it needs to be kept in mind that these texts reflect a soteriological orientation whose concerns are more of a prescriptive type than predominantly descriptive. Unlike attempts in later traditions to provide complete maps of the territory to be crossed, the early discourses content themselves with pointing out the main signposts of the path to be traveled. Thus what can be discovered are snapshots of the network of ideas that inform the early Buddhist conception of rebirth, not a complete coverage that provides explanations of every aspect of rebirth.

The topics I will be examining in this chapter are dependent arising as the doctrinal background for the early Buddhist conception of rebirth (1), the recollection of one's own past lives and the intermediate existence (2), the principle of karma that underpins the rebirth doctrine (3), and the significance of the affirmation of a continuity beyond a single life as part of right view, the forerunner of the path to awakening in early Buddhist soteriology (4).

1. Dependent Arising

A central aspect of early Buddhist thought is the doctrine of dependent arising (*paṭicca samuppāda*). The early discourses consider dependent arising to be such a key doctrine among the teachings of the Buddha that the seeing of *paṭicca samuppāda* equates to seeing the Dharma.[7] In what follows I first explore the common presentation of dependent arising by way of twelve links and then turn to two of the links in particular: consciousness and name-and-form.

7. MN 28 at MN I 190,37 and its parallel MĀ 30 at T 1.26.467a9.

The Twelve Links

The most common form of presentation for the teaching on dependent arising involves twelve links, which are:

- ignorance
- (volitional) formations
- consciousness
- name-and-form
- six senses
- contact
- feeling
- craving
- clinging
- becoming
- birth
- old age and death

According to contemporary scholarship, this formulation of dependent arising by way of twelve links probably involves an implicit criticism of a Vedic creation myth.[8] Instead of describing the creation of the world, the point made is to reveal the conditioned genesis of *dukkha*. The term *dukkha*, often and somewhat misleadingly translated as "suffering," is a term whose meaning ranges from what is outright painful to what is of an unsatisfactory nature.[9] To emerge from the predicament of being afflicted by *dukkha* is the goal of the early Buddhist path of practice.

The chief aspect of the early Buddhist doctrine of dependent arising is the principle of specific conditionality itself, which operates in relation to each of the twelve links. A succinct and recurrent formulation of the principle of specific conditionality, found, for example, in a discourse in the *Saṃyukta-āgama*, reads as follows:[10]

> Because there is this, that is; because this arises, that arises.

8. Jurewicz 2000; see also Gombrich 2003, 11–14 and Jones 2009.

9. See the discussion in Anālayo 2003, 243–45.

10. SĀ 348 at T 2.99.98a16–17.

Parallels in the *Saṃyutta-nikāya* and in Sanskrit fragments report similar statements.[11] The same principle of specific conditionality also informs the cessation mode of dependent arising, in that with the removal of ignorance the remaining links also come to an end.

An application of the basic principle of specific conditionality can alternatively take up shorter listings, which can cover only five, nine, or ten links. The discourses present several such variant listings, confirming that the twelve-link presentation is just a particularly prominent exemplification of the basic principle of specific conditionality.

The term "birth," *jāti*, as part of the standard expositions of dependent arising should, according to a discourse in the *Saṃyutta-nikāya* and its parallels, be understood to refer to the birth of living beings.[12] Later exegesis interprets this twelve-link model as extending over three consecutive lifetimes. Such an interpretation can be found in the *Jñānaprasthāna*, for example, an important canonical work in the Sarvāstivāda Abhidharma collection.[13] In contrast the *Vibhaṅga*, an early and similarly important canonical work in the Theravāda Abhidharma collection, presents an alternative mode of interpretation of the standard depiction of dependent arising, which applies each of the twelve links to a single mind moment.[14] This at first sight striking difference is not school-specific. The three-life interpretation can also be found in the *Paṭisambhidāmagga*, a work of Abhidharmic nature found in the fifth basket of the Theravāda Pāli canon,[15] whose presentation in several respects builds on the

11. SN 12.22 at SN II 28,18 (to be supplemented from the preceding discourse, SN 12.21 at SN II 28,7) and SHT VI 1457 R1, Bechert and Wille 1989, 143, and Waldschmidt 1958, 388 (§3); see also Speyer 1909/1970, 105,15.

12. SN 12.2 at SN II 3,6 and its parallels in Sanskrit fragments, Tripāṭhī 1962, 162,7 (§16.14), as well as in SĀ 298 at T 2.99.85b11, T 2.124.547c24, and D 4094 *ju* 140b1 or Q 5595 *tu* 161a8.

13. T 26.1544.921b17 states that two links pertain to the past (ignorance and formations), two to the future (birth and old age together with death), and the remaining eight links pertain to the present.

14. Vibh 144,2; on the interpretation that understands birth to refer to the momentary arising of a mental event, proposed by Buddhadāsa, see, e.g., Bucknell and Stuart-Fox 1983, 104 and Seeger 2005.

15. Paṭis I 52,19.

Vibhaṅga.[16] Conversely, a massive compendium that builds on the *Jñāna-prasthāna*, the **Mahāvibhāṣā*,[17] asserts that the operation of all twelve links could take place within a single mind moment.[18] In sum, it seems that, from the perspective of Sarvāstivāda and Theravāda Abhidharma and exegesis, the two interpretations proposed are not mutually exclusive, but rather complementary perspectives.

These complementary presentations in early Abhidharma and exegetical compendia can be considered to agree with what also emerges from a study of the early discourses, in that the doctrine of dependent arising concerns a basic principle of conditionality that, although not confined to rebirth, nevertheless most certainly applies to being reborn.

Consciousness and Name-and-Form

A detailed exposition of dependent arising can be found in the *Mahānidāna-sutta* and its parallels, which offer indications that are significant for a proper appreciation of the early Buddhist doctrine of rebirth. The teaching in this discourse is addressed by the Buddha to his personal attendant Ānanda with the express purpose of throwing into relief the profundity of dependent arising.

This exposition in the *Mahānidāna-sutta* and its parallels traces dependent arising back from old age and death via birth and so on, until reaching the conditional dependence of name-and-form on consciousness. Next the *Mahānidāna-sutta* and its parallels present consciousness and name-and-form as standing in a reciprocal conditional relationship to each other, a relationship that in turn helps to appreciate the early Buddhist conception of rebirth.

The *Dīrgha-āgama* parallel to the *Mahānidāna-sutta* formulates this reciprocal relationship in the following way, a statement found similarly in the parallel versions:[19]

16. See, e.g., Warder 1982, xxxv.

17. See, e.g., Cox 1995, 34.

18. T 27.1545.118c7.

19. DĀ 13 at T 1.1.61b20, with parallels in DN 15 at DN II 56,31, MĀ 97 at T 1.26.580a1, T 1.14.243c2, and T 1.52.845b11.

> Name-and-form conditions consciousness and consciousness conditions name-and-form.

This statement requires some unpacking. In early Buddhist thought, "consciousness" stands for the mind's ability to be conscious of something. "Form" represents the material side of experience, which also includes the fine-material dimension of celestial realms recognized in early Buddhist cosmology. "Name" stands for the functions of the mind apart from consciousness.[20] In the context of dependent arising an understanding of name as including consciousness, such as found in later tradition, would not work. On such a reading, the reciprocal conditional relationship between consciousness and name-and-form would result in presenting consciousness as self-conditioning.

According to a definition found in a discourse in the *Saṃyutta-nikāya* and its *Ekottarika-āgama* parallel, "name" stands for the following mental factors:[21]

- feeling
- perception
- intention
- contact
- attention

In the context of the early Buddhist analysis of experience, "feeling" represents the hedonic tone of experience in terms of it being pleasant, painful, or neutral. "Perception" stands for the matching of experience with

20. See, e.g., Harvey 1993b, 32, Ñāṇamoli 1994, 56, Ñāṇavīra 1987/2001, 76, Hamilton 1996, 125, Reat 1996/1998, 45, Ñāṇananda 2003, 5, Anālayo 2011a, 71n221, and 2017b.

21. SN 12.2 at SN II 3,34 and its parallel EĀ 49.5 at T 2.125.797b28. The same type of definition can also be found, e.g., in MN 9 at MN I 53,11 or EĀ 46.8 at T 2.125.778c24. Skilling 1993, 158 notes a discourse quotation in Vasubandhu's *Pratītyasamutpāda-vyākhyā* that defines "name" with the help of the factors feeling, perception, intention, contact, and attention. Probably under the influence of later developments, discourses preserved by Mūlasarvāstivāda and Sarvāstivāda transmission lineages instead tend to define "name" as equivalent to the four immaterial aggregates, thereby including consciousness; see, e.g., MĀ 29 at T 1.26.463c25, SĀ 298 at T 2.99.85a28, Tripāṭhī 1962, 160,1 (§16.7), and D 4094 *ju* 140a3 or Q 5595 *tu* 160b8.

concepts and thereby for cognition and recognition. "Intention" covers the purposive dimension, that which reacts to experience or its potential. "Contact" ensures the conjunction of the other factors in experience, their coming together in a particular time- and space-instant with the material dimension of contact taking the form of the experience of resistance (*paṭigha*) and the nominal dimension of contact taking the form of designation (*adhivacana*). "Attention" is responsible for noticing and observing a particular aspect out of whatever situation is experienced.

These aspects of the mind in conjunction are responsible for the coming into being of "name," that is, for the formation of concepts, for how we refer to and name things, be this mentally or verbally, and categorize them. Therefore feeling, perception, intention, contact, and attention taken together make up the "name" part in the compound name-and-form. Out of these five factors, volition in the sense of the mental factor of intention is of further importance for appreciating the doctrine of karma, which serves as the background for rebirth in Buddhist thought. I will return to volition later in this chapter.

The range of name-and-form as the conceptual and material aspects of experience encompasses the whole gamut of what is experienced by consciousness. Here name as well as form depend not only on each other but also on consciousness. The conceptual and material properties of an object require consciousness in order to be experienced. In turn, consciousness depends on name-and-form as that which provides the content of what consciousness is aware of.

This reciprocal conditioning of consciousness and name-and-form presents a basic matrix of experience, a continuous interplay between consciousness on the one hand and name-and-form on the other that, according to the early Buddhist analysis, builds up the world of experience. The reciprocal conditioning between consciousness and name-and-form explains the continuity of one's experiences during life without an unchanging agent. It thereby functions as the counterpart to the early Buddhist doctrine of notself, *anattā*, according to which there is no permanent entity in any aspect of experience.[22] In early Buddhist thought,

22. Gombrich 2009, 9 clarifies the implication of the *anattā* doctrine as follows: "all the fuss

the assertion of the doctrine of notself does not imply a denial of the existence of anything subjective in experience. It only means that subjective experience is a process devoid of a permanent entity, that it is a changing stream of consciousness that depends on a changing process of name-and-form, and vice versa.

Here it also needs to be kept in mind that, in contrast to later tradition, early Buddhist thought does not postulate that all phenomena are of only momentary existence and disappear as soon as they have appeared.[23] Instead, in its early Buddhist usage consciousness refers to a continuously changing process of being conscious. Later tradition goes further and envisions consciousness as a staccato-like series of micromoments of being conscious, each of these micromoments passing away immediately on having come into existence. This form of presentation makes the continuity of conscious experience more difficult to appreciate.

By way of illustration, instead of using the noun "consciousness," which could give the misleading impression of a permanent entity, to convey the early Buddhist position one might speak just of "being conscious," thereby better conveying the sense of a process. Only in later times does this process come to be seen as "b-e-i-n-g c-o-n-s-c-i-o-u-s," a series of infinitesimally brief moments that at high speed arise and disappear on the spot.

Dependent Arising and Rebirth

Returning to the *Mahānidāna-sutta* and its parallels, the reciprocal conditioning between the changing processes of consciousness and name-and-form has a direct bearing on the topic of rebirth. The relevant passage proceeds as follows in the *Dīrgha-āgama* version:[24]

---

and misunderstanding can be avoided if one inserts the word 'unchanging', so that the two-word English phrase becomes 'no unchanging self'. . .for the Buddha's audience *by definition* the word *ātman/attā* referred to something unchanging."

23. The theory of momentariness appears to have developed after the closure of the canonical Abhidharmas; see for more detail von Rospatt 1995, 15–28. The assumption by Griffiths 1982, 283–84 that the doctrine of rebirth stands in contrast to the teaching of notself does not hold for the early Buddhist position on rebirth, which does not involve the notion of momentariness.

24. DĀ 13 at T 1.1.61b8–10.

> [The Buddha said]: "Ānanda, in dependence on consciousness there is name-and-form. What is the meaning of this? If consciousness did not enter the mother's womb, would there be name-and-form?" [Ānanda] replied: "No."

The parallel versions report the Buddha making a similar statement.[25] In other words, at the moment of conception the same basic principle is in operation that also governs continuity during the life of an individual. This principle involves a reciprocal conditioning between consciousness and name-and-form. Of these interrelated processes, it is the process of consciousness that "enters" the mother's womb, so to speak, a form of presentation that shows that the early Buddhist conception of rebirth is more complex than a simple mind-body duality.

The role of consciousness as that which is reborn can also be seen in relation to a possible departure of consciousness after conception. Here the *Dīrgha-āgama* version offers the following indication:[26]

> [The Buddha said]: "If consciousness were to depart from the womb, [if] the infant were to be destroyed, would name-and-form come to grow?" [Ānanda] replied: "No."

The corresponding part in three out of the four parallels involves two separate inquiries, one about consciousness departing from the womb, the other about consciousness being cut off in the case of a young boy or girl.[27] The answer in both cases is equally "No." The main point made in

25. DN 15 at DN II 63,1, MĀ 97 at T 1.26.579c16, T 1.14.243b18, and T 1.52.845b7.

26. DĀ 13 at T 1.1.61b11–12.

27. DN 15 at DN II 63,7+11, MĀ 97 at T 1.26.579c18+19, and T 1.14.243b19+21. T 1.52 does not take the form of a question-and-answer catechism and therefore has no direct parallel to the present exchange. The depiction in all versions of a departure of consciousness from the womb would point to the phenomenon of stillbirth. It remains open to speculation whether another stream of consciousness could take the place of the departed one. A somewhat related idea can be found in the report in a Pāli commentary that Sakka, the ruler in the Heaven of the Thirty-Three, during the delivery of the *Sakkapañha-sutta* (DN 21) passed away and was reborn right away in the same body, which happened so quickly that, out of the entire congregation present, only he and the Buddha noticed what happened; see Sv III

this way remains the same in the different versions, in that, for name-and-form to "come to grow," consciousness is the necessary condition, and this applies to conception, pregnancy, and childhood.

Conversely, according to the *Mahāvedalla-sutta* and its *Madhyama-āgama* parallel, at death, when the body will come to be bereft of vitality and heat, consciousness will depart.[28] In this way, consciousness appears to be what provides the transition from one body to another, or, to be precise, instead of "consciousness" one might speak of "being conscious" to preserve the nuance of a changing process. This role of consciousness or of being conscious as a transition from one life to the next finds confirmation in a discourse in the *Saṃyutta-nikāya* and its parallels. The question here is where a monk, who has just died, might have been reborn. The parallel versions agree in referring to what could have been reborn as his "consciousness."[29]

Such rebirth can according to early Buddhist cosmology involve a variety of forms. Besides human and animal rebirth, it can also take the form of rebirth in various celestial realms and thereby occur with a kind of "bodily form" that differs substantially from the material body of humans and animals. Celestial beings are recurrently portrayed in the early discourses as being able to move around at the speed of thought without being obstructed by anything material, all the while being able to see and

---

732,30. Although this case involves the same stream of consciousness being reborn, it does envisage that an already existing body (in this case a celestial one) can continue beyond the moment when consciousness departs, if in some way the needed support for the continuity of name-and-form is provided right away by a stream of consciousness being "reborn." A testimony to a related idea in Tibetan Buddhism would be what Snellgrove 1987, 498 refers to as a "'transfer of consciousness', whereby the adept...injects his 'life principle' into any recently dead body...of his choice." As mentioned above, however, the possibility that the departure of a particular stream of consciousness from the womb could be followed by the entry into the same womb of another stream of consciousness, such that the fetus can continue to live, remains speculative at least as far as the early Buddhist conception of rebirth is concerned, as I am not aware of clear-cut support for this idea among the early discourses.

28. MN 43 at MN I 296,9 and its parallel MĀ 211 at T 1.26.791c12.

29. SN 22.87 at SN III 124,10 and its parallels SĀ 1265 at T 2.99.347b10 and EĀ 26.10 at T 2.125.642c27; for a study and translation see Anālayo 2011b. In this particular case the monk's consciousness did not become established anywhere, as he passed away as an arahant.

hear. A similar ability is also attributed to proficient meditators, who are credited with the creation of a mind-made body that appears to be similar in type to the bodily form of celestial beings of the sense sphere.[30]

An alternative term sometimes used in relation to the process of rebirth is the *gandhabba*, which for want of a better translation one might render as "spirit." The *Assalāyana-sutta* and its parallels quote a statement according to which, for conception to be successful, the parents must unite, the mother has to be in season, and the *gandhabba* needs to be present.[31] The quotation stems from a discussion between a seer and a group of Brahmins, giving the impression that the choice of the term *gandhabba* in the *Assalāyana-sutta* and its parallels reflects terminology used in Brahminical circles, employed here without carrying any implications of a permanent self that it would have carried in its non-Buddhist usage.

Rebirth and the Underlying Tendencies

Further information on consciousness in relation to rebirth can be gathered from a discourse in the *Saṃyutta-nikāya* and its *Saṃyukta-āgama* parallel. According to the relevant statement, what one thinks relates to an underlying tendency in the mind that in turn forms the object for the establishing of consciousness. This then leads on to the dependent arising of birth and so on. The *Saṃyukta-āgama* passage proceeds as follows:[32]

30. On the mind-made body see also the discussions in, e.g., Upadhyaya 1971, 375–76, Eimer 1976, 55, Johansson 1979/1985, 35–39, Hamilton 1996, 144–64, Radich 2007, 224–87, Lee 2014, and Anālayo 2016a.

31. MN 93 at MN II 157,1 and its parallels MĀ 151 at T 1.26.666a10 and D 4094 *ju* 111a6 or Q 5595 *tu* 127b1. Another parallel, T 1.71.878b5, speaks rather of what "becomes the child," 為作子者. The *gandhabba* recurs as one of the three conditions for conception in MN 38 at MN I 265,36 and its parallel MĀ 201 at T 1.26.769b24, whereas another parallel, EĀ 21.3 at T 2.125.602c19, speaks rather of the "external consciousness," 外識, and in the next line of the "consciousness that wishes [to be reborn]," 欲識. On the *gandhabba* see also, e.g., Pischel and Geldner 1889, 77–81, Oldenberg 1894, 244–50, Windisch 1908, 14–27, Malalasekera 1937/1995, 746, Masson 1942, 121–23, Wijesekera 1945/1994, Upadhyaya 1971, 373–75, Wayman 1974, 231–34, McDermott 1980, 169–71, Hoffman 1987, 67–69, Karunaratne 1991, Harvey 1995, 105–8, Cuevas 1996, Langer 2000, 9–17, Blum 2004, 204, Oberlies 2005, Premasiri 2005, 525, Somaratne 2005, 176–77, Anālayo 2008b, Werner 2008, 38, and Hara 2009, 220–21.

32. SĀ 359 at T 2.99.100a24–26.

> If one intends, if one gives rise to deluded conceptualizations, those underlying tendencies form an object for the establishment of consciousness. Because there is an object for the establishment of consciousness, there is future birth, old age, disease, and death.

The *Saṃyutta-nikāya* discourse has basically the same statement.[33] In early Buddhist thought the underlying tendencies, *anusaya*, are latent dispositions in the mind. The present passage relates these tendencies underlying one's deluded thought processes to rebirth via their providing a basis for the continuity of consciousness in *saṃsāra*.

Such underlying tendencies are considered to be already present in an infant, even though a baby would not yet be in a position to display the corresponding mental states and actions. Here is a passage from the *Madhyama-āgama* that describes this state of affairs:[34]

> A young tender infant, sleeping on its back, has no notion of sensual pleasure in its mental faculty; how could its mind become entangled in sensual desire? Yet, because of the nature of its underlying tendency, one speaks of its underlying tendency to sensual desire...
>
> A young tender infant, sleeping on its back, has no notion of a living being in its mental faculty; how could its mind become entangled in hatred? Yet, because of the nature of its underlying tendency, one speaks of its underlying tendency to hatred.

33. The corresponding passage in SN 12.39 at SN II 66,8 reads: "what one intends, what one thinks about, what one has an underlying tendency toward, that is an object for the establishing of consciousness. There being an object, there is a support for consciousness. Consciousness being supported and coming to grow, there is the future production of renewed existence. There being the future production of renewed existence, there is future birth, old age, and death."

34. MĀ 205 at T 1.26.778c25–29.

Parallel versions to this passage take the same position.[35] Judging from these passages, the underlying tendencies accompany consciousness at the time of conception. In other words, consciousness at the time of conception is not seen as just a *tabula rasa* but rather carries with it, in a way that the early discourses do not further specify, imprints from the past life. This type of residual memory, if one may call it such, continues from one life to another. From an early Buddhist perspective, it thereby becomes an important source of influence on the newborn, in addition to hereditary traits resulting from the parents and the influences exerted by the environment.

The reciprocal conditioning of consciousness and name-and-form at the same time implies that this continuity of memory is in itself a changing and conditioned process. One of the conditions that influence the accessibility of memories from the past life would be the degree to which new memories from the present life impact the mind. Moreover, various more somatic skills, such as being able to walk, are not readily present to the infant, even though they were learned in a previous existence, but have to be acquired anew. Although such details are not worked out in the early discourses, the type of continuity envisaged clearly does not result in a completely identical replica of the mental knowledge, skills, and abilities of the previous person. By way of example, one might perhaps think of a river that, after running swiftly down a steep course, due to the geographical conditions turns into a lake that has an outlet on its opposite side. Much of the dirt carried along in the river by the swift flow of the water will sink to the ground once the water has entered the lake. The water that flows out of the lake, although clearly standing in continuity with the water that entered it, will no longer carry along such dirt. Similar to the flow of water into and out of the lake, the early Buddhist conception of rebirth involves a continuity from one life to another that does not imply a complete identity of its earlier and later manifestations.

35. MN 64 at MN I 433,11 and D 4094 *ju* 260a6 or Q 5595 *thu* 2b3; parts of the discussion of the underlying tendencies have also been preserved in SHT V 1279 V8–R5, Sander and Waldschmidt 1985, 202.

2. Recollection of Past Lives and the Intermediate Existence

According to the early Buddhist discourses, residual memories that have been carried over from one existence to another, even though usually not remembered in the normal waking state, can be retrieved through the cultivation of deep states of concentration and mindfulness. Such cultivation would enable access to what normally appear to be subconscious regions of the mind.

The Buddha's Preawakening Recollection of Past Lives

The Buddha himself is said to have developed this ability on the night of his awakening. The *Bhayabherava-sutta* and its parallel report the Buddha describing his own preawakening recollection of past lives, notably showing him as having no qualms in using the first-person personal pronoun when identifying who he had been in the past. This is in line with the point made earlier regarding the significance of the notself teaching in early Buddhism, which does not deny that there is an individualized form of continuity from one birth to another; it only denies that this continuity involves a permanent and unchanging agent. Here is an extract from the relevant passage in the *Ekottarika-āgama* parallel to the *Bhayabherava-sutta*:[36]

> I formerly arose there, with such a given name, such a family name, eating food like this, experiencing pleasure and pain like this. Passing away from there I was reborn here; dying here I was reborn there.

The passage above mentions the ability to recall one's former name, living circumstances, and death, details also mentioned in the *Bhayabherava-*

36. EĀ 31.1 at T 2.125.666b27–28, parallel to MN 4 at MN I 22,17; parts of the description of the Buddha's recollection of past lives are also preserved in the Sanskrit fragment parallels SHT IV 165 folio 15 R5–9, Sander and Waldschmidt 1980, 191, and SHT IX 2401 Rb+c, Bechert and Wille 2004, 195.

sutta. Such descriptions clearly express the continuity of a sense of identity even when the body has come to its end.

According to early Buddhist thought, it would follow that anyone who cultivates the mind up to the point where such recollection becomes possible would in principle be able to access such information. This in turn implies that the doctrine of rebirth is considered the outcome of an insight that is replicable through meditative practice rather than being just a metaphysical speculation.

According to the *Mahāpadāna-sutta* and its *Dīrgha-āgama* parallel, the Buddha developed recollection of his own former lives up to the point where he recalled having lived in all of the different realms recognized in early Buddhist cosmology (except for the Pure Abodes).[37] This confirms that the early Buddhist teachings on different realms of rebirth are considered an expression of the Buddha's own direct knowledge and experience.

Perhaps somewhat comparable to looking back over one's present life and understanding how some experiences had a decisive influence on what one did and has become, so presumably being able to recollect one's past lives offers a direct appreciation of how the intentional quality of one's former deeds shapes one's own present, an influence that continues over the transition from one life to another.

The Buddha's Preawakening Witnessing of the Rebirth of Others

On the night of his awakening, the Buddha reportedly proceeded from having recollected his own past lives to exploring the passing away and being reborn of other beings. In this way, he was able to ascertain the driving force causing living beings to migrate through the round of births and deaths, their being propelled onward in accordance with their karmic

37. DN 14 at DN II 50,6 and DĀ 1 at T 1.1.10b10, an indication not made in a Sanskrit fragment parallel, Waldschmidt 1956, 160–61. A similar indication can be found in MN 12 at MN I 82,1 and its parallel T 17.757.596b20; see also EĀ 31.8 at T 2.125.672a18. Since only nonreturners, who have reached the third of the four levels of awakening, will be reborn in the Pure Abodes, the Buddha could not have spent a past life in the Pure Abodes, as he realized awakening only in his last life.

deeds. An extract from the relevant passage in the *Ekottarika-āgama* parallel to the *Bhayabherava-sutta* reads as follows:[38]

> I saw living beings of various types being born and passing away, of good or bad appearances, in good or bad destinies, attractive or ugly, in accordance with their good or bad conduct.

The text continues by specifying that the Buddha was able to witness that those who had acted in unwholesome ways were reborn in bad realms of existence and those who had acted in wholesome ways in good realms of existence, a specification similarly found in the *Bhayabherava-sutta*. In this way, the vision of rebirth and the vision of the principle of karma are clearly presented as integral aspects of the Buddha's progress to awakening. According to the testimony of the early discourses, his awakening took place after he had cultivated recollection of his own past lives and had observed how other beings pass away and are reborn in accordance with their previous deeds.

The Intermediate Existence

Before turning to the doctrine of karma in the next section of this chapter, a few more words are required about the actual transition from one life to the next. In early Buddhist thought this transition appears to involve an intermediate existence. Although later traditions hold different opinions on this matter,[39] the idea of an intermediate existence is implicit in listings of different types of nonreturner. Nonreturners have reached the third of four levels of awakening recognized in early Buddhism (the preceding two being stream entry and once return) and are on the path to becoming arahants, fully awakened ones. In addition to three fetters overcome with stream entry (personality view, doubt, and dogmatic clinging to moral observances), nonreturners have eradicated the two fetters of sensual

38. EĀ 31.1 at T 2.125.666c4–5, a description found similarly in its parallel MN 4 at MN I 22,30.

39. For a survey of the Buddhist schools that accepted or rejected the intermediate existence see Bareau 1955, 291.

desire and aversion. With this high degree of mental purity reached, they are nonreturners in the sense that they are beyond returning to be born in the material realm, and will take birth only in heavenly realms referred to in early Buddhist cosmology as the Pure Abodes.

One such type of nonreturner attains the final goal of full awakening "in between."[40] The reference to such a nonreturner is preceded by a mention of one who attains the final goal at the time of death; it is followed by noting that another type of nonreturner attains the final goal on being reborn (which in this case is a spontaneous rebirth in a Pure Abode).[41] The context makes it clear that the one who attains the final goal "in between" must be doing so in some sort of intermediate existence.

This can be seen with particular clarity in a simile used in a discourse in the *Aṅguttara-nikāya* and its *Madhyama-āgama* parallel to illustrate two nonreturners who both belong to the type that attains the final goal "in between." Here is the *Madhyama-āgama* version:[42]

> It is just as if iron that is thoroughly ablaze and very hot is hit with a hammer. A burning splinter flies up into the air and, while moving upward, becomes extinguished...
>
> It is just as if iron that is thoroughly ablaze and very hot is hit with a hammer. A burning splinter flies up into the air and, while moving downward from having been up, becomes extinguished without reaching the ground.

40. See, e.g., SN 46.3 at SN V 69,24 and its parallels SĀ 736 at T 2.99.196c16 or SĀ 740 at T 2.99.197a25.

41. The commentary on SN 46.3, Spk III 143,22, tries to reconcile this reference with the denial of an intermediate existence in Theravāda orthodoxy by suggesting that one who attains the final goal in between will do so during the first half of the life in a Pure Abode. Bodhi 2000, 1902n65 comments that this "disregards the literal meaning" of the expression and "also overrides the sequential and mutually exclusive nature of the five types as delineated elsewhere in the suttas. If we understand the term *antarāparinibbāyī* literally, as it seems we should, it then means one who attains Nibbāna *in the interval between two lives*, perhaps while existing in a subtle body in the intermediate state. The *upahaccaparinibbāyī* then becomes one who attains Nibbāna 'upon landing' or 'striking ground' in the new existence, i.e., almost immediately after taking rebirth."

42. MĀ 6 at T 1.26.427a28–b8, parallel to AN 7.52 at AN IV 70,16.

In contrast, the type of nonreturner that attains the final goal on being reborn compares to a splinter that becomes extinguished upon hitting the ground. These illustrations, found similarly in the *Aṅguttara-nikāya* parallel, confirm that the nonreturners mentioned earlier attain the final goal in midair, so to speak. They also implicitly show that this can happen at different times in this interim existence, just as the burning splinter can become extinguished right away or else after moving for some time through the air. Apart from this indication, however, the early discourses do not provide details regarding the possible duration of such an intermediate existence.[43]

The transition from one life to another finds comparison in the simile of a flame, which with the support of wind can cross over a distance even without any fuel and is able to set fire to fuel that is not immediately contiguous to it.[44] Similar to the wind acting as a support for the flame, craving is considered to function as the support for the mind at the time of transition from one life to the next. Unlike the wind, which will abate on its own at some point, as long as craving continues in unawakened beings, immersed in ignorance, it is the bond that according to the early Buddhist analysis binds consciousness to present and future bodies. To be free from this bond requires that ignorance and craving be eradicated.

3. The Principle of Karma

The topic of craving relates to the issue of volition or intention, mentioned earlier as one of the components of "name." Volition operates within the network of conditions provided by the other components of name as well as by the reciprocal conditioning between consciousness and name-and-

43. On the intermediate existence see, e.g., de La Vallée Poussin 1926/1971, 32n1, Lin 1949, 52–54, Wayman 1974, Bareau 1979, Harvey 1995, 98–104, 2013, 59–60, Cuevas 1996, 2003, 40–44, Blezer 1997, 6–26, Kritzer 1997, 1998, 2000a, 2000b, 2008, 78–81, 2013, 2014, 11–12, Somaratne 1999, de Silva 2004, Langer 2007, 82–84, Lin 2011/2012, and Lee 2014, 70–75 (as already noted by Somaratne 1999, 152, Kalupahana and Tamura 1965, 730 are not correct in assuming that the intermediate existence is a later concept).

44. SN 44.9 at SN IV 399,26 and its parallels SĀ 957 at T 2.99.244a26, SĀ² 190 at T 2.100.443b1, and D 4094 *nyu* 88a6 or Q 5595 *thu* 135b2.

form. Karma in early Buddhist thought refers to such mental volition as well as to intentionally undertaken verbal and bodily deeds.[45] This needs to be distinguished from popular usage, in which the term "karma" stands for the results. Strictly speaking this usage is not correct—the appropriate term for the results of karma is *vipāka*.

In short, "karma" means "action." The doctrine of karma and its fruition proposes that actions, be these mental, verbal, or bodily, tend to have a result, be this in relation to oneself or to others. Similar to the reciprocal conditioning of consciousness and name-and-form, karma as volitional action also applies to the present life just as much as to the transition from one life to another.

To provide a simple example, the fact that my hitting the keys on the computer in front of me produces sentences on the screen could be considered an example of karma and its fruit. The mental action of choosing particular keys has as its result that the letters appearing on the screen make up a meaningful sentence, and the ethical quality of my intention, leading to these letters expressing a particular idea, has its fruition in whatever this part of my writing will eventually convey to the reader. All this exemplifies the basic notion of karma and its fruit.

Karma and Its Fruit

A discourse in the *Saṃyutta-nikāya* and its parallels clarify that what one experiences now is the fruition not just of past karma in the sense of one's past deeds, but also of factors like bodily disorders, change of climate, or external violence.[46] This shows that in early Buddhist thought the results of karma operate within a network of various causes and conditions; karma does not exercise its influence in a monocausal manner. The

45. AN 6.63 at AN III 415,7 and its parallels MĀ 111 at T 1.26.600a23 and D 4094 *ju* 200a1 or Q 5595 *tu* 228a4; see also the *Abhidharmakośabhāṣya*, Pradhan 1967, 192,9.

46. SN 36.21 at SN IV 230,13, SĀ 977 at T 2.99.252c21, and SĀ² 211 at T 2.100.452b14. The same presentation of karma as only one in a set of conditions recurs also for different experiences in AN 4.87 at AN II 87,29 and AN 5.104 at AN III 131,6, and for different types of disease in AN 10.60 at AN V 110,1. Wujastyk 2011, 32 comments on the factors listed in addition to karma in SN 36.21 that "this is the first moment in documented Indian history that these medical categories and explanations are combined in a clearly systematic manner."

doctrine of karma is therefore clearly not deterministic.[47] Instead, one's volitional decisions taken in the present moment are only one factor in a network of interrelated conditions that will influence one's future. The emphasis is often on this factor, however, because it is the one condition amenable to being brought under control through mental training.

Given that according to early Buddhist thought the original volition, just as its eventual result, operates within a wider network of various conditions, the actual working out of karma and its fruit can take a variety of forms. An example is the proposal in the *Cūḷakammavibhaṅga-sutta* and a range of parallels that being prone to anger has its karmic result in ugliness.[48] By way of extension beyond the present life, the same principle is then considered to be applicable to one's next life as well. However, this does not mean that everyone who fails to satisfy current ideals of beauty must have been angry in his or her past life. This would be falling prey to the error of monocausality. The point made by the *Cūḷakammavibhaṅga-sutta* and its parallels is only to delineate a basic tendency, not to present a form of determinism.

The nature of karma finds illustration in early Buddhist thought in a simile about a lump of salt.[49] According to this simile, a lump of salt will have a different effect on the drinkability of water if it is thrown into a small cup of water or into a large river; in the first case the water

47. That the early Buddhist karmic theory is not deterministic has been pointed out repeatedly in academic writings; see, e.g., Jayatilleke 1968, Gómez 1975, 82, Ñāṇaponika 1975, 91, Story 1975, 74, Fujita 1982, 151, Siderits 1987, 153, Jayawardhana 1988, 408, de Silva 1991, 273, Keown 1996, 340, Halbfass 2000, 102, Harvey 2000/2005, 23, 2007, 59, Hershock 2005, 6–7, Nelson 2005, 4, and Anālayo 2009a, 2–4. It is not clear to me why Obeyesekere 2002, 130, after correctly stating that according to the early Buddhist notion of karma "human pain and suffering can arise from nonkarmic causes. For example, illness can be caused by karma, but it can also be caused through the sole action of the bodily humours," nevertheless continues to qualify this early Buddhist notion of karma as "deterministic." Instead, in the words of Jayatilleke 1969, 28, "Buddhism, it may be noted, was opposed to all forms of determinism."

48. MN 135 at MN III 204,18 and its parallels MĀ 170 at T 1.26.705a29, T 1.78.887c27, T 1.79.889c27, T 1.80.892a28, T 1.81.897a9, T 17.755.589a27, the *Karmavibhaṅga* in Kudo 2004, 52,6 and 2007, 98,9, with its Tibetan counterpart in Lévi 1932, 185,25, and D 339 *sa* 301a4 or Q 1006 *shu* 312b8.

49. AN 3.99 at AN I 250,1 and MĀ 11 at T 1.26.433a21; see also Dhammadinnā 2014, 114.

will become undrinkable, but in the second case it will have only a rather minor effect. Similarly the effect of a particular deed depends on the overall moral development of the performer of this deed.

This in turn implies that a substantial change in one's moral conduct has considerable transformative potential. An illustration is the tale of the former brigand Aṅgulimāla. According to his story, reported in several discourses, even a murderer has in principle the potential of transforming himself and reaching full awakening within the same lifetime.[50]

Karma and Right View

The last moments of one's life are considered to be of particular importance for possibly tipping the scale of karmic fruition, especially if one upholds right view as death approaches. This idea emerges as part of an exposition of the intricacy of the early Buddhist notion of karma in the *Mahākammavibhaṅga-sutta* and its parallels, which declare that someone who is acting in a good and wholesome way nevertheless may experience negative results. Conversely someone who is doing evil may enjoy pleasant results. The reason given is that the ripening of karma is complex and not something that operates in a monocausal manner; nor do the results immediately follow the cause.

The exposition in the *Mahākammavibhaṅga-sutta* and its parallels needs to be understood in relation to the early Buddhist notion that faring on in the round of rebirth extends so far back into the past that a beginning point cannot be discerned.[51] This implies that the amount of deeds performed in the past must be staggering. Since a particular deed in the present need not result in instant fruition, the results of karma someone experiences now could be related to the ripening of some other

50. His attainment of full awakening is reported in MN 86 at MN II 104,1, SĀ 1077 at T 2.99.281a26, SĀ² 16 at T 2.100.378c29, T 2.118.509b23, T 2.119.511a19, and EĀ 38.6 at T 2.125.721a7; for a translation of SĀ 1077 and a comparative study see Anālayo 2008a.

51. See, e.g., SN 15.3 at SN II 179,21 and its parallels SĀ 938 at T 2.99.240c26 and SĀ² 331 at T 2.100.486a19; part of a corresponding statement has been preserved in Sanskrit fragment SHT 1.167 R3, Waldschmidt, Clawiter, and Holzmann 1965, 95. Another parallel, EĀ 51.1 at T 2.125.814a28, has no counterpart to this introductory statement, although the rest of the discourse makes it clear that the same basic principle holds.

deed from the distant past. That is, the case of one who acts wholesomely and experiences negative results should be understood to involve two dimensions: (a) the acting in wholesome ways now, which sooner or later will have good results, and (b) the experiencing now of the fruition of some unwholesome deed(s) from the more distant past. The same principle applies to the case of someone who is doing evil and enjoying pleasure. The evil deeds performed now will certainly have bitter results, but due to other good deeds carried out in the more distant past this person will first of all experience pleasure. The complexity that emerges in this way implies that it would be misleading to believe that the workings of karma can be proven or disproven by taking into account just a single life or even just the transition from one life to the next.

In fact the *Brahmajāla-sutta* and its parallels showcase how various wrong views arose because of recollecting just one previous life.[52] Their presentation implies that just taking into account the previous life is an insufficient basis for drawing conclusions, instead of which a whole range of previous lives would need to be surveyed in order to be able to appreciate the workings of karma.[53]

This could be illustrated with the case of students sitting an exam. It would not work to assess the impact of prior preparation on good results by taking into account only what these students did the day before the exam. A good student might have prepared for months for the exam and taken the last day off to relax, whereas a bad student could have neglected studies until the last day and then tried to make up for that by frantically learning until late in the night. Proper assessment of the impact of exam preparation on the results requires taking into account a much longer period of time than just the day before. Moreover, even sustained

52. For a comparative study see Anālayo 2009b.

53. Tradition singles out five deeds as being of immediate fruition rather than involving an uncertain number of lives. These are murder of one's mother, father, or an arahant, being responsible for a schism in the monastic community, and physically attacking a Buddha so that his blood flows; see, e.g., the *Mahāvyutpatti* 2323–28 (§122), Sakaki 1916/1962, 172, and the discussion by Silk 2007. In terms of my simile below of the students and the exam, this would compare to the case of a student who for whatever reason has been disqualified from taking the exam. In such a case it can be concluded that the student in question will definitely not pass the exam.

preparation over a long period does not assure good results. Some exam questions may be formulated in such a confusing manner that even a good student will fail, and others could be so self-evident that even a bad student manages to pass, two examples illustrating the nondeterministic nature of karma. All that can be said with certainty is that those who prepare themselves well tend to get better results.

In the same way, the exact working out of the results of karma is hard to gauge.[54] Only a basic pattern can be discerned in that evil will eventually have its fruition in painful experience, just as wholesomeness will eventually have pleasant results.

The *Mahākammavibhaṅga-sutta* and its parallels agree in identifying the holding of right view as a factor that can counterbalance the ripening of evil deeds from the past at the time of passing away and being reborn.[55] This puts a spotlight on the last moments of a particular life as being of particular importance for influencing and even determining the conditions of the next life through the adoption and upholding of right view at that time. The topic of right view is indeed central for appreciating the position of the doctrine of rebirth in the early Buddhist teachings.

4. The Significance of Right View

The standard definition of wrong view in the early discourses explicitly covers the denial of rebirth and of the fruition of karma. An example of such an occurrence is a passage that considers it a highly deplorable condition if, in spite of being so fortunate as to be born at a time when the teachings of a Buddha are available, one holds wrong view and denies rebirth and the results of karma.[56]

54. Griffiths 1982, 289 explains that "Buddhist karmic theory is no open-and-shut determinism wherein it is possible to calculate with precision the karmic accounts, as it were, of any given individual. Things are much more complex than that."

55. MN 136 at MN III 214,21 and its parallels MĀ 171 at T 1.26.708b21 and D 4094 *ju* 267a7 or Q 5595 *thu* 10b3. Becker 1993, 13 notes that later "schools of Buddhism...placed increasing emphasis on the holding of right views at the moment of death and...[even] considered this to be more important than living a moral life in determining one's future rebirth."

56. AN 8.29 at AN IV 226,12 and its parallels MĀ 124 at T 1.26.613b24 and EĀ 42.1 at T

The Denial of Rebirth

The *Brahmajāla-sutta* and its parallels list the denial of rebirth as an annihilationist view. This view affirms that annihilation takes place once the body breaks up at death, in the sense that nothing survives the death of the material body.[57]

The *Sāmaññaphala-sutta* states that one of six well-known teachers existing at the time of the Buddha flatly denied rebirth, adopting precisely the wording used in the standard definition of wrong view.[58] According to the position attributed to him, a human being is made of the four elements and will just come to be extinguished at death. This goes to show that such a materialist position was already in vogue in ancient India. Moreover, since the doctrines of these six teachers recurrently feature as being the very opposite of what the Buddha teaches, this type of view is clearly considered as contrary to the Buddhist position. The *Dīrgha-āgama* version describes his view as follows:[59]

> [As for] the four elements a human being has received, when he passes away the earth element returns to earth, the water [element] returns to water, the fire [element] returns to fire, and

---

2.125.747a26, as well as a discourse quotation in the *Sūtrasamuccaya*, Pāsādika 1989, 7,8 and T 32.1635.50b27; parts of this exposition have also been preserved in Sanskrit fragment Or. 15009/64 v5–6, Nagashima 2009, 139. The formulation in these discourses speaks of the denial of the existence of "another world" and of the fruit of wholesome and unwholesome deeds. The expression "another world" occurs in the *Pāyāsi-sutta* in the context of a discussion about rebirth, making it clear that it refers to being reborn in another world; see DN 23 at DN II 316,13, DĀ 7 at T 1.1.42c2, MĀ 71 at T 1.26.525b16, and T 1.45.831a13, and for an extract from this discussion in the next chapter, see p. 45.

57. DN 1 at DN I 34,7, DĀ 21 at T 1.1.93a26, T 1.21.269b9, a Tibetan discourse parallel, Weller 1934, 56,6 (§185), a discourse quotation in T 28.1548.660a21, a discourse quotation in D 4094 *ju* 151b3 or Q 5595 *tu* 174b6, and a Sanskrit fragment parallel, SHT X 4189 V4–5, Wille 2008, 307; for a translation of the relevant section in DĀ 21 and a comparative study see Anālayo 2009b.

58. DN 2 at DN I 55,15.

59. DĀ 27 at T 1.1.108b26–c1; this has already been translated by Meisig 1987, 145 and MacQueen 1988, 41. A comparable tenet in the parallels T 1.22.271b28 and the *Saṅghabhedavastu*, Gnoli 1978, 221,6 (see also Vogel 1970, 11,10), is attributed to another of the six teachers, as already noted by Bapat 1948, 109.

> the wind [element] returns to the wind: they are all destroyed and the [sense] faculties return to space.
>
> When a person is dead, his body is carried on a bier, put in the cemetery and cremated, his bones become grey-colored or turn to dust. Whether foolish or wise, all are destroyed at death; they are of a nature to be annihilated.

According to the passage mentioned above, to live at the time when the Buddha's liberating teachings are available and hold such wrong view is considered a predicament comparable to being born dumb and dull, unable to understand the meaning of what is being said.[60] Both predicaments similarly obstruct one from benefiting from the Buddha's liberating teachings.

The contrast made in the early discourses between the early Buddhist teaching on rebirth and this materialist position implies that the doctrine of rebirth was not a belief unanimously accepted in ancient India.[61] It seems highly improbable that the rebirth doctrine in early Buddhist thought should be attributed to the wish to accommodate the presumed appeal of the notion of rebirth among contemporaries of the Buddha and his followers.[62]

The same can also be seen from the central position accorded to the denial of rebirth as an instance of wrong view. A notion taken over from the ancient Indian setting just to placate popular beliefs would hardly have been invested with such a vital function in the early Buddhist sote-

60. See above note 56.

61. Jayatilleke 1969, 8 notes that "as is evident from the Buddhist and the non-Buddhist literature, there was a variety of views on the question of survival at the time covering almost every possibility that one can think of." Jayatilleke 1963/1980, 372 concludes that "it is false to say that rebirth was universally accepted by the Indian religious tradition prior to the advent of Buddhism."

62. Jayatilleke 1969, 8–9 points out that it is "not correct to say (as many scholars have done) that the Buddha took for granted the belief in rebirth current in society at the time. . .the Buddhist theory of survival has its origin in the Enlightenment of the Buddha and not in any traditional Indian belief." Premasiri 1996, 138 adds that "the evidence contained in the various scriptural sources including the Pali Canonical scriptures does not favor the conclusion that Buddhism would have accepted the doctrine of rebirth because it was a well established belief in the pre-Buddhist background."

riological scheme. Identifying as wrong view the materialist position, which affirms that the death of the body equals the annihilation of a living being, only makes sense if this position was indeed considered diametrically opposed to the general thrust of the Buddha's teachings and therefore as detrimental to their understanding as being dumb and dull.

Different Types of Right View

Right view functions as the precursor to the noble eightfold path that according to the early Buddhist scheme of mental training needs to be undertaken in order to reach liberation.[63] This need not be taken to imply, however, that rebirth must be accepted on blind faith in order to be able to embark on this path, since alternative modes of describing right view exist. One of these is the exact opposite of wrong view and thus affirms rebirth and the results of karma.[64] Another definition instead speaks of insight into the four noble truths.[65] Although the four noble truths build on the notion of rebirth, the basic attitude and practices they convey can be put to use without affirming rebirth.

The fact that the discourses present such an alternative definition of right view leaves open the possibility that someone may engage in practices related to the Buddhist path to liberation without necessarily pledging faith in rebirth. It does not leave open the possibility of denying rebirth outright, however, since that would amount to holding wrong view.

The point that emerges in this way is that one who wishes to embark on

63. MN 117 at MN III 71,23 and its parallels MĀ 189 at T 1.26.735c13 and D 4094 *nyu* 44a4 or Q 5595 *thu* 83b4.

64. See, e.g., AN 10.176 at AN V 268,1 and its parallel SĀ 1039 at T 2.99.272a4 (both instances are preceded by a corresponding description of wrong view, which has a counterpart in a discourse quotation in the *Abhidharmakośavyākhyā*, Wogihara 1936, 409,19).

65. See, e.g., MN 141 at MN III 251,12; in spite of differences in formulation, the parallels MĀ 31 at T 1.26.469a15 and T 1.32.816a17 make basically the same point. Another parallel, EĀ 27.1 at T 2.643b23, only refers to right view, without drawing out its implications; for a translation and study of EĀ 27.1 see Anālayo 2006a. Collins 1982, 92 distinguishes three types of right view: "firstly, that of a general and pan-Indian pro-attitude to the belief system of *karma* and *saṃsāra*; secondly, that of knowledge of Buddhist doctrine and the motivation to accept and introject it; and thirdly, that of progress towards, and attainment of, liberating insight."

the Buddhist path of practice need not affirm rebirth as a matter of mere belief. The question of rebirth might simply be set aside as something that such a person is unable to verify at present, without going so far as to deny rebirth and affirm that there is nothing that continues beyond the death of the body.

Further advice related to the same problem of how to approach positions on rebirth that one is unable to corroborate from one's own experience can be found in the *Apaṇṇaka-sutta*. The discourse reports how the Buddha gave counsel to a group of householders on how to resolve for themselves the contradiction between those teachers who deny rebirth and those teachers who affirm it.[66] The advice given by the Buddha is to reflect on the consequences of holding these two opposing views. Such reflection will according to the *Apaṇṇaka-sutta* lead to the conclusion that the affirmation of rebirth (besides being from an early Buddhist viewpoint an affirmation of what is actually correct) encourages one to act in wholesome ways, unlike the denial of rebirth.

In line with this suggestion, someone wishing to embark on the Buddhist path to awakening might then take the position that, inasmuch as the doctrine of rebirth encourages one to act in wholesome ways, following a teaching that is based on this doctrine is meaningful, even though one is unable to verify rebirth on one's own and thus unable to affirm its truth from personal experience.

Another comparable piece of advice can be found in the *Kālāma-sutta* (also known as the *Kesamutti-sutta*), where the Buddha similarly gives a teaching to householders confronted with different views held by various teachers. Here, too, he recommends that the householders reflect on the wholesome and unwholesome consequences of these views. A difference when compared to the *Apaṇṇaka-sutta*'s advice is that in the Pāli version of the *Kālāma-sutta* the Buddha considers it fitting that the members of his audience have doubts about the different views they encounter.[67]

66. MN 60 at MN I 401,30; part of the description of the view that denies rebirth has been preserved in Sanskrit fragment SHT III 966 Bd, Waldschmidt, Clawiter, and Sander-Holzmann 1971, 226 (identified by J.-U. Hartmann in Bechert and Wille 1996, 272).

67. AN 3.65 at AN I 189,6: *alaṃ vicikicchituṃ*.

In the *Madhyama-āgama* parallel he instead instructs them not to have doubts.[68]

Besides this difference, when evaluating the advice given in the *Apaṇṇaka-sutta* and the *Kālāma-sutta* it also needs to be kept in mind that their audiences are not a gathering of disciples of the Buddha.[69] In other words, the teachings given here are not addressed to those who have decided to follow the path of liberation taught by the Buddha and consider themselves his disciples.[70]

Speculation and Direct Knowledge

The advice given to those who are disciples of the Buddha is that they should not waste their time by speculating about precisely what they were in the past and what they will be in the future. Such advice can be found in the *Sabbāsava-sutta* and its parallels,[71] where it forms part of an encouragement given by the Buddha that his disciples should rather give attention to cultivating meditative insight and progress to stream entry.

What the *Sabbāsava-sutta* and its parallels consider as problematic is not the idea of having been someone else in the past as such but rather engaging in theoretical speculations. In contrast to the critical attitude evinced in the *Sabbāsava-sutta* and its parallels, the early discourses regularly commend recollection of one's own past lives as one of the three

68. MĀ 16 at T 1.26.438c12: 汝等莫生疑惑; see also Bodhi 2012, 74. The same difference recurs between an acknowledgment of the appropriateness of doubt in relation to various views in vogue in the ancient Indian setting, found in SN 42.13 at SN IV 350,15, and its parallel MĀ 20 at T 1.26.447a22, where the Buddha rather discourages having doubts.

69. In MN 60 at MN I 401,22 the householders explicitly indicate that they do not have firm faith established in any particular teacher. AN 3.65 at AN I 188,22 and MĀ 16 at T 1.26.438b29 portray different ways in which the householders greet the Buddha on arrival, which implies that some of them feature merely as interested visitors and do not consider themselves as disciples of the Buddha.

70. Story 1975/2010, 101 comments on AN 3.65 that "the true meaning of the Kālāma Sutta [is] not the licence to doubt everything and to go on doubting, which many people today are all too eager to read into it."

71. MN 2 at MN I 8,4 and its parallels MĀ 10 at T 1.26.432a16, T 1.31.813b11, EĀ 40.6 at T 2.125.740b21, and D 4094 *ju* 92b5 or Q 5595 *tu* 105b5. Carrithers 1983, 54 explains that "for the Buddha the specific details of transmigration were never so important as the principle underlying it: human action has moral consequences, consequences which are inescapable, returning upon one whether in this life or another."

higher knowledges, *abhiññā*. These three higher knowledges correspond to the realizations attained by the Buddha on the night of his awakening, mentioned above, covering recollection of one's own past lives, the direct witnessing of the rebirth of others in various realms of existence, and the gaining of awakening through the eradication of the influxes, *āsava*. The *Saṅgārava-sutta* and its Sanskrit-fragment parallel report the Buddha identifying the epistemological foundation of his own realization of awakening to be precisely such higher knowledge, *abhiññā*.[72]

The decisive difference between the higher knowledges concerned with rebirth and the speculations described in the *Sabbāsava-sutta* and its parallels is of an epistemological type, inasmuch as *abhiññā* is considered to yield direct experiential knowledge, thereby being far removed from mere theorizing.

Another dimension of the second higher knowledge regarding the rebirth of others in various realms of existence comes to the fore in the *Naḷakapāna-sutta* and its parallels. These report that the Buddha would at times declare the rebirth and level of realization attained by deceased disciples, giving as the rationale for such declarations that this can serve as an inspiration for others to emulate those disciples.[73]

Nevertheless, other passages indicate that concern with such issues should not be taken to extremes, hence the *Mahāparinibbāna-sutta* and its parallels report an occasion when the Buddha censured Ānanda (or in the parallel versions unnamed monks) for continuing to inquire about the rebirth of particular individuals.[74] As already evident from the *Sabbāsava-sutta* and its parallels, overall importance should be given to progressing to stream entry oneself and thereby entering the stream that will lead to putting an end to rebirth. The *Mahātaṇhāsaṅkhaya-sutta* and its parallels in turn confirm that one who has attained penetrative insight into dependent arising, *paṭicca samuppāda*, has lost all interest in speculating about what he or she might have been in the past or what he or she

72. MN 100 at MN II 211,23 and fragment 348r1–2, Zhang 2004, 12–13.

73. MN 68 at MN I 465,12 and its parallel MĀ 77 at T 1.26.545b26.

74. DN 16 at DN II 93,13 (see also SN 55.8 at SN V 357,10) and its parallels in a Sanskrit fragment version, Waldschmidt 1951, 168,8 (§9.17), as well as DĀ 2 at T 1.1.13a29, T 1.5.163b7, T 1.6.178b27, and the Mūlasarvāstivāda *Vinaya*, T 24.1448.26c8, with its Tibetan counterpart in Waldschmidt 1951, 169,9 (§9.17).

might become in the future.[75] Here, again, direct realization is considered superior to theoretical speculation.

The notion of direct realization finds its most evident expression in the early discourses in the four stages of awakening, which also stand in direct relationship to the idea of rebirth. According to early Buddhist thought, a stream enterer will only be reborn seven lives at most, a once returner will be reborn in this world once, and a nonreturner will be reborn once in a Pure Abode.[76] An arahant has reached total freedom from rebirth, reflected in the standard description of the attainment of full liberation in terms of "birth is destroyed."[77]

In this way, from the wrong view to be avoided by one embarking on the Buddhist way of practice all the way up to the final consummation of such practice through the attainment of the four levels of awakening, rebirth is an integral component of early Buddhist thought.[78]

Summary

The early Buddhist doctrine of dependent arising describes a conditional interrelationship between consciousness, on the one hand, and mental activities (grouped under the header of "name") and the experience of matter ("form") on the other hand. This conditional interrelationship explains continuity during a single life and from one life to another without needing to bring in a permanent entity that continues to live or is

75. MN 38 at MN I 264,37 and its parallel MĀ 201 at T 1.26.769a10.

76. See, e.g., AN 3.86 at AN I 233,13 and its parallel SĀ 820 at T 2.99.210b29; for a discourse quotation regarding the prospective rebirth of a stream enterer see the *Abhidharmakośavyākhyā*, Wogihara 1936, 554,6.

77. See, e.g., DN 2 at DN I 84,11 and its parallels, DĀ 20 at T 1.1.86c7, T 1.22.275c26, and a parallel in the Mūlasarvāstivāda *Vinaya*, Gnoli 1978, 250,30.

78. Premasiri 2001/2006, 209 comments that "one might contend that the first Truth of the unsatisfactory nature of life...may be understood without the hypothesis of rebirth, but it becomes completely meaningful only under that hypothesis." Premasiri 2005, 521 concludes that "the Buddhist doctrine of liberation (*vimutti*) derives its meaning and significance primarily from its teaching concerning the inevitability of...a repeated series of births and deaths...the ultimate goal of Buddhism, and the way of life recommended in order to attain it, would lose much of its significance if the teaching concerning rebirth is not considered as a cardinal tenet of the system."

reborn. Actual conception is envisaged in terms of a descent of consciousness, which appears to imply the continuity of residual memories but not of the entirety of the mental processes of the deceased person. The transition of such consciousness from one life to another, or rather the transition of such a process of being conscious, seems to involve an intermediate existence of unspecified duration.

Through meditative training, memories of past lives are considered to become accessible to recollection, which can involve memory of one's name, living circumstances, and death in a past form of existence. The form of rebirth taken is seen to follow the law of karma, in the sense that the ethical quality of one's volitional deeds, in particular the impact of craving as an outgrowth of ignorance, has an effect in this life and in the future. Such an effect is not envisaged as operating in a monocausal manner. Alongside karma, a range of other conditions can influence the quality and circumstances of one's present life. The early Buddhist doctrine of karma is therefore not deterministic. Nor are the results of karma seen as having only an immediate effect. Rather, they can come to fruition even after a long interval, once conditions for ripening are appropriate. This in turn makes it impossible to prove or disprove the doctrine of karma based on taking into account only a single life or the passing on from one life to the next.

The early Buddhist path of practice has right view as its forerunner. Whereas right view does not necessarily require accepting rebirth on mere faith, it does require maintaining an open attitude to what is beyond the sphere of one's direct verification and avoiding the adoption of a firm position that flatly denies rebirth.

The doctrine of rebirth is an integral and essential component of early Buddhist thought and cannot be reduced to a taking over of popular notions from the ancient Indian background. Tradition considers rebirth and its working mechanics to have been verified by the Buddha himself on the night of his awakening. Rebirth is also intrinsically intertwined with the different levels of awakening recognized in early Buddhist thought.

Due to its centrality for Buddhist thought, the notion of rebirth has been defended in debate by Buddhists of various times. To such debates I turn in the next chapter.

II. Debates on Rebirth

Introduction

The Buddhist doctrine of rebirth without an unchanging agent and in accordance with karma (in the sense of volition operating within a wider network of conditions) was, and still forms, a topic of recurring debate. In what follows I survey instances that reflect the main topics raised by such debates ranging from ancient times to the contemporary setting. I begin by surveying the undeclared questions—a set of opinions debated in ancient India, some of which are related to rebirth—in regard to which the Buddha reportedly refused to take a position (1). Then I turn to instances of debate concerning the topic of rebirth in ancient India (2), in China during the early imperial period (3), and in modern times (4).

1. The Undeclared Questions

Right View and Speculative Views

The early discourses depict the setting in ancient India at the time of the Buddha as teeming with various philosophers and recluses ready to debate their respective views. In line with the contrast between theoretical speculation about past lives and direct realization, briefly described in the previous chapter, early Buddhist texts repeatedly express an attitude of disinterest in debating theories of various types. Such rejection of speculative views, several of which concern rebirth, has found an eloquent expression in the *Aṭṭhaka-vagga* of the *Sutta-nipāta*, a text also preserved in Chinese translation.[79] This has led some scholars to perceive a substantial

79. Sn 766–975 and T 4.198.74b8–189c23, translated by Bapat 1945 and 1950.

difference between the rejection of views enunciated in this text and the remainder of the early discourses,[80] in which the need for right view in particular and the affirmation of rebirth feature as central components of early Buddhist thought.

Yet the warning sounded in the *Aṭṭhaka-vagga* and its parallel against entanglement in views is but an implementation of right view in the sense of the four noble truths, inasmuch as the main task is to recognize how craving and attachment manifest in dogmatic adherence to one's own opinions.[81] Right view becomes "rightly" directed once it sees through craving and attachment, in particular with regard to one's own cherished positions.

80. See, e.g., Gómez 1976, Vetter 1990, 44–52, and Burford 1991, 45–70. It is not clear to me whether Fronsdal 2016 should also be included in this list. The title of his study and translation of the *Aṭṭhaka-vagga* announces the topic to be "the Buddha *before* Buddhism"; the collection is then introduced in Fronsdal 2016, 10 with the comment that "it may well be that these teachings lay at the heart of the earliest tradition. Many of the rest of the surviving teachings could be considered elaborations, adaptations, and digressions from these early foundational teachings." Yet in the final part of his study Fronsdal 2016, 141 convincingly refutes the argument that certain teachings are not mentioned in the collection because they were not yet formulated, pointing out that this "ignores the fact that different genres of texts may emphasize very different ideas. Poetry, for example, is not a common place for referring to numerical lists." In addition, Fronsdal 2016, 146 reasons that the *Aṭṭhaka-vagga* "may well represent the teaching emphasis of one person or group. Rather than being chronologically earlier relative to some other early Buddhist teachings, the *Book of the Eights* may have its origin with a particular Buddhist group in a particular location." This successfully undermines claims that the *Aṭṭhaka-vagga* is best read as preserving some sort of precanonical Buddhism substantially different in orientation and values from what can be found in common in the four main Pāli *Nikāya*s and their parallels.

81. Norman 2003, 519 concludes his study of the *Aṭṭhaka-vagga* by stating that "there is, however, no reason whatsoever for believing that the form of Buddhism taught in the [Aṭṭhaka-]vagga represents the whole of Buddhism at the time of its composition, and that everything not included in it must be a later addition." Bodhi (2017, 39) points out that such a conclusion "would have bizarre consequences. It would in effect reduce the Dhamma to a collection of poems and aphorisms with only the barest unifying structure"—a conclusion that overlooks that these discourses "have a different purpose than to provide a comprehensive overview of the Dhamma. As works mostly in verse, their primary purpose is to inspire, edify, and instruct rather than to provide systematic doctrinal exposition"; see also the detailed discussion in Fuller 2005, 148–53. For an appraisal of the philosophy underlying the *Aṭṭhaka-vagga* see Jayawickrama 1948/1978, 45–57 and Premasiri 1972, and on its poetic nature Shulman 2012/2013.

The *Aggivacchagotta-sutta* makes a closely related point by indicating that the Buddha had put away holding a "view," *diṭṭhi*, since he had "seen," *diṭṭha*, the impermanent nature of the five aggregates.[82] The *Saṃyukta-āgama* parallels to the *Aggivacchagotta-sutta* express the same insight in a different way by stating that the Buddha had "seen" the four noble truths.[83]

Another relevant text is the *Brahmajāla-sutta* and its parallels, which provide an analysis of sixty-two standpoints for views from the perspective of their genesis in the misinterpretation of certain experiences or incorrect ways of reasoning.[84] This results in a thorough analysis of the view-formation process as the outcome of craving.[85] Such discourses fit with and complement the presentation in the *Aṭṭhaka-vagga* and its Chinese parallel. In sum, these passages flesh out the early Buddhist interest in the vision that comes from seeing through views rather than clinging to them, which easily results in becoming involved in vain disputes.

The Poisoned Arrow of Speculative Views

Disinterest in debate for its own sake also comes to the fore in the Buddha's refusal to take up any of a set of positions that, judging from the frequency of their appearance in the early discourses, were a topic of much interest in ancient India. Several of the debated positions relate to rebirth and therefore are of relevance to the main topic of this chapter.

82. MN 72 at MN I 486,11.

83. SĀ 962 at T 2.99.245c21 and SĀ² 196 at T 2.100.445b8.

84. The analysis of different views can be found in DN 1 at DN I 12,29, DĀ 21 at T 1.1.89c23, T 1.21.266a4, a Tibetan discourse parallel, Weller 1934, 14,30, a discourse quotation in T 28.1548.656b19, and a discourse quotation in D 4094 *ju* 143a5 or Q 5595 *tu* 164b3; for Sanskrit fragment parallels see Anālayo 2009b, 226n23.

85. Bodhi 1978/1992, 9 explains that, according to the presentation in the *Brahmajāla-sutta*, "the Buddha does not trouble to refute each separate view because the primary focus of his concern is not so much the content of the view as the underlying malady of which the addiction to speculative tenets is a symptom." In the words of Katz 1982/1989, 150, the discourse presents a "psychoanalysis of metaphysical claims." Fuller 2005, 115 concludes that "the *Brahmajāla-sutta*...is a clear example of *sammā-diṭṭhi* signifying that all views have been transcended."

According to the *Cūḷamāluṅkya-sutta*, concern with such views had also affected one of the Buddha's monastic disciples, who was ready to leave the Buddhist order unless he received from the Buddha a definite declaration in relation to these positions. Here is the *Madhyama-āgama* list of the views regarding which he wanted the Buddha to take a clear position of either acceptance or else refusal:[86]

> The world is eternal, the world is not eternal; the world is finite, the world is infinite; the soul (*jīva*) is the same as the body, the soul is different from the body; a Tathāgata comes to an end, a Tathāgata does not come to an end, a Tathāgata both comes to an end and does not come to an end, a Tathāgata neither comes to an end nor does not come to an end.

The *Cūḷamāluṅkya-sutta* and its parallels agree that the Buddha refused to adopt any of these positions, comparing the pursuit of wanting these positions to be affirmed or rejected to someone who has been struck by a poisonous arrow. Instead of allowing the arrow to be removed in order to prevent the poison from spreading throughout the body, this person first wants to get replies to a whole series of largely irrelevant questions related to the incident of being shot. The refusal to take up any of the various positions in the passage translated above, illustrated with the simile of the poisoned arrow, reflects an attitude adopted consistently by the Buddha in other discourses.[87]

86. MĀ 221 at T 1.26.804a26–28, with parallels in MN 63 at MN I 426,10 and T 1.94.917b18.

87. The reason(s) for the Buddha's refusal to take up any of these positions has been a recurrent topic of scholarly discussion; see, e.g., Oldenberg 1881/1961, 256–63, Schrader 1904/1905, Beckh 1919, 118–21, Keith 1923/1979, 62–67, Thomas 1927/2003, 201–2, de La Vallée Poussin 1928, Organ 1954, Murti 1955/2008, 36–50, Nagao 1955/1992, 38, Frauwallner 1956/2003a, 141–42, Jayatilleke 1963/1980, 470–76, Smart 1964/1976, 34–35, Kalupahana 1975, 177–78, Lamotte 1976, 2003–5, Collins 1982, 131–38, Pannikar 1989/1990, 61–76, Tilakaratne 1993, 109–21, Harvey 1995, 84–87, Vélez de Cea 2004, Manda 2005, Karunadasa 2007, 2013, 129–49, and Anālayo 2017c, 13–14.

The Reason for Setting Aside Speculative Views

The reason for such refusal, for considering these positions as irrelevant as the various questions the person shot with a poisoned arrow wants to pursue, can best be appreciated by considering the actual positions listed. The first of these proposes that the world is eternal or else is not eternal; another affirms that the soul and the body are the same or else are different.

That there is nothing eternal in the world is a basic tenet of early Buddhist thought, for which reason one would hardly expect the Buddha to have any qualms about asserting this.[88] Therefore the reason for refusing to take up one of the two positions concerned with the world and thereby reject the other—for example, affirming that "the world is not eternal" and rejecting that "the world is eternal"—must be related to the way the questioners employed the term "world." The connotations it held for them must have been mistaken from an early Buddhist viewpoint. Instead of being a self-sufficient independent entity on which something can be predicated, in early Buddhist thought the "world" is rather the dependently arisen result of sense experience.

That implicit premises are the problem at stake becomes clearer with the two positions regarding the soul, *jīva*. According to the early Buddhist analysis, such a soul does not exist. Therefore it is hardly meaningful to make any statement about its relationship to the body, independent of whether this relationship is construed as being one of identity or of difference. As an aside, the refusal to affirm the identity of soul and body or their separateness in a way ties in with a point made in the previous chapter, in that early Buddhist thought in general, and its conception of rebirth in particular, is not based on a simple mind-body duality.

The same basic principle, evident from the questions regarding the world and the soul, also holds for a Tathāgata, where the taking of a position about what happens to a Tathāgata at death would first of all require clarifying what the term "Tathāgata" actually refers to. According to the

88. See, e.g., the proclamation made according to Ud 3.10 at Ud 33,15 by the Buddha that all forms of existence, *bhava*, are entirely impermanent, a statement found similarly in a counterpart in the *Mahāvastu*, Senart 1890, 418,11.

Pāli commentarial tradition, those who advocated any of the four positions on a Tathāgata after death did so by mistaking the term "Tathāgata," an expression in common usage in ancient Indian circles to refer to a fully realized one, as implying an actually existing living being, *satta*.[89] This would explain why, from an early Buddhist perspective, any predication about a Tathāgata after death is considered not suitable for being either taken up or rejected, on a par with a pronouncement on the relationship of the soul to the body or the nature of the world, in that all of these positions are considered to be based on wrong premises from the start.

The Destiny of an Awakened One after Death

The need to set these speculative views aside without attempting to take a position in relation to them was not always fully appreciated by the Buddha's own disciples, as the *Cūḷamālunkya-sutta* has already shown. A discourse in the *Saṃyutta-nikāya* and its Sanskrit fragment parallel report that the recently ordained Anurādha, on being confronted with the four positions regarding the destiny of a Tathāgata after death, proclaimed that there was a way apart from these four alternatives of declaring what happens to a Tathāgata after death.[90] This reply earned him the ridicule of his visitors, since the four alternatives formulated in the tetralemma form exhaust the possibilities that could be proposed according to ancient Indian logic. The episode involving Anurādha confirms that refusing to take up any of these four positions is not an implicit pointer to a position apart from these four.

The freedom of a fully awakened one from all possible types of future rebirth is a recurrent feature in the early discourses, being for example

89. Sv I 118,1: *satto tathāgato ti adhippeto*; see also Ps III 141,21, Spk II 201,4, and Mp IV 37,22: *tathāgato ti satto*. Gnanarama 1997, 236 comments that this implies that "those questions have been asked either due to eternalist or nihilist or sceptic points of view." Manda 2005, 716–15 adds that "Buddhaghosa does not intend to imply that a *tathāgata* is a normal person. On the contrary, it is clearly natural for him to regard a *tathāgata* as an enlightened one. The only question is whether a *tathāgata*. . .exists in this world as a *satta* or a living being."

90. SN 22.86 at SN III 116,20 and Sanskrit fragment Kha ii 3 R2, de La Vallée Poussin 1913, 579; according to another parallel, SĀ 106 at T 2.99.32c16, he simply clarified that, although these positions had indeed been left undeclared, this was not because the Buddha was bereft of knowledge and vision. This would have been a much wiser position to take.

part of the standard pericope that describes the gaining of full awakening with the phrase "birth is destroyed."[91] Thus the refusal to take up one of the four positions on a Tathāgata after death must indeed be related to misconceptions related to the term itself, such as taking it to stand for an actually existing living being.

The problem seen in the reification of a "living being," *satta*, recurs in a discourse in the *Saṃyutta-nikāya* and its *Saṃyukta-āgama* parallels. A Buddhist nun clarifies this issue in the following manner:[92]

> There is only a collection of empty aggregates,
> there is no "living being" [as such].
> Just as when the various parts are assembled,
> the world calls it a chariot,
> [so] in dependence on the combination of the aggregates
> there is the appellation "a living being."

Here the example of a chariot illustrates the notion of a living being. If the chariot is taken apart, one would hardly continue to call the different parts "a chariot." This does not imply that the term "chariot" has no meaning at all. The different parts spread on the ground are certainly not a chariot, but once they are placed together in a way that enables them to function, the result does become a chariot and it is possible to drive it. So the simile does not deny that a chariot or a being exists at all. The point is only that there is no substantial entity that corresponds to the notion of a chariot or a living being. Whether one closely inspects a chariot or a living being, one finds only a changing process of conditioned parts or aggregates whose mutual cooperation is responsible for the functional phenomenon referred to as a chariot or a being.

91. One of numerous examples for the use of this pericope would be the Buddha's own awakening, described in, e.g., MN 4 at MN I 23,24 and its parallel EĀ 31.1 at T 2.125.666c18; for another example see above note 77.

92. SĀ 1202 at T 2.99.327b8–10 (for a full translation of SĀ 1202 see Anālayo 2014d, 125–26), parallel to SN 5.10 at SN I 135,19 and SĀ[2] 218 at T 2.100.454c28; see also Enomoto 1994, 42 and D 4094 *nyu* 82a7 or Q 5595 *thu* 128b2. Whereas SN 5.10 identifies the nun as Vajirā, the parallels instead introduce her by the name of Selā.

This would make it clear why any proposition on the condition after death of a Tathāgata, as long as this comes with substantialist connotations, cannot be properly answered. Among four types of question recognized in early Buddhist thought, it falls into the last category, questions that are to be set aside.[93]

2. Debating Rebirth in Ancient India

Misunderstandings of the Teaching on Rebirth

The early discourses show some monk disciples of the Buddha seriously misunderstanding the core teaching on rebirth in general. The *Mahātaṇhāsaṅkhaya-sutta* and its parallels report a monk coming to the mistaken conclusion that it is this very same consciousness that will be reborn.[94] According to the *Mahāpuṇṇama-sutta* and its parallels, another monk came to the similarly mistaken conclusion that the teaching on notself implies that there is nobody who will be affected by the fruition of karma.[95]

In both cases the Buddha made it clear that the respective monks had thoroughly misunderstood his teachings. By way of clarifying both mistakes, the Buddha pointed to the principle of conditionality, or dependent arising. This in turn suggests that it was a lack of appreciation of this cardinal doctrine of early Buddhist thought and its implications that had fueled the misunderstanding of both monks. The same holds for later discussions, in that proper appreciation of the implications of dependent

93. DN 33 at DN III 229,20 (see also AN 4.42 at AN II 46,5) and its parallels in a Sanskrit fragment, Stache-Rosen 1968, 106 (§4.26), DĀ 9 at T 1.1.51b1, and T 1.12.230a4; see also the *Saṅgītiparyāya*, T 1536 at T 26.401b27, and the *Abhidharmakośabhāṣya*, Pradhan 1967, 292,12 (§5.22).

94. MN 38 at MN I 258,14 and MĀ 201 at T 1.26.767a9; part of his statement has been preserved in Sanskrit fragment SHT V 1114b1, Sander and Waldschmidt 1985, 109. Norman 1991/1993, 256 draws attention to passages that reflect ideas similar to this view in the *Bṛhadāraṇyaka Upaniṣad* 4.4.2 and 4.4.22, which supports the impression that the monk in question had not fully left behind ideas inherited from the general Indian religious background.

95. MN 109 at MN III 19,12 (= SN 22.82 at SN III 103,27) and the parallels SĀ 58 at T 2.99.15a12 and D 4094 *nyu* 56a6 or Q 5595 *thu* 98a4.

arising would make it clear how early Buddhist thought can combine a denial of an unchanging self with the affirmation of continuity beyond death.

Experiments to Prove the Materialist Position

As briefly mentioned in the first chapter of my study, the early discourses give the impression of having come into being in a setting where the idea of rebirth was far from universally accepted. Hence it comes as no surprise that at times the early Buddhists had to defend this doctrine when facing those who rejected the idea of any form of survival after death. The *Pāyāsi-sutta* and its parallels record a prolonged debate between the materialist Pāyāsi and the Buddhist monk Kumārakassapa on precisely this topic. In addition to the early Buddhist discourses that report their discussion, a similar debate is also recorded in a Jain text.[96] This goes to show that the need to defend teachings on rebirth against materialist challenges was shared by the Buddhist and Jain communities alike.

The *Pāyāsi-sutta* and its parallels report that Pāyāsi brought up various experiments carried out to prove that the whole of personal reality consists of the body alone. According to the description of these experiments, criminals were executed in various ways to determine whether some immaterial substance or soul could be seen to escape at the moment of their passing away. Here are some of the experiments reported in the *Dīrgha-āgama* parallel to the *Pāyāsi-sutta*:[97]

> In the village that is my fief some person committed thievery. The inspectors caught him, led him to me, and told me: "This man is a thief, may you punish him." I replied: "Take that man,

96. Bollée 2002; a comparison of the Buddhist and Jain versions of this discourse has been undertaken by Leumann 1885, 470–539 and Ruben 1935, 143–51; see also Frauwallner 1956/2003b, 193–94 and Ganeri 2014.

97. DĀ 7 at T 1.1.44a10-17; for a translation and comparative study of DĀ 7 see Anālayo 2012b and 2013b. In the parallel DN 23 at DN II 333,5 the investigation only takes place once the criminal is dead by opening the container and watching closely whether some soul, *jīva*, can be seen to escape. In MĀ 71 at T 1.26.528b26 the investigation takes place while the criminal is being cooked; see also T 1.45.833b28.

> bind him, and put him into a big cauldron, cover it with soft leather and with a thick layer of mud, so that [the covering] is firm and thick—let there be no leak. Dispatch people to surround it and boil it over fire."
>
> Then I wanted to observe and come to know whether his spirit goes out at some place. Leading my retinue we surrounded the cauldron and watched, but none of us saw his spirit come or go at any place. We opened the cauldron again to look and did not see the spirit coming or going at any place. For this reason I know that there is no other world.

The reference to an "other world" is to rebirth in some other form of existence. An alternative procedure adopted with another thief is described as follows:[98]

> I told my attendants to take and bind that man, take off his skin while he was alive, and seek the consciousness, yet we all did not see it. I again told my attendants to cut off the flesh and seek the consciousness, yet we still did not see it. I again told my attendants to sever the tendons and veins and seek the consciousness between the bones, yet we still did not see it. I again told my attendants to break the bones and extract the marrow to seek the consciousness inside the marrow, yet we still did not see it. Kassapa, for this reason I know that there is no other world.

Yet another thief reportedly received the following treatment:[99]

> I told my attendants: "Take that man and weigh him." My attendants took him while he was alive and weighed him. Then

98. DĀ 7 at T 1.1.44b7–12, with parallels in DN 23 at DN II 339,10, MĀ 71 at T 1.26.528c25, and T 1.45.833c22.

99. DĀ 7 at T 1.1.44c25–45a3, with parallels in DN 23 at DN II 334,19, MĀ 71 at T 1.26.528b1, and T 1.45.833a29.

> I told the attendants: "Take this man and slowly kill him without damaging his skin or flesh." They followed my instruction and killed him without any damage. I again told my attendants: "Again weigh him." He was heavier than before.
>
> Kassapa, we weighed that man when he was alive, when his consciousness was still there, his complexion was pleasing, he was still able to speak, and his body was light. When he was dead we weighed him again, when his consciousness had become extinct, he had lost his complexion, he was unable to speak, and his body had become heavy. For this reason I know that there is no other world.

It is remarkable that already in ancient India we find the idea of trying to test religious doctrine by conducting various experiments in such a manner. This holds independent of whether one considers the text to be reporting what Pāyāsi had actually told his attendants to do or whether he had only made up these descriptions for the sake of debate. In both cases the basic assumption behind the description given of these experiments is that, for anything to exist, it needs to be physically measurable in some way.

Since in reply to the earlier experiments Kumārakassapa had denied the possibility that the consciousness to be reborn can be seen, the last experiment then assumes that there should at least be some other evidence for it, such as weight. The body should be lighter after the departure of consciousness, but the experiment finds the opposite.

The materialist position taken by Pāyāsi foreshadows an attitude that continues to emerge again and again in debates surrounding rebirth right up to modern times. According to this attitude, the entire range of mental experiences is a mere byproduct of matter and can be accounted for in material terms, hence anything that is not observable and measurable in material terms has no claim to being real at all.

In the setting of the *Pāyāsi-sutta* and its parallels, Kumārakassapa is quick to challenge the assumptions underlying the epistemological position taken by Pāyāsi, which he does with the help of similes. He points out that, on granting the validity of this type of approach, one would have to grant to the congenitally blind the claim that, since they do not see certain things, these do not exist.[100]

Pāyāsi's expectation that the mind should manifest as an easily visible physical phenomenon at the time of death is like someone chopping up fire sticks and pounding them to dust in an attempt to find the fire that they can produce if used properly.[101] Or else it is like someone who has heard the sound of a conch being blown and then addresses the conch with a request for more sound, or in some versions of the discourse even goes so far as to hit the conch, kick it with the foot, or threaten to smash it, all done in an attempt to hear its beautiful sound again.[102] These replies exemplify the type of answer with which Buddhists of later times will try to meet the materialist challenge by rejecting its premises as invalid.

Continuity without an Unchanging Agent

The use of similes to counter materialistic assumptions in a debate about rebirth recurs again in the Indian context in subsequent times. The *Milindapañha* reports another Buddhist monk by the name of Nāgasena in debate with a king known in the Pāli tradition under the name Milinda, presumably a Bactrian Greek king who lived during the second century B.C.E.[103] The king appears puzzled by the idea of rebirth without a lasting agent or soul. In order to illustrate this concept, Nāgasena employs the simile of a lamp. In a Chinese parallel to the *Milindapañha* the relevant exchange proceeds as follows:[104]

100. DN 23 at DN II 328,3 and its parallels DĀ 7 at T 1.1.43c29, MĀ 71 at T 1.26.527a24, and T 1.45.832b27.

101. DN 23 at DN II 341,1 and its parallels DĀ 7 at T 1.1.44c2, MĀ 71 at T 1.26.529a17, and T 1.45.834a13.

102. DN 23 at DN II 337,23 and its parallels DĀ 7 at T 1.1.45a22, MĀ 71 at T 1.26.528a9, and T 1.45.833a12.

103. On Milinda see, e.g., Arunasiri 2002.

104. T 32.1670A.698b8-13. The relevant part of the parallel T 32.1670B.708c21 has already been translated by Guang Xing 2007, 141; for a translation of this passage in both versions see Demiéville 1924, 115–16. The corresponding simile in the Pāli version can be found at Mil 40,20.

Nāgasena asked the king: "If a person lights a lamp, would it reach up to the time of the [next] day's dawn?"

The king replied: "A lamp with [sufficient] oil lit by a person would reach up to the time of dawn."

Nāgasena said: "Did [the flame] on the wick in the lamp during the first watch of the night continue to be the original flame on the wick? Did the original flame continue until midnight? Did it continue until the time of the [next] day?"

The king replied: "It did not [continue to be] the original flame."

Nāgasena said: "Regarding the lamp lit from the first watch of the night until midnight, has the lamp been lit again? Has the lamp been lit again at the time of dawn?"

The king replied: "No."

The point Nāgasena makes is that the flame continues throughout the night, even though this is not always the same flame, nor has there been a need to introduce another flame. This illustrates the Buddhist position that there is a continuity of consciousness, even though the consciousness of one particular moment is not just the same as the consciousness of another moment.

Expressed in doctrinal terms, the doctrine of *anattā* denies the assumption that throughout the night it is exactly the same flame that is burning. However, it does not deny that there is a continuity of the lamp burning and producing light—just that this continuity is merely a process without any unchanging substantial core.

Applying the same imagery to the case of rebirth, Nāgasena then gives the example of using the flame of this lamp to light another lamp.[105]

If for example with the wick in a lamp one lights another one, the burning of the original wick continues on the new wick.

105. T 32.1670A.700a10, with its counterparts in T 32.1670B.715c3–4 and Mil 71,19; see also Demiéville 1924, 154 and Guang Xing 2007, 173.

Such similes employed by Nāgasena reflect the need to provide some self-evident and easily understandable illustration of the principle of rebirth to an audience not accustomed to the early Buddhist doctrines of rebirth and notself.

The same difficulty of communicating an idea that does not easily fit existing notions and ideas becomes evident when turning to the situation in China from about the second century C.E. onward, where the proponents of Buddhism had to find ways of making the teachings on rebirth and karma comprehensible to their Chinese audience.[106]

3. Discussions on Rebirth in China during the Early Imperial Period

For most Chinese of the early centuries of the present era, the notion of an indeterminate survival after death was to some degree in conflict with existing beliefs.[107] A particular challenge in explaining the Buddhist idea of rebirth was to differentiate it from the notion of a perishable soul apparently fairly common in the Chinese setting.[108]

106. Needless to say, the teachings on rebirth that arrived in China would have come from various Buddhist traditions and in a piecemeal fashion, hence they can hardly be expected to correspond exactly to the early Buddhist perspective on the matter. In fact the same already applies to the *Milindapañha* just mentioned, as on a number of occasions this work reflects thought that developed subsequent to the early Buddhist period. It is only in relation to DN 23 and its parallels that it can safely be assumed that the doctrine debated reflects the early Buddhist conception of rebirth.

107. Yü 1987, 379 points out that "the belief that the departed soul actually enjoys the sacrificial food offered by the living was widely held in the popular culture of Han China. . .on the other hand, the idea that the individual soul can survive death indefinitely seems to have been alien to the Chinese mind." As Teiser 1996, 202 notes, from the viewpoint of traditional Chinese society, "a strict reading of the doctrine of karma throws into question the efficacy of traditional ancestral offerings."

108. Commenting on Han Buddhism, Zürcher 1959/1972, 11–12 explains that "the Chinese (not unreasonably) were unable to see in the doctrine of rebirth anything else than an affirmation of the survival of the 'soul' (*shen* 神) after death," resulting in "attacks of traditionalists who hold [the soul] to be 'annihilated'. . .at the moment of physical death." Liebenthal 1952, 346 quotes from sixth- to seventh-century documents the statement "many think that body and soul perish together."

Arguments against Rebirth and Karma

As in the case of Pāyāsi, materialism appears to have been of considerable influence in some Chinese circles, leading to a reasoning of this type:[109]

> When the body dissolves, the soul diffuses into nowhere; when the wood disintegrates, the fire dies lacking support. Such is the rule.

From such a perspective, the question then arises:[110]

> How could there be in this world a mind. . .that can perceive without a body?

The same position also finds expression in the two-pronged proposal that either the mental is part of existence, hence it cannot survive the body, or else it is not part of existence, in which case it would not be of relevance for an account of experience and it would not be possible to say anything about it. The passage in question proceeds as follows:[111]

> Though the corporeal and the uncorporeal are distinguished by their origin, both belong to Existence. [Argument. First alternative] Belonging to Existence, they are [both] rooted in Life. How is it possible that something survives when the root from which it grows is cut?
>
> [Second alternative] Not belonging to [Existence and] Life, [the soul] would be beyond our reach and altogether unfathomable, there would be no possibility to say anything about it.

109. Translated by Liebenthal 1952, 356. For passages quoted in this section of my exploration I have relied on translations provided by others, in contrast to chapter 1 and the first two sections of chapter 2, in which translations are my own.

110. Translated by Park 2012, 167 from a Daoist treatise.

111. Translated by Liebenthal 1952, 348.

In short, how could something, which during life clearly depends on the body, survive when the body breaks apart?[112]

> When the body has gone, to what should the soul apply itself and survive? If [the soul] survives [in the corpse], that would contradict its [function of] animating. If it [survives] in a disembodied state, then why should it incarnate in a body and [stay there during its lifetime] without ever leaving it? If it is unable ever to leave the body [during its lifetime], then both live together [and die together]. That seems to be the conclusion.

The same is briefly expressed as part of a criticism of the belief in a "ghost":[113]

> What sustains the life of man are vitality (*ching*) and spirit (*ch'i*). When man dies, vitality and spirit disappear. When this happens, the body begins to rot. Finally it becomes dust. Where could the ghost be?

The notion of karma also came in for criticism as something that cannot be verified and therefore as being just a belief accepted by simple people.[114]

> A wealth of evidence is quoted which is unverifiable. . .[yet] this doctrine. . .has credit with the simple fellow. . .[it] is a sham teaching fit for the purpose of pious propaganda, but untenable scientifically.

A particular difficulty the Buddhist conception of karma encountered on arrival in China was a prevalent belief that individuals share the retribution for deeds performed by their ancestors.[115] Such a notion of collective

112. Translated by Liebenthal 1952, 349.

113. Translated in Poo 1990, 60.

114. Translated by Liebenthal 1952, 375–76.

115. Zürcher 1980, 136–38 speaks of a "conception of collective guilt," which takes the form

guilt along family lines contrasts sharply with the individualist aspect of the Buddhist conception of karma, according to which one is the heir of one's own deeds, not of the deeds of others.[116]

Defending the Rebirth Doctrine

An argument raised in ancient China in defense of the rebirth doctrine is that conditions are responsible for continuity. The continuity of this process from one body to another finds illustration in the simile of the flame that is able to cross over a distance between one piece of wood and another, comparable to the argument employed by the monk Nāgasena and the illustration already found in the early discourses.[117] The relevant passage proceeds as follows:[118]

> You think instead that soul and body together perish! How sad!. . .transformations go on without interruption. Causes and

of "the belief (a) that the supplicant is burdened by the sins of his forbears and, in turn, is likely to commit sins implicating his children and grandchildren; (b) that his own redemption also implies that of his deceased relatives; but also (c) that he himself can only be exonerated and expect promotion if those relatives are discharged," which stands in contrast to "the fact that in Buddhism *karman* and retribution are, in principle, strictly individual, and that the whole concept of collective inherited guilt is not admitted." Bokenkamp 2007, 165 comments that "Buddhist karma entailed the idea that one's birth parents are not the true source of one's being, that there is no such thing as collective guilt within the family, and that one suffers the consequences of one's own deeds from previous lives. These were difficult pills to swallow" in the Chinese setting.

116. Yün-Hua 1986, 161 explains that "the lack of a rebirth doctrine in pre-Buddhist China had limited the Chinese idea of retribution to one's present lifetime. Consequently, if any retributive effect took place beyond the doer's life span, it would be left to his descendants to face. It is only in the Buddhist doctrine that the doer must face the consequences of his own deeds, either in the present or in his future life." Eventually, however, as pointed out by Teiser 1988, 460, "a synthesis of Indian and Chinese concepts" regarding the underworld took place, where "the Indian notion of karma and the Chinese principle of bureaucracy formed a seamless administrative net." Assandri 2013, 9 explains that the Buddhist doctrine "introduced the element of the morality of the individual's life as a possible determinant for the destination in the after-life. Thus, the post-mortem fate of the deceased came to be seen as dependent not only on correct mourning, care and commemoration by the descendants, but also on the moral qualities of the deceased's life"; see also Assandri and Wang Ping 2010, 148.

117. See above note 44.

118. Translated by Liebenthal 1952, 357–58; on the fire simile see also Fung 1953, 288–89.

> conditions co-operate and pass on their impulses...fire leaping from wood to wood can be compared to the soul transmigrating through bodies...the second body being different from the first one, we know how strongly our will [to live] yearns for continued existence. A fool, when he sees a body dissolving at the end of a life, believes that the will [to live] of the soul also perishes.

Other rebuttals consider the position taken by their opponents to be due to the influence of worldly literature that makes people believe that only what can be perceived by the senses is real. Thus the rejection of the Buddhist doctrine of rebirth is attributed to:[119]

> the worldly literature that cannot see beyond the borderlines of one incarnation, and thus makes those who seek after the truth believe that it can be found among the things perceivable by our senses.

Such a predicament then elicits the following comment:[120]

> Oh, these master-minds, these super-intellects, who believe only in hard facts!...those who today with a hazy mind try to illumine the dark [recesses of the universe] are they, unable to recognize what they are losing, capable of discerning what they may win?

In short, the argument is: since the mind is not made out of matter, why should it die along with the body?[121]

> [The] spirit is not made from matter, ... [it] joins it but does not die with it ... if it were created from matter and died with it, it would be matter itself.

119. Translated by Liebenthal 1952, 364.

120. Translated by Liebenthal 1952, 379–80.

121. Translated by Liebenthal 1952, 384.

Near-Death Experiences in Ancient China

A new element in the discussion on rebirth comes from near-death experiences, already known in China from the period before the arrival of Buddhism.[122] During such near-death experiences meetings reportedly took place with persons whose identity and timing of death the revived person could subsequently confirm.[123]

One case, for example, involves a meeting in the world beyond with a former neighbor who had been dead for seven or eight years. The neighbor relates that he had buried some cash beneath the bed in his house. After returning from the world beyond, the revived person informs the wife of the deceased. She indeed finds the cash in the place indicated by the revived person, based on the information received from the world of the dead.[124] Or else in two similar cases a man and a woman both going through near-death experiences meet for the first time in the world beyond and, based on the information exchanged in the other world, after reviving find each other again and get married.[125]

A noteworthy aspect of such near-death reports in the ancient Chinese setting is that experiences during a time of being to all appearances dead, at least from the viewpoint of this world, take place in the other world within the setting of a thoroughly bureaucratized administration.[126] Regularly the fact that the person in question is able to return to life is related to an error made in the registers of this administrative system, on the discovery of which the person in question is then allowed to return among the living.[127]

122. McClenon 1991, 326 notes that "the NDE [near-death experience] motif existed in Chinese folklore previous to the entrance of Buddhism. Since ancestral worship was a major component of their religious practice, Chinese people were particularly curious regarding the nature of the afterlife. This interest probably granted NDE narratives special rhetorical power for shaping religious ideologies."

123. Campany 1990, 100.

124. Campany 1990, 96.

125. Campany 1990, 109 and 118.

126. Harper 1994, 17 notes that "by no later than the end of the fourth century B.C. the underworld already resembled a bureaucratic state"; see also, e.g., Pirazzoli-t'Serstevens 2009, 975.

127. Cedzich 2001, 25 comments that "the world beyond was imagined as a complex administration with headquarters inside China's five sacred mountains. . .the vast bureaucracy was

One such report describes five hundred clerks busily correlating different types of animal birth with the actions of people they have been recording.[128] In another such tale the Heavenly Emperor offers to restore to someone his wife, who had passed away three years prior, and then orders the census entry of the wife to be moved to the register of the living. The wife indeed comes back to life, along with the husband.[129]

In this way, alongside showing a lively continuity of the debate on rebirth, the setting in China also reflects the influence of new notions mirroring the cultural setting, where persons who go through a near-death experience find themselves facing a huge bureaucracy responsible for administering the world beyond. I will return to the topic of near-death experiences (and the impact of cultural notions and beliefs on these) in the first part of the next chapter.

4. Debates on Rebirth in Modern Times

Misinterpretations of Karma and Rebirth

Most of the themes encountered so far continue in discussions of rebirth in modern times. One recurrent source of misunderstanding remains karma, which at times is considered to be putting the blame on the one who suffers.[130] This does not apply to the early Buddhist conception of

---

ruled by the Yellow (or Celestial) Emperor, who supervised detailed registers of the living and the dead that determined the individual life mandates of all humans. When these registers indicated that a person's allotted time had expired, the person was summoned to the other world and died. The name of the deceased was accordingly transferred from the register of life to that of the dead." Seidel 1987, 232 notes that even "the liturgy to save the dead is modelled after the judicial paperwork necessary for freeing a condemned prisoner. Gifts (with a flavor of bribes) are prepared, and an official petition is drawn up humbly submitting the case to the highest celestial gods, with an appeal for amnesty."

128. Gjertson 1980, 58–59; see also Kao 1985, 169–70.

129. Gjertson 1981, 290. Another story with a somewhat opposite effect involves a husband who during a visit to the netherworld finds out that his deceased wife should have been returned to the living, as she had been summoned by mistake, but was intercepted by a chief attendant of the administration in the netherworld who preferred to keep her for himself, as he was struck by her beauty; see Duyvendak 1952, 264.

130. An example of the extremes to which such a misunderstanding can lead is provided by Edwards 1996, 42, who describes the following consequences that according to his assess-

karma. Identifying karma as volition is in fact the opposite of fatalism, since it puts the spotlight on one's volitional decisions in the present moment. In other words, far from than encouraging a fatalist attitude, the doctrine of karma is meant to encourage taking responsibility for one's present actions with the understanding that these have far-reaching consequences.[131] The central concern that emerges from the early Buddhist notion of karma is how to react skillfully in the present situation.[132]

Such a formulation of the doctrine of karma certainly does not imply that those who suffer deserve it, simply because karma is not the only cause of suffering. Besides not attributing all responsibility to the past deeds of an individual, the teachings on reacting skillfully that inform the conception of karma in early Buddhist thought are precisely about how to avoid suffering when faced with the vicissitudes of life.

In order to appreciate the early Buddhist conception of karma, it needs to be kept in mind that it does not involve monocausality. It does not posit a single cause, such as one's deeds in the past, as the sole condition responsible for one's present situation. Therefore to approach a situation of suffering from the viewpoint of the early Buddhist theory of karma is not about giving rise to guilt and blaming but about responding to suffering, be it one's own or that of others, in wholesome ways. In short, karma is predominantly about taking the right "action" now.

---

ment result for one who believes in karma: "The suffering individual in his view *deserves* to suffer because he committed evil acts in this or else in a previous life. It is not only not our duty to help him but it would seem on karmic principles that it is our duty *not* to help him...as far as I can see...karma is completely vacuous as a principle of moral guidance." Edwards 1996, 43 then goes further by proposing that "karma provides no guidance on how to act but it does have implications concerning the appropriate attitude towards successful and unsuccessful people, towards those who are happy and those who are suffering: we should applaud and admire the former and despise or even hate the latter." As a final conclusion, Edwards 1996, 44 then arrives at the proposal that the law of karma entails that, "since the Jews deserved extinction, the Nazis were not really criminals and should not have been prosecuted."

131. Stevenson 1987/2001, 232 and 231 comments that some "Westerners find the idea of chance somewhat appealing, and to the extent that they do so, they may think that of reincarnation uncongenial." "If a person cannot accept responsibility for the outcome of one life, he will not welcome being asked to assume it for two or more lives."

132. Bodhi 2015, 189 explains that "the ultimate implication of the Buddha's teaching on kamma and rebirth is that human beings are the final masters of their own destiny."

A related problem is the attempt to verify the workings of karma. As the exposition of karma in the *Mahākammavibhaṅga-sutta* and its parallels (discussed in the previous chapter) shows,[133] at times those who do what is good are not seen to experience positive results, and those who perform evil can be observed to be living in joy and pleasure. The complexity of karma, at least in its early Buddhist formulation, leaves room for such observations, with the caveat that they need to be contextualized. Doers of good and evil will both in the end meet with the respective fruits of their deeds. These fruits do not ripen immediately, however, but can, according to the early Buddhist concept of karma, do so even after several lifetimes, making it impossible to prove or disprove the workings of karma using empirical evidence from the present life of a person.

Another problem is that the early Buddhist teaching on continuity from one life to another is assumed to be based on a simple mind-body duality.[134] Yet the reciprocal conditioning between consciousness and name-and-form, as presented in the *Mahānidāna-sutta* (discussed in the previous chapter), shows that this is not the case.[135]

The same reciprocal conditioning also makes it clear that the early Buddhist conception of the principles governing rebirth is in harmony with its teachings on the absence of a permanent self, *anattā*. This serves to clear up another recurrent misunderstanding, namely the assumption that rebirth conflicts with the teaching on notself.[136] The doctrine of

133. See above p. 25.

134. See, e.g., Batchelor 2010/2011, 38, who assumes that to explain rebirth one needs to "posit an impermanent, non-physical mental process to account for what is reborn. This unavoidably leads to a body-mind dualism." Batchelor 2010/2011, 38 then reports how he came to rebel against what he saw as implicit in the idea of rebirth as follows: "I rebelled against the very idea of body-mind dualism. I could not accept that my experience was ontologically divided into two incommensurable spheres: one material, the other mental. Rationally, I found the idea incoherent." Batchelor 2015, 300 then concludes that "Buddhist proponents of rebirth...opt for a body-mind dualism. They maintain that mind and matter are ontologically separate 'substances' (Sanskrit: *dravya*) and thus fundamentally incommensurable."

135. See above p. 9, *pace* Edwards 1996, 14–15, who reasons that "reincarnation logically presupposes an extreme form of dualism," hence "to refute reincarnationism it is quite sufficient to show that the extreme form of dualism is untenable."

136. Willson 1984/1987, 16 comments that "amateur writers on Buddhism never tire of

dependent arising can be considered as the other side of the coin of the teaching on *anattā*: the two require each other rather than standing in some sort of opposition to each other.

Yet another problem sometimes raised is how to reconcile rebirth with the observable current human-population growth and our knowledge of the evolution of the human species.[137] This problem does not affect the early Buddhist conception of rebirth, which operates on the notion of various realms of existence into which (or from which) rebirth can take place.[138] Similarly to the inability to prove or disprove karma based on empirical evidence from the present life of a person, the population growth on the planet Earth provides evidence neither in favor of, nor in contrast to, the early Buddhist teaching on rebirth.

Alongside the continuity of several themes in the debate around rebirth, what appears to be a new contribution in recent times is the suggestion that the historical Buddha did not teach rebirth.[139] Such an apparently apologetic move, presumably in order to render Buddhist teachings more palatable to a contemporary audience, is hard to reconcile with the textual material that we have at our disposal, as would have become evident

making the absurd claim that the teaching of rebirth is somehow contradicted by the principle of Selflessness." This seems to hold not only for "amateur writers on Buddhism," given that Batchelor 1997, 36 reasons as follows: "a central Buddhist idea, however, is that no such intrinsic self can be found. . .how do we square this with rebirth?" This mode of reasoning stands in continuity with the type of argument raised by Christian catechists, active in Sri Lanka in the nineteenth century, when debating Buddhist beliefs; see, e.g., Young and Somaratna 1996, 82–83.

137. This problem has been raised by Edwards 1996, 225–26.

138. Jayatilleke 1969, 43 comments on the argument regarding the increase in human population that "this objection would be valid if the theory required that any human birth at present presupposes the death of a prior human being on this earth. Such a theory would also make it impossible for human beings to evolve out of anthropoid apes since the first human beings to evolve would not have had human ancestors."

139. Story 1975/2010, 15 comments that "there are certain persons today who try to maintain that the Buddha did not teach rebirth. Whether they propagate this view in the mistaken belief that by so doing they make Buddhism more acceptable to the modern mind, which they imagine is completely wedded to materialism, or because they wish to convert Buddhism and Buddhists to the materialist-annihilationist view which the Buddha expressly repudiated. . .they are sufficiently refuted in every expression of the Buddha's teaching."

from the survey of several key passages in the first chapter of my study. In fact such attempts have been criticized as involving a form of intellectual dishonesty.[140]

An examination of the earliest textual sources at our disposal makes it indubitably clear that teachings on rebirth are an integral part of the early Buddhist thought to which we have access through the texts. This leaves little ground for the hypothesis that the historical Buddha did not teach rebirth or even that he taught rebirth only as an expedient means, without himself accepting it.[141]

Confirmation Bias

For the continuing debate around the topic of rebirth, it is helpful to keep in mind the problem of selective attention under the influence of what cognitive psychology refers to as "confirmation bias" or "my-side bias," as a result of which data will easily be misjudged and misunderstood.[142] The impact of such "confirmation bias" or "my-side bias" on the processing and evaluation of data has a considerable bearing on the debate regarding

140. Story 1975/2010, 92 argues that "to maintain that the Buddha did not teach rebirth is surely the most curious aberration that has ever made its appearance in Buddhism. It places upon one who holds it the burden of proof that most of the statements attributed to the Buddha were not made by him at all...for one claiming to be a Buddhist to maintain that the Buddha did not teach rebirth is an intellectual dishonesty of the worst kind...even if the doctrine of rebirth were not true, *it is true that the Buddha taught it*. The denial of that fact constitutes a lie."

141. Jayatilleke 1969, 1–2 identifies as "misconceptions" the following notions: "the Buddha utilised the doctrines of rebirth and *karma*...to impart ethical teachings but did not himself believe in these doctrines" and "the Buddha was not interested or held no specific views about the question of human survival or life after death. He roundly condemned speculation about the past or the future (i.e. about prior lives or future lives) as unprofitable and mistaken. He was only concerned with man's present state of anxiety, suffering and dissatisfaction and the solution for it."

142. An example is the interpretation by Batchelor 2010/2011, 100 of the unanswered questions as showing that "by refusing to address whether mind and body are the same or different or whether one exists after death or not, he [the Buddha] undermines the possibility of constructing a theory of reincarnation." Yet *jīva* does not refer to the "mind," and the *tathāgata* does not stand for "one" in general but much rather for an "awakened one." Besides misunderstanding the formulation, this suggestion also misjudges the Buddha's refusal to give a reply to these questions.

rebirth. The basic working mechanism of this bias can be described as follows:[143]

> Individuals will dismiss and discount empirical evidence that contradicts their initial views but will derive support from evidence, of no greater probativeness, that seems consistent with their views. Through such biased assimilation even a random set of outcomes or events can appear to lend support for an entrenched position, and both sides in a given debate can have their positions bolstered by the same set of data...
>
> The biased assimilation processes underlying this effect may include a propensity to remember the strengths of confirming evidence but the weaknesses of disconfirming evidence, to judge confirming evidence as relevant and reliable but disconfirming evidence as irrelevant and unreliable, and to accept confirming evidence at face value while scrutinizing disconfirming evidence hypercritically.

The effect of this tendency is not mitigated by intelligence,[144] nor does higher education provide an effective vaccination against the impact of confirmation bias.[145] Thus the danger of such bias is not merely confined to the faithful, who all too eagerly accept anything as truth and fact as long as it confirms their beliefs. It similarly holds sway over skeptics, who

143. Lord, Ross, and Lepper 1979, 2099. Hart et al. 2009, 579 point out that the strength of such bias is such that "people are almost two times...more likely to select information congenial rather than uncongenial to their pre-existing attitudes, beliefs, and behaviors."

144. West, Meserve, and Stanovich 2012, 515 found that "more intelligent people were not actually less biased...cognitive ability provides no inoculation at all from the bias blind spot—the tendency to believe that biased thinking is more prevalent in others than in ourselves." Stanovich, West, and Toplak 2013, 262 conclude that "individuals of higher intelligence are often just as likely to engage in biased reasoning as people of lesser intelligence."

145. Greenhoot et al. 2004, 219 report from their research that "the data here suggest that it is entirely possible to engage students in a curriculum on scientific reasoning and have them perform at a high level on the general concepts when tested about those concepts and the generation of scientifically valid conclusions, yet fail to use those concepts effectively when reasoning scientifically about real-world issues—particularly those with scientific solutions that may be at odds with their own existing prior beliefs."

just as eagerly dismiss anything as false and fake as long as it conflicts with their preconceived notions. In fact confirmation bias has been shown to have had a considerable effect on science itself. The basic pattern at work is as follows:[146]

> One can see confirmation bias both in the difficulty with which new ideas break through opposing established points of view and in the uncritical allegiance they are often given once they have become part of the established view themselves.

Summary

The Buddhist doctrine of rebirth has continued to be a topic of debate from ancient India up to modern times. In the Indian setting at the Buddha's time, the destiny of a liberated one after death appears to have aroused much interest. Closer inspection shows that the Buddha's refusal to agree to one of the preformulated propositions must be related to unwarranted assumptions implicit in the positions taken on this topic.

A theme that persists throughout centuries of debate is the assumption that a continuity of the mind beyond death is to be rejected by recourse to physical measurements based on a materialistic point of view. Already the early discourses report drastic "experiments" undertaken by an Indian materialist to prove that nothing continues beyond death.

A new contribution made to the discussion on rebirth in China can be found in reports of near-death experiences. These are couched in terms reflecting the ancient Chinese worldview to such an extent that the world beyond is experienced as thoroughly bureaucratized, a clear pointer to the subjectivity that can influence such reports.

A contribution made in modern times is the attempt to deny the rebirth dimension of early Buddhism. As the previous chapter would have made amply clear, this does not concord with what emerges from the historical-critical study of the textual material at our disposal.

146. Nickerson 1998, 197, a conclusion preceded by a survey of such cases in the history of science.

Both sides in the controversy, the faithful just as much as the skeptic, are prone to be influenced by confirmation bias or my-side bias, reading data in such a way that it confirms their predetermined ideas. This makes itself felt in relation to research for evidence related to the idea of rebirth. It is to such research that I turn in the next chapter.

III. Evidence Considered Supportive of Rebirth

Introduction

From the topic of debate related to rebirth, discussed in the last chapter, with the present chapter I move on to evidence adduced in support of rebirth in modern times. This is of course contested ground, and those who affirm just as those who reject rebirth are equally prone to read confirmation of their respective beliefs into the data, seen as either proving rebirth beyond doubt or else being insufficient to draw any type of conclusion that might question the current scientific paradigm, according to which the mind is a product of the brain.

In what follows my aim is to present a balanced survey of the main relevant contributions. I introduce each topic with a brief reference to a comparable phenomenon known from the history of Buddhist and other religious traditions in order to establish the continuity of such topics since ancient times, in line with what emerged in the previous chapter. Due to the mass of information available, I am only able to give brief summaries; in fact, even doing just that, what follows is still the longest of the four chapters in this book.

In relation to my surveys of contemporary research related to rebirth, I need to put on record that with these topics I am outside my own area of expertise. Therefore all I can offer is a selection of what to me seems relevant from perusing the publications of which I have become aware, without being able to assess these in the way an expert could. Although I have endeavored to cover what seemed relevant, quite probably I have overlooked significant publications, be these supportive or critical.

Nevertheless, within the confines of my awareness of relevant material and my understanding of what it implies, I hope to present a reasonably accurate survey that adopts a moderate position and avoids strongly dogmatic attitudes, be these based on scientific or religious grounds.

My exploration covers the following areas of research, from the viewpoint of their potential relevance to the question or rebirth: near-death experiences (1), past-life regression (2), children's memories of a past life (3), and xenoglossy (4).[147]

1. Near-Death Experiences

As mentioned in the preceding chapter, near-death experiences were already reported in ancient China and continue to be recorded up to the modern day.[148] Such near-death experiences, often referred to in the relevant literature with the abbreviation NDE, are a widespread phenomenon and as such attested in various cultures. Besides China, India, and Tibet, for example, near-death experiences have been reported from a range of non-Western cultures and peoples, including Africans, hunter-gatherer cultures in North and South America, Aboriginal Australians, the Māori of New Zealand, and others from the Pacific area, such as Guam and Hawai'i.[149]

The topic has come to the forefront of public and academic interest in recent decades, as developments in health care have enabled the resuscitation of patients who only a few decades ago would have stood little chance of survival. This has led to an increase in the occurrence of near-death experiences and made such cases considerably more conspicuous.

147. I have not included mediumistic communications in this survey, as I am uncertain to what degree this can be considered to provide convincing evidence in support of the rebirth hypothesis.

148. See, e.g., Feng and Liu 1992; on attitudes in contemporary China toward such experiences see Kellehear, Heaven, and Gao 1990.

149. For a survey of relevant research see, e.g., Belanti, Perera, and Jagadheesan 2008 and Kellehear 2009.

From Ancient to Contemporary Reports of Near-Death Experiences

The early Buddhist discourses repeatedly portray the Buddha and chief disciples visiting various heavens and returning to report their encounters with celestial beings. Such visits appear to have been originally conceived of as being undertaken with a mind-made body.[150] As already briefly mentioned in the first chapter, the creation of such a mind-made body as the outcome of meditative expertise is held to result in the ability to leave the physical body behind and move around at the speed of thought, without being obstructed by anything material, yet at the same time being able to see and hear.

The early discourses also report frequently that celestial beings come to pay a visit to the Buddha or his disciples. One such instance involves a lay disciple who has just passed away and been reborn in a heaven. As a celestial being he approaches the Buddha at night and speaks a poem, which the next morning the Buddha then reports to his disciples.[151]

An otherworld journey that has some features in common with near-death experiences, except for the fact that it does not involve being close to death, is the tale of King Nimi found in a discourse in the *Majjhima-nikāya* and its parallels. Because of his exemplary conduct, King Nimi has been invited to visit heaven by the divine ruler of the Heaven of the Thirty-Three. Asked by the celestial charioteer, who has come to fetch him, which way he prefers to be driven to reach his heavenly destination, King Nimi prefers to be taken in such a way that he can see both the regions where evildoers suffer for their deeds and the regions where those who act well enjoy the fruits of their wholesome conduct. After completion of the journey he arrives in the Heaven of the Thirty-Three and is offered the option to remain. He declines, since he prefers to go back to earth and continue his wholesome conduct.[152]

150. See in more detail Anālayo 2016a.

151. MN 143 at MN III 262,8 (= SN 2.20 at SN I 55,12) and the parallels SĀ 593 at T 2.99.158c3, SĀ[2] 187 at T 2.100.441c15, and EĀ 51.8 at T 2.125.820a25.

152. MN 83 at MN II 80,19 (see also Jā 541 at Jā VI 127,32), MĀ 67 at T 1.26.515a3, EĀ 50.4 at T 2.125.809c17, T 3.152.49b14, and the *Bhaiṣajyavastu* of the Mūlasarvāstivāda *Vinaya*, Dutt 1984, 113,4 and D 1 *kha* 55b6 or Q 1030 *ge* 51b3.

Perhaps the most well-known instance of influence of near-death experiences on a Buddhist text is the so-called *Tibetan Book of the Dead*, a work considerably later than the early discourses. This text provides guidance for what is to be expected on passing away.[153] Actual near-death experiences are described in versions of the scripture on the Medicine King, Bhaiṣajyaguru, another comparatively late text. The relevant passage reports that deceased persons, on being brought for the reckoning of their actions in front of the ruler of the underworld, King Yāma, can be made to return to their body through devotional activities performed on their behalf toward Bhaiṣajyaguru. They revive as if waking up from a dream.[154] Because of recollecting the karmic consequences of their good and bad deeds, they will be transformed by this experience and behave in wholesome ways for the rest of their lives.

In addition to being attested in Buddhist sources, the notion that on passing away one will encounter deceased friends and relatives is found, for example, in the so-called *Egyptian Book of the Dead*;[155] in fact it has been argued that the descriptions in this text derive from acquaintance with near-death experiences.[156] Another relevant text is the Myth of Er in Plato's *Republic*, which involves a soldier who has died in battle. The tale goes that, after an interval of several days during which his corpse did not decompose, he revived on his funeral pyre and then related the experiences he had had in the otherworld.[157]

Turning to Christian sources, what immediately comes to mind as a related notion is the resurrection of Jesus himself, as well as his famous

153. The classic translation of this work is Evans-Wentz 1927/2000; for a study see, e.g., Cuevas 2003.

154. Schopen 1978, 61,27 (Sanskrit) and 98,3 (Tibetan), with Chinese parallels in T 14.449.403c25, T 14.450.407b22, and T 14.451.415c8; see also T 21.1331.536a2.

155. Walker and Serdahely 1990, 105–6; for descriptions of otherworld experiences in Zoroastrianism see Skjærvø 2013.

156. Schumann and Rossini 1995/1998, 110–12. Ross 1979, 31 notes the continuity of the tenets evident in this ancient text "today among most of the religious tribes of the Sudan."

157. *Republic* 10.614–21; on the Myth of Er, as well as other such tales, see, e.g., Platthy 1992, Bremmer 2002, 90–96, and van der Sluijs 2009.

resuscitation, if it can be called such, of Lazarus.[158] An apparent reference to a visit to the otherworld can be found in St. Paul's Second Epistle to the Corinthians. In this epistle St. Paul briefly refers to a visit to heaven, presumably experienced by himself.[159]

St. Gregory the Great, who served as pope in the sixth century, reports episodes in which souls are taken away from their body as if by mistake and then come back to life.[160] One such episode concerns a Spanish hermit monk who recalls his visit to hell.[161] In another tale a person has just died. When it is found out that another person by the same name should have been brought to the nether regions, the first person is sent back to life.[162] After miraculously reviving, he finds out that at the very time of his revival another person of the same name indeed passed away.

In recent times, accounts of comparable experiences have multiplied, so much so that an entire journal is dedicated to research on near-death experiences,[163] and a range of monographs and other publications tackle various aspects of such experiences.

A continuity with modern accounts can be seen in the following features of medieval episodes:[164]

> external proofs that are remarkably similar to the kind of evidence brought forward in contemporary near-death literature: the transformation of the visionary, unusual physical and emotional symptoms, signs that he was truly dead, and extraordinary powers, such as the ability to predict his own death or that

158. John 11:43. On resurrection from a Buddhist perspective see Gethin 1996.

159. 2 Corinthians 12:2. On Gnostic Christianity and near-death experiences see Bain 1999.

160. Moricca 1924, 285,6: *nonnulli quasi per errorem extrahuntur e corpore, ita ut facti exanimes redeant*; on the role of St. Gregory the Great as the forefather of accounts of visions of the otherworld see also, e.g., Dinzelbacher et al. 1990, 267.

161. Moricca 1924, 285,17.

162. Moricca 1924, 286,22.

163. *The Journal of Near-Death Studies*, published by IANDS (International Association for Near Death Studies).

164. Zaleski 1987, 84.

> of others, or to know things that he could not have found out through normal means.

A noteworthy difference also emerges when comparing contemporary accounts to medieval descriptions of otherworld journeys:[165]

> gone are the bad deaths, harsh judgment scenes, purgatorial torments, and infernal terrors of medieval visions; by comparison, the modern other world is a congenial place...a garden of unearthly delights...[166]
>
> The most glaring difference is the prominence in medieval accounts of obstacles and tests, purificatory torments, and outright doom...modern accounts, on the other hand...are shaped throughout by optimistic, democratic, "healthy-minded" principles that transparently reflect a contemporary ideology and mood...
>
> These comparative observations force us to conclude that the visionaries of our own age are no more free of cultural influence than those of less pluralistic eras...the otherworld journey story...is through and through a work of the socially conditioned religious imagination.

Indeed, reports of the otherworldly dimension of near-death experiences are clearly influenced by the cultural setting of the one who experiences them. Whereas Chinese meet the Yellow Emperor presiding over a vast bureaucracy administering the affairs of the dead and the living, Indians will meet the messengers of Yāma, the Lord of the Dead in Hindu thought. An element of continuity from China to India is the motif of

165. Zaleski 1987, 7, 189, and 190.

166. Nevertheless, frightful and even hellish experiences do at times occur also in contemporary near-death experiences; see, e.g., Kastenbaum 1979, 19–22, Greyson and Bush 1992, Rommer 2000, and Bush 2002 and 2009.

mistaken identity, where the recently deceased has been mistaken for someone else, is released when this is found out, and then revives.[167]

Contemporary Western accounts tend to place considerably less emphasis on decisions made by authoritative figures. This can best be illustrated by an element in one near-death experience, where the one responsible for taking account of the life of the recently deceased turns out to be a computer.[168]

Nevertheless, it also needs to be noted that near-death experiences at times contrast with the expectations and beliefs of the patient.[169] An exemplification of this pattern is when Christian patients during a near-death experience encounter a spiritual being and, full of awe, ask whether the one they are meeting is Jesus, only to be told: "No."[170]

Leaving aside the intriguing descriptions of the otherworld as well as the various features that the transition to that world can involve,[171] such as at times a tunnel experience or an encounter with a dazzling source of light, for my present purpose of particular relevance are cases when patients during near-death experiences apparently see or hear. Often they report doing so with more clarity than usual, even though due to their physical condition of being comatose or having cardiac arrest they should not be able to have such conscious experiences. This type of recollection conflicts with the paradigmatic assumption in much of contemporary science that the brain is the source of mental activities, which is perhaps also the most central objection to the notion of rebirth in present times.

167. The prominence of the motif of mistaken identity in Indian near-death experiences, for example, emerges from the cases studied in Osis and Haraldsson 1977/1986, 154–84, Pasricha and Stevenson 1986/2008, and Pasricha 1993/2008 and 1995/2008.

168. Zaleski 1987, 129 reports that "one woman who revived from cardiac arrest tells of watch ing details of her life being noted down; in her case, the recording angel was a computer."

169. Already Moody 1975/1986, 140 observed that "many persons have stressed how unlike their experiences were to what they had been led to expect in the course of their religious training." On the limited impact of societal notions of the nature of near-death experiences on actual reports of their occurrence see also Athappilly, Greyson, and Stevenson 2006.

170. One such case is reported in Rawlings 1978/1980, 98 and another in Rommer 2000, 28.

171. On similarities between these aspects of near-death experiences and children who appear to remember the intermission period between a past and the present life see Sharma and Tucker 2005.

The Case of Pam Reynolds

A striking case for veridical perceptions during a near-death experience is that of Pam Reynolds, who at the age of thirty-five was diagnosed with a giant basilar-artery aneurysm close to the brain stem, a rupture of which would have caused her immediate death.[172] In order to remove the aneurysm, the brain surgeon put her into hypothermic cardiac arrest.[173] She was anesthetized, her heartbeat and breathing were stopped, the body cooled down to 60 degrees Fahrenheit (corresponding to about 15 to 16 degrees Celsius), and blood drained from her head. Her eyes had been taped shut, and into her ears molded speakers had been inserted, which emitted repeated loud clicks to enable monitoring of any possible brainstem activity.

Pam Reynolds reports that she experienced being outside of her body and able to see her own partly shaven head and the surgeon holding the bone saw. She also overheard a discussion between the chief surgeon and another female cardiac surgeon regarding the artery and vein in her right groin being too small, therefore those in the left groin would be used instead.[174] Next she moved through a tunnel and encountered deceased relatives and an incredibly bright light, features found often, but not invariably, in near-death experiences.

Particularly noteworthy is that, alongside her description of the operation procedure, she correctly reported the conversation between the chief surgeon and the female cardiac surgeon. In her physical condition, with the molded speakers clicking in her ears, it is not easy to conceive of how she could have heard such a conversation.[175] It is equally remarkable that

172. My account of the case is based on Sabom 1998, 37–47. For critical appraisals of the case see, e.g., Woerlee 2005a, 2005b, and 2011. Augustine 2007, 227 argues that "Reynolds did not report anything that she could not have learned about through normal perception"; for critical replies see Sabom 2007 and Tart 2007, and for replies to these Augustine 2007, 276–82.

173. For a brief note on other near-death-experience cases involving hypothermic cardiac arrest see, e.g., Beauregard et al. 2012.

174. Sabom 1998, 185 and 184 comments that "the conversation actually occurred and. . .its content was accurately recalled," even though the molded "speakers occlude the ear canals and altogether eliminate the possibility of physical hearing."

175. As part of his critical appraisal of the case, Woerlee 2011, 7 argues that "if a disem-

she should have vivid experiences of the otherworld, and later retain clear memories of these experiences, even though for quite some time she would have been without the brain functions that are considered to be required for memory and apperception.[176] Parnia and Fenwick (2002, 9) state that

> memory is a very sensitive indicator of brain injury and the length of amnesia before and after unconsciousness is an indicator of the severity of the injury. Therefore, events that occur just prior to or just after loss of consciousness would not be expected to be recalled...[regarding] reports of patients being able to "see" and recall detailed events occurring during the actual cardiac arrest, such as specific details relating to the

---

bodied conscious mind can pass through several concrete floors without experiencing any apparent resistance, then it will certainly not interact in any way with the infinitely less solid air pressure variations of sound waves in air caused by speech or music. Accordingly, an apparently disembodied conscious mind is unable to hear sound waves in air." Based on this premise and a detailed discussion of the operation procedure, Woerlee 2011, 19 then comes to the conclusion that "the fact that Reynolds did hear these sounds indicates the earplugs did not totally block out all sounds." His presentation seems to me to be unconvincing, since the very assumption that hearing is impossible for a disembodied consciousness is at stake in the discussion and therefore cannot be used as a premise to draw conclusions on the degree to which the earplugs blocked out sounds. Nor does it seem convincing that the clicks, delivered at a rate of 11.3 per second, were, according to Woerlee 2011, 9, "no more than an ignored background noise," in between which Reynolds could hear the conversation. Sabom 2007, 259 notes that "after these speakers were molded into each external auditory canal, they were further affixed with 'mounds of tape and gauze to seal securely the ear piece into the ear canal'...making it extremely unlikely that Reynolds could have physically overheard" a conversation in the operation room. Thompson 2015, 307 notes that, whereas she could "have been able to hear the sound of the saw through bone conduction," her "ability to hear what the cardiac surgeon said may seem less likely, but to my knowledge no one has tried to replicate the auditory stimulus conditions to determine whether speech is comprehensible through those sound levels or during the pauses between the clicks." Yet it is not easy to imagine hearing speech coherently through pauses in clicks delivered at such a fast rate. Moreover, as Holden 2009, 199 points out, "she never mentioned even hearing clicks, more or less feeling distracted by them or struggling to hear through them. Her own perception of her accurate hearing was that it occurred through nonphysical processes."

176. Long and Perry 2010, 104 argue that "Near-death experiences that occur during cardiac arrest while under general anesthesia are perhaps the strictest test of the possibility of consciousness residing outside of the body. By conventional medical thinking, neither a person under anesthesia nor a person experiencing cardiac arrest should have a conscious experience like that of an NDE."

> resuscitation period verified by hospital staff...For this memory to take place, a form of consciousness would need to be present during the actual cardiac arrest itself.

Verified Information Apparently Obtained During Near-Death Experiences

The case of Pam Reynolds is not the only one where information, seemingly obtained during a near-death experience, could later be verified. A series of patients apparently able to describe in detail the resuscitation procedures carried out in relation to their own body after cardiac arrest, witnessed by them from a vantage point above, have been compared with a control group. The control group consisted of cardiac patients who did not have a near-death experience and who were asked to imagine as vividly as possible resuscitation procedures, with the result that many of them made major errors.[177] This contrasts to the accurate and detailed descriptions furnished by those who did have a near-death experience. A problem here was that the control group had not actually undergone cardiac arrest.[178] To make up for this deficiency, another similar study was carried out with a control group that did go through a resuscitation but without having a near-death experience. The results confirmed the earlier study, in that those who did not have a near-death experience made more errors in their descriptions.[179] Such findings make it less probable that memories of resuscitation procedures reported by those who have had near-death experiences are entirely the product of vivid imagination.[180]

An example of seemingly veridical perceptions concerns a near-death experience of a patient who experienced complications when giving birth to her first child.[181] The patient recalls leaving the body and apparently being able to see her mother in the waiting room smoking a cigarette.

177. Sabom 1982, 115–61.

178. Blackmore 1993, 120.

179. Sartori 2008, 273–74.

180. See, e.g., Siegel 1981, 160, who argues that the "hypothesis of hallucinogenic induction of near-death experiences is supported by hard data."

181. Cook, Greyson, and Stevenson 1998, 391.

This surprised her, because her mother did not smoke. On later investigation her mother admitted to having tried a cigarette on that occasion because she felt so nervous. In another case the patient, during an experience of being out of the body caused by cardiac arrest, was reportedly able to observe that her mother had moved her chair from the waiting room to the hallway and sat there, a detail that the mother later confirmed.[182]

Two cases involve very nearsighted patients who during near-death experiences suddenly found themselves apparently able to see various details that would have been beyond their normal range of vision.[183] The patients in both cases described moving out of the body and floating up, at which point they noticed that the top part of the light fixture in the room was quite dirty, something that could not be seen from below. Another two cases involve patients seemingly able to tell the nurse what dress or shoes she wore during the resuscitation, which in each case, given their physical condition, they should not have been able to see.[184]

Another patient was found in a public park in a comatose condition and brought to the hospital in an ambulance.[185] In order to prepare the patient for intubation, the nurse removed the upper part of his dentures and put them aside. After prolonged resuscitation the patient was revived but remained in a coma for another week. During subsequent recovery, he chanced on the nurse and, according to the report given, not only recognized her but even asked her where his dentures were and then described to the astonished nurse exactly where she had put his dentures when preparing him for intubation. Further questions apparently elicited from the patient a detailed description of the resuscitation procedure, which he remembered to have witnessed from above, being outside of his body.

Another example concerns a migrant worker who during a visit to a particular city had a heart attack and was rushed to the hospital at night, where she subsequently had a cardiac arrest and was resuscitated. She recalls being out of her body and moving outside of the hospital, where

182. Kelly, Greyson, and Stevenson 1999/2000, 515–16.

183. Ring and Valarino 1998, 60–61.

184. Ring and Lawrence 1993, 227–28.

185. Van Lommel 2010, 20–21.

she apparently happened to see on the ledge of the third floor of the north wing of the hospital building a tennis shoe, which she described in detail to a social worker after recovery.[186] The story continues that, when the social worker checked, she indeed found the tennis shoe on the ledge described. According to the report of the social worker, the ledge was situated on a higher level than the location of the patient in the hospital and therefore outside the range of her normal vision.

A similar story involves a red shoe, this time found on the roof of the hospital.[187] Here, too, the vision of the shoe is part of a memory of a near-death experience during resuscitation; the placing and color of the shoe were later seemingly confirmed by another patient who went up on the roof to check.

Another example concerns a patient who during an operation experienced leaving his body and then was apparently able to observe the surgeon "flapping his arms as if trying to fly."[188] Being conscious again, he reported his observation to his cardiologist, who confirmed that the surgeon had a habit of flattening his sterilized hands against his chest in order to avoid touching anything, and would then give instructions to his assistants by pointing with his elbows.

In yet another such story the patient not only gave an accurate account of the operation procedures but was also apparently able to describe the nervous behavior of the physiotherapists (who felt responsible for having occasioned a deterioration of the patient's condition). The observations seem to have been communicated as soon as the patient was able to speak again.[189]

If these cases are correctly reported, the details given would make it less probable that mere familiarity with hospital procedures and expectations generated by the nowadays fairly well publicized accounts of near-death

186. Clark 1984, 243; for a critical appraisal of this story see Ebbern, Mulligan, and Beyerstein 1996, with a reply in Clark 2007, and a reply to that in Augustine 2007, 273–75.

187. Ring and Valarino 1998, 67.

188. Cook, Greyson, and Stevenson 1998, 399.

189. Sartori, Badham, and Fenwick 2006, 80 conclude that "the patient's description of what happened while he was unconscious was extremely accurate and was reported immediately as soon as the patient regained full consciousness."

experiences are entirely responsible for the descriptions given. However, it needs to be kept in mind that at times information could indeed stem from a different source. In the case of the tennis shoe on the ledge, mentioned above, a follow-up examination has led to the suggestion that such a shoe would have been easily visible from the ground, leaving open the possibility that the patient overheard a conversation on this topic by other patients, who could have seen the shoe, and then unconsciously wove this into her memory of the near-death experience. Clearly caution is required before coming to firm conclusions based on such reports.

Children and the Blind

Particularly striking among near-death experiences are cases that concern small children. A fair number of cases involve children who were apparently able to report various details that happened during resuscitation procedures, even though the children in question, due to their physical condition, should not have been able to witness these and be able to recall them later.[190] Instances of such near-death experiences can seemingly even happen with children who have just been born or who are in the incubator, and who only years later are able to communicate to others their experiences.[191]

In addition to instances involving children, another type of case with similarly striking features is near-death experiences by the blind, some of whom have been blind from birth. Yet during near-death experiences such patients report visions, some of which have later been verified.[192] This is remarkable because it contrasts with what we know about the visual imagination of the blind:[193]

> There are no visual images in the dreams of the congenitally blind; individuals blinded before the age of 5 also tend not to

190. For a survey of near-death experiences by children see, e.g., Morse et al. 1986, Ring and Valarino 1998, 97–121, Atwater 2003, and van Lommel 2010, 71–79.

191. Sutherland 2009, 92.

192. For surveys see Ring and Valarino 1998, 73–95 (or else Ring and Cooper 1999/2008), Fox 2003, 212–34, and Long and Perry 2010, 83–92.

193. Ring and Cooper 1997, 126–27.

> have visual imagery...[yet] not only were their NDEs unlike their usual dreams, but in the case of those blind from birth, they stood out as radically different precisely because they contained visual imagery, whereas their dreams had always lacked this element.

Although near-death experiences of children and the blind, as well as apparently verified information obtained during such experiences, are certainly significant, often the evidence they provide does not allow individual verification.[194] In the two cases involving shoes on a ledge outside or on the roof, the verification comes from someone who went to check out of disbelief. If one then indeed finds the shoe in the described place, it becomes quite understandable that the initial disbelief is replaced by confidence. Yet it is equally understandable that a shift from initial disbelief to confidence does not necessarily happen when one just reads or hears such a story, without having been able to witness it directly.

The problem of relying on secondhand testimony can be illustrated with another description of a near-death experience during cardiac arrest, according to which the patient was able to see details of the surgery schedule board outside and notice the hairstyle of the head nurse as well as the fact that the anesthesiologist was wearing nonmatching socks. Closer inspection brought to light that the entire story was fabricated and the patient in question never existed.[195] The possibility that such accounts may be fake, or at least the outcome of self-delusion on the part of the patient, can only really be set aside once correct recall during a near-death experience can be proven under control conditions. Yet, due to the accidental nature of cardiac arrests, combined with the inability to predict whether a cardiac arrest will lead to the patient having a near-death expe-

194. As noted by Greyson 2014, 354, "the accuracy of out-of-body perceptions during NDEs challenges the conception that they are hallucinations. However, the evidence, although at times corroborated by independent witnesses, consists of uncontrolled observations reported spontaneously after the fact."

195. This case has been discussed in Ring and Lawrence 1993, 225.

rience, it remains a daunting challenge to reproduce such type of evidence under control conditions.[196]

What remains the perhaps most prominent result for my present purposes lies not so much in individual instances of verified information, be it a shoe on the roof or a surgeon flapping his arms, but in the very fact that during a period devoid of normal brain activity the patients have experiences that they later on recall vividly. This is a recurring feature of near-death experiences that by now has been documented so extensively that there can hardly be any doubt about its factuality:[197]

> Individuals reporting NDEs often describe their mental processes during the NDE as remarkably clear and lucid and their sensory experiences as unusually vivid, equaling or even surpassing those of their normal waking state. Reports of NDEs from widely divergent cultures confirm that people have consistently reported, from different parts of the world and across different periods of history, having had complicated cognitive and perceptual experiences at times when brain functioning was severely impaired.

Such experiences are not easily reconciled with the prevalent notion that mental activities depend entirely on the brain:[198]

> Complete brain anoxia with absent electrical activity in cardiac arrest is incompatible with any form of consciousness, according to present scientific knowledge, making the finding of an explanation for NDEs a challenging task for the ruling physicalist and reductionist view of biomedicine.

196. On unsuccessful attempts to set up perceptual targets in places where near-death experiences are likely to occur, positioned in such a way that they are outside the normal range of vision and could only be perceived by someone having an out-of-body experience, see, e.g., Augustine 2007, 230–34, Greyson 2007, 242–43, and Holden 2009, 203–11.

197. Greyson 2010, 40.

198. Facco and Agrillo 2012, 4.

The question does not appear to be solved by assuming that some remnant of brain activity is still possible during cardiac arrest:[199]

> The issue is not, however, whether there is *any* brain activity, but whether there is the type of brain activity that is considered necessary for conscious experience. Such activity is detectable by EEG, and it is abolished both by anesthesia and by cardiac arrest...Thus it is not plausible that NDEs under anesthesia or in cardiac arrest can be accounted for by a hypothetical residual capacity of the brain to process and store complex information under those conditions.

In this way the findings from near-death experiences invite a reconsideration of the relationship between the brain and the mind:[200]

> Every experience has correlations with brain activity, but that correlation does not imply that the brain activity *caused* the experience...as an analogy...if someone listening to music were also being monitored for brain activity, such activity would be evident, but no one would conclude that the origin of the music was in the brain.

2. Past-Life Regression

From the prospective perspective afforded by reports of near-death experiences, with the remainder of this chapter I shift to the retrospective perspective afforded by recollections of past lives (and deaths). As already mentioned in the first chapter, according to early Buddhist doctrine residual memories from past lives, even though usually not remembered in the normal waking state, can be retrieved through the cultivation of deep

199. Greyson, Kelly, and Kelly 2009, 227. Agrillo 2011, 7 concludes that "basically, it is hard to believe that NDEs can be entirely accounted for in terms of some hypothetical residual brain capacity to process and store such complex experiences under those critical conditions."

200. Holden, Greyson, and James 2009, 11–12.

states of meditation. Such ability to recollect one's own past lives features as one of the insights gained by the Buddha on the night of his awakening.

A case documenting such recall has been reported from Thailand by Ian Stevenson. A Buddhist nun of about twenty years of age while meditating unexpectedly experienced memories of two past lives as an infant.[201] For the most recent of these two lives she was apparently able to give information about the names of the parents of the previous person and the location where they lived. She described that the father had a hole in one tooth and that he had regularly played a musical instrument to soothe the infant, and that the mother had a scar on her face and was holding the infant in her arms when it died, whereas the father at that time was out of the house trying to get medicine. According to Stevenson's report, as far as he had been able to ascertain the nun had no prior contact with the family in question, yet all these details turned out to be correct.

An avenue for accessing such memories that does not require meditation practice has increasingly come into use in recent times, namely hypnotic regression. Before surveying relevant cases, however, a few words on the working mechanism of memory are required as a background for appreciating past-life memories in the remainder of this chapter.

The Workings of Memory

Thanks to research in cognitive psychology it has over quite some time become clear that memory does not work in a way comparable to a tape recorder or a copy machine, faithfully producing an exact replica of what was originally experienced. The shortcomings of memory result in several main avenues for inaccurate recall, which can be captured under the headings "transience," "absent-mindedness," "blocking," "misattribution," "suggestibility," and "bias":[202]

> *Transience* involves decreasing accessibility of information over time, *absent-mindedness* entails inattention or shallow

201. This is the case of Pratomwan Inthanu; see Stevenson 1983b, 140–70.

202. Schacter 1999, 183, who adds a seventh shortcoming that is not relevant to the present context.

> processing that contributes to weak memories of ongoing events or forgetting to do things in the future, and *blocking* refers to the temporary inaccessibility of information that is stored in memory. . .*misattribution* involves attributing a recollection or idea to the wrong source, *suggestibility* refers to memories that are implanted as a result of leading questions or comments during attempts to recall past experiences, and *bias* involves retrospective distortions and unconscious influences that are related to current knowledge and beliefs.

An easily overlooked problem is that memory, far from being merely reproductive, is rather of a constructive nature,[203] in that

> remembering appears to be far more decisively an affair of construction, rather than one of mere reproduction. . .when a subject is being asked to remember, very often the first thing that emerges is something of the nature of [an] attitude. The recall is then a construction, made largely on the basis of this attitude. . .[Thus remembering] is an imaginative reconstruction. . .[and] is thus hardly ever really exact.

At the time of trying to recall, the mind constructs the information anew. It is this act of constructing or reconstructing that will determine the way the information is being remembered. In an illustrative experiment subjects were given the task of remembering the description of a house from the viewpoint of a prospective burglar or a prospective buyer of the house.[204] After a first recall, some subjects were asked to shift perspective (e.g., "buyer" instead of "burglar") and consequently were able to recall details they had earlier been unable to remember, whereas a control group that did not change perspective did not show a similar increase in ability to recall additional details on the second occasion. These experiments show that the attitude during information retrieval influences the way

203. Bartlett 1932, 205, 207, and 213.

204. Anderson and Pichert 1978.

things are remembered. Another experiment complements these findings by showing the following:[205]

> Imagining actions led subjects to remember that they had actually performed the actions when in fact they had not. . .[this] increased with the number of imaginings, as did subjects' confidence about their erroneous responses.

Besides, not only on the occasion of trying to recall something that took place in the past, but already at the time when something is experienced that is to be memorized, information is not simply taken in. Rather, information is stored in the mind together with inferences, and often enough one is not aware of the fact of having drawn such inferences.[206] On later recall of the past event, one is frequently no longer able to distinguish between the original data and the inference drawn. This has the following result:[207]

> Subjects apparently experience the recollection of. . .events that never happened as quite real, as real as the recall of. . .events that actually had occurred. "False memories" may be a misnomer, at least from the subject's viewpoint.

This rather sobering perspective on the limitations of memory is to be kept in mind as a backdrop when evaluating the various recollections of past lives surveyed in the remainder of this chapter.

Therapeutic Benefits

Recollection of past lives in early Buddhist thought serves to enable meditative adepts to witness their own past experiences prior to the present

205. Goff and Roediger 1998, 28.

206. Bransford and Johnson 1973, 391 explain that "processes of making inferences. . .occur quite frequently in the normal course of comprehending. Generally, we may not be aware of them."

207. Roediger 1996, 85.

life and thereby verify for themselves the truth of the Buddhist perspective on *saṃsāra*, the round of rebirths. By now regression therapy has acquired a to some degree comparable function by way of evoking memories experienced by the patients as pertaining to a past life. The potential of offering relief lies not in the mere experiencing of past-life images as such but rather in their at times quite specific relation to present psychological problems.[208] Needless to say, the successful employment of hypnotic regression in therapy does not imply that the memory of a past life is veridical.[209] From the viewpoint of the therapist, the accuracy of such memories is in fact of little relevance:[210]

> Whether the former lifetimes that are "relived" are fantasies or actual experiences lived in a by-gone era does not matter to me as a therapist—getting results is important. I have found past-life regression consistently helpful, often resulting in immediate remission of chronic symptoms that do not return, even after months and years.

The increasing use of past-life regression in therapy gives the impression that such a type of recollection can be produced almost on demand and would satisfy the criterion of being replicable by others. The question remains, however, whether verifiable information can be obtained in this way.

208. Woods and Barušs 2004, 604 and 606 note that "no measurable psychological benefits were found to be associated with the presence of past-life imagery" as such, which may be because "past-life imagery is more effective when targeted toward the treatment of specific psychological disorders."

209. Stevenson 1994, 190 points out that a "regressed patient may, moreover, seem to remember some traumatic experience in the 'previous life' that is relevant to present symptoms, and he or she may feel better afterward. These events, however, are not evidence that the patient did remember a real previous life."

210. Fiore 1979/1986, 6.

Verified Information Apparently Obtained from Past-Life Regression

The question of verifiability can easily turn into a debate that at times manifests the problem of confirmation bias already mentioned in the previous chapter. An illustrative example is the case of Bridey Murphey. Under hypnosis an American woman had spoken in Irish brogue, reporting with much detail a past life under the name of Bridey Murphey in the nineteenth century. The promotion of the case by one American newspaper was followed by a debunking of the case by a rival newspaper, with the result that in public opinion the case is considered a hoax, even though this does not reflect the actual state of affairs.[211]

Nevertheless, research has shown that hypnotic suggestion can lead to the creation of imaginary past lives. In a subsequent hypnotic session some such patients can even be made to reveal the source of information that they unconsciously employed to embellish the supposed past life with details.[212] Another study has shown that those "who report memories of past lives exhibited greater false recall and false recognition" compared to those who did not report such memories.[213] Other studies have highlighted the degree to which past-life memories elicited through regression are influenced by the beliefs and expectations of the hypnotist.[214]

Yet another study involved three groups undergoing past-life regression, each of which was given different priming. One group was introduced to past-life therapy in positive terms, the second in neutral terms,

211. Wilson 1981, 80 concludes his survey of the case by stating that "the Bridey Murphey affair...[is] more of an object lesson about the competitive methods of rival US newspaper groups in the fifties than about the truth or otherwise of the phenomenon Bridey Murphey brought to public attention. Although many people now think that the Bridey Murphey affair has all been dismissed as a hoax, the real truth of the matter is far more complex." Based on a detailed rebuttal of the debunking of the case, Ducasse 1960, 13–14 even concludes that "the temptations to wishful thinking and to emotionally biased conclusions are even greater on the side of...the vested 'scientific common sense of the epoch' than on the side of the protagonists of *prima facie* paradoxical views."

212. Kampman and Hirvenoja 1978.

213. Meyersburg et al. 2009, 402.

214. Spanos et al. 1991 and Spanos 1994; Spanos 1996, 141–42 concludes that "past-life personalities are...contextually generated, rule-governed, goal-directed fantasies. Subjects construct these fantasies to meet the demands of the hypnotic regression situation."

and the third in highly skeptical terms. Of the first group, 85 percent did experience a past life, of the second group 60 percent, and of the third group only 10 percent. This does document the influence of subjectivity on such experiences.[215] At the same time, however, it is also remarkable that 10 percent of those who were told that past-life therapy is "crazy" and "ridiculous" still had such an experience.[216] Alongside clear awareness of the potential pitfalls of past-life regression, this suggests that the resulting experiences need not be entirely the product of the influence of the hypnotist. Nor does wishful imagination seem to be always the sole source, given that some patients find their expectations not met at all by the type of past-life memory that emerges under hypnosis.[217]

A study based on data obtained from over a thousand regressions shows a distribution of former lives over various periods of the past that corresponds to our knowledge of the increase in world population during previous centuries.[218] Another result of the same study was that in several

215. After describing the experiment and results, Baker 1992, 161 concludes that this shows past-life regression phenomena to be "the results of suggestions made by the hypnotist, expectations held by the subject, and the demand characteristics of the hypnoidal relationship."

216. In fact Lucas 1993, 51 notes that "the most obvious barrier to regression work is a belief system that is strongly skeptical of the concept of past lives."

217. Freedman 2002, 35 reports working with clients who had been made to believe by a psychic that they had spectacular past lives. On being regressed their expectations remained unfulfilled, as they rather experienced much less glorious and unimpressive past-life memories. This type of failure suggests that the regression experience cannot be entirely the product of wishful thinking, otherwise there would have been no reason for the imagination of such clients to fail to produce what they were expecting.

218. Wambach 1978, 137–38. Wambach 1978, 124–25 also notes that the regressed lives were distributed almost exactly 50:50 between past lives as a female and as a male. However, Venn 1986, 413 objects to this as relevant evidence on the grounds that "a 50:50 ratio is precisely what she should have expected, given an equal probability of obtaining either a male or a female personality," adding that no control-group data had been gathered from nonregressed subjects. Yet a finding to some degree related is reported by Tucker 2013, 136–37, based on a statistical analysis of children who remember past lives of someone whose cause of death is known. Once those who had a natural death are examined on their own, an approximate rate of 50:50 results between males and females. In the case of those who died an unnatural death, however, over 70 percent are male. The reason could be that men are more likely to engage in high-risk behavior, including fights, and therefore more often suffer a violent death, a suggestion borne out by statistics of violent deaths in countries like the United States.

cases those regressed thought that their account contained details that were historically not accurate, yet subsequent research brought to light that these details were actually correct.[219]

One case involves a person with no previous knowledge of Spanish who remembers having been a woman in sixteenth-century Spain. Over a hundred facts that emerged under hypnosis apparently proved true after detailed research had been conducted in Spain, North Africa, and the Caribbean; some pieces of information were only found in old obscure Spanish sources or archives.[220] Not even a single error was seemingly detected, and two facts that at first appeared to be errors, as they contradicted the authorities in Spain, on further research turned out to be true as well.[221] Such results could hardly be expected if the memory were the

219. Wambach 1978, 112 reports that in "instances in which my subjects felt that their data were wrong, according to their own view of history, research showed that their unconscious had presented them with a more accurate picture...If past-life recall is fantasy, one would expect our conscious knowledge of history to provide the images. When the images contrast with what we believe to be true, and yet prove on careful study to be accurate, then we must look anew at the concept of past-life recall as fantasy."

220. Tarazi 1990, 316–17 mentions as examples the date "of the first publication of the Edict of Faith on the Island of Hispaniola; Spanish laws governing shipping to the Indies; types of ships used in the Mediterranean and the Atlantic, and details about them; dates and contents of the Spanish indexes of prohibited books and how they differed from the Roman Index; names of priests executed in England in 1581 and 1582, and the method of execution; and information about a college in Cuenca. Over a dozen facts did not seem to be published in English at all but only in Spanish. A few could only be found in the Municipal and others in the Diocesan Archives in Cuenca, Spain."

221. Tarazi 1990, 321 reports that the first concerns "the description of the building that housed the tribunal of Inquisition. The Government Tourist Office in Cuenca reported it as 58 Calle de San Pedro. This building did not even slightly resemble the one she recalled...later...I found that the Tribunal had been moved in December 1583 from the given address to an old castle overlooking the town, which fits Antonia's description perfectly" (Antonia is the name of the previous personality). The second was a reference to a college in Cuenca, for which no supportive evidence could be located, until eventually such evidence turned up "in an old seven-volume work in Spanish (Astrain, 1912–1925). I checked and found that Vol. II (pp. 131, 595) mentioned the founding of a college in Cuenca in the mid-16th century. Even a person who reads Spanish is not likely to wade through this tome unless involved in historical research." Tarazi 1990, 329 concludes that "it takes a great stretch of the imagination to believe that a person who neither speaks nor reads Spanish would go to a university with which she had no affiliation and pore through seven large volumes in old Spanish to find a few lines about a college in Cuenca."

result of cryptomnesia, of memories acquired in the present life whose original source has been forgotten. Therefore,[222]

> it does not seem reasonable to dismiss the entire narration. . .in view of the great amount of recondite, yet accurate information revealed. If all information and all possible explanations are considered, it seems consistent with parsimony to suggest that [the patient] L.D. showed knowledge of obscure details in 16th-century Europe and America that she did not learn normally.

Another case involves memories of a life spent in eighteenth-century England, a country to which the hypnotized person had never been before. A research trip to the area apparently corroborated a range of details. One example concerned the names of two villages that either no longer existed or had in the meantime been named differently; both names turned out to be correct on consulting older maps. Another example is the use of an obsolete term only employed at that time in that part of England.[223] The patient also seems to have described a house correctly, some features of which were only discernible when entering the house to verify aspects of its construction that in the meantime had changed.[224]

Particularly noteworthy is her apparent memory of an event during that past life in which she had hurt her foot and had been given a ride by someone who was transporting stones from ruins to use for the floor of his house. Riding on the cart she noticed designs made on these stones. Her memories of this detail during the hypnotic session were apparently sufficient to make a drawing. The research team found that in the meantime this particular house had been turned into a chicken shed. According to the report given, removing the overlay of chicken droppings from the floor led to finding a stone with the design she had earlier described.[225]

222. Tarazi 1990, 334.

223. Ramster 1994, 75–76 and 77.

224. Ramster 1994, 84–85.

225. Ramster 1994, 87 reports that the patient "has found the very stone that she had drawn

If these two case studies are to be trusted, in the sense of being reported correctly, then alongside fantasy and influence by the hypnotist the possibility that such regressions can yield historically accurate information will have to be taken seriously.

Besides the possibility that individual instances of past-life regression might at times contain historically accurate information, another noteworthy feature of this approach in general is that it does enable some degree of personal experimentation. Whereas near-death experiences occur relatively rarely, past-life regression seems to be possible for most of those willing to try. From this it follows that such a hypnotic procedure would offer an option for those who are interested in testing things out, even without needing to go through the demanding meditative preparation that according to early Buddhist sources is required in order to be able to recollect past lives at will.[226] Past-life regression would enable anyone interested to have a personal experience and then decide whether the story remembered does in some way stand in a meaningful relationship to experiences, attitudes, and behavior patterns of one's present life.

3. Children's Memories of a Past Life

Recall of past lives by children has a clear advantage over hypnotic regression, as it makes it less probable that such memories are a case of cryptomnesia, of recalling things earlier learned but whose original source has in the meantime been forgotten. Children who remember what they perceive as a past life often begin to relate information at a rather early age of around two or three years, at times even earlier, as soon as they are able to speak. This leaves little time and occasion for them to acquire detailed information and then forget its source.

As for Buddhist precedents, whereas recollection of past lives through meditation practice is a recurrent topic in the early discourses and

---

in Sydney, a feat far beyond any element of chance as it was in a place, in a country, she had never been to."

226. On the tendency in later Buddhist texts to present recollection of past life as not necessarily requiring meditative expertise see Schopen 1983.

apparently considered of general availability to those willing and able to cultivate the required meditative expertise, the ability of even small children to recollect a past life is not a commonly reported phenomenon in early Buddhist textual sources.

A case can be found in texts somewhat later than the early discourses, namely a Pāli *jātaka* tale and its parallel in the Mūlasarvāstivāda *Vinaya*.[227] The story goes that as a small infant a prince realizes that, having reigned in the past, he had in turn been reborn in hell in retribution for acts committed as the king of the country. In order to avoid another rebirth in hell, the prince pretends to be a mute cripple so as not to become the successor to the throne.

Children's ability to recognize items pertaining to the person whose previous life they remember is a well-known feature of Tibetan Buddhism, where successors to a particular ecclesiastical role prove themselves as the rebirth of the previous holder of this position through recognition tests.[228]

Cases of children who recall an apparent past life have been studied especially by Ian Stevenson, hence in what follows I rely in particular on his findings. The detail and number of cases that he and his colleagues have documented, together with the criticism that has sometimes been raised, defy any attempt at easy summarization, so that I can only provide selected examples, and even these stripped down to the few aspects that to me seem particularly striking. The reader would be well advised to consult the full report of each case for a proper appreciation of its value (as well as other cases I have not included). I might also mention that in some cases I tend to be less convinced than Ian Stevenson of their merit, although this would at least in part be due to the difference between reading a written report and actually meeting its protagonists. But even with only written

227. Jā 538 at Jā VI 4,1 and D 1 *kha* 254a3 or Q 1030 *ge* 236b2; see also, e.g., T 3.152.20b9, T 3.167.408b11, T 3.168.410c7, and Tamai 2017 for a Tocharian version.

228. Samuel 1993/1995, 151 notes that, for example, "the 14th Dalai Lama is the present-day member of a series of rebirths stretching back through historical time to the 1st Dalai Lama and before him to the early Tibetan kings"; for a study of the historical beginnings of such rebirth lineages in the different traditions of Tibetan Buddhism see Schwieger 2015, 17–31, and for a description of the *tulku* tradition by one of its members Thondup 2011.

reports to assess the situation, several of the cases he has recorded strike me as impressive, and I think fraud as an explanation for all of them can safely be discarded.[229]

In what follows I first survey cases where children recall rather specific information about the previous person they believe to have been,[230] and then turn to the related aspect of their exhibiting behavior that fits the previous person. Then I take up cases where information has been documented in some form before attempts were made to verify details concerning the previous person. Finally I examine birthmarks and birth defects. These types of case often overlap, in that most children exhibit both forms of recollection, informational and behavioral, and some such cases have been documented before verification and some of them involve birthmarks. My taking these up separately is only to facilitate presentation. Since children's memories of past lives provide a background to my exploration in the next chapter, I dedicate more space to these than I afforded to the topics of near-death experiences and rebirth regression.

Specific Information Recalled and Behavioral Continuities

A case from Sri Lanka features a boy born in a Buddhist family who at less than two years of age began to relate details of a former life in a Christian family living in a different place and with no discernible prior connection to his present family.[231] Among a series of recognitions made when brought to the place of the other family, he apparently knew the path to a well that in the meantime had fallen out of use and become overgrown with weeds, recognized the bench in the classroom and the pew in church on which the previous person had sat, and found his way

229. Brody 1979, 770 comments that "while acknowledging the possibility of occasional deceptive strengthening of a case, it seems to me unlikely that the complex effort necessary to construct a fraudulent picture, or the rewards for doing so, have occurred with sufficient frequency to account for the bulk of the observations" made by Ian Stevenson (here in particular in his study of Sri Lankan cases).

230. For a summary of the famous case of Shanti Devi see Stevenson 1960, 66–67; the account of the case in Lönnerstrand 1998 is too unscientific for my purposes, for which reason I have not included Shanti Devi in my survey.

231. This is the case of Gamini Jayasena; see Stevenson 1977, 43–76.

unaided to the boarding house where the previous person had lived when attending school, noting that an olive tree, which in the meantime had been cut down, was missing. In line with his memories of having been a Christian, he reportedly resisted Buddhist practices and forms of worship in his present family.

A Sri Lankan girl, who at the age of three began to relate information concerning a past life, was apparently able to lead the way to the former house via a shortcut through paddy fields unknown to all those who accompanied her on this occasion,[232] and recognized the correct house and entered it through a side entrance not visible from the road, an entrance regularly used by the previous personality.[233] Among various correct details, such as recognizing the bed of the former person, her water pot, rice dish, and drums, she also seems to have displayed knowledge of money buried in a cigarette tin in the house; this had been found accidentally during repair works, several months after the death of the former person. The girl exhibited a precocious ability at cooking and showed her own mother how to weave coconut leaves, two skills characteristic of the previous personality.[234]

Another Sri Lankan case involves male twins, both of which recalled a past life. One of them in particular furnished a wealth of verified details of the former life in an unrelated family dwelling in a different village.[235] He apparently knew that the previous person had made a footprint in freshly placed concrete, which later had been destroyed during building work, and was also able to point out where he had scratched his name and the date of that time into concrete, something unknown even to the members of the previous family but confirmed on examination.

232. The feature of recognizing an old road recurs in the case of Suleyman Andary from Lebanon. Stevenson 1980, 69 reports that without any guidance from others the child led the way to the house of the previous person "over an abandoned and barely visible path," instead of taking the recently built paved road that would have been an obvious choice.

233. This is the case of Disna Samarasinghe; see Story 1975/2010, 132–47 and Stevenson 1977, 77–116.

234. Matlock 1990, 202 notes as a general feature that "behavioral memories may include skills possessed by the previous persons, but unlearned by the subjects."

235. This is the case of Indika Ishwara; see Stevenson 1997a, 1970–2000.

A Burmese girl, at the time of starting to speak and being between one and two years old, began to relate details of a previous life.[236] Visiting the house of the deceased person she remembered having been before, the girl apparently pointed to a glass bottle containing coins and was able to give the correct count and value of the coins in it. This was not visible from the outside and had not been previously ascertained by other members of the family. She was also able to state correctly the contents of a closed purse that, just as the coins in the bottle, belonged to the previous personality. She also reportedly recognized clothing belonging to the previous personality, even though this fact of ownership was not known to anyone present and was only ascertained later. Her ability in this respect impressed her father, a practicing Roman Catholic, sufficiently to make him give up his former rejection of the possibility of rebirth.

A boy in Lebanon between three and four years of age started to relate a former life in which he was killed in battle.[237] Among a number of verified details of that previous life, the child was seemingly able to report correctly how much money the previous person had in his pockets when he was killed. He also showed knowledge of various personal items, such as pointing out that in the closet of the deceased a shirt was missing, and that in the pocket of a jacket of the dead subject one of four fountain pens was missing, as well as correctly identifying the previous persona's valise among four valises and the key to this valise among three keys.

At the age of about three years another boy from Lebanon is reported to have related several verified details of a former life.[238] Brought to visit the house of the former family, he is credited with pointing out that in the previous person's room pictures had been removed from the walls (Stevenson verified that the walls did not show any marks that a picture had been there) and that the bed was now in a different position in the room. He also apparently remembered that a servant maid had flirted with a

236. This is the case of Ma Than Than Sint; see Stevenson 1983b, 253–68.

237. This is the case of Mounzer Haïdar; see Stevenson 1980, 17–51 (on the birthmark in this case see the critical comments in Rogo 1985/2005, 55–56 and the reply by Stevenson 1986, 234). When evaluating cases from Lebanon, it needs to be kept in mind that most of these involve Druzes, who believe in rebirth.

238. This is the case of Rabih Elawar; see Stevenson 1980, 117–58.

man through the window of their house, an episode the rest of the former family had forgotten until he reminded them of it. In addition, the child seems to have known various details of the new motorcycle of his former life's friend, such as remembering a saying the two had written on it and its license number. The two had been riding this motorcycle together when they collided with a truck, as a result of which the former person died. In line with his past-life memory of this accident, the little boy was markedly afraid of trucks and would run into the house when he saw one.

A case from Turkey features a boy who before being able to speak showed a marked phobia of airplanes.[239] Between the ages of two and three he began relating memories of a past life in which he had died in an airplane crash. In addition to various correct details given about the previous personality, he apparently related that the former person once stole a tray in his parents' house and sold it to be able to buy a ticket for a football game, a misdeed only known to the two friends with whom he had gone to see the game. Another item of rather private information was his recollection of having exchanged watches with a friend, and that his watch had distinct teeth marks on its case. He also correctly attributed the previous person's death to freezing after the airplane in which he had been traveling had crashed on a mountain. This is remarkable insofar as the villagers and the family all believed that the former person had died instantly from the airplane crash itself. Only by consulting an official from Turkish Airlines could it be verified that the previous person indeed must have died of freezing.

A boy in India at close to three years refused to perform a simple task, alleging that this was beneath his caste dignity (which for his present birth was incorrect). Questioned further, he related a past life as a Brahmin who had been shot by his brother.[240] He is credited with a number of recognitions, such as finding his way unaided to the house of the previous personality, recognizing relatives, or describing exactly how he was shot.

239. This is the case of Erkan Kılıç; see Stevenson 1980, 272–98. Similarly to evaluating children from Lebanon, assessing cases from Turkey requires taking into account that these often involve communities who believe in rebirth, in this instance the Alevis.

240. This is the case of Gopal Gupta; see Stevenson 1975, 70–106.

When meeting the former person's wife, he reportedly behaved coolly and then explained that he was upset because she had refused to lend him money, with which the previous personality had been planning to appease his brother. This episode, as part of the events that culminated in the situation where the former person was shot by his infuriated brother, was apparently a domestic secret; in fact the wife fainted on hearing the child state this openly. On the assumption that the case is reported correctly, it is not easy to conceive how by normal means the boy could have had access to such private information concerning an unrelated family living in a different town in India.[241]

The above cases show children seemingly able to provide rather specific information about the past life of another person. The number of cases and the care with which they have been investigated makes it improbable that all of them should be considered just products of fantasy. It is also not entirely straightforward to conceive of the source of the information given by the children as being cryptomnesia, due to the tender age at which they start to relate their memories.

Cryptomnesia can in fact be excluded in another case from Turkey, as the child in question was born deaf and mute. Nevertheless, when aged between two and three years he apparently communicated memories of a past life with the help of gesturing.[242] It took some time for others to make sense of his gestures, but eventually it became clear that he remembered a life in the same village of a man who had drowned. Taken to the house of the previous person, through gesturing he was able to point out various objects that had belonged to the deceased. Due to the child's congenital deafness,[243] it does not seem easily conceivable that he could have somehow been given or picked up information about the deceased person.

241. Stevenson 1975, 103 comments: "I do not see how we can believe that he acquired his information through any normal channel of communication."

242. This is the case of Süleyman Zeytun; see Stevenson 1980, 260–71.

243. Stevenson 1980, 267–68 reports one of the present-life brothers stating that "he would not hear a cannon discharged near him," adding that the subject was exempted from the otherwise obligatory military service in Turkey after examination in the military hospital led to the diagnosis: "congenital deaf-mute."

The suggestion of cryptomnesia, or else of some other paranormal process of information conveyance, seems even less plausible when children exhibit rather specific behavior and skills corresponding to the previous person they remember to have been.[244] Unusual behavior is in fact a general feature of many cases, insofar as children tend to act as if they were still the deceased person, speaking to elders as if these were still their children and ordering them around or else showing emotions appropriate to the relationships the previous personality had with certain persons. In what follows, I survey some examples of more specific types of behavior.[245]

An example from Thailand involves a boy who at the time of beginning to speak, being just one year and eight months old, started to relate memories of a past life as a young Laotian man who had been killed, a murder case not known to his parents who did not have any direct relationship with the family of this Laotian man.[246] At the age of three he reportedly would beat a post with a stick, shout the names of his murderers and threaten to kill them in revenge. At times he would behave like an adult, for instance exhibiting a sexual interest in women entirely inappropriate for a small child. Besides various detailed recognitions, including the bicycle of the Laotian, the Thai boy showed distinct Laotian behavior in his food preferences, eating manners, and way of speaking, in contrast to those of his family who were all Thais, living in a Thai village. His use of Laotian words could be an example of xenoglossy, the ability to communicate in a language apparently not learned in the present life, a feature of some cases to which I return in the last part of this chapter.

Another child in Thailand remembered a past life during which she stayed for a period of time at a monastery.[247] As a small girl of about

244. Braude 1992 nevertheless argues for psi as an explanation of past-life memories even in the case of behavioral abilities or skills; for a philosophical argument related to psi as against rebirth see Sudduth 2016.

245. Pasricha 1990/2005, 233 reports from her study of Indian cases "behavioral features. . .unusual for the subject's family. . .[but] concordant with his statements concerning a previous life. Such behavior might include: unusual likes or dislikes toward food, clothes, persons, and themes of play; phobias of bladed weapons, wells, and guns. . .most of them related to the previous personality's mode of death."

246. This is the case of Bongkuch Promsin; see Stevenson 1983b, 102–39.

247. This is the case of Ratana Wongsombat; see Stevenson 1983b, 12–48.

two years, on being taken for the first time to the monastery, she reportedly not only recognized monastics and knew her way around the place (including recognition of changes to the buildings that had happened in the meantime), but also was able to execute correctly the traditional forms of worship and offerings to the Buddha statue without being instructed. After that she apparently went on her own to sit down cross-legged in meditation posture for half an hour, without having been told by anyone to do so or having witnessed this being done by others earlier at her home. The spontaneous sitting in meditation of a young child is a feature that recurs in my case study in the next chapter.

A continuity of religious behavior from a previous life is also documented in three cases from Sri Lanka, each of which remembered having been a Buddhist monk in a previous life.[248] All three boys apparently had a keen interest in Buddhist practices from a very young age, wanted to dress as a monk, and showed precocious ability in reciting Pāli and performing religious ceremonies. One of the three families in which the respective boys were born had little interest in religion and another family was Roman Catholic, making it safe to assume that the behavioral features would not have been due to influences in the family.

Another case from Sri Lanka concerns a girl who, when less than a year old, began to exhibit a marked resistance to being bathed, so much so that it took three people to hold her and get her bathed.[249] She also showed a fear of buses, continuously crying during a journey on which she was taken at six months of age and on other occasions hiding her face when seeing a bus. She did not react in such a way to any other vehicles. When able to speak, she expressed memories of a past life as a girl who, walking along a road after a heavy rain, had been splashed by a bus driving too close to her. She lost her balance and fell into a paddy field by the side of the road, where she drowned. Brought to the village of the former personality, the girl reportedly recognized the place where the accident had happened, as well as members of the former family and their house.

248. Haraldsson and Samararatne 1999; for the first case see also Haraldsson 1991, 247–57.

249. This is the case of Shamlinie Prema; see Stevenson 1977, 15–42.

Particularly remarkable are the distinct reactions exhibited by her to water and buses at less than one year of age.[250]

Another girl in Sri Lanka at less than two years of age started to relate details of a past life as a man in a family with which her present family had had no personal contact, apparently providing a wealth of specific details as well as subsequently recognizing members of the former family who were unknown to her present family.[251] She conveyed the fact that the father of the former person was a bus driver by way of making steering gestures, as she did not yet have the vocabulary to express the idea of driving. One of the details she is credited with concerns her description of an aunt washing the burned part of a machine in a well. The aunt had indeed washed a piece of loom machinery that had become blackened with soot from an oil lamp. The girl had a phobia of wells; the former person had died after falling into a well. She also showed distinctly boyish behavior, such as climbing trees and playing cricket, which in the Sri Lankan setting are highly unusual for a girl. When angered she was ready to pound others with her fists as a boy would do and preferred to wear trousers; when made to wear a girl's dress, she would wear boys' shorts under it.

A comparable case involves a Burmese girl who at the age of two or three started to relate an unverified past life as a Japanese soldier, killed when gunned down by an airplane of the Allied Forces who were driving the Japanese out of Burma during the final stages of World War II.[252] Similarly to the Sri Lankan girl just mentioned, she showed pronounced masculine behavior.[253] From an early age she resisted wearing girls' clothes,

250. Stevenson 1977, 40 highlights that these reactions took place at a very young age, before she had even begun to speak, making it improbable that cryptomnesia could offer a plausible explanation of the case.

251. This is the case of Ruby Kusuma Silva; see Stevenson 1977, 163–202.

252. This is the case of Ma Tin Aung Myo; see Stevenson 1983b, 229–41. In this case the previous person has not been identified, unlike the other cases discussed in this chapter. Due to the strong behavioral features, I felt it nevertheless appropriate to mention this case. In fact the Japanese soldier was known to the mother of the girl, so that qualifying the case as an "unverified past life" only refers to the fact that his name is not known, therefore it has not been possible to identify him with anyone who had lived in Japan.

253. A picture of her standing between her sister and brother can be found in Stevenson

wore her hair short as done in Burma only by boys, and preferred to play with boys, especially playing at being a soldier with toy guns. Her refusal of female dress was so strong that she eventually had to leave the school she was attending, since the school authorities insisted that she should dress as a girl. She also showed a severe phobia of airplanes, to the extent that she would cower and cry when one flew over her—ways of reacting that were presumably related to the way the Japanese soldier had been killed. The girl also apparently showed behavior traits appropriate to a Japanese, such as having difficulties with the hot climate and food in Burma, both of which differ from the situation in Japan, or a preference for half-raw fish of the type Japanese tend to consume.

This case relates to a feature of a number of cases that involve Burmese children who remember a past life as a Japanese soldier in Burma. Such children are reported to have spoken a strange language when they were very young, which members of their family could not understand.[254] Similarly to the Thai boy speaking Laotian, mentioned earlier, such instances could involve xenoglossy (although it has not been possible to ascertain whether these children indeed spoke Japanese). I will take up xenoglossy in more detail in the final section of this chapter.

Cases Documented Before Verification Attempts

With the options of cryptomnesia and paranormal communication offering fairly improbable explanations for the cases surveyed so far, another option to be taken seriously remains paramnesia, the inability

---

1983b, 237, which shows her hairstyle and dress being of a masculine type (in the Burmese cultural setting). Stevenson 1983b, 236 also reports her performing the extended Draw-a-Person test, which corroborated her decidedly masculine orientation. Another example of a girl recollecting a past life as a male and behaving like a boy in the present life is the case of Ampan Petcherat from Thailand, Stevenson 1983b, 69.

254. In a survey of features common to such type of cases, Stevenson 1983b, 217 notes that "informants for several of these cases reported having heard the subject speaking (when he was young) a language that they could not understand. They assumed, from the child's behavior or statements, that the language he was speaking was Japanese. Unfortunately, these cases all occurred in areas where, at the time the cases developed, there were no Japanese-speaking people who might have positively identified the child's strange language."

to distinguish between real and fantasy memories.[255] This could lead the respective families to report statements attributed to the child with richer detail and precision than they had originally had. The possibility of paramnesia points to the need to exercise caution when evaluating the reported abilities of the children surveyed so far and leave room for the possibility of, perhaps quite unintentional, narrative embellishment by the families concerned. This possibility can be excluded only in those rare cases when information given by the child was documented before attempts at verification led to identifying the previous person and to meetings between the child and the other family, with its resultant information exchange.[256]

An example of documentation prior to verification from Sri Lanka concerns a boy who at the age of eight months started to exhibit a fear of lorries, to the extent that the word "lorry" (an English loanword in Sinhalese) would suffice to get him to do things he did not want to do.[257] At less than two years he began to communicate information regarding a past life in a different village, often using gestures to express information for which he did not yet have the appropriate vocabulary. The previous person had died after stepping onto a road and being struck by a lorry. Among the various details apparently familiar to him from that past life were two place names that in the meantime had fallen out of use and were only known among elderly people in the village.[258] Besides his fear of lorries, another apparent behavioral continuity with the previous person was his request to be given cigarettes and arrack, a distilled alcoholic drink

255. Tucker 2005/2014, 38 sums up that the "possibility of faulty memory by informants is the most likely normal explanation for many of our cases."

256. For a survey of such cases and a new case in Turkey see Keil and Tucker 2005; for a case in Europe see Stevenson 2003/2008, 210–23.

257. This is the case of Sujith Lakmal Jayaratne; see Stevenson 1977, 234–80 and, for criticism of this case raised by B. N. Moore, the summary in Edwards 1996, 258–59. Another Sri Lankan case with written documentation before verification is that of Indika Guneratne; see Stevenson 1977, 203–34. Here Stevenson himself arrived early enough to take down correct information given by the boy concerning a former life as a deceased member of an unrelated family living in a different town.

258. Stevenson 1977, 277 comments that "this case is certainly one of the strongest known to me because of the recording in writing of sixteen items stated by Sujith before they were verified."

that the previous person had been producing, trading, and consuming; none of the members of his present family drank or smoked. Even when drinking water he would do so in the manner typical of arrack drinkers in Sri Lanka, including belching and wiping his mouth.

In three cases in Sri Lanka, assistants of Ian Stevenson were able to arrive on the scene before a corresponding previous personality was recognized.[259] This enabled them to take down various statements made by the three girls in question and then proceed themselves to identify a corresponding deceased person. In the first of these three cases, the location of the previous personality was over two hundred kilometers away from the town of the girl's present life, and the two families concerned were to all appearances not previously acquainted with each other.[260] Several of the statements she made about the past life were rather specific, and they turned out to be correct.

In the second case, besides various verified details about the family of the previous personality, the girl also correctly described earlier features of the boutique run by the previous person's father and of the former house, even though in both cases these features had in the meantime changed. The roof of the boutique had earlier been made of coconut leaves, but in the meantime this had been replaced by tiles; the walls of the house had been painted in a different color.[261] The two families involved did not appear to have known each other prior to the development of the case.

The third girl remembered dying in a landslide in a different part of the country and as part of a family unrelated to her present one.[262] When her present father took her to the tea estate where the landslide had happened, she started to scream and refused to proceed, whereupon he had to abandon his plan to reach the site. Besides providing various correct details about the previous personality, the girl also showed behavioral continuities with the former life that were out of keeping with her present living

259. For another case in Sri Lanka that was also documented before verification see Haraldsson 1991, 235–43.

260. This is the case of Thusitha Silva; see Stevenson and Samararatne 1988, 221–25.

261. This is the case of Iranga Jayakody; see Stevenson and Samararatne 1988, 225–29.

262. This is the case of Subashini Gunasekera; see Stevenson and Samararatne 1988, 229–35.

situation, including the use of specific words appropriate for dwellers on a tea estate.

Another example of previous documentation is a girl from India who, when aged between two and three, started to relate details of a past life that were taken down in writing before an attempt was made to verify them.[263] She apparently gave a wealth of correct details reflecting close acquaintance with the life of an otherwise unrelated Indian woman who had lived in a different town and passed away five years before her birth. Besides speaking at a young age with an unusual accent, appropriate for the location of the previous personality, the girl also showed remarkable fearlessness with snakes, in line with the fact that the previous person had kept a pet cobra. When the girl was at school at the age of six, a wild cobra fell from a tree and the other children ran away in fear. The girl instead reportedly went up to the cobra and patted it on the hood, whereupon the cobra moved away.

Another case in India features a boy who at the age of three started to give details of a past life that were recorded on tape and in writing.[264] Besides various details about the previous life of an otherwise unrelated and unknown family, he reportedly gave a correct account of how the former person was shot dead by dacoits who had attacked the house at night. At the time of relating this, the boy had apparently not encountered dacoits in his present life, nor did his present father own a gun. As an otherwise fairly aggressive child, he showed a marked phobia of the dark and warned his present father not to go out in the dark, lest he might be killed.

A case from India involves a boy who at little over three years of age began to relate a past life as a Brahmin in a different town.[265] Various details about what he saw as his former life experiences were published by

263. This is the case of Kumkum Verma; see Stevenson 1975, 206–40.

264. This is the case of Ajendra Singh Chauhan; see Mills and Lynn 2000, 283–85 and Mills 2004.

265. This is the case of Jagdish Chandra; see Stevenson 1975, 144–75 and, for criticism of this case, e.g., Nicol 1976, 14–15 and Edwards 1996, 256–57.

his father, a lawyer, in a newspaper before an attempt was made to identify someone whom these descriptions would fit.[266] Besides furnishing rather accurate information, on being brought to the town of the previous personality he apparently found his way to the former home without any aid through a tangle of narrow streets, such that Ian Stevenson on his way back, after visiting the house, lost his way. This case also involves behavioral continuities, as in relation to eating manners and food preferences the child behaved like a Brahmin, even though his present family were not Brahmins. He also showed an interest in *bhang*, a preparation made of cannabis, which for a child is rather unusual.

The same pattern of details being published in a newspaper before an attempt at verification was made, a procedure adopted by the same lawyer, holds for the case of another Indian boy who as soon as he was able to speak began to relate a past life in another town.[267] The information he was able to give matched the life of a young man who had died. When taken to the town of the former person, one of his various recognitions apparently involved pointing out the place where a staircase had been to a house that in the meantime had fallen into ruin, such that no trace of the staircase remained. He is also credited with having been able to identify a room where some gold treasure had been buried, which a subsequent search was indeed able to recover in the room he had indicated.

A significant behavioral aspect of this case is that the child was reportedly able to play *tabla*, an Indian type of drum that the previous person had played but that was not in use in the child's present family. He also kept complaining to his present family regarding the much better living conditions he was used to from his former life. According to the report given, he secretly took to eating meat and drinking alcohol when about five years old; the rest of his family were vegetarians and teetotalers.

266. Stevenson 1975, 171 reports that his father "was a prominent and respected lawyer of Bareilly. When his son began to talk of a previous life, he called in various colleagues of the bar, who themselves interrogated Jagdish Chandra. Then he openly published details of the case in a newspaper before trying to get in touch with the previous family. Thus I believe that a fraudulent contrivance of this case by him is out of the question."

267. This is the case of Bishen Chand Kapoor; see Stevenson 1975, 176–205.

Another interesting aspect is that he seemingly was able to read and speak some Urdu, whereas the language spoken in his present family was Hindi. This aspect of the case suggests xenoglossy.

Cases mentioned so far have been from countries in which rebirth is an accepted belief. Nevertheless, while in themselves rare, cases where documentation has been possible before verification have also been found in settings less supportive of such beliefs, such as the United States.

A boy in the United States at the age of three gave various verified details of a former life as a pilot who died when fighting the Japanese during World War II.[268] He apparently gave the name of the boat correctly from which he would take off as well as the name of another pilot. Already at the age of two he had nightmares about crashing with his plane, as had indeed happened to the former person after his engine was hit during Japanese shooting and the plane started burning. In this case the information given by the boy was videotaped before verification. At the age of four he showed good knowledge of fighting planes, for instance noting that Corsairs often get flat tires, the correctness of which was confirmed by a military historian. He appeared to have a behavioral memory habit that manifested on being seated in a car, when he would perform a series of hand movements that mirrored what a pilot does when putting on earphones and adjusting the microphone in an airplane.

The case just described shows that children with past-life memories are not found only in a cultural setting where rebirth is an accepted notion; in fact the father of the American boy was highly skeptical of his son's tales until verification showed them to be correct. In this case, however, the father was at least open enough to allow the evidence to unfold and eventually convince him. The same does not necessarily happen with other

268. This is the case of James Leininger; see Tucker 2013, 63–87. Stevenson 1974a, 396 reports that in general "subjects (and their parents) of some American cases have expressed. . .fears [of ridicule or ostracism] to me, and often have only revealed the cases known to them with much trepidation." On negative reactions among American families to a child with apparent memories of a past life see also Stevenson 1983a, 744 and, for a psychological evaluation of cases involving American children, Tucker and Nidiffer 2014. A survey of European cases of memories believed to be from a past life can be found in Stevenson 2003/2008.

cases in a setting in which belief in rebirth is not an acceptable notion, leading either to ignoring it or else even to active attempts at suppression.[269] In the average Western setting, it would not be surprising for a child who relates memories from a past life not to be taken seriously, and insistence by the child may even lead to him or her being silenced.[270]

Active attempts at suppression can also be seen in an Indian setting that involves a boy whose Muslim parents did not believe in rebirth. At two years of age he started to remember a previous life, giving various verified details from the past life and relating a birthmark he had to a spear wound from which the previous person died.[271] Although this convinced his parents, Ian Stevenson reports that a group of Muslims from the neighborhood tried to disrupt the case's investigation, considering it offensive to their belief that no rebirth can take place; later the parents of the boy had to face criticism and threats for having cooperated.[272] This is not the only instance of opposition by Muslims to research related to rebirth.[273]

Even in countries where rebirth is accepted, parents are not necessarily

269. Regarding the tendency to ignore evidence and beliefs related to rebirth, a telling example is the question posed by Mills 1994, 4 in her introduction to a study of Amerindian rebirth beliefs: "Why then has it taken more than 500 years of contact for a single book to appear that describes the role of reincarnation in North American indigenous culture?" In the case of Alaska, Stevenson 1987/2001, 37–38 reports that several professionally trained persons (four of whom were anthropologists) working for longer periods with the Tlingit were for the most part unaware of the existence of rebirth beliefs among the people they were dealing with.

270. Willson 1984/1987, 18 points out that "normally, especially in the West, a young child who talks of its previous life soon learns not to." Stevenson 1987/2001, 95 reasons that an "unknown number of cases are suppressed, even within the subject's own family. This is particularly likely to happen in cultures, such as those of Western countries, where the majority of people do not believe in reincarnation."

271. This is the case of Nasruddin Shah; see Stevenson 1997a, 400–17.

272. Stevenson 1997a, 414. On Muslim cases in India see also Mills 1990 and 2006.

273. Mills 1990, 182 reports that "in four cases the Moslem relatives showed considerable hostility to the investigation of the case because reincarnation is against their doctrine. . .[however] opposition from the Moslems involved blocked further investigation in only two of the twenty-six cases in this study."

supportive of their children having such memories.[274] Apparently belief in rebirth, therefore,

> has little bearing on the attitudes informants adopt toward a particular case. The belief makes credible for them the statements of a child who talks about it without, as often happens when a Western child talks of a previous life, thinking that either he or they have lost their minds. But this does not necessarily mean that they enjoy what they hear.[275]

Another pattern of children remembering past lives relates to a prominent feature of near-death experiences, namely the influence of beliefs held in the respective cultures in which the cases occur. With children remembering past lives, this becomes evident in aspects such as the average intermission period between the death of the previous person and the birth of the present child,[276] the frequency of the occurrence of change of sex from one life to the next, and the manifestation of birthmarks.

Compared to past-life regression, it is remarkable that children who remember past lives often involve recently deceased previous personalities in relatively close geographical locations. This appears to be related to a general pattern of children having memories of lives that ended suddenly,

274. Rawat and Rivas 2007, 118 report from India that there "is a wide spread superstition that children who recall a past life die young. We see the parents, besides scolding and beating the child, resorting to various odd practices like putting a child on a potter's wheel and then moving it in anticlockwise direction or filling his mouth with soap or filth just to make the child to forget and not to delve in the remembrances of a past life." Stevenson 1997a, 396n10 notes that "in a series of 69 Indian cases 29 (41 %) of the parents of the subjects suppressed or tried to suppress their child from speaking about a previous life."

275. Stevenson 1975, 30.

276. Particularly noteworthy here is that in several cases the interval between death and birth is too short to allow for the normal period of gestation, making it clear that the mother was already pregnant when the previous person presumably to be reborn as her child had not yet died. In relation to one such case in which actual birth had already occurred, Story 1975/2010, 166 reasons that the psychic current of the deceased "must have projected itself into the body of the new-born child, permanently displacing the personality of the individual whose karma had actually formed the body in the womb"; see also Matlock 1990, 211 and above note 27.

often in violent ways. In other words, it seems such memories occur with much higher frequency in relation to past lives that came to an end unexpectedly. Presumably as a result of the person not having been able to live that life fully, what is perceived by the individual as a rebirth perhaps takes place soon and comparatively close by, which in turn would stand a better chance of being spontaneously remembered.[277] In contrast, past lives at a more distant time in the past would then be less prone to being spontaneously remembered and would instead require past-life regression or meditative practice to be recalled. This might explain at least in part why only some children have such memories.

From the viewpoint of the early Buddhist conception of rebirth it is of interest that several of the cases that have been investigated clearly counter a deterministic conception of karma. Comparing a single past life to the present situation of the children does not evince a clear-cut relationship between the ethical qualities of deeds in the former life and present results. Some recollections involve past lives as dacoits, for example, who committed major crimes, and others show that the belief that suicide leads to a lower rebirth is contrary to the evidence that children's memories can provide.[278] Such cases could only be accommodated by a nondeterministic theory of karma, which allows for the relationship between deed and fruition to involve an indeterminate timespan ranging over a series of successive lives.[279]

277. A finding to some extent related, reported by Cook et al. 1983, 131, is that "the incidence of violent death among the presumed previous personalities was much higher in unsolved cases than in solved cases...[which could] result from the relatively easy penetration of memories of a violent death combined with a lesser ability to remember names that permit identifying the person who died violently." The point seems to be that the violent nature of the death ensured that at least that much is remembered, even if other details are forgotten.

278. Stevenson 1987/2001, 220 notes that the cases he and his colleagues have researched "disprove the belief expounded in some religions that persons who commit suicide live in Hell for centuries or even for eternity."

279. Stevenson 1987/2001, 253 comments that, even though a clear-cut relationship between conduct in one life and socioeconomic situation in the next life cannot be established, "this does not mean that conduct in one life cannot have effects in another...the subjects frequently demonstrate interests, aptitudes, and attitudes corresponding to those of the persons whose lives they remember...one child counts every rupee he can grasp, like the acquisitive

Birthmarks and Birth Defects

Beginning with Buddhist precedents, a description related to birthmarks, if they can be called such, could be the report that the Buddha was endowed with thirty-two special marks of bodily beauty whose recognition enabled fortune tellers to predict his future destiny already at the time when he had just been born.[280] A Pāli discourse records various deeds the Buddha-to-be is held to have performed in previous lives, leading to the acquisitions of these marks.[281] The point of the description is to relate what he had done in those lives to the result of his having a particular mark of bodily beauty now.

Although official Christian doctrine does not affirm rebirth, and so of course does not have a basis for such an interpretation of birthmarks, a phenomenon that is at least to some extent related is the manifestation of stigmata.[282] A famous case of the actual arising of stigmata is St. Francis of Assisi, whose hands and feet are reported to have shown visible signs, as if pierced by nails, comparable to the wounds to be seen on depictions of the crucified Jesus.[283]

Similar to research on children remembering past lives, in the case of birthmarks and defects Ian Stevenson has studied in detail a wealth of

---

businessman whose life he remembers, but another gives generously to beggars, just as the pious woman whose life she remembers did. One young boy aims a stick at passing policemen, as if to shoot them, as did the bandit whose life he remembers, but another solicitously offers medical help to his playmates in the manner of the doctor whose life he remembers."

280. Sn 693, the *Buddhacarita* 1.69, Johnston 1936/1995, 8 (see also T 4.192.3a25 and T 4.193.61a27), the *Lalitavistara*, Lefmann 1902, 104,9 (see also T 3.186.496b4 and T 3.186.557b3), the *Mahāvastu*, Senart 1890, 32,9, the *Saṅghabhedavastu*, Gnoli 1977, 53,21, with its parallels in T 24.1450.109b24 and D 1 *ga* 285a7 or Q 1030 *nge* 268a7, and several Buddha biographies preserved in Chinese translation: T 3.184.464c14, T 3.185.474a23, T 3.189.627b21, T 3.190.697a3, and T 3.191.941a15.

281. DN 30 at DN III 145,22–179,10; for a study see Anālayo 2017a, 103–22.

282. The term "stigmata" harks back to St. Paul's Letter to the Galatians 6:17, where he proclaims that he bears on his body the marks (*στίγματα*) of Jesus.

283. Amoni 1880, 180,5: *manus, et pedes ejus in ipso medio clavis confixæ videbantur*. The description implies that the marks appeared in the place where the nails are shown in pictorial depictions. In the case of real crucifixion, the nails would be driven through the wrists, not through the palm of the hands. As noted by Stevenson 1997a, 38n2, the "stigmata correspond to the mental image the stigmatist has of the crucifixion, not necessarily to the physical experience of Jesus."

instances. In what follows I present a brief summary of what to my mind are particularly striking examples, recommending that the reader consult the full report of the cases in the original publications for a full assessment of their value.

A case in Turkey involves two children born in different families who at a little over a year old remembered past lives as husband and wife.[284] The couple had been brutally murdered by being hit on the head with a blacksmith's hammer. At his birth, the boy's head was soft and had to be kept in cotton wadding for two months, only after which the skull hardened. The girl had a red birthmark on top of her head, the area of which was soft, and she suffered from strong headaches when young. Both presumably related to the way the former persons had been killed. Among various details of the former lives remembered by each of the two, particularly worthy of note is that apparently the boy correctly recalled private debts owed to the former person by others.

Another case in Turkey involves a boy who began narrating events of a previous life at the age of three, describing his former house and family, as well as his death.[285] On being taken to the village of the former personality, at the age of six he recognized the house and wife, and at the age of eight he recognized the man who, he believed, had murdered the previous person. Not only were the two families concerned unacquainted with each other, but the former family only knew that the man in question had disappeared; it was only when the child related the details of the murder that a corpse that had been buried elsewhere could be identified as being of the man in question. At birth the boy had grooves on two fingers of the right hand and the finger between these two was shortened, corresponding to his memory that he put up his right hand in an effort to deflect the blade with which he was being attacked, whereupon his hand was cut. The murderer next cut off his head, apparently reflected in a birthmark the boy had running around the back of his neck.

Yet another boy in Turkey at the age of two started to relate various verified details of a former life, including the name of the one who had

284. These are the cases of İsmail Altınkılıç and Cevriye Bayrı; see Stevenson 1980, 194–259.
285. This is the case of Yusuf Köse; see Stevenson 1997a, 1344–51.

murdered the past personality during an election riot.[286] The postmortem report and the records of the trial describe a wound on the head caused by an unspecified solid object. The boy had to have an operation soon after his birth, as he had an opening in his skull through which part of the meninges were extruding, apparently closely corresponding to the wound the deceased had received on his head.

A boy in Thailand at the age of two repeatedly expressed fear as soon as any woman came to the house.[287] When asked about the reason for acting in this manner, he related that in a past life he had been stabbed by a woman, giving various verified details about the previous personality. He had a birthmark on the chest that, according to the testimony of the woman convicted for the murder, corresponded in location to the wound caused by her stabbing the former person.

Another boy in Thailand aged between three and four kept asking to be taken to see his wife and children, giving the name and various details of the former person.[288] Starting from the market of the village of the former person, he was apparently able to lead the way to the correct house and there recognized family members and objects that had belonged to the deceased, including the place where the man had been shot, as well as pointing out changes that had been made to the house in the meantime and noting that furniture and books were missing. He had two birthmarks on his head, presumably corresponding to the wounds caused by the entry and exit of the bullet that had killed the previous person (the birthmark at the back of the head was smaller, in keeping with the detail that he seemed to have been shot from behind; a wound caused by a bullet's entry tends to be smaller than the one caused by its exit).[289]

Birthmarks on the head apparently corresponding to the wounds caused by the entry and exit of the bullet that had killed the previous person occur also in the case of a boy from India who, when aged between one

286. This is the case of Mehmet Samioğlu; see Stevenson 1997a, 1442–54.

287. This is the case of Som Pit Hancharoen; see Stevenson 1997a, 276–91.

288. This is the case of Chanai Choomalaiwong; see Stevenson 1997a, 300–23.

289. For a summary of this pattern in other cases see also Stevenson 1997a, 932.

and two, began to speak and refer to a past life.[290] The boy knew how the previous person had been killed, described some rather unique features of the home, and recognized the shop owned by the former personality. He apparently used nicknames when seeing the children of the previous person, conforming to the latter's usage, and spontaneously slapped a stool when entering and leaving the shop, conforming to the somewhat macho behavior characteristic of the former person. Other behavioral features are his apparent familiarity with how to drive a car and play the tape deck in it, something outside of his present-life experience but in conformity with the fact that the previous person had owned and driven a car.

A Sri Lankan girl at the age of three began giving subsequently verified details of a previous life as a male incense maker in an unrelated family in a rather distant part of the country.[291] She had a cluster of birthmarks on her chest, apparently corresponding to the location where during a fatal accident the tire of a bus had run over the previous person, a location confirmed by the postmortem report. When taken to the former place of incense production, she noticed that the packets in which the incense was sold had been changed. She not only knew with precision which procedure the past person had employed to make incense but also correctly gave the names of the local brands of the incense sold.

A boy in Burma at the age of about eight months was taken by his parents to the nearby monastery, on arriving at which he started crying with such vehemence that the parents had to return home.[292] At the age of three he began to relate a previous life, indicating with the help of gestures, due to his lack of vocabulary, that in the nearby monastery he had been hit on the head. When he could speak fully, he reported having been the head monk of the monastery, who had been killed when a deranged visitor had hit him on the head. Since birth the boy had had a hairless depression on the head, apparently corresponding to where the head monk had been struck. He displayed fear when taken to the monastery and a recurrent

290. This is the case of Toran Singh; see Mills 1989, 156–71 (see esp. 171 on a complication of the case caused by divergent birth dates).

291. This is the case of Purnima Ekanyake; see Haraldsson 2000/2006.

292. This is the case of Maung Myo Min Thein; see Stevenson 1997a, 1454–66.

concern about protecting his head. As a small boy he showed behavior typical of a monk and displayed precocity in learning the recitation of Buddhist texts.

Female twins in Sri Lanka showed masculine behavior traits, to the extent of urinating while standing and stroking their faces as if to feel a beard's growth, in line with their memories of having been males who had been killed by the police during an insurgency.[293] Both were able to relate verified details of the lives of the two men. One of the two former persons had been shot by the police when trying to escape; the girl remembering this life was able to show the way to the place where this had happened and had a birthmark apparently corresponding to the bullet wound. Both showed a phobia of jeeps of the type used by police in Sri Lanka.

Regarding the occurrence of such birthmarks and defects, it needs to be noted that these do not invariably manifest in those who remember having died by violent means. In fact concern with birthmarks and defects features among culturally conditioned phenomena. Both tend to be given importance predominantly in places where there is a commonly held belief that such physical features reflect the influence of a previous life, to the extent that at times dead bodies are physically marked somewhere in the hope that, on being reborn, the child will have a birthmark in the corresponding place.

Thus the question of whether a bodily mutilation at the time of death carries over to the next life, if that is indeed what these cases point to, depends on the individual. Just as not all of those who meditate on the crucified Jesus acquire stigmata, similarly not all those who remember a past life that ended violently are born with birthmarks or defects related to injuries received at that time.[294]

293. This is the case of Sivanthie and Sheromie Hettiaratchi; see Stevenson 1997a, 1940–70.

294. Stevenson 1997b, 185 reasons that, similar to "the importance of intense concentration in the occurrence of stigmata...a person suddenly shot, stabbed, or struck will inevitably concentrate attention on the wounded part." This would imply that the carry-over effect of such experiences to what appears to be the next life would be related to the victim's reaction to the inflicted pain.

4. Xenoglossy

Xenoglossy refers to the ability to communicate in a language that the person in question to all appearances has not learned in the present life. Cases can be divided into the two categories of "recitative xenoglossy," the ability to repeat by rote without necessarily understanding the text, and "responsive xenoglossy," which requires that the language be understood and that the one who exhibits this ability be able to reply to questions in that language.

By way of introducing a Buddhist textual precedent, the *Lalitavistara* and the **Abhiniṣkramaṇa-sūtra* depict an ability of the Buddha as a child that has a distant relation to xenoglossy. They report that the young prince was sent to school to learn writing. As part of his inquiry as to what the teacher would teach him, he listed a broad variety of scripts with which he apparently was already familiar, most of which his teacher had never even heard of.[295]

In the Christian tradition xenoglossy is recorded by St. Luke in his Acts of the Apostles. The apostles, being filled with the Holy Spirit, began to speak in languages they had earlier not learned and that could be understood by those who were native speakers.[296] Examples of such ability continue to be found in hagiographic texts of the Middle Ages.[297]

As already mentioned in earlier parts of this chapter, apparent xenoglossy occurs in several cases of children seemingly remembering past lives.[298]

Recitative Xenoglossy

A case of recitative xenoglossy concerns a girl in India who happened to remember two past lives.[299] For one of these two lives she was able to give

295. Lefmann 1902, 125,19 and T 3.187.559b13 as well as T 3.190.703c10.

296. Acts 2:4.

297. For a study of women from the later Middle Ages credited with such abilities see Cooper-Rompato 2010.

298. For further examples see the survey in Stevenson 1974b, 2–8 (xenoglossy in general) and 14–18 (xenoglossy of children remembering past lives), and for a case in Europe Stevenson 2003/2008, 22–23.

299. This is the case of Swarnlata Mishra; see Stevenson 1966/1974, 67–91.

a substantial amount of correct information that had been documented before verification, including items of a rather private nature such as knowing that the husband of the deceased had taken a certain amount of money from a box in which she had kept money, which the former husband confirmed and declared to have been known only to him and his deceased wife. From the other life, however, she appeared to remember songs in Bengali, a language unknown in her present family. At the age of five or six she would sing these and at the same time perform the appropriate dance; in fact she apparently needed to do both together, in that the dancing was required for her to be able to sing (which seems to reflect the relationship of body kinesthetics to memory). Two songs were later identified as deriving from poems by Rabindranath Tagore. Her present family had no phonograph or radio, and she had not yet been to the movies at the time she began to perform the songs.[300]

Recitative xenoglossy, in the form of the ability to recite in an unlearned language, recurs in my case study in the next chapter, which differs insofar as the posture assumed when reciting is not a dance but rather sitting in meditation.

Responsive Xenoglossy

Three cases of responsive xenoglossy have been studied in detail by Ian Stevenson and others.[301] One of these cases concerns an Indian woman able to converse in Bengali; in this case this ability emerged when she was no longer a child. Instead she was a grown-up woman from Maratha by the name of Uttara who at times spontaneously changed into a Bengali woman by the name of Sharada. As Sharada, she no longer understood Marathi or any of the other languages that Uttara knew but instead

300. Rogo 1985/2005, 148 concludes that the case is not strong since it cannot "be ruled out that the girl had, at sometime unbeknown to her parents, learned the songs from records." However, it needs to be noted that this would also require that she somehow learned the appropriate dance, which is less easily done than just learning a song. As Stevenson 1966/1974, 88 points out, "she must have herself practiced the songs and dances before she could have reached the skill in them she showed on the very first occasion when she revealed her ability to perform them to her family" at a time when she was between five and six years old.

301. Stevenson 1974b, 1984, and Stevenson and Pasricha 1980.

was only able to converse in Bengali, which she was able to do fluently. Although sharing the same body, Uttara and Sharada lived in seeming ignorance of each other, in the sense that neither remembered what the other had done, which invests the present case with features of the possession type.[302] Sharada also showed ignorance of modern-day appliances. In contrast, she appeared to be quite well informed about various aspects of Bengal in the nineteenth century,[303] and she also behaved like a married Bengali woman (Uttara was not married).[304]

Sharada's ability in Bengali has met with different evaluations. Several persons who met her asserted that she spoke fluently and remarked that she did not use any of the English loanwords that had become part of modern Bengali since the nineteenth century. A trained linguist, however, based on examining two tape recordings, considered her Bengali to have been learned as a second language and in the twentieth century.[305] Although this trained linguist did not meet Sharada personally and therefore based his evaluation on the limited material available through two tape recordings, the assessment of her language ability remains equivocal.

Two other cases are based on hypnotic regression and thus share to some extent the limitations, discussed above, of information acquired through such means. Both cases involve American housewives, one of whom manifested a male personality by the name of Jensen who might have lived in seventeenth-century Sweden, and the other a female personality by the name of Gretchen who would have lived in Germany in the nineteenth century. These previous lives remain unverified. In both cases it appears that the two housewives had not learned the respective languages previously but under hypnosis were able to exhibit abilities in conversing in Swedish or German, respectively. In the Jensen case, Stevenson himself considers possession somewhat more likely as an interpretation,

302. On the somewhat blurred dividing line between possession and rebirth cases see Stevenson 1966/1974, 376–77.

303. Stevenson 1984, 88–99 notes Sharada's ability to give a correct genealogy of her Bengali family, including data not mentioned in any official publication of this genealogy, and her knowledge of somewhat obscure places in Bengal as well as of a particular temple.

304. Stevenson 1984, 99–105.

305. Stevenson 1984, 127–32.

compared to rebirth.[306] As for the Gretchen case, the German spoken comes with errors of the type that a native speaker would not make.[307]

In sum, so far evidence from responsive xenoglossy for the case of rebirth has been considered inconclusive.[308]

Summary

Throughout my survey in this chapter, I at least briefly noted textual antecedents when introducing each topic, in order to show the deep roots of near-death experiences and various dimensions of memories of former lives in ancient religious beliefs. Although individual instances of the type surveyed above are amenable to a range of different interpretations and fall short of providing definite proof of rebirth, the body of data that has emerged so far changes the status of the idea that rebirth can occur from a religious creed into a reasonable belief supported by a body of evidence.[309]

Near-death experiences pose a challenge to the assumption that mental activity is solely the product of the brain. Past-life regression opens up an avenue for personally trying out whether memories that are subjectively

306. Stevenson 1974b, 85 considers possession a slightly more probable hypothesis than rebirth to explain the manifestation of the Jensen personality; on the subject's development of mediumistic abilities see also Stevenson 1974b, 57–59.

307. Since German is my native language, I am able to assess the material myself. Expressions like "ich beistehen der Hausfrau. Das Kinder," "ich gehe der Kirche," "warum er kommen wieder und wieder," and "ich habe reden alles. Warum der Fragen wieder und wieder," found in the transcripts in Stevenson 1984, 172, 176, 182, and 189, clearly involve grammatical errors of a type that a native speaker would not make. Stevenson 1984, 26 considers the possibility that the location referred to by Gretchen might have been a village located in an area where the inhabitants' native language would have been Polish, German only being their second language. This "would adequately account for the imperfections in Gretchen's German, supposing that Polish was her mother tongue," although, as he notes himself, this would then require an explanation as to why she did not speak Polish on being regressed to that life.

308. For critical assessments see, e.g., Samarin 1976, Roll 1982, 186–89, Thomason 1984, 1987, 1988, and 1996.

309. Dell'Olio 2010, 122 argues that "we don't need conclusive evidence for a rational belief since most of the beliefs we consider to be rational do not have conclusive evidence." Carter 2012, 65 concludes that "reincarnation provides a rational and coherent explanation for the data from past-life memory cases. At this point, it would appear that reincarnation provides the *best* explanation of the data."

experienced as belonging to a past life can be accessed, whatever their historical value.

Children's memories of past lives and the documented cases of birthmarks as well as birth defects taken together are not easily dismissed as the wishful imagination of the faithful. Instead, the body of evidence collected by Ian Stevenson and others offers considerable support for the assumption that at least some of these cases do reflect genuine memories from the past. In the case of xenoglossy, however, the instances studied so far appear to be not as convincing as some of the documented children's memories and birthmarks. It is to another case of xenoglossy that I turn in the next chapter.

IV. Case Study in Pāli Xenoglossy

Introduction

With this chapter I return to focus on Buddhist sources, in particular to a set of Pāli texts in the form in which they have been chanted by a young boy in Sri Lanka. His case stands in continuity with children's memories of past lives that I explored in the previous chapter. My examination begins with a brief survey of the case history (1), followed by the background to the chants (2). Then I examine errors and variants compared to the presently available editions of the respective Pāli texts (3) as well as significant omissions and additions (4).

1. The Case History

By way of introducing the case, I first report my personal contact with Dhammaruwan, the reciter of the chants. Then I summarize his recollections of events related to his present-life experiences as a child able to recite texts in Pāli that he does not recall having learned or overheard from others in this life. After that I turn to his memories of when he learned those chants in the past and report the verification of the recordings of the chants as genuine by an audio engineer.

Personal Contacts

As already mentioned briefly in the introduction to this book, I personally know Dhammaruwan from the time I lived in Sri Lanka in the 1990s. At that time I was in charge of a meditation center on the outskirts of Kandy, and Dhammaruwan's house was in the vicinity of the meditation center. He mainly stayed in Colombo but regularly came to the house in Kandy. Due to his interest in meditation, we naturally came to know each other.

Although I knew of his past-life memories, we rarely spoke about this since it was a matter of limited interest to me. What was of considerable interest to me was his rather unusual way of chanting Pāli texts. Traditional Sri Lankan Pāli chanting tends to be quite swift; in fact often several monks chant together so that, when one of them has to take a breath, the others can continue. Dhammaruwan's chanting is in contrast very measured and slow. It is also much more melodious than standard Sri Lankan recitations.

At that time I was doing PhD research on the *Satipaṭṭhāna-sutta*. To complement what I could gather from an academic perspective by approaching this discourse also from a traditional viewpoint, I had begun to memorize and recite it regularly.[310] For this purpose Dhammaruwan gave me useful practical advice, in the course of which we developed a closer friendship.

The Present-Life Story

Dhammaruwan was born on November 18, 1968, in Matale.[311] At an age of about two years he would sit in meditation spontaneously and then start chanting, as well as at times saying things in a language not understood by his mother, who tried to hush him up. This feature of the present case is similar to the Burmese children who remember previous lives as Japanese soldiers and who apparently spoke for some time in early childhood in a language not understood in their families.[312] It also bears similarity to the case of the Thai child who at the age of two, presumably as a

310. The PhD thesis was published as Anālayo 2003; on the benefit of using traditional modes of learning a discourse alongside modern academic research, in relation to the *Satipaṭṭhāna-sutta*, see also Anālayo 2014c.

311. The following is a summary based on an interview conducted on March 21, 2016. The interview comes in two parts, as halfway through Dhammaruwan requested a break. When quoting directly from the interview, I use the numbers 1 and 2 to distinguish between the first and the second recording.

312. This is the case of Ma Tin Aung Myo and others like her; see above p. 98.

result of remembering a former life spent for a considerable time living in a monastery, spontaneously sat in meditation.[313] Another parallel obtains with the case of the Indian girl who was able to perform dances and sing in Bengali, a language unknown in her family.[314]

Returning to Dhammaruwan's story, at a later time he and his mother went from Matale to Kandy to stay with Bertie and Rosa Seneviratne, who became his stepparents. When Dhammaruwan was about three years old, his chanting of a part of the *Dhammacakkappavattana-sutta* was overheard by someone in the house, at a time when Bertie and Rosa had gone to India, leading to the eventual realization that he was chanting a Pāli text. On their return, Bertie encouraged the boy to continue and regularly made recordings of the chants, copies of which he would give to interested visitors. By the time he had become an adult, Dhammaruwan had lost the ability to perform these chants.

Before that happened, visitors who witnessed the chants included, according to his recollections, several eminent monks, Presidents R. Premadasa (1923–93) and J. R. Jayewardena (1906–96),[315] the Indian meditation teacher Anagārika Munindra (1915–2003),[316] as well as the American professor Ian Stevenson (1918–2007).[317] In an interview conducted by me, Dhammaruwan reports:[318]

> As a child I was very, very shy and didn't want, didn't like people coming and looking at me chanting and stuff like that. So because of that, they thought, my father thought, that more

313. This is the case of Ratana Wongsombat; see above p. 96.

314. This is the case of Swarnlata Mishra; see above p. 113.

315. I have not verified the dates of the persons listed, thus these are only meant as an approximation.

316. For Dhammaruwan's recollections of meetings with Munindra see Knaster 2010, 43, 49, and 82.

317. An attempt to locate a corresponding file in the archives of Ian Stevenson's research at the University of Virginia has not been successful, according to the reply by the research coordinator (December 1, 2016), who on behalf of Jim Tucker tried to locate records of the case.

318. 2–00.25 until 2–01.49; here and below I have slightly corrected the text to avoid grammatical errors.

> publicity or more of these people trying to make a fuss out of this, he will lose this ability, so he tried to keep it very, very quiet. And he made people promise first, before listening to the tapes or coming to see me, they first make a promise, even people who want to do research, like Ian Stevenson, made a promise: "You can see him provided you don't make this public, for your knowledge okay, but not to make it public for others."

The shyness became worse when on one occasion he was brought to a monastery in a car to meet the head monk. People had come to know of it and a great crowd had assembled. He reports:[319]

> People, wearing white, jump into the vehicle, like a mob, to see what this child is. And it's very scary when that happens. Only if it happens to you, you will know. As a child, people. . .with these eyes which are. . .like wanting to swallow you, like that type of look. . .this was such a shock for me, I started crying very, very hard. . .So I was crying very loudly like that, and from that day onwards I was really, really scared to even do any chanting.

The Past-Life Story and a Verification of the Recordings

According to Dhammaruwan's memories, he learned the Pāli chants in a former lifetime in India, where he had been born as the son of a Brahmin and trained in memorization of the Vedas. He had gone forth as a Buddhist monk and become a student of the eminent monk Buddhaghosa at Nālandā. After being trained as a *bhāṇaka*, a reciter, together with other monks who had similarly been trained, he was chosen to accompany Buddhaghosa from India to Sri Lanka. Having come to Sri Lanka, he stayed with Buddhaghosa at the Mahāvihāra in Anurādhapura, of which he remembers various details.

319. 2–04.38 until 2–05.53.

He reports that in his present life he was taken on a tour of the Mahāvihāra by President J. R. Jayewardena:[320]

> I used to exactly say: "This is where I used to live, this is where my senior monk used to live"...and then they were excavating in those areas, and I said: "This is the right place and not that place." And they dug and they said: "The child was right."

Buddhaghosa lived in the fifth century and traveled from India to Sri Lanka to translate the commentaries kept there from the local Sinhala to Pāli.[321] He is particularly renowned for compiling the *Visuddhimagga*, a manual of practice and doctrine that has become the chief reference point for Theravāda meditation and exegesis.

What we know about Buddhaghosa would accord with the outlines provided by Dhammaruwan's memories, in that it seems quite probable that Buddhaghosa would have come to Sri Lanka accompanied by other monks who had trained as *bhāṇaka*s.[322] They would have been a meaningful asset in his work, since it would be much faster to have a *bhāṇaka* remember and recite a particular passage than to have to go through a whole stack of palm-leaf manuscripts in order to locate the same.

Beyond such probabilities, however, there seems little hope that such a past life as a monk disciple of Buddhaghosa could ever be verified. In fact, due to the father's insistence that nothing should be published and the time that has passed since then, even apparent recognitions made by Dhammaruwan in his childhood are not easily confirmed. Moreover, even if it should be possible to provide extensive documentation in this

320. 1–16.22 until 1–17.55.

321. On the life of Buddhaghosa see, e.g., Law 1923, Buddhadatta 1944, and Ñāṇamoli 1956/1991, xxviii–xl.

322. Buddhadatta 1944, 83 comments that "we may surmise that he came here not alone but with a band of learned monks." According to von Hinüber 2015, 357–58, "it seems that Buddhaghosa was invited to the Mahāvihāra and that he came from South India, where there was a strong Theravāda tradition, as a kind of 'foreign expert', or perhaps as a leader of a group of experts, because it seems that some of his South Indian fellow monks joined him in Ceylon."

respect, this would simply add one more case to the already large number of such children's memories documented by Ian Stevenson and others.

Instead, what does appear to be a more promising avenue of research is the recordings of his chants, and it is to these that the remainder of this chapter is dedicated. Unfortunately these chants have not been systematically recorded. Thus at present it is no longer possible to arrive at a comprehensive survey of the material; in fact it is at times not even certain whether a particular text is not recited in full due to problems of recording or limitations of memory.

The father made copies of the recordings of the chanting and passed these on to friends and visitors. Not knowing Pāli himself, he would not have been in a position to keep an inventory of the material, and the stricture he had imposed on other researchers must have contributed to a lack of thorough documentation of the chanted material.

What at present can still be done is to verify the recorded material. For this purpose, one tape with chants, presumably a copy of an original recording, has been examined by a professional audio-recording and mastering engineer.[323] The engineer notes that he could not detect any rustling of paper throughout the recording, which suggests that the original performance was made from memory. Regarding a dating of the recordings, he offers the following assessments:

> Prior to the first child utterance, I hear genuine "tape print through" which is very hard to simulate in a digital manner. This kind of print through occurs with cassette tapes which have been stored for a very long time. It would be very costly to simulate print through in a way that would fool an audio expert. For example, the print through on this tape has particular characteristics that sound genuine to me and a "mixed up delay" very much like print through that would be difficult to create convincingly through editing and delay. This is evidence

323. The engineer is Bob Katz, president of Digital Domain, Inc., who in his final report written on January 2, 2017, introduces himself as "a professional audio recording and mastering engineer with almost 50 years of experience."

> that this is a genuine original cassette recording made in the time period between about 1970–1985 and stored for a very long time...
>
> The distinct sound character of the built-in microphone of this type of recorder and the characteristic AGC (automatic gain control) are very hard to simulate. Since only the mike preamp of these machines and not their line input had this type of AGC, it would be very difficult and costly to make a modern digital recording and play it back into a very old cassette machine in order to simulate an old recording, and even then the engineer would have to recreate the print through which would be very difficult. So it's highly unlikely that this recording has been faked by modern digital methods.

Having examined a photograph of the label on one of the cassettes, the engineer also confirms that this type of cassette was manufactured by Philips, released in 1978 and only made until 1981. Taken together, the results of his examination seem to offer sufficiently strong confirmation that the recording indeed stems from a copy made of an oral recitation performed at some time in the 1970s (or early 1980s, depending on how much time elapsed between the original recording and the copying).

2. The Chanted Texts and Their Background

The Transmission of the Pāli Canon

The Pāli discourses to which we nowadays have access in printed form are the final product of a prolonged oral and written transmission. Originally delivered orally and passed on as such in India, one branch of this oral transmission in the Pāli language reached Sri Lanka during the second century B.C.E., and about two centuries later the texts were written down.[324]

Alongside the written transmission, oral recitation continued to be of

324. On the transmission of the Pāli texts to Sri Lanka see, e.g., Malalasekera 1928/1994 and Adikaram 1946/1994.

importance. For the situation in India, we know from the accounts of the Chinese pilgrim Fǎxiǎn that even in the early fifth century C.E. oral transmission was still continuing.[325]

The written transmission of the Pāli texts spread beyond Sri Lanka, resulting in distinct editions with their respective variant readings from Burma and Thailand, alongside the Sri Lankan edition. In my study of the chants below, I will consult these three editions together with the European edition by the Pali Text Society (PTS).

Textual Memory

In their attempt to transmit textual material orally, the early Buddhist reciters, *bhāṇaka*s, would have had the Vedic oral tradition as their model.[326] Long before the time of the Buddha, the oral transmission of the Vedas had acquired a high degree of precision. This was achieved by systematically training reciters from their early youth onward.[327] These would begin learning texts by rote and only much later study the meaning of what they had learned (this provides background to Dhammaruwan's memory that he had been a Brahmin trained in recitation).

According to research in cognitive psychology, someone may be able to remember a text that he or she does not understand at all with more precision than someone who has understood the text well.[328] This explains a tendency evident when comparing different versions of a Buddhist text

325. T 51.2085.864b17. Bechert 1992, 53 explains that "oral tradition continued to exist side by side with written scriptures for many centuries"; see also Demiéville in Renou and Filliozat 1953/2001, 403, de Jong 1974/1979, 241, and Sander 1991, 141–42.

326. See, e.g., Lévi 1915, 441, Gombrich 1990, 23, and von Hinüber 1991, 123.

327. See, e.g., von Hinüber 1989, 67 and Bronkhorst 2016, 164.

328. The experiment in question presented texts with instructions about the use of Microsoft Word and Microsoft Excel to three groups of readers, asking them to remember the text and subsequently testing their memory through a recognition task in which the participants had to decide whether a particular statement had been made in the original text. Of these participants, the first group had no experience with computer software, the second group had some experience, and the third group had advanced knowledge of computer software. Caillies, Denhière, and Kintsch, 2002, 284 report that "contrary to our expectations, the beginner participants recognized true targets faster than the other two groups. . .our interpretation is that the answers of the beginners were based mainly upon the surface features of the text."

transmitted by oral means, namely the occurrence of errors that appear to reflect insufficient attention to the meaning. Such instances are not merely absentmindedness but need to be understood as part of an overall pattern where, for ease of memorization, formal aspects of a text are given more importance than its content.

The Chanted Texts

For the purpose of the present study, I have selected the following thirteen texts out of the recordings at my disposal:[329]

- DN 15 *Mahānidāna-sutta*
- DN 16 *Mahāparinibbāna-sutta*
- DN 22 *Mahāsatipaṭṭhāna-sutta*
- SN 22.59 *Anattalakkhaṇa-sutta*
- SN 46.14 *Gilāna-sutta* (1)
- SN 46.15 *Gilāna-sutta* (2)
- SN 46.16 *Gilāna-sutta* (3)
- SN 56.11 *Dhammacakkappavattana-sutta*
- AN 10.60 *Girimānanda-sutta*
- Khp 5 / Sn 258–69 *(Mahā-)maṅgala-sutta*
- Khp 6 / Sn 222–38 *Ratana-sutta*
- Khp 9 / Sn 143–52 *Metta-sutta*
- Dhp *Dhammapada*

The first of these, the *Mahānidāna-sutta*, offers a detailed exposition of the early Buddhist conception of conditionality. This discourse already came up in chapter 1, as it provides the important indication that the early Buddhist notion of rebirth does not involve a simple mind-body dualism. Although the chanting has not preserved the full discourse, the relevant passage on the reciprocal conditioning of consciousness and name-and-form is part of the recited text.

The chanting has only a few extracts from the *Mahāparinibbāna-sutta*, the longest discourse in the Pāli canon, containing various episodes that lead up to the Buddha's passing away.

329. Several other recordings available to me are from the *Paṭṭhāna*.

The *Mahāsatipaṭṭhāna-sutta* presents detailed instructions on mindfulness practice. The recitation has preserved the full discourse, including a long section expounding the four noble truths. In the Pāli original this section appears to be the result of an addition of text that originally was of a commentarial nature.[330] This reflects a fairly recurrent pattern of textual expansion that can be detected through a comparative study of various transmission lineages of a text.

The *Anattalakkhaṇa-sutta* expounds the nature of notself, an exposition addressed to the first five disciples of the Buddha. The discourse makes it clear that notself refers to the lack of control and the impermanent and therefore ultimately unsatisfactory nature of all aspects of subjective experience, a topic already broached in chapter 1 as well.

The three *Gilāna-sutta*s reflect an important aspect of oral recitation, namely its function as a *paritta*, a protective chant. The act of chanting such texts functions as a source of merit and power, held in tradition to be able to effect even physical healing in the audience. This is indeed what the three discourses report, namely that hearing a recitation of the awakening factors led to recovery from disease.

The *Dhammacakkappavattana-sutta* is reckoned to have been the Buddha's first sermon, in which he disclosed the four noble truths. Insight into the four noble truths is another topic already taken up in chapter 1 in relation to right view.

Another text related to the genre of *paritta*, whose recitation is considered to have healing power, is the *Girimānanda-sutta*, which lists ten meditative perceptions. One of these concerns various diseases that can arise in the body, among which those caused by karma are mentioned. This exemplifies a point made in chapter 1, in that the early Buddhist doctrine of karma is not deterministic, as karma is only one in a range of possible causes for falling sick.

A set of three discourses that may well be the most often memorized texts in the Theravāda tradition are the *(Mahā-)maṅgala-sutta*, the

330. For a detailed study see Anālayo 2014b, 91–100.

Ratana-sutta, and the *Metta-sutta*.[331] These are for the most part in verse, as is the *Dhammapada*, of which the chanting contains just a few stanzas.

3. Errors and Variants

In what follows I first survey instances in the recitations that appear to be the result of errors of memory; I then take up variants, in the sense of wording, be it single words or whole phrases of the chanted text, that differs from one or more of the four main editions of the Pāli canon consulted in this study.

I would like to mention at the outset that, due to my longstanding personal acquaintance with Dhammaruwan, I feel certain that he would not be speaking falsehood or intentionally be taking part in some fraudulent activity. However, this is a personal assessment, which in what follows I have to set aside in order to examine the case as critically as possible. For this purpose I will at times explore scenarios of possible deception and fraud that I personally find highly improbable.

Now, whatever the veridical status of Dhammaruwan's memories, the recordings of a small boy chanting in a rather unusual manner an impressive amount of Pāli texts remain a fact—recordings that have been authenticated by a professional engineer as the result of a genuine oral recitation performed at some time in the 1970s (or early 1980s). In relation to these recordings, the main question to be kept in mind in what follows is whether Dhammaruwan could have learned the texts he chants in his present life, be this by being intentionally taught to do so or by picking them up accidentally through overhearing. In the case of a young child in Sri Lanka who lives in a household in which English is spoken in addition to Sinhala, the most probable options would be:

331. The order of Dhammaruwan's recitation corresponds to the order of these three discourses adopted in the *Khuddakapāṭha*. A difference is that in the *Khuddakapāṭha* two other texts come in between the *Ratana-sutta* (Khp 6), and the *Metta-sutta* (Khp 9), namely the *Tirokuḍḍa-sutta* (Khp 7) and the *Nidhikaṇḍa-sutta* (Khp 8). Nevertheless, the *Khuddakapāṭha* seems the more probable source given the semblance between the texts chanted by Dhammaruwan and collections of texts for *paritta* purposes, for which the *Khuddakapāṭha* appears to have provided a starting point; see also below notes 439–41.

- a printed text in Sinhala script
- a manuscript in handwritten Sinhala script
- a printed text in Roman script

Memory Errors

The distinction between what are just errors and what should be considered variants is not as straightforward as it may appear at first sight. In fact a perusal of the variants found in the printed editions will show several cases that one would more naturally classify as simple errors. Nevertheless, a few errors in the chanting can be safely set aside as such and need not enter the discussion of variants; consequently in what follows I survey such cases and their implications for assessing the recorded chanting. Before taking up such errors, I should mention that overall the quality of the chanting is impressive. For a small child to be able to recite such substantial portions of text, if indeed done from memory, would be a remarkable feat.

Besides mistakes, also not included in the survey of variants are two types of phrases that are a typical feature of oral performance. Even though these are not mentioned at all in the editions or only mentioned in some, they do not involve a substantial difference. For the sake of completeness, however, I briefly mention them here.

One of these occurrences is an expression of homage, which takes the form *namo tassa bhagavato arahato sammāsambuddhassa*, "Homage to the Blessed One, the Worthy One, the Fully Awakened One." This is a standard way of expressing respect toward the Buddha in a traditional setting, used when reciting a Pāli text or giving an oral teaching. This formula occurs twice in the chants, but in both cases it is not mentioned in any of the four consulted editions.[332]

The other is the introductory phrase *evaṃ me sutaṃ*, "Thus have I heard."[333] Although this is at times not found in all editions or else found

332. DN 22: 1–00.05 and SN 56: 00.00.

333. The phrase has been repeatedly discussed in Buddhist academic writings; for a survey of the discussion see Anālayo 2014a, 41–45.

only in some of them,[334] the term is clearly implied and would be recited in any oral performance to signal the onset of the discourse. Neither such absence nor the lack of written testimony of the standard expression of homage is a significant variant.

Turning to actual errors, the occurrence of slips of attention can be documented from passages in the *Mahāsatipaṭṭhāna-sutta* that have been preserved in parallel recordings, evidently made at different times. The overlap in recited texts brings to light two instances where one recording has the correct term but the other recording of the same passage has a wrong term. One of these two instances involves an incorrect declination of the interrogative pronoun *katama*, "which?," resulting in *katamo*.[335] The second instance has in one recording the correct plural form *vuccanti*, "are called," but the other recording instead has the incorrect singular *vuccati*, "is called."[336]

Another related type of instance involves the three closely similar *Gilāna-sutta*s, where a particular mistake occurs only in two of them. According to a phrase found in each of these three discourses, the seven awakening factors lead to awakening. Here the phrase should be the plural form "lead to," as the awakening factors are plural. Yet the first occurrence of this phrase in the chanting has the singular "leads to," *saṃvattati*.[337] In the case of the second discourse the same phrase has the correct plural form *saṃvattanti*, but the third discourse again has the mistaken singular form *saṃvattati*.[338]

A confusion between *saṃvattati* and *saṃvattanti* can easily occur, since the body of each discourse takes up the awakening factors singly,

334. The phrase is absent from all four editions in the case of SN 22: 29.10 and AN 10: 00.00; it is found in only some editions in the case of SN 46: 00.00, 08.01, 17.00, and SN 56: 00.12.

335. DN 22: 3–26.09 has *katame*, but DN 22: 5–10.34 has the incorrect *katamo*. The same type of error recurs in DN 22: 6–21.41 and 6–22.46, which have *katamo*, yet the correct form would be *katamā*. An instance where this type of error is found in both recordings of the same passage is DN 22: 3–17.10 (= 5–01.31), which have *katama* when the correct form would be *katamo*.

336. DN 22: 5–11.14 has *vuccanti*, but DN 22: 3–26.52 has the incorrect *vuccati*.

337. SN 46: 02.58.

338. SN 46: 19.16.

indicating in each case that it "leads to" awakening, where the form *saṃvattati* is correct. Thus the mistake of using the singular when the plural is required seems to be caused by a simple slip of attention. As mentioned above, a key feature of memorization in line with the Vedic tradition appears to be the giving of only limited attention to the meaning. This could easily lead to missing a difference that is rather minor, involving merely the need to add an *n* to the otherwise identical term.

The same error of confusing singular and plural forms occurs also in the chanting of a passage in the *Mahāparinibbāna-sutta*, where the introduction correctly refers to five "disadvantages" with the plural *ādīnavā*. The body of the exposition then uses the singular *ādīnavo* for each single "disadvantage," but the final statement at the end uses the incorrect singular for summing up the five "disadvantages," *ādīnavo* instead of *ādīnavā*.[339] Here the five previous occurrences of *ādīnavo* seem to have influenced the pronunciation of the last instance of the term in the passage, where the grammar instead required a shift back to the plural form that had been used at the outset.

A definite instance of mispronunciation due to an apparent slip of attention can be seen on one occasion, as this error is then rectified right away. The correct term *gimhe*, "in the summer," has been mispronounced as *gimhi*, and this is immediately followed by adding the correct °*he*, as if to make up for the error. As a result, the recording now has the term *gimhihe*, an impossibility from the viewpoint of Pāli language.[340] This gives the impression that on this occasion an error occurred, was noticed, and then rectified immediately.

Another type of error that can easily occur during recitation is the repetition of a phrase or term that has just been recited. An example of this can be found in the chanting of the *Mahāsatipaṭṭhāna-sutta*. The discourse follows each of its various exercises with a recurrent paragraph that describes how practice should be undertaken. According to the first part of this paragraph, *satipaṭṭhāna* meditation should be practiced internally, externally, and both internally and externally. In the case of

339. DN 16: 13.41.

340. Khp/Sn: 14.02.

contemplation of feeling, the instruction for internal contemplation reads *iti ajjhattaṃ vā vedanāsu vedanānupassī viharati*, enjoining that "one dwells contemplating feelings in regard to feelings internally." The next part then brings up the need to contemplate arising, passing away, and both. Here the first part reads in Pāli *samudayadhammānupassī vā vedanāsu viharati*, "one dwells contemplating the nature of arising in feelings." In the chanting, however, the phrase *vedanānupassī* appropriate for the description of internal and external practice has made its way also into the next section, resulting in the phrase *samudayadhammānupassī vā vedanāsu vedanānupassī viharati*, "one dwells contemplating the nature of arising in feelings, contemplating feelings."[341] The intrusion of *vedanānupassī* also occurs for "passing away" and "arising and passing away."[342] This departure from the standard phrasing happens only in relation to feelings, not in relation to any of the other exercises found under the other three *satipaṭṭhāna*s, making it fair to conclude that an error has occurred.

An example also related to the term *samudaya*, here in its alternative sense of "origin" instead of "arising," can be seen in the *Mahānidāna-sutta*. In this discourse an exposition on conditionality recurrently points to a particular cause with the phrase *es' eva hetu etaṃ nidānaṃ esa samudayo esa paccayo*, "just this is the root, this is the cause, this is the origin, this is the condition." But in one instance in the chanting the part *esa samudayo* is missing, so that the phrase becomes *es' eva hetu etaṃ nidānaṃ esa paccayo*, "just this is the root, this is the cause, this is the condition."[343] This, too, can safely be taken to be an error of memory that has led to a loss of "this is the origin," *esa samudayo*, in this string of near synonyms.

A similar loss of a term in a string of near synonyms can be observed in the same *Mahānidāna-sutta* in relation to the phrase *yehi ākārehi yehi liṅgehi yehi nimittehi yehi uddesehi*, "by the attributes, by the features, by the signs, by the characteristics." In the first instance of the phrase

341. DN 22: 2–07.56.

342. DN 22: 2–08.08 and 2–08.22.

343. DN 15: 15.37.

the second term *yehi liṅgehi* is not found,[344] and that even though the sentence continues right away with the corresponding formulation *tesu ākāresu tesu liṅgesu tesu nimittesu tesu uddesesu*, where the term *liṅga* does occur. The term *liṅga* also features in subsequent uses of both the *yehi ākārehi* (etc.) and the *tesu ākāresu* (etc.) formulas. Clearly the omission of *liṅga* on the first occurrence is due to a slip of attention.

Whereas the cases mentioned so far are not in themselves problematic, apart from showing a slip of memory or oversight, other cases point to a lack of knowledge of Pāli language and grammar. An example is a listing of the factors of the noble eightfold path. Here the last member should be "right concentration," yet the chanting mentions as the last factor *sammā sammādiṭṭhi*, "right right view."[345] The doubling of "right" makes little sense, and "right view" has already been mentioned at the outset. One would expect this type of error to occur more easily in the case of a reciter who is not well versed in Pāli.

The instructions for contemplating the hindrance of "doubt" in the *Mahāsatipaṭṭhāna-sutta* require a grammatical shift from the accusative *vicikicchaṃ* in the introductory phrase to the nominative *vicikicchā* in the subsequent phrase. This shift is lost in the chanting, which uses *vicikicchaṃ* even in the subsequent phrases.[346]

The same problem of lack of adjustment to what is required grammatically becomes more prominent with a catechism on the impermanent nature of the five aggregates. The first of the five aggregates is *rūpa*, "material form," a term that in Pāli is neuter. The query as to whether material form is permanent or impermanent then takes the form *rūpaṃ niccaṃ vā aniccaṃ vā*, where the terms "permanent," *nicca*, and "impermanent," *anicca*, are governed by the gender of *rūpa* and therefore share with it the *-aṃ* ending.

When the same type of question is applied to the next aggregate of feeling, the formulation requires adjustment, since the term for feeling, *vedanā*, is feminine. Yet the chant proceeds with the formulation *vedanā*

344. DN 15: 17.43.

345. DN 22: 6–21.36.

346. DN 22: 2–20.42 and 2–20.57.

niccaṃ vā aniccaṃ vā, instead of adjusting this to the correct form *vedanā niccā vā aniccā vā*.[347] The chanting continues in the same way with the next aggregate of perception, *saññā*, also feminine, and the subsequent formations, *saṅkhārā*, which are in the masculine plural. In each of these cases the expression used is *niccaṃ vā aniccaṃ vā*, appropriate only for the first case of *rūpa* and the last item of consciousness, *viññāṇa*.

In the written original of this passage in the various editions, only the first and last aggregate are spelled out in full—the middle three are abbreviated. The fact that the chant uses the incorrect declination for the middle three terms shows that the abbreviated part has been supplemented by someone who does not know Pāli grammar. The same problem continues for the subsequent exposition in the same discourse, where the terms in the correct formulation *yaṃ kiñci rūpaṃ atītānāgatapaccuppannaṃ*, "whatever material form, past, future, or present," recur in the chant in relation to feeling in the form *yaṃ kiñci vedanā atītānāgatapaccuppannaṃ*, instead of adjusting to the different gender by reading *yā kāci vedanā atītānāgatapaccuppannā*.[348] The same lack of adjustment continues throughout the passage for this and the next two aggregates.[349] Clearly the whole exposition is based on simply repeating the terms from the formulations used for material form without implementing the required grammatical changes.

This finding implies that, at the time of recitation, the reciter did not have a proper knowledge of Pāli grammar, otherwise one would expect him to have noticed that he was making a whole series of grammatical errors.

This also implies that, if someone made the child recite, those responsible for doing so were not acquainted with Pāli grammar. During recitation one might at times, due to a slip of attention, make at least minor errors. But from someone who prepares a text that a child is going to be made to recite, it can safely be expected that the rules of grammar will be followed when supplementing a whole section of text that in the written original is abbreviated, if such rules are known. The incorrect recitation

347. SN 22: 36.52.

348. SN 22: 41.23; see also 41.26, 41.35, 41.53, 41.59.

349. See SN 22: 42.26, 43.27, 43.31, 43.57, 44.02.

of the passage discussed above requires either a mistakenly written original or a text learned by heart some time ago and recited rather automatically by someone who is not paying attention to the requirements of Pāli grammar.

Minor Variants

Leaving aside the cases discussed above as probable memory errors, in what follows I survey other instances where the chanting differs from what is found in the standard Pāli editions consulted in this study. For this purpose I distinguish between "minor variants," variants that concern different spellings of a term,[350] and "major variants," which involve the addition or lack of a whole term or even of several terms. This distinction is merely for the purpose of ease of presentation and is not intended to convey that all major variants are invariably more important than those designated as minor variants. Whereas some major variants involve several terms and even phrases and for this reason are indeed highly remarkable, the same category also accommodates the absence of the quotative *iti*, which is considerably less significant.

Based on the distinction between minor and major variants and on the count of editions in which a variant is found, I present a series of tables to convey the main pattern that emerges from comparing the recitations to the printed editions. The tables list from left to right the editions that differ from the wording employed in the chanting. Here the abbreviation B^e stands for the Burmese Chaṭṭha Saṅgāyana edition of Myanmar, C^e for the Ceylonese Buddha Jayanti edition of Sri Lanka, E^e for the European PTS edition, and S^e for the Siamese Red Elephant edition of Thailand. Where the respective edition has a corresponding term in its notes on variants, the abbreviation for this edition carries an asterisk*.

To the right of the editions comes a column that gives the rate of frequency of the term in question in the chanted text, where 1 stands for a single occurrence. To the right of that comes the location of the term in question, which combines an abbreviation for the text, such as DN

350. Also included in this category are very occasional differences in the placing of a term, in the sense of the same term occurring before instead of after another word.

for *Dīgha-nikāya*, and a number combination that indicates the time at which the term occurs in the recording.

The first case, for example, is DN 22: 1–33.21. This stands for the twenty-second discourse in the *Dīgha-nikāya* (which is the *Mahāsatipaṭṭhāna-sutta*). The "1" signifies that this is the first of several recordings of this discourse, and "33.21" stands for the occurrence being roughly at about 33 minutes and 21 seconds from the start of the recording.

The *(Mahā-)maṅgala-sutta*, the *Ratana-sutta*, and the *Metta-sutta* occur once in the *Khuddakapāṭha* and again in the *Sutta-nipāta*. Since these discourses are found twice in the Pāli canon, I have consulted both extant versions from each of the studied editions. I refer to variants found in both with the combined abbreviation Khp/Sn. The single Khp or Sn then reflects the rare occasion when a particular variant is found in only one of these two.

Where more than one occurrence of the same variant can be identified in the same text, I list the other occurrences in a footnote (this includes cases where the term in question is conjugated or declined differently). Within occurrences of the same type, the listing follows the order of the texts as they are found in the Pāli canon, which is also the order adopted for the full transcriptions given in the appendix. The table proceeds from multiple occurrences to single occurrences, beginning with B^e and followed by the other editions in alphabetical order. Subsequent tables have the same survey for two, three, and four editions.

MINOR VARIANTS IN A SINGLE EDITION:

B^e				2	DN 22: 1–33.21[351]
B^{e*}				2	Khp/Sn: 12.48[352]
B^{e*}				2	Khp/Sn: 18.25[353]
B^e				1	DN 22: 1–28.00

351. DN 22: 1–36.06. Another instance of the same variant occurs also in C^e, hence I have entered it separately; see DN 22: 1–30.41.

352. Khp/Sn: 13.22.

353. Khp/Sn: 19.20 (the second instance does not note the variant).

B^e				1	DN 22: 1–39.07
B^e				1	DN 22: 3–29.01[354]
B^e				1	DN 22: 6–24.14
B^e				1	AN 10: 04.15
B^e				1	AN 10: 08.03
B^e				1	AN 10: 12.27
B^e				1	AN 10: 12.40
B^e				1	AN 10: 12.42
B^e				1	AN 10: 13.06
B^e*				1	Khp/Sn: 10.40
B^e				1	Khp/Sn: 11.40
B^e*				1	Khp/Sn: 13.08
B^e				1	Khp/Sn: 15.05
B^e				1	Khp/Sn: 18.03
B^e				1	Khp/Sn: 18.09
B^e				1	Khp/Sn: 18.52
B^e*				1	Khp/Sn: 19.08
B^e*				1	Khp/Sn: 19.37
B^e				1	Khp/Sn: 20.49
B^e*				1	Khp/Sn: 20.52
B^e*				1	Khp/Sn: 21.24
B^e				1	Khp/Sn: 21.31
	C^e			1	DN 15: 24.23
	C^e			1	DN 16: 11.08
	C^e			1	DN 16: 15.08
	C^e			1	DN 22: 1–21.56
	C^e			1	DN 22: 2–14.01
		E^e*		9	DN 15: 08.13[355]
		E^e		2	DN 16: 11.50[356]

354. Another instance of the same variant occurs also in C^e, hence I have listed it separately; see DN 22: 4–16.41.

355. DN 15: 10.12, 13.02, 14.29, 16.09, 21.16, 21.37, 22.01, 23.13 (only the first instance has a note on the variant corresponding to the chanting).

356. DN 16: 15.12.

		E^{e}*		1	DN 15: 21.20[357]
		E^{e}		1	DN 15: 08.57
		E^{e}		1	DN 15: 11.31
		E^{e}		1	DN 16: 00.04
		E^{e}		1	DN 22: 1–41.48
		E^{e}		1	SN 56: 01.00
		E^{e}		1	SN 56: 01.08
		E^{e}		1	SN 56: 01.39
		E^{e}		1	AN 10: 20.59
		E^{e}		1	Khp: 21.35
		E^{e}		1	Dhp: 23.26
			S^{e}	7	DN 22: 3–01.54[358]
			S^{e}	2	DN 22: 1–15.54[359]
			S^{e}	1	DN 15: 21.29
			S^{e}*	1	DN 16: 21.18
			S^{e}	1	DN 22: 1–38.37
			S^{e}	1	AN 10: 05.28
			S^{e}	1	Khp/Sn: 10.46[360]
			S^{e}	1	Khp/Sn: 13.16
			S^{e}	1	Khp/Sn: 19.38
			S^{e}	1	Khp: 11.23
			S^{e}*	1	Khp: 19.04
			S^{e}	1	Dhp: 23.13
			S^{e}*	1	Dhp: 25.09

The table above shows a particularly high count of variants in the Burmese edition. A closer look at the type of texts listed in the sixth column brings to light that the great majority of variants are from the *Khuddakapāṭha*/

357. A second occurrence of the term also varies in C^{e}, which has therefore been entered separately in the list; see DN 15: 21.41.

358. DN 22: 3–03.20, 3–04.45, 3–06.05, 3–07.26, 3–08.46, 3–10.04.

359. DN 22: 1–18.16.

360. In the case of C^{e}, the variant is found only in Khp.

Sutta-nipāta (Khp/Sn), which only corresponds to a fraction of the recitations studied here. In other words, this aspect of the table reflects an idiosyncrasy of the Burmese edition of the three texts from the *Khuddakapāṭha/Sutta-nipāta* collection. If the *Khuddakapāṭha/Sutta-nipāta* occurrences were to be left aside, the table for minor variants in a single edition would show a considerably more balanced distribution among the four editions.

From the viewpoint of my present research, the high frequency of variants in the Burmese edition is anyway of no particular relevance, since one would not expect that those who in the 1970s in Sri Lanka might have taught recitation to the child employed the Burmese edition for that purpose. At that time the different editions had not yet been digitized, so that consultation of the Burmese edition (as well as the Ceylonese and Siamese editions) required knowledge of the relevant script. Whereas for someone in Sri Lanka the script of the Ceylonese edition would of course have posed no problem, to be able to consult the Burmese or Siamese editions would have required the ability to read Pāli in the Burmese and Siamese scripts (which differ substantially from the Roman and the Sinhala alphabets), a type of expertise probably only found among a limited number of scholars and monks in the country.

Minor Variants in Two Editions:

B^e	C^e			1	DN 22: 1–17.04
B^e	C^e			1	DN 22: 1–30.41
B^e	C^e			1	DN 22: 4–16.18
B^e	C^{e*}			1	AN 10: 04.17
B^e		E^e		1	SN 56: 28.34
B^{e*}		E^e		1	Khp/Sn: 02.07[361]
B^e			S^e	16	DN 22: 2–04.43[362]
B^e			S^e	9	DN 22: 1–25.18[363]

361. In the case of E^e, the variant is found only in Khp.

362. DN 22: 2–04.50, 2–04.59, 2–05.05, 2–05.16, 2–05.24, 2–05.36, 2–05.45, 2–05.56, 2–06.04, 2–06.16, 2–06.25, 2–06.38, 2–06.47, 2–07.01, 2–07.11.

363. DN 22: 1–28.32, 1–31.11, 1–33.52, 1–36.31, 1–39.38, 1–42.25, 1–45.18, 2–02.36.

B^{e}			S^{e}	2	DN 22: 1–01.12[364]
B^{e}			S^{e}	2	DN 22: 1–16.21[365]
B^{e}			S^{e}	1	DN 16: 09.38
B^{e}			S^{e}	1	DN 22: 1–38.43
B^{e}			S^{e}	1	DN 22: 1–39.02
B^{e}			S^{e}	1	DN 22: 1–42.00
B^{e}			S^{e}	1	DN 22: 3–28.35[366]
B^{e*}			S^{e*}	1	SN 56: 16.53
B^{e}			S^{e}	1	AN 10: 08.06
	C^{e}	E^{e*}		1	DN 15: 21.41
	C^{e}	E^{e*}		1	DN 22: 1–33.25
	C^{e*}	E^{e}		1	Khp/Sn: 17.31
	C^{e*}		S^{e*}	4	SN 56: 05.00[367]
	C^{e*}		S^{e*}	4	SN 56: 05.36[368]
	C^{e}		S^{e*}	2	DN 22: 3–27.15[369]
	C^{e}		S^{e*}	2	DN 22: 4–14.32[370]
	C^{e*}		S^{e*}	1	DN 16: 20.02
	C^{e*}		S^{e*}	1	DN 16: 20.12
	C^{e}		S^{e}	1	DN 22: 1–27.55
		E^{e}	S^{e}	1	SN 56: 04.21

The survey of minor variants found in two editions shows a considerably more equal distribution among the three Asian editions than was the case for those found in one edition. This confirms that the unequal distribution in the previous table does indeed reflect the idiosyncrasy of the Burmese edition of the three *Khuddakapāṭha/Sutta-nipāta* discourses.

364. DN 22: 6–34.06.

365. DN 22: 1–18.41.

366. Another instance in a different place of the same variant occurs also in C^{e}, hence I have listed this separately; see DN 22: 4–15.51.

367. SN 56: 08.46, 09.22, 10.02.

368. SN 56: 10.39, 11.16, 11.56.

369. DN 22: 4–14.23.

370. DN 22: 6–20.45.

Remarkable in the present case are the relatively few occurrences in the PTS edition (E^e), which among minor variants found in a single edition was more prominent.

Minor Variants in Three Editions:

B^e	C^e	E^e		1	DN 22: 3–15.39
B^{e*}	C^{e*}	E^{e*}		1	DN 15: 02.08
B^e	C^e		S^e	8	DN 22: 1–01.24[371]
B^e	C^e		S^e	4	DN 22: 6–29.06[372]
B^e	C^e		S^e	3	DN 22: 2–23.33[373]
B^e	C^e		S^e	2	DN 16: 13.21[374]
B^e	C^e		S^e	1	DN 15: 22.11
B^e	C^e		S^e	1	DN 15: 23.24
B^e	C^e		S^e	1	DN 15: 24.12
B^e	C^e		S^e	1	DN 16: 20.57
B^e	C^e		S^e	1	DN 16: 21.25
B^e	C^e		S^e	1	DN 22: 1–39.10
B^e	C^e		S^e	1	DN 22: 4–15.51
B^e	C^e		S^e	1	SN 56: 22.30
B^e		E^e	S^e	1	SN 56: 17.22
B^e		E^{e*}	S^e	1	SN 56: 27.28
B^e		E^e	S^e	1	DN 22: 3–14.27
B^e		E^e	S^e	1	AN 10: 03.36
B^e		E^{e*}	S^e	1	AN 10: 05.49
	C^{e*}	E^e	S^e	1	DN 16: 02.36

In the table with minor variants in three editions, the variant with the highest frequency of eight occurrences involves the difference between

371. DN 22: 2–24.13, 2–24.25, 2–24.37, 2–24.52, 2–25.07, 6–30.42, 6–34.18.

372. DN 22: 6–29.40, 6–30.20, 6–30.54.

373. DN 22: 2–23.52, 2–26.53.

374. DN 16: 16.36.

atthaṅgama and *atthagama*, "disappearance." The chanting quite distinctly uses *atthagama*, thereby differing from all three Asian editions.[375]

Minor Variants in Four Editions:

B^e	C^e	E^e	S^e	5	DN 16: 17.24[376]
B^e	C^e	E^e	S^e	4	DN 22: 1–06.13[377]
B^e	C^e	E^e	S^e	4	SN 22: 30.51[378]
B^e	C^e	E^e	S^e	2	DN 16: 01.01[379]
B^e	C^e	E^{e*}	S^e	2	DN 22: 3–31.35[380]
B^e	C^e	E^e	S^e	1	DN 15: 09.00
B^e	C^e	E^e	S^e	1	DN 15: 22.09
B^e	C^e	E^e	S^e	1	DN 15: 23.27
B^e	C^e	E^e	S^e	1	DN 15: 24.35
B^e	C^e	E^e	S^e	1	DN 16: 21.41
B^e	C^e	E^e	S^e	1	DN 16: 04.05
B^e	C^e	E^e	S^e	1	DN 22: 1–21.58
B^e	C^e	E^e	S^e	1	DN 22: 3–26.27
B^e	C^e	E^{e*}	S^e	1	DN 22: 6–22.56
B^e	C^e	E^{e*}	S^e	1	DN 22: 6–23.01
B^e	C^e	E^e	S^e	1	DN 22: 6–26.44
B^e	C^e	E^e	S^e	1	DN 22: 6–30.13
B^e	C^e	E^e	S^e	1	SN 56: 27.34
B^e	C^e	E^e	S^e	1	AN 10: 02.19
B^e	C^e	E^e	S^e	1	AN 10: 07.49
B^e	C^e	E^e	S^e	1	AN 10: 07.53
B^e	C^e	E^e	S^e	1	AN 10: 07.58
B^e	C^e	E^e	S^e	1	AN 10: 08.50

375. DN 22: 1–01.24, 2–24.13, 2–24.25, 2–24.37, 2–24.52, 2–25.07, 6–30.42, 6–34.18.

376. DN 16: 18.01, 18.33, 19.03, 19.41.

377. DN 22: 1–06.17, 1–06.26, 1–06.29.

378. SN 22: 32.03, 33.12, 35.38.

379. DN 16: 06.00.

380. DN 22: 4–19.03.

Be	Ce	Ee	Se	1	AN 10: 12.39
Be	Ce	Ee	Se	1	Khp/Sn: 08.29
Be	Ce	Ee	Se	1	Khp/Sn: 05.01[381]

The table of minor variants in all four editions reflects the degree to which the chanting does not follow any of these. Here another item could be added that I have not included in the table above, namely the peculiar pronunciation in the recitations of the term *seyyathīdaṃ*, "for example," as two separate terms.[382] This expression is indeed a combination of the two terms *seyyathā* and *idaṃ*, so that a separation as such is meaningful.[383] However, in the recitations the first term is pronounced as *seyyathi*, followed by *idaṃ*. It remains unclear to me how to explain this, but its repeated occurrence in various chants (fourteen times in four different texts) makes it clearly a distinct mark of the recitations that could hardly have been inspired by any of the existing editions or manuscripts.

The net result of the survey of minor variants makes it improbable that the chanting was based on any of the editions that would have been readily available in Sri Lanka in the 1970s or early 1980s.

Major Variants

Major Variants in a Single Edition:

Be				4	DN 22: 1–41.25[384]
Be				2	DN 22: 1–03.28[385]
Be				1	DN 22: 1–27.55
Be				1	DN 22: 1–39.08
Be				1	AN 10: 01.49

381. In the case of Ce and Ee, the variant is found only in Khp.

382. DN 15: 08.25, 10.25, 11.45, 13.14, 14.43, 16.21, DN 22: 1–17.13, 3–26.19, 3–27.35, 6–21.09, SN 56: 02.56, 05.20, 06.21, AN 10: 07.17.

383. Childers 1875/1993, 474 explains, under his entry for *seyyathā*, that "with foll. *idaṃ* it takes the form *seyyathidaṃ*, an adv. meaning 'as follows, namely'."

384. DN 22: 1–44.13, 2–01.41, 2–04.14. Several instances of the same variant occur also in Ce, hence I have listed these separately; see DN 22: 1–09.54 etc.

385. DN 22: 2–04.26. Several instances of the same variant occur also in Ce, hence I have noted them separately; see DN 22: 2–09.14 etc.

	Ce			2	DN 15: 10.34[386]
	Ce			1	DN 15: 14.59
	Ce			1	DN 22: 2–24.58
	Ce			1	DN 22: 2–29.43
	Ce			1	DN 22: 3–13.59[387]
		Ee*		6	SN 22: 45.45[388]
		Ee*		1	DN 15: 07.33
		Ee		1	SN 22: 34.48
		Ee		1	SN 56: 04.26
		Ee*		1	SN 56: 17.57
			Se*	1	DN 15: 01.43
			Se	1	DN 16: 05.02
			Se	1	DN 22: 3–14.26
			Se	1	SN 56: 27.55
			Se	1	SN 56: 18.02

Major variants in single editions, in the sense of involving terms that either are found in addition or else are absent, show an equal distribution among the four editions.

Major Variants in Two Editions:

Be	Ce			10	DN 22: 1–09.54[389]
Be	Ce			7	DN 22: 2–09.14[390]
Be	Ce			7	DN 22: 2–09.01[391]
Be	Ce			1	DN 22: 1–38.56

386. DN 22: 2–10.36.

387. Several instances of the same variant occur also in Be, hence I have listed them separately; see DN 22: 2–09.01 etc.

388. SN 22: 45.50, 45.55, 46.01, 46.07, SN 56: 04.51 (only the last mentions the variant).

389. DN 22: 1–12.23, 1–15.27, 1–20.49, 1–24.14, 1–27.08, 1–30.13, 1–32.52, 1–35.34, 1–38.07.

390. DN 22: 2–14.03, 2–14.30, 2–23.41, 2–27.23, 3–00.21, 3–12.14.

391. DN 22: 2–13.50, 2–23.10, 2–26.41, 2–36.46, 3–11.40, 6–32.53.

B^{e*}		E^{e*}		2	SN 56: 15.40[392]
B^{e*}		E^{e*}		1	DN 15: 09.09
B^{e}		E^{e}		1	SN 56: 27.21
B^{e}			S^{e}	3	DN 22: 2–04.40[393]
	C^{e}	E^{e}		2	DN 15: 10.29[394]
	C^{e}		S^{e}	4	SN 22: 31.09[395]
		E^{e*}	S^{e*}	1	DN 22: 1–04.17
		E^{e*}	S^{e*}	1	AN 10: 07.08

With major variants in two editions, occurrences involving the Ceylonese and PTS editions have the same frequency. A difference found in the Ceylonese edition concerns an additional type of bone mentioned in the contemplation of a decaying corpse;[396] a difference found in the PTS edition concerns an additional synonym for expressing the idea of a "moment" in the concluding section of the *Dhammacakkappavattana-sutta*.[397] The chanting differs in both cases, making it improbable that it would have been based on either of these two editions.

Major Variants in Three Editions:

B^{e}	C^{e}		S^{e}	1	DN 22: 1–39.13
B^{e}	C^{e}		S^{e}	1	DN 22: 3–13.32[398]
B^{e}	C^{e}		S^{e}	1	DN 22: 3–13.48
B^{e}	C^{e}		S^{e}	1	DN 22: 3–16.14
B^{e}	C^{e}		S^{e}	1	DN 22: 3–19.49
B^{e}		E^{e*}	S^{e}	1	DN 22: 3–22.51
B^{e}		E^{e}	S^{e*}	1	SN 56: 00.53
	C^{e}	E^{e*}	S^{e*}	1	AN 10: 14.05

392. SN 56: 16.41.

393. DN 22: 2–04.58, 2–05.14.

394. DN 15: 10.31.

395. SN 22: 32.21, 33.29, 34.44.

396. DN 22: 1–38.56.

397. SN 56: 27.21.

398. This case combines major variants in three editions with a minor variant in one edition.

The impression that the chanting does not follow either the Ceylonese or the PTS edition finds further confirmation when one examines major variants in three editions. The first five instances listed in the table are sizable differences that involve several terms or whole phrases, differences that affect the meaning. In all these cases the chanting differs from the Ceylonese edition. Differences from the PTS edition are less pronounced, but one of them, for example, concerns an additional question in the text.[399] Had the PTS edition been used as the basis, this question should have been part of the recitation.

Major Variants in Four Editions:

B^e	C^e	E^e	S^e	9	DN 15: 02.38[400]
B^e	C^e	E^e	S^e	3	SN 46: 07.00[401]
B^e*	C^e	E^e*	S^e	2	DN 22: 1–16.37[402]
B^e	C^e	E^e*	S^e	2	DN 22: 3–28.42[403]
B^e	C^e	E^e	S^e	1	DN 15: 16.06
B^e	C^e	E^e	S^e	1	DN 15: 10.34
B^e	C^e	E^e	S^e	1	DN 22: 2–29.12
B^e	C^e	E^e	S^e	1	SN 46: 17.53[404]
B^e	C^e	E^e	S^e	1	SN 56: 22.47
B^e	C^e	E^e	S^e	1	AN 10: 01.20
B^e	C^e	E^e	S^e	1	AN 10: 06.05
B^e	C^e	E^e	S^e	1	Khp/Sn: 06.09[405]

The table with major variants in all four editions completes the picture that already emerges from the previous tables. Two differences of

399. SN 56: 00.53.

400. DN 15: 03.09, 03.36, 04.05, 04.33, 05.03, 05.31, 06.01, 06.31.

401. SN 46: 15.55, 23.43.

402. DN 22: 1–18.56.

403. DN 22: 4–15.59 (the variant in E^e is only noted in this second instance).

404. SN 46: 17.53. This could also be a memory error, resulting from accidentally taking over the phrase, found additionally in the recitation, from the preceding discourses.

405. In the case of E^e, the variant is found only in Sn.

particular importance are the recurrent addition of the "brain" to listings of the anatomical parts as well as an additional listing of *devas* in the final part of the recitation of the *Dhammacakkappavattana-sutta*. I will return to these two cases below, as they deserve a more detailed discussion.

The above tables show that the recitations do not agree with any of the four consulted editions. This is the case to such a degree as to make it safe to conclude that none of these, be it in print or in manuscript form, has been employed as a basis for teaching the child what to chant.

Already at this point it seems considerably more probable that the chants are indeed recitations learned in the distant past. This would explain why the recitations do not follow any of the consulted editions and would also explain why, alongside remarkable precision, at times memory errors can be identified that betray a lack of familiarity with Pāli grammar. In view of the nature of oral recitation discussed earlier, and given a considerable distance between the postulated time of learning and the time of recitation, it would be understandable for such errors to occur.

4. Omissions and Additions

Loss of Text

In three cases a substantial portion of text has been lost in the chanting, which I have left out of the listing of variants, in line with my policy for the memory errors already surveyed earlier.[406]

The first of these three occurs in relation to the instructions for contemplation of feeling in the *Mahāsatipaṭṭhāna-sutta*. The instructions are given for each of the three type of feelings (pleasant, painful, and neutral) and in each case for those that are of a worldly and of an unworldly type. The chanting misses out the case of the unworldly painful feeling.[407] This appears to be a loss caused by the repetitiveness of the text, leading to an

406. Another possible loss of text due to memory slip, also not included in the list of variants, is the lack of the concluding phrase *pañcasu nīvaraṇesu* at DN 22: 2–23.20. Although this could be an error of recall, it is also possible that this part has been cut off in the recording, as there is a background noise as if the tape recording has been stopped. Due to this uncertainty, I do not consider this particular instance further in my discussion.

407. DN 22: 2–06.31.

accidental jumping ahead to the next phrase. In principle this could occur also with a written original by jumping a line and therefore need not be a loss of memory.

Another loss of text, considerably more substantial, concerns the final part of the *Mahāsatipaṭṭhāna-sutta*, which in all editions gives a prediction of realization within a variable period of time. This prediction is applied to descending time periods of seven, six, five, four, three, two, and one year(s) of practice, followed by the same numerical series from seven to one month(s), and further down to half a month and seven days. The chanting does not have this progressive series at all but just mentions the period of seven years.[408]

In this case one might in fact query whether this is really a loss of memory or whether this might not be an alternative version of the discourse. The recited text continues smoothly and makes sense as it is. Nevertheless, a parallel preserved in Chinese translation also has a comparable series of predictions, working through descending periods of time.[409] The existence of this passage in the Chinese *Madhyama-āgama* shows that this progressive series of predictions was already known at a comparatively early time in the transmission of the early discourses, early enough to be reflected in the Theravāda and Sarvāstivāda textual lineages. This makes it more probable that the absence of such a descending series of time periods in the chanting is an error of memory.

Independent of whether this is a memory error or a genuine reproduction of the original, however, this substantial difference is remarkable insofar as it supports the impression already gained from the survey of variants, that it seems highly improbable that these chants could be the result of some sort of text extant in Sri Lanka in the 1970s or early 1980s. For someone trying to produce recordings of Pāli texts that can be passed off as reflecting memories of a past life, it would make little sense to introduce such a massive loss of text. Nor would it be reasonable to expect such a loss of text to occur when reading out a written original or reproducing it after having just learned it a moment ago.

408. DN 22: 6–33.52.

409. MĀ 98 at T 1.26.584b16.

The same holds for the third case of textual loss, which concerns the *Mahānidāna-sutta*. The part that precedes the missing passage works backward through the links of dependent arising, namely old age and death, birth, becoming, clinging, craving, and feeling, each time showing how the link just mentioned is a condition for the preceding item. After having explained that feeling conditions craving, the text found in all editions takes a detour by exploring several other related topics, before coming back to the topic of how the next link of contact conditions feeling. The chanting does not have this detour at all and directly proceeds from the exposition of how feeling conditions craving to how contact conditions feeling.[410]

As in the case of the final section of the *Mahāsatipaṭṭhāna-sutta*, where a similar presentation can be found in a Chinese parallel, the detour taken in the *Mahānidāna-sutta* is also found in Chinese parallels.[411] This makes it more probable that the absence of this detour is an omission in the recitation due to a lapse of memory.

Such omission reflects a memory error typical of oral transmission, whereby the associations called up by the preceding item directly lead on to the next but one by mistake. The memory errors mentioned earlier, and the three instances of loss mentioned now, make it clear that the chanting is based on genuine oral recall. Alongside an impressive ability to reproduce long portions of text from memory, this also shows clear signs of the typical drawbacks of oral recall. It is thus highly improbable that the recorded recitations could have been based on a written original, extant in the 1970s or early 1980s in Sri Lanka, that in some way was used to make the child chant. Alongside the differences found in the case of variants, the major loss of text attested in the recording clearly points to a genuine oral performance.

The possibility of such a major loss of text in the oral transmission of Pāli discourse material is a relatively recent discovery. In an article published in 2005 I drew attention to one such case, where a Pāli discourse

410. DN 15: 15.45.

411. DN 15 at DN II 58,31, with its parallels DĀ 13 at T I 60c19, T 14 at T I 242b18, MĀ 97 at T I 579a1, and T 52 at T I 844c17.

whose title mentions six purities only covers five in its actual text, whereas a Chinese *Āgama* parallel has all six.[412] That this is indeed a case of loss of text becomes evident from the Pāli commentary on this discourse, which reports various opinions voiced by reciters in an attempt to reconcile the title of the discourse with its content. One of the alternative solutions to the dilemma proposed mentions that, according to the reciters from India, a sixth purity concerned with the nutriments should be added to the discourse. This is precisely the additional purity found in the Chinese *Āgama* parallel.[413] This conclusively shows that text has indeed been lost at some point during the transmission of the Pāli discourse from India to Sri Lanka.

Before the publication of this article, as far as I am able to tell, the possibility of such a major textual loss in Pāli discourse material had not yet been documented. This makes it safe to discard the possibility that someone in the 1970s or early 1980s, trying to produce a recitation of Pāli texts that could be passed off as genuine oral recall from ancient times, would have come up with the idea of introducing instances of major loss of text in order to make sure the chanting appeared authentic. At that time, such a major loss of text would just have been perceived as a serious mistake best avoided in order not to jeopardize unnecessarily the credibility of the chants.

The Brain in the Listing of Anatomical Parts

In this and the next section I take up two cases of addition already mentioned briefly above as major variants not found in any of the four editions. The first of these is a reference to the "brain," *matthaluṅga*, in listings of the anatomical parts of the human body. Among the recited texts such listings are found in the *Mahāsatipaṭṭhāna-sutta* (twice) and the *Girimānanda-sutta* (once), neither of which in any edition has the

412. Anālayo 2005, 104–5, followed by a full translation and study in Anālayo 2008c and a comparative study in Anālayo 2011a, 635–39. The comparative study of *Majjhima-nikāya* discourses and their *Madhyama-āgama* parallels by Minh Chau 1964/1991 does not mention this major difference.

413. Ps IV 94,23 (commenting on MN 112) and MĀ 187 at T 1.26.732b14.

brain in the main text.[414] In the case of the *Mahāsatipaṭṭhāna-sutta*, the brain is noted as a variant in the Burmese and PTS editions; in the case of the *Girimānanda-sutta* it does not even feature as a variant.[415]

The absence of the brain in canonical listings of constituents of the human body is a standard feature of the Pāli discourses, which regularly include only thirty-one anatomical parts in such instructions. The brain occurs elsewhere among Pāli discourse and *Vinaya* literature and thus was obviously known as part of the human body,[416] but for whatever reason it was not considered an item to be mentioned in such listings in Pāli discourses. The brain is found in the Chinese *Āgama* parallels to the *Mahāsatipaṭṭhāna-sutta*.[417]

In listings of the anatomical parts in later Pāli texts like the *Khuddakapāṭha* and the *Paṭisambhidāmagga*, the brain is explicitly included,[418] and the *Visuddhimagga* by Buddhaghosa also mentions the brain.[419] The late nature of this inclusion finds reflection in a different positioning of the brain, which is found either at the end of the whole list or else in the midst of the list, after feces.

The impression that in the Theravāda tradition the brain came gradually to be included in listings of anatomical parts finds unexpected confirmation in a version of the *Girimānanda-sutta* that was transmitted to Tibet during the early fourteenth century by a Sri Lankan monk who was living in India.[420] The original he had brought for translation into Tibetan has been identified as a Theravāda version.[421] In the case of this alternative

414. DN 22: 1–16.37, 1–18.56, and AN 10: 06.05.

415. In the case of the *Satipaṭṭhāna-sutta* (MN 10), Trenckner 1888/1993, 533,9 mentions a Burmese edition that lists the brain after referring to the feces.

416. The brain is mentioned explicitly in Sn 199. Vin I 274,16 even reports a case of successful brain surgery by Jīvaka, who also took care of the medical needs of the Buddha and his disciples; for a survey of the cures performed by Jīvaka see, e.g., Zysk 1982.

417. The brain is mentioned in the Chinese parallels to DN 22, MĀ 98 at T 1.26.583b8 and EĀ 12.1 at T 2.125.568a20: 腦.

418. Khp 2,9 and Paṭis I 7,7.

419. Vism 240,24 and 260,11; see also 349,33 and 359,9.

420. Skilling 1993, 90n1 quotes a colophon according to which the monk was dwelling at Bodh Gayā, *rdo rje gdan bzhugs pa*.

421. Skilling 1993, 73 explains that a set of thirteen texts, which includes this version of the

Theravāda version of the *Girimānanda-sutta*, extant in Tibetan translation, the listing of anatomical parts does mention the brain.[422]

Not only the fact that the brain is included in this version of the *Girimānanda-sutta* but also other variations compared to the Pāli version of this discourse make it safe to conclude that the Tibetan translation reflects a version of the text that came into being independently from what was written down in Sri Lanka and served as the basis for the Pāli editions now extant.[423] Given the apparent tendency to include the brain in such listings in Theravāda texts, it would be natural if versions of the *Girimānanda-sutta*, and by implication also other texts that have such listings (such as the *Mahāsatipaṭṭhāna-sutta*), came to reflect this tendency by incorporating the term.

This in turn implies that the chants do indeed accurately reflect a development that apparently took place in a transmission lineage of Theravāda Pāli discourses that ended up being preserved in Tibetan translation. In contrast, had the chants been in some way based on a written text available in the twentieth century in Sri Lanka, those preparing the texts for recitation would hardly have included the brain in a listing of the anatomical parts. Although the Tibetan text had been translated into French already toward the end of the nineteenth century,[424] the problem is not

---

Girimānanda-sutta (D 38 or Q 754), all of which were translated in collaboration with the same monk, are "the only *group* of Theravādin texts in the *Kanjur*."

422. D 38 *shes ka* 277a3: *glad pa* or Q 754 *sher tsi* 293b8: *klad pa*; mentioned right at the end of the list. Glass 2007, 164 and 225, however, takes *glad pa* / *klad pa* to refer to the "head." Yet *klad pa* as an equivalent of *klad pa rgyas*, conveying the sense of "brain," is attested in Negi 1993, 87, and Uebach 2005, 143 lists the brain ("Hirn, Gehirn") as one of the meanings of *klad pa*, alongside the head or the skull. In fact a reference to the whole head would not fit the context, as the actual list also does not mention other anatomical units like the torso, the arms, or the legs. In view of the tendency evident in other texts to add precisely the brain to such listings of anatomical parts, it can safely be concluded that this is also the appropriate meaning for *glad pa* or *klad pa* in the present context.

423. A translation of the Tibetan version can be found in Anālayo 2016b, 100–104, see esp. notes 5–9 and 15 on differences (besides the reference to the brain) when compared to its Pāli parallel AN 10.60.

424. Feer 1883, 146; for a survey of scholarship on the group of Theravāda texts translated into Tibetan, among which D 38 or Q 754 occurs, see Skilling 1993, 98–100. A brief reference to the whole set can be found in an entry in the *Encyclopaedia of Buddhism* (published

just that awareness of this alternative would require someone in Sri Lanka who knew French.[425] It would also require an understanding of the significance of the additional reference to the brain.

The problem here is that a proper understanding of the impact and dynamics of early Buddhist oral transmission is a relatively recent development. Groundbreaking in this respect are a work published in German in 1994 and an in-depth study in English in 1997.[426] An intentional addition of the brain to the listing of anatomical parts in the *Mahāsatipaṭṭhāna-sutta* and the *Girimānanda-sutta* only becomes really meaningful once there is a clear appreciation of the dynamics of oral transmission and its impact on such listings. Such appreciation could hardly have been in existence in the 1970s or early 1980s, making it safe to conclude that the mention of the brain is not the result of someone creating on purpose a text or chant of these two discourses at that time in Sri Lanka.

The Devas' *Acclaim of the Buddha's First Sermon*

The other case of addition to be discussed occurs in the final part of the *Dhammacakkappavattana-sutta*. The discourse reports that, after the Buddha had given his first teaching, the news of this event was passed on by *deva*s of various celestial realms. This is the scene portrayed on the cover of the present book, which shows a Gupta-period image from Sārnāth that portrays the Buddha with his hands in the gesture of "setting in motion the wheel of Dharma," a standard expression used to symbolize that he had started to teach. Below the seated Buddha in the center is the wheel of the Dharma with an antelope on each side, reflecting the location where the discourse was spoken, and the first five disciples who listen with respectfully raised hands.[427] The Buddha is flanked by a *deva*

in Sri Lanka) by van Zeyst 1971, 153, which only gives the title (as "Giri, Ānanda"), without further information about its contents.

425. To my knowledge the first discussion in English of this transmission of Theravāda texts to Tibet is Skilling 1993, which is thus later than the time when the chants were recorded.

426. Von Hinüber 1994 and Allon 1997.

427. Regarding the other two figures alongside the five monk disciples, Huntington 1986, 40 explains that "the female and the dwarf/child are probably donor figures present as patrons of the image."

on each side, one of whom appears to be raising its right hand to its ear as if listening, perhaps a pictorial reference to the hearing of the celestial proclamation that the Buddha has set in motion the wheel of Dharma.

Regarding the *Dhammacakkappavattana-sutta*'s report of this celestial proclamation, after mentioning different divisions of *deva*s of the sense sphere, all Pāli editions conclude with a single reference to the *deva*s of the Brahmā world, the *brahmakāyikā devā*. Instead of just this single reference, the chanting has a long listing of various *deva*s reflecting subdivisions of the Brahmā world.[428] These are as follows:

- *brahmapārisajjā devā*
- *brahmapurohitā devā*
- *mahābrahmā devā*
- *parittābhā devā*
- *appamāṇābhā devā*
- *ābhassarā devā*
- *parittasubhā devā*
- *appamāṇasubhā devā*
- *subhakiṇṇakā devā*
- *vehapphalā devā*
- *avihā devā*
- *atappā devā*
- *sudassā devā*
- *sudassī devā*
- *akaniṭṭhakā devā*

Such a listing of subdivisions of the Brahmā realm is absent from any of the four Pāli editions of the *Dhammacakkappavattana-sutta*. It is also not found in any of the Chinese parallels to this discourse.[429] A parallel in the Mūlasarvāstivāda *Vinaya* preserved in Chinese translation follows a reference to what corresponds to the *brahmakāyikā devā* with the Chinese counterpart to the *akaniṣṭha deva*s (corresponding to the last in the list

428. SN 56: 22.47.

429. For a detailed study with translations see Anālayo 2012a and 2013a.

above),[430] without bringing in any of the others. Even this class of *devas* is not mentioned in the corresponding version of the Mūlasarvāstivāda *Vinaya* preserved in Sanskrit and in Tibetan translation, whose listings do not proceed beyond a single reference to the *devas* of the Brahmā world.[431]

A list of *devas* similar to the above can be found in a different context in the *Vibhaṅga*, a work of the Theravāda *Abhidharma* collection, with the difference that it additionally mentions a type of *deva* that is devoid of perception.[432] Such *devas* would have been unable to hear or pass on the good news of the Buddha's setting into motion the wheel of Dhamma, hence it is only natural that the chanting of the *Dhammacakkappavattana-sutta* does not include them.

Among Pāli discourses, to some extent comparable listings of realms of the Brahmā world, although with some differences, can be found in the *Sāleyyaka-sutta* and the *Saṅkhāruppatti-sutta*.[433] Together with the *Vibhaṅga* passage, these two discourses point to a tendency for descriptions of such celestial realms to become more detailed.[434]

430. T 24.1450.128a23: 阿迦尼吒天.

431. Gnoli 1977, 137,7 and Waldschmidt 1957, 157,11.

432. Vibh 424,3, which besides standing alone in mentioning the *asaññasattā devā*, speaks of the *subhakiṇṇā devā* and *akaniṭṭhā devā*, whereas the chanting refers to these as the *subhakiṇṇakā devā* and the *akaniṭṭhakā devā*. The listing in the *Vibhaṅga* serves to correlate each of these *devas* with the respective level of absorption attainment and indicates the lifespan to be expected on being reborn in the corresponding realm. Gethin 1997, 194 provides a convenient survey of the resulting cosmological map; see also Masefield 1983, 85.

433. MN 41 at MN I 289,17 (the same listing would also be part of the next discourse MN 42, which is nearly identical with MN 41, hence the main body of its discourse is abbreviated) and MN 120 at MN III 102,25. Both listings differ by not mentioning the three subdivisions of the Brahmā realm corresponding to the first absorption (*brahmapārisajjā devā*, *brahmapurohitā devā*, *mahābrahmā devā*), and by adding the *ābhā devā* and the *subhā devā* (the last is not found in the B^e and S^e editions of MN 41, nor in the B^e and C^e editions of MN 120) before the listings of the subdivisions of the second and third absorption respectively.

434. Masson 1942, 23 speaks of a tendency toward increasing lists of heavenly realms with the passage of time, "les catalogues se sont gonflés avec le temps," mentioning the case of MN 41 and MN 120 as two long lists exhibiting a detailed acquaintance with the matter; see also de La Vallée Poussin 1926/1971, 3n1 and Marasinghe 1974, 50–51. This tendency to subdivide realms that correspond to the second and third absorption is not an exclusively Theravāda preoccupation, as such subdivisions can also be found, for example, in the *Mahāvastu*, Senart 1890, 348,19, although this listing does not have a counterpart to the *parīttaśubhā devā*, which are, however, mentioned in another listing in the same work, Sen-

Considering these two listings from the viewpoint of their respective parallels, a *Saṃyukta-āgama* parallel to the *Sāleyyaka-sutta* only mentions the main realms, without giving any further divisions into their respective subrealms.[435] The *Saṅkhāruppatti-sutta* does not have a parallel properly speaking, although a *Madhyama-āgama* discourse shows some similarities.[436] This discourse lists the main realms, without giving any further division into subrealms.[437]

The second of these two cases is of less significance, since this *Madhyama-āgama* discourse is in general quite different from the *Saṅkhāruppatti-sutta*. This does not apply in the same way to the case of the *Sāleyyaka-sutta*, however, so that in this case the *Saṃyukta-āgama* discourse is a proper parallel. This parallel shows that developing increasingly detailed listings of celestial realms is a tendency that manifests in particular in Theravāda discourses. In other words, a comparative study brings to light that in the case of the *Sāleyyaka-sutta* the apparent interest in subdivisions of the Brahmā world was strong enough among Theravāda reciters to affect the discourse itself. This is in line with the case of the *Mahāsatipaṭṭhāna-sutta* mentioned above, where a similar interest in additional detail led to a rather substantial section being incorporated in the Pāli version of the discourse.[438] It would be fully in keeping with the

art 1890, 360,19. In fact the same tendency to increasing differentiation can also be seen in the Jain tradition, where, according to Bruhn 1983, 59, one can discern a "multiplication of segments in cosmography."

435. SĀ 1042 at T 2.99.273a15 mentions only 光音 and 遍淨, corresponding to the *ābhassarā* and the *subhakiṇṇā devā*. The rest of the exposition is abbreviated, 乃至, as a result of which only the highest realm of the Pure Abodes finds explicit mention, 阿伽尼吒, corresponding to the *akaniṭṭhā devā* mentioned last in the *Sāleyyaka-sutta*. For a translation of SĀ 1042 see Anālayo 2006b and for a comparative study also Anālayo 2011a, 263–68.

436. That MĀ 168 differs quite substantially from MN 120 had already been noted by Minh Chau 1964/1991, 143; see also Schmithausen 1987, 355n204 and Anālayo 2011a, 679.

437. MĀ 168 at T 1.26.700c5: 梵身天, corresponding to the *brahmakāyikā devā*, T 1.26.700c13: 晃昱天, corresponding to the *ābhassarā devā*, T 1.26.700c22: 遍淨天, corresponding to the *subhakiṇṇā devā*, and T 1.26.701a1: 果實天, corresponding to the *vehappalā devā*. MĀ 168 then continues with the immaterial realms and does not mention the Pure Abodes at all.

438. See above note 330.

same tendency if a Theravāda version of the *Dhammacakkappavattana-sutta* were to incorporate a detailed listing of *devas* of the Brahmā realm in its final part.

This is in fact the case for a version of the *Dhammacakkappavattana-sutta* found as part of the *Catubhāṇavārapāḷi*, a Sri Lankan collection of Pāli *paritta* texts for recitation purposes. The relevant part in the *Catubhāṇavārapāḷi* does have the detailed list of *devas*.[439]

Now the *Catubhāṇavārapāḷi* comprises a range of different Pāli texts.[440] Of the discourses chanted by Dhammaruwan, this collection has counterparts to the three *Gilāna-suttas* (SN 46.14–16), the *Girimānanda-sutta* (AN 10.60), the *Metta-sutta* (Sn 143–52), the *Ratana-sutta* (Sn 222–38), and the *(Mahā-)maṅgala-sutta* (Sn 258–69). Not included in the

439. Ānandajoti 2009, 70–73. Saddhatissa 1991/2001, 130 explains that "because many thousands of deities assemble to listen to this discourse, people believe that on occasions of reciting it deities are pleased and so protect the listeners." This would provide a reason for expanding the list of *devas* listening to the original delivery of the discourse (and thus presumably expected to be present also during its subsequent recital). On the role of *devas* in relation to *paritta* recitation in general, de Silva 1981, 136 reports that at first, "when *paritta* was employed for exorcism, the gods were informed of demons who were stubborn and unyielding. Later, when *paritta* became a prophylactic and benedictive ceremony freely performed for a variety of purposes, and when there was no particular complaint to be made to the gods, the message would have assumed the form of a formal invitation extended to them" to be present during the recitation.

440. According to the listing given in Trenckner, Andersen, and Smith 1924, 93*–94*, the texts included in this collection are as follows: *Saraṇattaya*, *Dasasikkhāpada*, *Sāmaṇerapañha*, *Dvattiṁsākāra*, *Paccavekkhaṇā*, *Dasadhamma*, *Maṅgala-sutta*, *Ratana-sutta*, *Karaṇīyametta-sutta*, *Khandha-paritta*, *Metta-sutta*, *Mettānisaṁsa*, *Mora-paritta*, *Canda-paritta*, *Suriya-paritta*, *Dhajagga-paritta*, *Mahākassapatherabojjhaṅga*, *Mahāmoggallānatherabojjhaṅga*, *Mahācundatherabojjhaṅga*, *Girimānanda-sutta*, *Isigili-sutta*, and *Āṭānāṭiya-sutta*, to which an alternative longer version of the *Catubhāṇavārapāḷi* adds *Dhammacakkapavattana-sutta*, *Mahāsamaya-sutta*, *Āḷavaka-sutta*, *Kasibhāradvāja-sutta*, *Parābhava-sutta*, *Vasala-sutta*, and *Saccavibhaṅga-sutta* (the addition is placed before the last item in the shorter list, the *Āṭānāṭiya-sutta*); see also, e.g., Karunaratne 1977 and de Silva 1981, 5–6. Skilling 1992, 118 comments that "the earliest definite reference to the four *Bhāṇavāra* that I am aware of is an inscription of Kassapa V, dated *circa* 929–39 A.C., from the Jetavana area in Anurādhapura." Harvey 1993a, 79 notes the Sri Lankan belief that "the compilation of *parittas* known as Catubhāṇavāra-pāli. . .was put together in the fourth century AD, though it may have been compiled by as late as the tenth century"; for a survey of evidence regarding the historical development of *paritta* in general see also de Silva 1981, 16–22 (or de Silva 1991/2001, 140–42) and Abeynayake 2016.

Catubhāṇavārapāḷi are the three *Dīgha-nikāya* discourses (DN 15, DN 16, DN 22), the *Anattalakkhaṇa-sutta* (SN 22.59), and the *Dhammapada* (Dhp).[441] Out of the chanted material studied in this chapter, what recurs in the *Catubhāṇavārapāḷi* corresponds to about 25 percent in terms of textual length.

In what follows I briefly survey the chanted texts that do have a parallel in the *Catubhāṇavārapāḷi*. In the case of the list of *devas*, the chanting differs from all four editions but agrees with the *Catubhāṇavārapāḷi*. Should the chanting have been based on a version of the *Catubhāṇavārapāḷi*, it could reasonably be expected that it would conform to this collection also on other occasions where it differs from the four editions. In the table below I refer to the *Catubhāṇavārapāḷi* with the abbreviation "Catubh" in an additional column that comes after the four main editions. A comparison with the chants yields the following result for the relevant instances from the above tables:

441. Skilling 1992, 119–20 notes that "the *Catubhāṇavāra* is not, however, recited or even generally known in Burma today, and its exact status in the past remains to be determined...the standard collection used in Burma today consists of 11 texts called simply *Paritta*...the *Sīrimaṅgala-paritta*, a modern collection settled during the U Nu period, contains the 11 texts of the *Paritta*, to which it adds another 20 texts to make a total of 31." According to the survey given in Skilling 1992, 178–79, this expanded Burmese version contains three of the texts chanted by Dhammaruwan that are not found in the *Catubhāṇavārapāḷi*, namely DN 22, SN 22.59, and Dhp (as well as material from the *Paṭṭhāna*; see above note 329), although this Burmese *paritta* version lacks AN 10.60. A check of this Burmese collection shows that its version of the *Dhammacakkappavattana-sutta* (SN 56.11) does not include the expanded list of *devas* and thus could not have been the basis for Dhammaruwan's chanting; see Aung Than 1990, 89. In fact, given that it is in Burmese script, it is rather improbable anyway that it would have served as the original used for chanting in Sri Lanka, besides the fact that it also does not include a version of the *Girimānanda-sutta* and thus in this respect also differs from the *Catubhāṇavārapāḷi*. The fact that some of the material chanted by Dhammaruwan overlaps with collections of texts for *paritta* purposes is not surprising. Given the importance of *paritta* performance for a monastic in the traditional setting, it would be natural for texts in such a collection to be easily remembered, simply because they would have been more frequently recited by him than any other text he had also memorized.

MINOR VARIANTS IN FOUR EDITIONS COMPARED TO THE *CATUBHĀṆAVĀRAPĀḶI*:

B^e	C^e	E^e	S^e	Catubh	1	SN 56: 27.34
B^e	C^e	E^e	S^e	Catubh	1	AN 10: 02.19
B^e	C^e	E^e	S^e	Catubh	1	AN 10: 07.49
B^e	C^e	E^e	S^e	Catubh	1	AN 10: 07.53
B^e	C^e	E^e	S^e	Catubh	1	AN 10: 07.58
B^e	C^e	E^e	S^e	Catubh	1	AN 10: 08.50
B^e	C^e	E^e	S^e	Catubh	1	AN 10: 12.39

MAJOR VARIANTS IN FOUR EDITIONS COMPARED TO THE *CATUBHĀṆAVĀRAPĀḶI*:

B^e	C^e	E^e	S^e	Catubh*	3	SN 46: 07.00[442]
B^e	C^e	E^e	S^e		1	SN 46: 17.53
B^e	C^e	E^e	S^e		1	SN 56: 22.47
B^e	C^e	E^e	S^e		1	AN 10: 01.20
B^e	C^e	E^e	S^e	Catubh	1	AN 10: 06.05
B^e	C^e	E^e	S^e	Catubh	1	Khp/Sn: 06.09[443]

In the case of three major variants the chanting conforms to the *Catubhāṇavārapāḷi*. One of these concerns the additional listing of *deva*s and another one is also of a substantial type, involving a whole phrase. For the remaining ten variants (of which one involves three instances), the chanting differs not only from the four editions but also from the *Catubhāṇavārapāḷi*. Considered together with the fact that about 75 percent of the chanted material is anyway without a parallel in the *Catubhāṇavārapāḷi*, it seems fair to conclude that Dhammaruwan's recitation was not based on a version of this *paritta* collection.

442. SN 46: 15.55, 23.43.

443. See above note 405.

According to the assessment by a Pāli scholar well versed in South and Southeast Asian manuscript cultures, the chants contain a number of variants that are distinctly un–Sri Lankan.[444] This makes it highly improbable that the chants were based on an original of the type that would have been available in the second half of the twentieth century (or for that matter in the early twenty-first century) in Sri Lanka.

One of the major variants where the chanting disagrees with the *Catubhāṇavārapāḷi* is the reference to the brain in the *Girimānanda-sutta*, discussed above.[445] Not only is the brain not mentioned in the version of the *Girimānanda-sutta* found in the *Catubhāṇavārapāḷi*, but in another text found in this collection the brain does occur as part of a list of anatomical parts, yet this is found in a different place in this list. Whereas in the *Girimānanda-sutta* chanted by Dhammaruwan the brain occurs in the midst of the list, after feces, in the listing of anatomical parts in the *Catubhāṇavārapāḷi* the brain stands at the end of the list.[446] This reflects the pattern mentioned earlier, where the late inclusion of the brain in lists of anatomical parts finds its reflection in differing positions. Had the *Catubhāṇavārapāḷi* been influencing Dhammaruwan's chants, one would expect either that the brain would not be mentioned in the *Girimānanda-sutta* at all or else that an addition of the brain to the *Girimānanda-sutta* would at least follow the precedent of placing it at the end of the list rather than opting for the alternative location in the midst of the list.

In sum, the occurrence of the same list of *deva*s in the *Catubhāṇavārapāḷi* and in the *Dhammacakkappavattana-sutta* chanted by Dhammaruwan does not seem to be reflecting an influence of the former on

444. The scholar is G. A. Somaratne, who reedited the first volume of the *Saṃyutta-nikāya* for the PTS (1998) and who served as chief editor of the Dhammachai Tipiṭaka Project (Thailand) for the pilot edition of the first volume of the *Dīgha-nikāya* and thus is very familiar with the Pāli-discourse manuscript traditions of South and Southeast Asia (on which see the survey by von Hinüber 2016, 951–54). According to Somaratne's assessment, minor variants like *guṇagaṇṭhikajātā* (DN 15: 02.08), *avenipātadhammo* (DN 16: 01.01), *opaneyyiko* (DN 16: 02.36), *añjalikaraṇeyyo* (DN 16: 04.05), *añjanto* (DN 22: 1–06.13), *upekkho* (DN 22: 6–30.13), and *suhujū* (Sn: 17.31) are distinctly un–Sri Lankan and would make it highly improbable that a Sri Lankan text served as a basis for the recitations.

445. AN 10: 06.05.

446. Ānandajoti 2009, 16.

the latter. Instead, it rather confirms that Theravāda versions of the *Dhammacakkappavattana-sutta* did indeed end up incorporating the detailed listing of *devas*.[447]

Summary

The recitations of thirteen texts, studied in this chapter, show several errors typical of oral performance, ranging from minor mispronunciation to substantial loss of text. The recited texts depart in various ways from the Pāli editions consulted, making it safe to conclude that they were not based on a published edition available in the second half of the twentieth century in Sri Lanka. Given that several variants are distinctly un–Sri Lankan, it also seems rather improbable that a Sri Lankan manuscript served as a basis for the chants.

The recitations recurrently include the brain in listings of anatomical parts, thereby departing from all consulted editions. That the brain did indeed eventually become part of such a list in a version of the *Girimānanda-sutta* is attested by a Tibetan translation of a Theravāda version of this discourse carried out in the fourteenth century. The recitation of the *Dhammacakkappavattana-sutta* has a substantial additional part that mentions different realms of the Brahmā world, which a *paritta* collection shows to have indeed become part of this discourse in a Theravāda lineage of textual transmission.

In sum, the evidence surveyed above suggests that Dhammaruwan's chanting of these texts as a child is a genuine case of xenoglossy, in the sense of involving a recitation of material in Pāli that he did not learn and was not made to recite in this way in his present life in Sri Lanka.

447. In fact another such instance can be found in a Laotian *paritta* recitation. Langer 2012, 33 reports that, as part of a recitation of the *mātikā*s of the *Dhammasaṅgaṇī* and the *Paṭṭhāna*, in this particular case "a list of *devas* was sandwiched between the two Abhidhamma parts." "When examining the list of *devas* more closely, it turned out to be an elaborated version of a passage from the Dhammacakkappavattanasutta." Langer 2012, 33n38 explains that the "chanting names all the gods individually while the canonical passages group the Brahmā gods together as *brahmakāyikā devā*."

Conclusion

Rebirth is an integral component of the teachings of the historical Buddha in the way these have been preserved in the earliest textual materials at our disposal. The early Buddhist doctrine of rebirth does not involve a simple mind-body duality, nor does it posit an unchanging entity to be reborn. Instead, continuity during life and beyond is conceived of as a changing process of a plurality of interrelated mental and physical phenomena that operate under the overarching influence of a complex set of causes and conditions. Centrally important conditions here are one's own intentional actions (karma) at the bodily, verbal, and mental level. Operating within a wider network of conditions, karma and its fruit are not deterministic, and the time period for a deed to produce its fruit can vary greatly, such that karmic fruition can take place at a time far removed from the original deed.

The idea of ascertaining whether anything survives death by carrying out experiments and physical measurements is already attested in ancient India. Through the ages, the debate on rebirth continues to revolve around the theme of credibility and verification. The overarching importance of scientific modes of thought and procedure in contemporary times has had a considerable impact on the debate around rebirth. On the one hand, Buddhist apologetics have come to pretend that the Buddha did not really teach rebirth. Such a position avoids conflict with the notion that rebirth is impossible, as the mind is considered to be merely a product of the brain and therefore unable to survive when the brain ceases to function. On the other hand, research related to rebirth has brought to light evidence of various types and varying quality in support of the belief in some form of survival of mental processes beyond the death of the body.

Studies of near-death experiences in different cultures show the impact of subjective and culturally influenced conditioning on otherworld experiences. At the same time, the very occurrence of such experiences during what clinical documentation shows to be a period of severe impairment or even nonfunctionality of the brain is not easily reconciled with the assumption that all mental events are in the final count reducible to activities in the brain.

Documentation of apparently correct information provided by children who recollect what they perceive as past lives, behavioral continuities between the past and the present personalities, together with birthmarks and deformities seemingly related to the deceased person, have significantly contributed to changing the notion of rebirth from a religious creed to a reasonable belief.[448]

The case of xenoglossy studied in this book further strengthens the growing body of evidence in support of such a reasonable belief. Close inspection of the Pāli texts chanted by a small boy in the 1970s gives the impression that he did not learn these, in the form in which he recites them, at that time in Sri Lanka.

Besides providing evidence in support of the possibility of xenoglossy, the present case also has an advantage over many other cases insofar as it does not depend only on having to take on trust the memories of the child or others who have been in contact with him. In order to enable the reader to take personal verification further than is usually possible, the publisher has agreed to dedicate a webpage to the present research that allows downloading or listening to recordings of two pieces of evidence, the *Girimānanda-sutta* (AN 10.60) and the *Dhammacakkappavattana-sutta* (SN 56.11).[449] The ability to hear the chants for oneself adds

448. Stevenson 1980, 369–70 concludes on the cases he has assembled that "reincarnation seems to me, as of now, the most satisfactory interpretation of them. This is far from saying that any single case, or all the known cases together, offer anything like a proof of reincarnation. But...formerly such belief rested on philosophical arguments or docile acceptance of scriptural dogma...but [the]...growing body of evidence...permits a rational belief in reincarnation, even though this evidence falls short of being decisive. And for the future, there is the possibility that further and improved investigations of cases of this type may develop stronger evidence of a quality that will permit a firmer conclusion."

449. The publisher's website is at http://www.wisdompubs.org/rebirth-early-buddhism. The making available of central evidence in this way is in line with a suggestion by Visoni 2010,

another dimension to the information provided in the last chapter in written form.

Nevertheless, certainty about what happens or does not happen after death will become accessible to each of us only at an uncertain point in time in the future, namely when we die ourselves. At that point in time death and its implications will indeed become a matter of personal and direct experience. The present study can only collect information to enable one better to appreciate the early Buddhist teachings regarding rebirth and to evaluate for oneself how far the body of evidence presented here suffices for a belief in the possibility of some continuity beyond death.

In the final count, it seems to me that what remains of central importance is to learn to face mortality, one's own and that of others, rather than turning a blind eye to it. I doubt this challenge can be met by resorting to arguments and counterarguments in the debate on rebirth. Instead, it requires diligent practice of mindfulness of death, by way of giving full recognition to the indubitable fact of mortality.[450] In fact in early Buddhist thought the "deathless," *amata*, can be realized while one is still alive. It is not a state or condition reached only after one has passed away.

> The path to the deathless is diligence;
> Negligence is the path to death.
> The diligent do not "die";
> As if dead are those who are negligent.[451]

---

101 that, "in order to generate more knowledge and interest among the scientific community concerning research of C[ases] O[f the] R[eincarnation] T[ype], I suggest that as much material as possible—such as audio and video recordings—should be placed on the Internet, so that a larger number of scholars can get access to the studies, and would thus be able to identify more easily the strengths and weaknesses of the cases."

450. See in more detail Anālayo 2016b, 200–207.

451. Dhp 21, a stanza that has similarly worded parallels in the Gāndhārī *Dharmapada* 115, Brough 1962/2001, 135, the Patna *Dharmapada* 14, Cone 1989, 108, and the *Udānavarga* 4.1, Bernhard 1965, 126 (which in the last line has *sadā*, "always," instead of *yathā*, "as if").

Transcriptions

Introduction

In what follows I present transcripts of the Pāli chants by Dhammaruwan selected for study in this book, arranged in sequence according to their placing in the Pāli canon. Words in the transcripts that differ from any of the main editions consulted are underlined; an underlined ellipsis marks a place where one or more of the editions has additional material. In the footnotes to these underlined occurrences I first refer to the recordings, combining an abbreviation for the text with the count of minutes and seconds of the approximate time when this particular phrase occurs in the recording.[452] This is followed by the variants in the four Pāli editions consulted (B^e^: Burmese, C^e^: Ceylonese, E^e^: Pali Text Society, and S^e^: Siamese), from which I only note those that make a clearly audible difference.[453] The same goes for the annotation in these editions, from which I only record variants mentioned in the edition's notes if these correspond

452. In relation to the abbreviations used to refer to the chanted texts, in the case of discourses from the *Saṃyutta-nikāya* and *Aṅguttara-nikāya* I simplify these by just referring to the section of the collection. Thus SN 22.59 becomes SN 22; SN 46.14, SN 46.15, and SN 46.16 become SN 46; SN 56.11 becomes SN 56; and AN 10.60 becomes AN 10. In the case of the *Khuddakapāṭha* and *Sutta-nipāta* I use Khp and Sn, combining the two abbreviations when variants are found in both. For these two as well as for the *Dhammapada* I just use the respective abbreviation without any numbering, which in the last case is Dhp.

453. I ignore differences such as between the *niggahīta* and *m*, whether consonants are aspirated or unaspirated, cerebral or dental, and the lengthening of vowels, since to try to determine these with precision in the recordings, whose quality is not always clear, involves various degrees of uncertainty. In addition, it also needs to be kept in mind that to some degree Dhammaruwan's chanting must be influenced by his present-life dialect as a Sinhalese. In order to avoid any possible influences in this respect, it seems to me best to note only clearly audible differences as a basis for my discussion. The strength of my argument in

to the reading in question. The footnotes appended to the titles of the texts give information about the location of the discourse in the Pali Text Society edition and the parts of the discourse covered by the recording.[454]

DN 15 *Mahānidāna-sutta*[455]

evaṃ me sutaṃ. ekaṃ samayaṃ bhagavā kurūsu viharati kammāsadhammaṃ nāma kurūnaṃ nigamo.

atha kho āyasmā ānando yena bhagavā ten' upasaṅkami. upasaṅkamitvā bhagavantaṃ abhivādetvā ekamantaṃ nisīdi. ekamantaṃ nisinno kho āyasmā ānando bhagavantaṃ etad avoca:

acchariyaṃ bhante abbhutaṃ bhante yāva gambhīro cāyaṃ bhante paṭiccasamuppādo gambhīrāvabhāso ca, atha ca pana me uttānakuttānako viya khāyatī ti.

mā h' evaṃ ānanda avaca, mā h' evaṃ ānanda avaca. gambhīro cāyaṃ, ānanda,[456] *paṭiccasamuppādo gambhīrāvabhāso ca. etassa ānanda dhammassa ananubodhā appaṭivedhā evam ayaṃ pajā tantākulakajātā guṇagaṇṭhikajātā*[457] *muñjapabbajabhūtā apāyaṃ duggatiṃ vinipātaṃ saṃsāraṃ nātivattati.*

atthi idappaccayā jarāmaraṇan ti iti puṭṭhena satā ānanda atthi' ssa[458] *vacanīyaṃ. kim paccayā jarāmaraṇan ti iti ce vadeyya, jātipaccayā jarāmaraṇan ti icc' assa vacanīyaṃ.*

---

chapter 4 relies in part on the quantity of variants, so it seems best to exercise restraint in this respect and avoid inflating their number with uncertain variants.

454. The software I have been using gives differing counts of seconds depending on whether a recording is played from the beginning or only started close to the place in question. Therefore the count of seconds is only an approximation, and its function is predominantly to enable readers to relate the discussion and tables in chapter 4 to the corresponding place here in the transcripts. This would give those who wish to consult the actual recordings a rough indicator as to where the passage can be found.

455. The recording corresponds to the first part of DN 15 at DN II 55,1–64,2; however, a whole section of the discourse is missing in the chanting, corresponding to DN II 58,31–61,34.

456. DN 15: 01.43. S^e without *ānanda* (but noted as a variant).

457. DN 15: 02.08. B^e: *kulagaṇṭhikajātā* (with *guṇagaṇṭhikajātā* noted as a variant), C^e: *guḷāguṇḍikajātā* (with *guṇagaṇḍhikajātā* noted as a variant), and E^e: *gulāguṇṭhikajātā* (with *guṇagaṇṭhikajātā* noted as a variant).

458. DN 15: 02.38. B^e, C^e, E^e, and S^e: *atthī ti 'ssa*.

atthi idappaccayā jātī ti iti puṭṭhena satā ānanda atthi 'ssa[459] *vacanīyaṃ. kim paccayā jātī ti iti ce vadeyya, bhavapaccayā jātī ti icc' assa vacanīyaṃ.*

atthi idappaccayā bhavo ti iti puṭṭhena satā ānanda atthi 'ssa[460] *vacanīyaṃ. kim paccayā bhavo ti iti ce vadeyya, upādānapaccayā bhavo ti icc' assa vacanīyaṃ.*

atthi idappaccayā upādānan ti iti puṭṭhena satā ānanda atthi 'ssa[461] *vacanīyaṃ. kim paccayā upādānan ti iti ce vadeyya, taṇhāpaccayā upādānan ti icc' assa vacanīyaṃ.*

atthi idappaccayā taṇhā ti iti puṭṭhena satā ānanda atthi 'ssa[462] *vacanīyaṃ. kim paccayā taṇhā ti iti ce vadeyya, vedanāpaccayā taṇhā ti icc' assa vacanīyaṃ.*

atthi idappaccayā vedanā ti iti puṭṭhena satā ānanda atthi 'ssa[463] *vacanīyaṃ. kim paccayā vedanā ti iti ce vadeyya, phassapaccayā vedanā ti icc' assa vacanīyaṃ.*

atthi idappaccayā phasso ti iti puṭṭhena satā ānanda atthi 'ssa[464] *vacanīyaṃ. kim paccayā phasso ti iti ce vadeyya, nāmarūpapaccayā phasso ti icc' assa vacanīyaṃ.*

atthi idappaccayā nāmarūpan ti iti puṭṭhena satā ānanda atthi 'ssa[465] *vacanīyaṃ. kim paccayā nāmarūpan ti iti ce vadeyya, viññāṇapaccayā nāmarūpan ti icc' assa vacanīyaṃ.*

atthi idappaccayā viññāṇan ti iti puṭṭhena satā ānanda atthi 'ssa[466] *vacanīyaṃ. kim paccayā viññāṇan ti iti ce vadeyya, nāmarūpapaccayā viññāṇan ti icc' assa vacanīyaṃ.*

iti kho ānanda nāmarūpapaccayā viññāṇaṃ, viññāṇapaccayā nāmarūpaṃ, nāmarūpapaccayā phasso, phassapaccayā vedanā, vedanāpaccayā taṇhā, taṇhāpaccayā upādānaṃ, upādānapaccayā bhavo, bhavapaccayā

459. DN 15: 03.09. B^e^, C^e^, E^e^, and S^e^: *atthī ti 'ssa.*

460. DN 15: 03.36. B^e^, C^e^, E^e^, and S^e^: *atthī ti 'ssa.*

461. DN 15: 04.05. B^e^, C^e^, E^e^, and S^e^: *atthī ti 'ssa.*

462. DN 15: 04.33. B^e^, C^e^, E^e^, and S^e^: *atthī ti 'ssa.*

463. DN 15: 05.03. B^e^, C^e^, E^e^, and S^e^: *atthī ti 'ssa.*

464. DN 15: 05.31. B^e^, C^e^, E^e^, and S^e^: *atthī ti 'ssa.*

465. DN 15: 06.01. B^e^, C^e^, E^e^, and S^e^: *atthī ti 'ssa.*

466. DN 15: 06.31. B^e^, C^e^, E^e^, and S^e^: *atthī ti 'ssa.*

jāti, jātipaccayā jarāmaraṇaṃ...[467] *sokaparidevadukkhadomanass' upāyāsā sambhavanti. evam etassa kevalassa dukkhakkhandhassa samudayo hoti.*

jātipaccayā jarāmaraṇan ti iti kho pan' etaṃ vuttaṃ. tad ānanda iminā p' etaṃ pariyāyena veditabbaṃ, yathā jātipaccayā jarāmaraṇaṃ. jāti ca[468] *hi ānanda nābhavissa sabbena sabbaṃ sabbathā sabbaṃ kassaci kiṃhici, seyyathi idaṃ*[469] *devānaṃ vā devattāya, gandhabbānaṃ vā gandhabbattāya, yakkhānaṃ vā yakkhattāya, bhūtānaṃ vā bhūtattāya, manussānaṃ vā manussattāya, catuppadānaṃ vā catuppadattāya, pakkhīnaṃ vā pakkhittāya,*[470] *sarīsapānaṃ vā siriṃsapattāya,*[471] *tesaṃ tesañ ca...*[472] *ānanda sattānaṃ tathattāya jāti nābhavissa, sabbaso jātiyā asati jātinirodhā api nu kho jarāmaraṇaṃ paññāyethā ti?*

no h' etaṃ bhante.

tasmātih' ānanda es' eva hetu etaṃ nidānaṃ esa samudayo esa paccayo jarāmaraṇassa, yad idaṃ jāti.

bhavapaccayā jātī ti iti kho pan' etaṃ vuttaṃ. tad ānanda iminā p' etaṃ pariyāyena veditabbaṃ, yathā bhavapaccayā jāti. bhavo ca[473] *hi ānanda nābhavissa sabbena sabbaṃ sabbathā sabbaṃ kassaci kiṃhici, seyyathi*

467. DN 15: 07.33. E^e continues after *jarāmaraṇaṃ* with *jarāmaraṇapaccayā* (with a note that some manuscripts omit this).

468. DN 15: 08.13. E^e: *va* (with *ca* noted as a variant).

469. DN 15: 08.25. Here and elsewhere, my departure from the standard spelling *seyyathīdaṃ* is on purpose, as throughout the chants of different texts this expression is clearly pronounced as two separate terms, the first of which is pronounced as ending on an *-i* (from the viewpoint of Pāli language, the compound is a combination of *seyyathā* and *idaṃ*. Therefore, when pronouncing them separately, the first term should end on an *-ā* instead of an *-i*).

470. DN 15: 08.57. E^e: *pakkhattāya*.

471. DN 15: 09.00. B^e: *sarīsapānaṃ vā sarīsapattāya* (with *siriṃsapānaṃ* and *siriṃsapattāya* noted as variants), C^e, E^e, and S^e: *siriṃsapānaṃ vā siriṃsapattāya* (with *sarīsapānaṃ* and *sarīsapattāya* noted in E^e as variants, and just *sarīsapānaṃ* noted in C^e as a variant).

472. DN 15: 09.09. B^e: *ca hi*, E^e: *va hi*.

473. DN 15: 10.12. E^e: *va*.

idaṃ[474] *kāmabhavo vā*[475] *rūpabhavo vā*[476] *arūpabhavo vā hi,*[477] *sabbaso bhave asati bhavanirodhā api nu kho jāti paññāyethā ti?*

no h' etaṃ bhante.

tasmātih' ānanda es' eva hetu etaṃ nidānaṃ esa samudayo esa paccayo jātiyā, yad idaṃ bhavo.

upādānapaccayā bhavo ti iti kho pan' etaṃ vuttaṃ. tad ānanda iminā p' etaṃ pariyāyena veditabbaṃ, yathā upādānapaccayā bhavo. upādānañ ca[478] *hi ānanda nābhavissa sabbena sabbaṃ sabbathā sabbaṃ kassaci kimhici, seyyathi idaṃ*[479] *kāmūpādānaṃ vā diṭṭhūpādānaṃ vā sīlabbatūpādānaṃ vā attavādūpādānaṃ vā, sabbaso upādāne asati upādānanirodhā api nu kho bhavo paññāyethā ti?*

no h' etaṃ bhante.

tasmātih' ānanda es' eva hetu etaṃ nidānaṃ esa samudayo esa paccayo bhavassa, yad idaṃ upādānaṃ.

taṇhāpaccayā upādānan ti iti kho pan' etaṃ vuttaṃ. tad ānanda iminā p' etaṃ pariyāyena veditabbaṃ, yathā taṇhāpaccayā upādānaṃ. taṇhā ca[480] *hi ānanda nābhavissa sabbena sabbaṃ sabbathā sabbaṃ kassaci kimhici, seyyathi idaṃ*[481] *rūpataṇhā saddataṇhā gandhataṇhā rasataṇhā phoṭṭhabbataṇhā dhammataṇhā, sabbaso taṇhāya asati taṇhānirodhā api nu kho upādānaṃ paññāyethā ti?*

no h' etaṃ bhante.

tasmātih' ānanda es' eva hetu etaṃ nidānaṃ esa samudayo esa paccayo upādānassa, yad idaṃ taṇhā.

vedanāpaccayā taṇhā ti iti kho pan' etaṃ vuttaṃ. tad ānanda iminā p' etaṃ pariyāyena veditabbaṃ, yathā vedanāpaccayā taṇhā. vedanā ca[482]

474. DN 15: 10.25; see the comments above in relation to DN 15: 08.25.

475. DN 15: 10.29. C^{e} and E^{e} without *vā*.

476. DN 15: 10.31. C^{e} and E^{e} without *vā*.

477. DN 15: 10.34. B^{e}, C^{e}, E^{e}, and S^{e} without *hi*, C^{e} also without *vā*.

478. DN 15: 11.31. E^{e}: *upādānaṃ va*.

479. DN 15: 11.45; see the comments above in relation to DN 15: 08.25.

480. DN 15: 13.02. E^{e}: *va*.

481. DN 15: 13.14; see the comments above in relation to DN 15: 08.25.

482. DN 15: 14.29. E^{e}: *va*.

hi ānanda nābhavissa sabbena sabbaṃ sabbathā sabbaṃ kassaci kimhici, seyyathi idaṃ[483] *cakkhusamphassajā vedanā sotasamphassajā vedanā ghānasamphassajā vedanā jivhāsamphassajā vedanā*[484] *kāyasamphassajā vedanā manosamphassajā vedanā, sabbaso vedanāya asati vedanānirodhā api nu kho taṇhā paññāyethā ti?*

no h' etaṃ bhante.

tasmātih' ānanda es' eva hetu etaṃ nidānaṃ...[485] *esa paccayo taṇhāya, yad idaṃ vedanā...*[486]

phassapaccayā vedanā ti iti kho pan' etaṃ vuttaṃ. tad ānanda iminā p' etaṃ pariyāyena veditabbaṃ, yathā phassapaccayā vedanā ti.[487] *phasso ca*[488] *hi ānanda nābhavissa sabbena sabbaṃ sabbathā sabbaṃ kassaci kimhici, seyyathi idaṃ*[489] *cakkhusamphasso sotasamphasso ghānasamphasso jivhāsamphasso kāyasamphasso manosamphasso, sabbaso phasse asati phassanirodhā api nu kho vedanā paññāyethā ti?*

no h' etaṃ bhante.

tasmātih' ānanda es' eva hetu etaṃ nidānaṃ esa samudayo esa paccayo vedanāya, yad idaṃ phasso.

nāmarūpapaccayā phasso ti iti kho pan' etaṃ vuttaṃ. tad ānanda iminā p' etaṃ pariyāyena veditabbaṃ, yathā nāmarūpapaccayā phasso. yehi ānanda ākārehi...[490] *yehi nimittehi yehi uddesehi nāmakāyassa paññatti hoti, tesu ākāresu tesu liṅgesu tesu nimittesu tesu uddesesu asati api nu kho rūpakāye adhivacanasamphasso paññāyethā ti?*

no h' etaṃ bhante.

yehi ānanda ākārehi yehi liṅgehi yehi nimittehi yehi uddesehi rūpakāyassa paññatti hoti, tesu ākāresu tesu liṅgesu tesu nimittesu tesu uddesesu asati api nu kho nāmakāye paṭighasamphasso paññāyethā ti?

483. DN 15: 14.43; see the comments above in relation to DN 15: 08.25.

484. DN 15: 14.59. Ce without *jivhāsamphassajā vedanā.*

485. DN 15: 15.37. Be, Ce, Ee, and Se: *esa samudayo.*

486. DN 15: 15.45. At this point a major portion of text is missing, corresponding to DN 15 at DN II 58,31–61,34 and thus three full pages in Ee.

487. DN 15: 16.06. Be, Ce, Ee, and Se without *ti.*

488. DN 15: 16.09. Ee: *va.*

489. DN 15: 16.21; see the comments above in relation to DN 15: 08.25.

490. DN 15: 17.43. Be, Ce, Ee, and Se: *yehi liṅgehi.*

no h' etaṃ bhante.

yehi ānanda ākārehi yehi liṅgehi yehi nimittehi yehi uddesehi nāmakāyassa ca rūpakāyassa ca paññatti hoti, tesu ākāresu tesu liṅgesu tesu nimittesu tesu uddesesu asati api nu kho adhivacanasamphasso vā paṭighasamphasso vā paññāyethā ti?

no h' etaṃ bhante.

yehi ānanda ākārehi yehi liṅgehi yehi nimittehi yehi uddesehi nāmarūpassa paññatti hoti, tesu ākāresu tesu liṅgesu tesu nimittesu tesu uddesesu asati api nu kho phasso paññāyethā ti?

no h' etaṃ bhante.

tasmātih' ānanda es' eva hetu etaṃ nidānaṃ esa samudayo esa paccayo phassassa, yad idaṃ nāmarūpaṃ.

viññāṇapaccayā nāmarūpan ti iti kho pan' etaṃ vuttaṃ. tad ānanda iminā p' etaṃ pariyāyena veditabbaṃ, yathā viññāṇapaccayā nāmarūpaṃ. viññāṇañ ca[491] *hi ānanda mātu kucchismiṃ*[492] *na okkamissatha, api nu kho nāmarūpaṃ mātu kucchismiṃ samucchissathā*[493] *ti?*

no h' etaṃ bhante.

viññāṇañ ca[494] *hi ānanda mātu kucchismiṃ*[495] *okkamitvā vokkamissatha, api nu kho nāmarūpaṃ itthattāya abhinibbattissathā ti?*

no h' etaṃ bhante.

viññāṇañ ca[496] *hi ānanda daharass' eva sato vocchissatha*[497] *kumārassa*[498] *vā kumārikāya vā, api nu kho nāmarūpaṃ vuddhiṃ virūḷhiṃ vepullaṃ āpajjissathā ti?*

no h' etaṃ bhante.

tasmātih' ānanda es' eva hetu etaṃ nidānaṃ esa samudayo esa paccayo nāmarūpassa, yad idaṃ viññāṇaṃ.

491. DN 15: 21.16. Eᵉ: *va.*

492. DN 15: 21.20. Eᵉ: *kucchiṃ* (with *kucchismiṃ* noted as a variant).

493. DN 15: 21.29. Sᵉ: *samucchijjissathā.*

494. DN 15: 21.37. Eᵉ: *viññaṇaṃ va.*

495. DN 15: 21.41. Cᵉ and Eᵉ: *kucchiṃ* (with *kucchismiṃ* noted in Eᵉ as a variant).

496. DN 15: 22.01. Eᵉ: *viññaṇaṃ va.*

497. DN 15: 22.09. Bᵉ, Cᵉ, Eᵉ, and Sᵉ: *vocchijjissatha.*

498. DN 15: 22.11. Bᵉ, Cᵉ, and Sᵉ: *kumārakassa.*

nāmarūpapaccayā viññāṇan ti iti kho pan' etaṃ vuttaṃ. tad ānanda iminā p' etaṃ pariyāyena veditabbaṃ, yathā nāmarūpapaccayā viññāṇaṃ. viññāṇañ ca[499] *hi ānanda nāmarūpe patiṭṭhaṃ na labhissatha, api nu kho āyati*[500] *jātijarāmaraṇaṃ dukkhaṃ samudayasambhavo*[501] *paññāyethā ti?*

no h' etaṃ bhante.

tasmātih' ānanda es' eva hetu etaṃ nidānaṃ esa samudayo esa paccayo viññāṇassa yad idaṃ nāmarūpaṃ.

ettāvatā kho ānanda jāyetha vā jīyetha vā mīyetha vā cavetha vā uppajjetha[502] *vā, ettāvatā adhivacanapatho, ettāvatā niruttipatho, ettāvatā paññattipatho,*[503] *ettāvatā paññāvacaraṃ, ettāvatā vaṭṭaṃ vattati itthaṃ*[504] *paññāpanāya, yad idaṃ nāmarūpaṃ saha viññāṇena.*

DN 16 *Mahāparinibbāna-sutta*[505]

...[506] *ādīnavā dussīlassa sīlavipattiyā. katame pañca?*

idha gahapatayo dussīlo sīlavipanno pamādādhikaraṇaṃ mahatiṃ bhogajāniṃ nigacchati. ayaṃ paṭhamo ādīnavo dussīlassa sīlavipattiyā.[507]

puna ca paraṃ gahapatayo dussīlassa sīlavipannassa pāpako kittisaddo abbhuggacchati. ayaṃ dutiyo ādīnavo dussīlassa sīlavipattiyā.

499. DN 15: 23.13. Eᵉ: *viññaṇaṃ va.*

500. DN 15: 23.24. Bᵉ, Cᵉ, and Sᵉ: *āyatiṃ* (*āyatiṃ* is also noted in Eᵉ as a variant).

501. DN 15: 23.27. Bᵉ and Cᵉ: *jātijarāmaraṇaṃ dukkhasamudayasambhavo*, Eᵉ and Sᵉ: *jātijarāmaraṇadukkhasamudayasambhavo.*

502. DN 15: 24.12. Bᵉ, Cᵉ, and Sᵉ: *upapajjetha.*

503. DN 15: 24.23. Cᵉ: *viññattipatho.*

504. DN 15: 24.35. Bᵉ, Cᵉ, Eᵉ, and Sᵉ: *itthattaṃ.*

505. The recording has extracts from DN 16, corresponding to DN II 85,13–86,20, DN II 90,8–91,5, DN II 93,21–94,14, and DN II 100,20–101,4. In the recording these do not occur in the sequence in which they are found in the discourse, as the recording starts with the passage at DN II 93,21, then has the one found at DN II 100,20, followed by the one at DN II 85,13 and then the one at DN II 90,8. In my study I follow the canonical positioning of these passages, not the order of the chanting. Each of these four sections is clearly a separate recording; the recited texts do not follow each other without interruption.

506. DN 16: 10.24. The recorded part lacks the introductory phrase *pañc' ime gahapatayo,* found in DN 16 at DN II 85,13.

507. DN 16: 11.08. Cᵉ: *sīlaṃ vipattiyā.*

puna ca paraṃ gahapatayo dussīlo sīlavipanno yaññad[508] *eva parisaṃ upasaṅkamati, yadi khattiyaparisaṃ yadi brāhmaṇaparisaṃ yadi gahapatiparisaṃ yadi samaṇaparisaṃ, avisārado upasaṅkamati maṅkubhūto. ayaṃ tatiyo ādīnavo dussīlassa sīlavipattiyā.*

puna ca paraṃ gahapatayo dussīlo sīlavipanno sammūḷho kālaṃ karoti. ayaṃ catuttho ādīnavo dussīlassa sīlavipattiyā.

puna ca paraṃ gahapatayo dussīlo sīlavipanno kāyassa bhedā paraṃ maraṇā apāyaṃ duggatiṃ vinipātaṃ nirayaṃ uppajjati.[509] *ayaṃ pañcamo ādīnavo dussīlassa sīlavipattiyā.*

ime kho gahapatayo pañca ādīnavo[510] *dussīlassa sīlavipattiyā.*

pañcime gahapatayo ānisaṃsā sīlavato sīlasampadāya. katame pañca?

idha gahapatayo sīlavā sīlasampanno appamādādhikaraṇaṃ mahantaṃ bhogakkhandhaṃ adhigacchati. ayaṃ paṭhamo ānisaṃso sīlavato sīlasampadāya.

puna ca paraṃ gahapatayo sīlavato sīlasampannassa kalyāṇo kittisaddo abbhuggacchati. ayaṃ dutiyo ānisaṃso sīlavato sīlasampadāya.

puna ca paraṃ gahapatayo sīlavā sīlasampanno[511] *yaññad*[512] *eva parisaṃ upasaṅkamati, yadi khattiyaparisaṃ yadi brāhmaṇaparisaṃ yadi gahapatiparisaṃ yadi samaṇaparisaṃ, visārado upasaṅkamati amaṅkubhūto. ayaṃ tatiyo ānisaṃso sīlavato sīlasampadāya.*

puna ca paraṃ gahapatayo sīlavā sīlasampanno asammūḷho kālaṃ karoti. ayaṃ catuttho ānisaṃso sīlavato sīlasampadāya.

puna ca paraṃ gahapatayo sīlavā sīlasampanno kāyassa bhedā paraṃ maraṇā sugatiṃ saggaṃ lokaṃ uppajjati.[513] *ayaṃ pañcamo ānisaṃso sīlavato sīlasampadāya*[514]

508. DN 16: 11.50. E^{e}: *yaṃ yad.*

509. DN 16: 13.21. B^{e}, C^{e}, and S^{e}: *upapajjati.*

510. DN 16: 13.41. B^{e}, C^{e}, E^{e}, and S^{e}: *ādīnavā.*

511. DN 16: 15.08. C^{e}: *sīlasampannā.*

512. DN 16: 15.12. E^{e}: *yaṃ yad.*

513. DN 16: 16.36. B^{e}, C^{e}, and S^{e}: *upapajjati.*

514. DN 16: 16.52. The written text in DN 16 at DN II 86,20 (and B^{e}, C^{e}, and S^{e}) continues with *ime kho gahapatayo ānisaṃsā sīlavato sīlasampadāya.*

. . .[515] *catunnaṃ bhikkhave ariyasaccānaṃ ananubodhā appaṭivedhā evam idaṃ dīgham addhānaṃ sandhāvitaṃ saṃsaritaṃ mamaññeva*[516] *tumhākañ ca. katamesaṃ catunnaṃ?*

dukkhassa bhikkhave ariyasaccassa ananubodhā appaṭivedhā evam idaṃ dīgham addhānaṃ sandhāvitaṃ saṃsaritaṃ mamaññeva[517] *tumhākañ ca.*

dukkhasamudayassa bhikkhave ariyasaccassa ananubodhā appaṭivedhā evam idaṃ dīgham addhānaṃ sandhāvitaṃ saṃsaritaṃ mamaññeva[518] *tumhākañ ca.*

dukkhanirodhassa bhikkhave ariyasaccassa ananubodhā appaṭivedhā evam idaṃ dīgham addhānaṃ sandhāvitaṃ saṃsaritaṃ mamaññeva[519] *tumhākañ ca.*

dukkhanirodhagāminiyā paṭipadāya bhikkhave ariyasaccassa ananubodhā appaṭivedhā evam idaṃ dīgham addhānaṃ sandhāvitaṃ saṃsaritaṃ mamaññeva[520] *tumhākañ ca.*

tayidaṃ bhikkhave dukkhaṃ ariyasaccaṃ anubuddhaṃ paṭividdhaṃ, dukkhasamudayaṃ[521] *ariyasaccaṃ anubuddhaṃ paṭividdhaṃ, dukkhanirodhaṃ*[522] *ariyasaccaṃ anubuddhaṃ paṭividdhaṃ, dukkhanirodhagāminī paṭipadā ariyasaccaṃ anubuddhaṃ paṭividdhaṃ, ucchinnā bhavataṇhā, khīṇā bhavanetti, n' atthi dāni punabbhavo ti.*

idam avoca bhagavā. idaṃ vatvā[523] *sugato athāparaṃ etad avoca satthā:*

catunnaṃ ariyasaccānaṃ
yathābhūtaṃ adassanā

515. DN 16: 16.59. The recording sets in with text found in DN 16 at DN II 90,8.

516. DN 16: 17.24. Be, Ce, Ee, and Se: *mamañ c' eva.*

517. DN 16: 18.01. Be, Ce, Ee, and Se: *mamañ c' eva.*

518. DN 16: 18.33. Be, Ce, Ee, and Se: *mamañ c' eva.*

519. DN 16: 19.03. Be, Ce, Ee, and Se: *mamañ c' eva.*

520. DN 16: 19.41. Be, Ce, Ee, and Se: *mamañ c' eva.*

521. DN 16: 20.02. Ce and Se: *dukkhasamudayo* (with *dukkhasamudayaṃ* noted in both as a variant). On this difference see, e.g., Woodward 1930/1979, 358n1, Weller 1940, Johansson 1973/1998, 24, Norman 1984, Anālayo 2006a, 150–51, and Harvey 2009, 218–19.

522. DN 16: 20.12. Ce and Se: *dukkhanirodho* (with *dukkhanirodhaṃ* noted in both as a variant); see also previous footnote.

523. DN 16: 20.57. Be and Se: *vatvāna*, Ce: *vatthā*.

saṃsitaṃ[524] *dīgham addhānaṃ*
tāsu tās' eva[525] *jātisu.*
tāni etāni diṭṭhāni
bhavanetti samūhatā
ucchinnamūlaṃ[526] *dukkhassa*
n' atthi dāni punabbhavo ti.[527]

. . .[528] *ānanda*[529] *dhammādāso dhammapariyāyo yena samannāgato ariyasāvako ākaṅkhamāno attanā va attānaṃ vyākareyya: khīṇanirayo 'mhi khīṇatiracchānayoni khīṇapettivisayo khīṇāpāyaduggativinipāto, sotāpanno 'ham asmi avenipātadhammo*[530] *niyato sambodhiparāyano ti?*

idh' ānanda ariyasāvako buddhe aveccappasādena samannāgato hoti: iti pi so bhagavā arahaṃ sammāsambuddho vijjācaraṇasampanno sugato lokavidū anuttaro purisadammasārathi satthā devamanussānaṃ buddho bhagavā ti.

dhamme aveccappasādena samannāgato hoti: svākkhāto bhagavatā dhammo sandiṭṭhiko akāliko ehipassiko opaneyyiko[531] *paccattaṃ veditabbo viññūhī ti.*

saṅghe aveccappasādena samannāgato hoti: supaṭipanno bhagavato sāvakasaṅgho, ujupaṭipanno bhagavato sāvakasaṅgho, ñāyapaṭipanno bhagavato sāvakasaṅgho, sāmīcipaṭipanno bhagavato sāvakasaṅgho, yad idaṃ cattāri purisayugāni aṭṭha purisapuggalā; esa bhagavato sāvakasaṅgho āhuneyyo pāhuneyyo dakkhiṇeyyo añjalikaraṇeyyo[532] *anuttaraṃ puññakkhettaṃ lokassā ti.*

ariyakantehi sīlehi samannāgato hoti akhaṇḍehi acchiddehi asa-

524. DN 16: 21.18. S^e^: *saṃsaritaṃ* (with *saṃsitaṃ* noted as a variant).

525. DN 16: 21.25. B^e^, C^e^, and S^e^: *tāsv' eva.*

526. DN 16: 21.41. B^e^, C^e^, E^e^, and S^e^: *ucchinnaṃ mūlaṃ.*

527. DN 16: 21.54. The recording stops with text found in DN 16 at DN II 91,5.

528. DN 16: 00.04. The recorded part lacks the introductory phrase in the written text in DN 16 at DN II 93,21: *katamo ca so. . .*

529. DN 16: 00.04. E^e^: *ānando.*

530. DN 16: 01.01. B^e^, C^e^, E^e^, and S^e^: *avinipātadhammo.*

531. DN 16: 02.36. C^e^, E^e^, and S^e^: *opanayiko.*

532. DN 16: 04.05. B^e^, C^e^, E^e^, and S^e^: *añjalikaraṇīyo.*

balehi akammāsehi bhujjissehi viññuppasatthehi aparāmaṭṭhehi samādhisaṃvattanikehi.

ayam kho so[533] *ānanda dhammādāso dhammapariyāyo yena samannāgato ariyasāvako ākaṅkhamāno attanā va attānaṃ vyākareyya: khīṇanirayo 'mhi khīṇatiracchānayoni khīṇapettivisayo khīṇāpāyaduggativinipāto, sotāpanno 'ham asmi avenipātadhammo*[534] *niyato sambodhiparāyano ti.*[535]

. . .[536] *tasmātih' ānanda attadīpā viharatha attasaraṇā anaññasaraṇā, dhammadīpā dhammasaraṇā anaññasaraṇā. kathañ c' ānanda bhikkhu attadīpo viharati attasaraṇo anaññasaraṇo, dhammadīpo dhammasaraṇo anaññasaraṇo?*

idh' ānanda bhikkhu kāye kāyānupassī viharati ātāpī sampajāno satimā vineyya loke abhijjhādomanassaṃ, vedanāsu vedanānupassī viharati ātāpī sampajāno satimā vineyya loke abhijjhādomanassaṃ, citte cittānupassī viharati ātāpī sampajāno satimā vineyya loke abhijjhādomanassaṃ, dhammesu dhammānupassī viharati ātāpī sampajāno satimā vineyya loke abhijjhādomanassaṃ.

evaṃ kho ānanda bhikkhu attadīpo viharati attasaraṇo anaññasaraṇo, dhammadīpo dhammasaraṇo anaññasaraṇo.

ye hi keci ānanda etarahi vā mamaṃ[537] *vā accayena attadīpā viharissanti attasaraṇā anaññasaraṇā, dhammadīpā dhammasaraṇā anaññasaraṇā, tamatagge me te ānanda bhikkhū bhavissanti. .* .[538]

533. DN 16: 05.02. Se without *so*.

534. DN 16: 06.00. Be, Ce, Ee, and Se: *avinipātadhammo*.

535. DN 16: 06.12. The recording stops with text found in DN 16 at DN II 94,14.

536. DN 16: 06.30. The recording sets in with text found in DN 16 at DN II 100,20.

537. DN 16: 09.38. Be and Se: *mama*.

538. DN 16: 10.15. The written text in DN 16 at DN II 101,4 continues with *ye keci sikkhākāmā ti*.

DN 22 *Mahāsatipaṭṭhāna-sutta*[539]

namo tassa bhagavato arahato sammāsambuddhassa[540]

evaṃ me sutaṃ. ekaṃ samayaṃ bhagavā kurūsu viharati kammāsadhammaṃ nāma kurūnaṃ nigamo. tatra kho bhagavā bhikkhū āmantesi: bhikkhavo ti. bhadante ti te bhikkhū bhagavato paccassosuṃ. bhagavā etad avoca:

ekāyano ayaṃ bhikkhave maggo sattānaṃ visuddhiyā sokapariddavānaṃ[541] *samatikkamāya dukkhadomanassānaṃ atthagamāya*[542] *ñāyassa adhigamāya nibbānassa sacchikiriyāya, yad idaṃ cattāro satipaṭṭhānā.*

katame cattāro?

idha bhikkhave bhikkhu kāye kāyānupassī viharati ātāpī sampajāno satimā vineyya loke abhijjhādomanassaṃ, vedanāsu vedanānupassī viharati ātāpī sampajāno satimā vineyya loke abhijjhādomanassaṃ, citte cittānupassī viharati ātāpī sampajāno satimā vineyya loke abhijjhādomanassaṃ, dhammesu dhammānupassī viharati ātāpī sampajāno satimā vineyya loke abhijjhādomanassaṃ.

kathañ ca...[543] *bhikkhave bhikkhu kāye kāyānupassī viharati?*

idha bhikkhave bhikkhu araññagato vā rukkhamūlagato vā suññāgāragato vā nisīdati pallaṅkaṃ ābhujitvā ujuṃ kāyaṃ paṇidhāya parimukhaṃ satiṃ upaṭṭhapetvā. so sato va assasati, sato va[544] *passasati.*

539. The recordings correspond to DN 22 at DN II 290,1–315,14 and thus to the full discourse, except for a missing piece at the end (DN II 314,14–315,7). The recordings have some degree of overlap, as the first four are consecutive from DN II 290,1 to 311,21. The fifth and sixth (judging from the tone of the voice, these two appear to be from a recording done at a different age) are also consecutive from DN II 305,14 to 315,14. The overlapping part covered by the fourth and fifth recording, alongside repeating the same variations that seem to be part of the base text, shows differences between the two chants in relation to what are clearly errors of memory. In order to distinguish between the six recordings, in the notes I add the numbers 1 to 6 before the timings.

540. DN 22: 1–00.05. This is a standard expression of respect usually employed at the outset of an oral recitation. Even though this is not mentioned in any of the editions consulted, this is of no further significance.

541. DN 22: 1–01.12. B^{e} and S^{e}: *sokaparidevānaṃ*.

542. DN 22: 1–01.24. B^{e}, C^{e}, and S^{e}: *atthaṅgamāya*.

543. DN 22: 1–03.28. B^{e}: *pana*.

544. DN 22: 1–04.17. E^{e} and S^{e} without *va* (but noted in both as a variant). The tendency

dīghaṃ vā assasanto: dīghaṃ assasāmī ti pajānāti, dīghaṃ vā passasanto: dīghaṃ passasāmī ti pajānāti. rassaṃ vā assasanto: rassaṃ assasāmī ti pajānāti, rassaṃ vā passasanto: rassaṃ passasāmī ti pajānāti. sabbakāyapaṭisaṃvedī assasissāmī ti sikkhati, sabbakāyapaṭisaṃvedī passasissāmī ti sikkhati. passambhayaṃ kāyasaṅkhāraṃ assasissāmī ti sikkhati, passambhayaṃ kāyasaṅkhāraṃ passasissāmī ti sikkhati.

seyyathā pi bhikkhave dakkho bhamakāro vā bhamakārantevāsī vā dīghaṃ vā <u>*añjanto*</u>*:*[545] *dīghaṃ* <u>*añjāmī*</u>[546] *ti pajānāti, rassaṃ vā* <u>*añjanto*</u>*:*[547] *rassaṃ* <u>*añjāmī*</u>[548] *ti pajānāti. evam eva kho bhikkhave bhikkhu dīghaṃ vā assasanto: dīghaṃ assasāmī ti pajānāti, dīghaṃ vā passasanto: dīghaṃ passasāmī ti pajānāti. rassaṃ vā assasanto: rassaṃ assasāmī ti pajānāti, rassaṃ vā passasanto: rassaṃ passasāmī ti pajānāti. sabbakāyapaṭisaṃvedī assasissāmī ti sikkhati, sabbakāyapaṭisaṃvedī passasissāmī ti sikkhati. passambhayaṃ kāyasaṅkhāraṃ assasissāmī ti sikkhati, passambhayaṃ kāyasaṅkhāraṃ passasissāmī ti sikkhati.*

iti ajjhattaṃ vā kāye kāyānupassī viharati, bahiddhā vā kāye kāyānupassī viharati, ajjhattabahiddhā vā kāye kāyānupassī viharati. samudayadhammānupassī vā kāyasmiṃ viharati, vayadhammānupassī vā kāyasmiṃ viharati, samudayavayadhammānupassī vā kāyasmiṃ viharati.

atthi kāyo ti vā pan' assa sati paccupaṭṭhitā hoti yāvad eva ñāṇamattāya paṭissatimattāya. anissito ca viharati, na ca kiñci loke upādiyati. evam pi <u>*. . .*</u>[549] *bhikkhave bhikkhu kāye kāyānupassī viharati.*

---

of B^e manuscripts to have a second *va* at this place has already been noted by Cousins 2015, 21n11, although this particular case does not support his suggestion that the second *va* is not found in C^e.

545. DN 22: 1–06.13. B^e, C^e, E^e, and S^e: *añchanto* (with *añjanto* noted in E^e and S^e as a variant). I need to mention that throughout the chants, here and elsewhere, the *-ñ-* in *-ñj-* is hardly pronounced. At first in fact I thought that in the present passage the chants were referring to *ajanto* and *ajāmī*, and it was only after more familiarity with the chants that I realized that the intended words must be *añjanto* and *añjāmī*.

546. DN 22: 1–06.17. B^e, C^e, E^e, and S^e: *añchāmī*; see the comments above on DN 22: 1–06.13.

547. DN 22: 1–06.26. B^e, C^e, E^e, and S^e: *añchanto*; see the comments above on DN 22: 1–06.13.

548. DN 22: 1–06.29. B^e, C^e, E^e, and S^e: *añchāmī*; see the comments above on DN 22: 1–06.13.

549. DN 22: 1–09.54. B^e and C^e: *kho*.

puna ca paraṃ bhikkhave bhikkhu gacchanto vā: gacchāmī ti pajānāti, ṭhito vā: ṭhito 'mhī ti pajānāti, nisinno vā: nisinno 'mhī ti pajānāti, sayāno vā: sayāno 'mhī ti pajānāti, yathā yathā vā pan' assa kāyo paṇihito hoti tathā tathā naṃ pajānāti.

iti ajjhattaṃ vā kāye kāyānupassī viharati, bahiddhā vā kāye kāyānupassī viharati, ajjhattabahiddhā vā kāye kāyānupassī viharati. samudayadhammānupassī vā kāyasmiṃ viharati, vayadhammānupassī vā kāyasmiṃ viharati, samudayavayadhammānupassī vā kāyasmiṃ viharati.

atthi kāyo ti vā pan' assa sati paccupaṭṭhitā hoti yāvad eva ñāṇamattāya paṭissatimattāya. anissito ca viharati, na ca kiñci loke upādiyati. evam pi...[550] *bhikkhave bhikkhu kāye kāyānupassī viharati.*

puna ca paraṃ bhikkhave bhikkhu abhikkante paṭikkante sampajānakārī hoti, ālokite vilokite sampajānakārī hoti, samiñjite pasārite sampajānakārī hoti, saṅghāṭipattacīvaradhāraṇe sampajānakārī hoti, asite pīte khāyite sāyite sampajānakārī hoti, uccārapassāvakamme sampajānakārī hoti, gate ṭhite nisinne sutte jāgarite bhāsite tuṇhībhāve sampajānakārī hoti.

iti ajjhattaṃ vā kāye kāyānupassī viharati, bahiddhā vā kāye kāyānupassī viharati, ajjhattabahiddhā vā kāye kāyānupassī viharati. samudayadhammānupassī vā kāyasmiṃ viharati, vayadhammānupassī vā kāyasmiṃ viharati, samudayavayadhammānupassī vā kāyasmiṃ viharati.

atthi kāyo ti vā pan' assa sati paccupaṭṭhitā hoti yāvad eva ñāṇamattāya paṭissatimattāya. anissito ca viharati, na ca kiñci loke upādiyati. evam pi...[551] *bhikkhave bhikkhu kāye kāyānupassī viharati.*

puna ca paraṃ bhikkhave bhikkhu imam eva kāyaṃ uddhaṃ pādatalā adho kesamatthakā tacapariyantaṃ pūraṃ nānappakārassa[552] *asucino paccavekkhati: atthi imasmiṃ kāye kesā lomā nakhā dantā taco maṃsaṃ nahāru aṭṭhi aṭṭhimiñjā*[553] *vakkaṃ hadayaṃ yakanaṃ kilomakaṃ pihakaṃ papphāsaṃ antaṃ antaguṇaṃ udariyaṃ karīsaṃ matthaluṅgaṃ*[554]

550. DN 22: 1–12.23. Bᵉ and Cᵉ: *kho.*

551. DN 22: 1–15.27. Bᵉ and Cᵉ: *kho.*

552. DN 22: 1–15.54. Sᵉ: *pūrannānappakārassa.*

553. DN 22: 1–16.21. Bᵉ and Sᵉ: *aṭṭhimiñjaṃ.*

554. DN 22: 1–16.37. Not in Bᵉ, Cᵉ, Eᵉ, or Sᵉ (but noted in Bᵉ and Eᵉ as a variant).

pittaṃ semhaṃ pubbo lohitaṃ sedo medo assu vasā kheḷo siṅghāṇikā lasikā muttan ti.

seyyathā pi bhikkhave ubhatomukhā mutoḷī[555] *pūrā nānāvihitassa dhaññassa, seyyathi idaṃ*[556] *sālīnaṃ vīhīnaṃ muggānaṃ māsānaṃ tilānaṃ taṇḍulānaṃ. tam enaṃ cakkhumā puriso muñcitvā paccavekkheyya: ime sālī, ime vīhī, ime muggā, ime māsā, ime tilā, ime taṇḍulā ti. evam eva kho bhikkhave bhikkhu imam eva kāyaṃ uddhaṃ pādatalā adho kesamatthakā tacapariyantaṃ pūraṃ nānappakārassa*[557] *asucino paccavekkhati: atthi imasmiṃ kāye kesā lomā nakhā dantā taco maṃsaṃ nahāru aṭṭhi aṭṭhimiñjā*[558] *vakkaṃ hadayaṃ yakanaṃ kilomakaṃ pihakaṃ papphāsaṃ antaṃ antaguṇaṃ udariyaṃ karīsaṃ matthaluṅgaṃ*[559] *pittaṃ semhaṃ pubbo lohitaṃ sedo medo assu vasā kheḷo siṅghāṇikā lasikā muttan ti.*

iti ajjhattaṃ vā kāye kāyānupassī viharati, bahiddhā vā kāye kāyānupassī viharati, ajjhattabahiddhā vā kāye kāyānupassī viharati. samudayadhammānupassī vā kāyasmiṃ viharati, vayadhammānupassī vā kāyasmiṃ viharati, samudayavayadhammānupassī vā kāyasmiṃ viharati.

atthi kāyo ti vā pan' assa sati paccupaṭṭhitā hoti yāvad eva ñāṇamattāya paṭissatimattāya. anissito ca viharati, na ca kiñci loke upādiyati. evam pi...[560] *bhikkhave bhikkhu kāye kāyānupassī viharati.*

puna ca paraṃ bhikkhave bhikkhu imam eva kāyaṃ yathāṭhitaṃ yathāpaṇihitaṃ dhātuso paccavekkhati: atthi imasmiṃ kāye paṭhavīdhātu āpodhātu tejodhātu vāyodhātū ti.

seyyathā pi bhikkhave dakkho goghātako vā goghātakantevāsī vā gāviṃ vadhitvā cātumahāpathe bilaso[561] *paṭavibhajitvā*[562] *nisinno assa. evam eva kho bhikkhave bhikkhu imam eva kāyaṃ yathāṭhitaṃ yathāpaṇihitaṃ*

555. DN 22: 1–17.04. B^e: *putoḷi*, C^e: *putoḷī*.

556. DN 22: 1–17.13; see the comments above in relation to DN 15: 08.25.

557. DN 22: 1–18.16. S^e: *pūrannānappakārassa*.

558. DN 22: 1–18.41. B^e (abbreviated) and S^e: *aṭṭhimiñjaṃ*.

559. DN 22: 1–18.56. Not in B^e (abbreviated), C^e, E^e, or S^e.

560. DN 22: 1–20.49. B^e and C^e: *kho*.

561. DN 22: 1–21.56. C^e: *khīlaso*.

562. DN 22: 1–21.58. B^e and C^e: *vibhajitvā*, E^e and S^e: *paṭivibhajitvā*.

dhātuso paccavekkhati: atthi imasmiṃ kāye paṭhavīdhātu āpodhātu tejodhātu vāyodhātū ti.

iti ajjhattaṃ vā kāye kāyānupassī viharati, bahiddhā vā kāye kāyānupassī viharati, ajjhattabahiddhā vā kāye kāyānupassī viharati. samudayadhammānupassī vā kāyasmiṃ viharati, vayadhammānupassī vā kāyasmiṃ viharati, samudayavayadhammānupassī vā kāyasmiṃ viharati.

atthi kāyo ti vā pan' assa sati paccupaṭṭhitā hoti yāvad eva ñāṇamattāya paṭissatimattāya. anissito ca viharati, na ca kiñci loke upādiyati. evam pi...[563] *bhikkhave bhikkhu kāye kāyānupassī viharati.*

puna ca paraṃ bhikkhave bhikkhu seyyathā pi passeyya sarīraṃ sīvathikāya chaḍḍitaṃ ekāhamataṃ vā dvīhamataṃ vā tīhamataṃ vā uddhumātakaṃ vinīlakaṃ vipubbakajātaṃ, so imam eva kāyaṃ upasaṃharati: ayam pi kho kāyo evaṃdhammo evaṃbhāvī etaṃ[564] *anatīto ti.*

iti ajjhattaṃ vā kāye kāyānupassī viharati, bahiddhā vā kāye kāyānupassī viharati, ajjhattabahiddhā vā kāye kāyānupassī viharati. samudayadhammānupassī vā kāyasmiṃ viharati, vayadhammānupassī vā kāyasmiṃ viharati, samudayavayadhammānupassī vā kāyasmiṃ viharati.

atthi kāyo ti vā pan' assa sati paccupaṭṭhitā hoti yāvad eva ñāṇamattāya paṭissatimattāya. anissito ca viharati, na ca kiñci loke upādiyati. evam pi...[565] *bhikkhave bhikkhu kāye kāyānupassī viharati.*

puna ca paraṃ bhikkhave bhikkhu seyyathā pi passeyya sarīraṃ sīvathikāya chaḍḍitaṃ kākehi vā khajjamānaṃ, kulalehi vā khajjamānaṃ, gijjhehi vā khajjamānaṃ supāṇehi vā khajjamānaṃ,[566] *sigālehi*[567] *vā khajjamānaṃ, vividhehi vā pāṇakajātehi khajjamānaṃ, so imam eva kāyaṃ upasaṃharati: ayam pi kho kāyo evaṃdhammo evaṃbhāvī etaṃ*[568] *anatīto ti.*

iti ajjhattaṃ vā kāye kāyānupassī viharati, bahiddhā vā kāye kāyānu-

563. DN 22: 1–24.14. Bᵉ and Cᵉ: *kho.*

564. DN 22: 1–25.18. Bᵉ and Sᵉ: *evaṃ.*

565. DN 22: 1–27.08. Bᵉ (abbreviated) and Cᵉ: *kho.*

566. DN 22: 1–27.55. Bᵉ: *kaṅkehi vā khajjamānaṃ, sunakhehi vā khajjamānaṃ, byagghehi vā khajjamānaṃ, dīpīhi vā khajjamānaṃ,* Cᵉ: *sunakhehi vā khajjamānaṃ,* Sᵉ: *suvānehi vā khajjamānaṃ* (Eᵉ notes additional terms as variants).

567. DN 22: 1–28.00. Bᵉ: *siṅgālehi.*

568. DN 22: 1–28.32. Bᵉ and S: *evaṃ.*

passī viharati, ajjhattabahiddhā vā kāye kāyānupassī viharati. samudayadhammānupassī vā kāyasmiṃ viharati, vayadhammānupassī vā kāyasmiṃ viharati, samudayavayadhammānupassī vā kāyasmiṃ viharati.

atthi kāyo ti vā pan' assa sati paccupaṭṭhitā hoti yāvad eva ñāṇamattāya paṭissatimattāya. anissito ca viharati, na ca kiñci loke upādiyati. evam pi...[569] *bhikkhave bhikkhu kāye kāyānupassī viharati.*

puna ca paraṃ bhikkhave bhikkhu seyyathā pi passeyya sarīraṃ sīvathikāya chaḍḍitaṃ aṭṭhisaṅkhalikaṃ[570] *samaṃsalohitaṃ nahārusambandhaṃ, so imam eva kāyaṃ upasaṃharati: ayam pi kho kāyo evaṃdhammo evaṃbhāvī etaṃ*[571] *anatīto ti.*

iti ajjhattaṃ vā kāye kāyānupassī viharati, bahiddhā vā kāye kāyānupassī viharati, ajjhattabahiddhā vā kāye kāyānupassī viharati. samudayadhammānupassī vā kāyasmiṃ viharati, vayadhammānupassī vā kāyasmiṃ viharati, samudayavayadhammānupassī vā kāyasmiṃ viharati.

atthi kāyo ti vā pan' assa sati paccupaṭṭhitā hoti yāvad eva ñāṇamattāya paṭissatimattāya. anissito ca viharati, na ca kiñci loke upādiyati. evam pi...[572] *bhikkhave bhikkhu kāye kāyānupassī viharati.*

puna ca paraṃ bhikkhave bhikkhu seyyathā pi passeyya sarīraṃ sīvathikāya chaḍḍitaṃ aṭṭhisaṅkhalikaṃ[573] *nimaṃsalohitamakkhitaṃ*[574] *nahārusambandhaṃ, so imam eva kāyaṃ upasaṃharati: ayam pi kho kāyo evaṃdhammo evaṃbhāvī etaṃ*[575] *anatīto ti.*

iti ajjhattaṃ vā kāye kāyānupassī viharati, bahiddhā vā kāye kāyānupassī viharati, ajjhattabahiddhā vā kāye kāyānupassī viharati. samudayadhammānupassī vā kāyasmiṃ viharati, vayadhammānupassī vā kāyasmiṃ viharati, samudayavayadhammānupassī vā kāyasmiṃ viharati.

atthi kāyo ti vā pan' assa sati paccupaṭṭhitā hoti yāvad eva ñāṇamattāya

569. DN 22: 1–30.13. Be (abbreviated) and Ce: *kho.*

570. DN 22: 1–30.41. Be: *aṭṭhikasaṅkhalikaṃ*, Ce: *aṭṭhikaṅkhalikaṃ.*

571. DN 22: 1–31.11. Be (abbreviated) and Se (abbreviated): *evaṃ.*

572. DN 22: 1–32.52. Be (abbreviated) and Ce: *kho.*

573. DN 22: 1–33.21. Be: *aṭṭhikasaṅkhalikaṃ.*

574. DN 22: 1–33.25. Ce and Ee: *nimaṃsaṃ lohitamakkhitaṃ* (with *nimaṃsalohitamakkhitaṃ* noted in Ee as a variant).

575. DN 22: 1–33.52. Be (abbreviated) and Se (abbreviated): *evaṃ.*

paṭissatimattāya. anissito ca viharati, na ca kiñci loke upādiyati. evam pi...[576] *bhikkhave bhikkhu kāye kāyānupassī viharati.*

puna ca paraṃ bhikkhave bhikkhu seyyathā pi passeyya sarīraṃ sīvathikāya chaḍḍitaṃ aṭṭhisaṅkhalikaṃ[577] *apagatamaṃsalohitaṃ nahārusambandhaṃ, so imam eva kāyaṃ upasaṃharati: ayam pi kho kāyo evaṃdhammo evaṃbhāvī etaṃ*[578] *anatīto ti.*

iti ajjhattaṃ vā kāye kāyānupassī viharati, bahiddhā vā kāye kāyānupassī viharati, ajjhattabahiddhā vā kāye kāyānupassī viharati. samudayadhammānupassī vā kāyasmiṃ viharati, vayadhammānupassī vā kāyasmiṃ viharati, samudayavayadhammānupassī vā kāyasmiṃ viharati.

atthi kāyo ti vā pan' assa sati paccupaṭṭhitā hoti yāvad eva ñāṇamattāya paṭissatimattāya. anissito ca viharati, na ca kiñci loke upādiyati. evam pi...[579] *bhikkhave bhikkhu kāye kāyānupassī viharati.*

puna ca paraṃ bhikkhave bhikkhu seyyathā pi passeyya sarīraṃ sīvathikāya chaḍḍitaṃ aṭṭhikāni apagatasambandhāni[580] *disā vidisāsu*[581] *vikkhittāni, aññena hatthaṭṭhikaṃ, aññena pādaṭṭhikaṃ, ...,*[582] *aññena jaṅghaṭṭhikaṃ, aññena ūraṭṭhikaṃ,*[583] *aññena kaṭaṭṭhikaṃ,*[584] *...,*[585] *aññena piṭṭhikaṇṭakaṃ,*[586] *...,*[587] *aññena sīsakaṭāhaṃ, so imam eva*

576. DN 22: 1–35.34. B^e (abbreviated): *kho.*

577. DN 22: 1–36.06. B^e: *aṭṭhikasaṅkhalikaṃ.*

578. DN 22: 1–36.31. B^e (abbreviated) and S^e (abbreviated): *evaṃ.*

579. DN 22: 1–38.07. B^e (abbreviated) and C^e: *kho.*

580. DN 22: 1–38.37. S^e: *apagatanahārusambandhāni.*

581. DN 22: 1–38.43. B^e and S^e: *vidisā.*

582. DN 22: 1–38.56. B^e: *aññena gopphakaṭṭhikaṃ,* C^e: *aññena gopaphaṭṭhikaṃ.*

583. DN 22: 1–39.02. B^e and S^e: *ūruṭṭhikaṃ.*

584. DN 22: 1–39.07. B^e: *kaṭiṭṭhikaṃ.*

585. DN 22: 1–39.08. B^e: *aññena phāsukaṭṭhikaṃ.*

586. DN 22: 1–39.10. B^e and C^e: *piṭṭhiṭṭhikaṃ* (C^e also has *aññena kaṭiṭṭhikaṃ* after this, instead of before it), S^e: *piṭṭhaṭṭhikaṃ.*

587. DN 22: 1–39.13. B^e: *aññena khandhaṭṭhikaṃ, aññena gīvaṭṭhikaṃ, aññena hanukaṭṭhikaṃ, aññena dantaṭṭhikaṃ.* C^e: *aññena khandhaṭṭhikaṃ, aññena gīvaṭṭhikaṃ, aññena dantaṭṭhikaṃ.* S^e: *aññena kaṇṭakaṭṭhikaṃ, aññena phāsukaṭṭhikaṃ, aññena uraṭṭhikaṃ, aññena aṃsaṭṭhikaṃ, aññena bāhuṭṭhikaṃ, aññena gīvaṭṭhikaṃ, aññena hanukaṭṭhikaṃ, aññena dantaṭṭhikaṃ* (E^e notes additional terms as variants).

kāyaṃ upasaṃharati: ayam pi kho kāyo evaṃdhammo evaṃbhāvī etaṃ[588] *anatīto ti.*

iti ajjhattaṃ vā kāye kāyānupassī viharati, bahiddhā vā kāye kāyānupassī viharati, ajjhattabahiddhā vā kāye kāyānupassī viharati. samudayadhammānupassī vā kāyasmiṃ viharati, vayadhammānupassī vā kāyasmiṃ viharati, samudayavayadhammānupassī vā kāyasmiṃ viharati.

atthi kāyo ti vā pan' assa sati paccupaṭṭhitā hoti yāvad eva ñāṇamattāya paṭissatimattāya. anissito ca viharati, na ca kiñci loke upādiyati. evam pi...[589] *bhikkhave bhikkhu kāye kāyānupassī viharati.*

puna ca paraṃ bhikkhave bhikkhu seyyathā pi passeyya sarīraṃ sīvathikāya[590] *chaḍḍitaṃ aṭṭhikāni setāni saṅkhavaṇṇūpanibhāni,*[591] *so imam eva kāyaṃ upasaṃharati: ayam pi kho kāyo evaṃdhammo evaṃbhāvī etaṃ*[592] *anatīto ti.*

iti ajjhattaṃ vā kāye kāyānupassī viharati, bahiddhā vā kāye kāyānupassī viharati, ajjhattabahiddhā vā kāye kāyānupassī viharati. samudayadhammānupassī vā kāyasmiṃ viharati, vayadhammānupassī vā kāyasmiṃ viharati, samudayavayadhammānupassī vā kāyasmiṃ viharati.

atthi kāyo ti vā pan' assa sati paccupaṭṭhitā hoti yāvad eva ñāṇamattāya paṭissatimattāya. anissito ca viharati, na ca kiñci loke upādiyati. evam pi...[593] *bhikkhave bhikkhu kāye kāyānupassī viharati.*

puna ca paraṃ bhikkhave bhikkhu seyyathā pi passeyya sarīraṃ sīvathikāya chaḍḍitaṃ aṭṭhikāni puñjakitāni terovassikāni, so imam eva kāyaṃ upasaṃharati: ayam pi kho kāyo evaṃdhammo evaṃbhāvī etaṃ[594] *anatīto ti.*[595]

iti ajjhattaṃ vā kāye kāyānupassī viharati, bahiddhā vā kāye kāyānupassī viharati, ajjhattabahiddhā vā kāye kāyānupassī viharati. samudaya-

588. DN 22: 1–39.38. B^{e} and S^{e}: *evaṃ*.

589. DN 22: 1–41.25. B^{e} (abbreviated): *kho*.

590. DN 22: 1–41.48. E^{e}: *sīvathikāyo*.

591. DN 22: 1–42.00. B^{e}: *saṅkhavaṇṇapaṭibhāgāni*, S^{e}: *saṅkhavaṇṇasannibhāni* (with *saṅkhavaṇṇūpanibhāni* noted in S^{e} as a variant).

592. DN 22: 1–42.25. B^{e} (abbreviated) and S^{e} (abbreviated): *evaṃ*.

593. DN 22: 1–44.13. B^{e} (abbreviated): *kho*.

594. DN 22: 1–45.18. B^{e} (abbreviated) and S^{e} (abbreviated): *evaṃ*.

595. End of tape 1, beginning of tape 2.

dhammānupassī vā kāyasmiṃ viharati, vayadhammānupassī vā kāyasmiṃ viharati, samudayavayadhammānupassī vā kāyasmiṃ viharati.

atthi kāyo ti vā pan' assa sati paccupaṭṭhitā hoti yāvad eva ñāṇamattāya paṭissatimattāya. anissito ca viharati, na ca kiñci loke upādiyati. evam pi...[596] *bhikkhave bhikkhu kāye kāyānupassī viharati.*

puna ca paraṃ bhikkhave bhikkhu seyyathā pi passeyya sarīraṃ sīvathikāya chaḍḍitaṃ aṭṭhikāni pūtīni cuṇṇakajātāni, so imam eva kāyaṃ upasaṃharati: ayam pi kho kāyo evaṃdhammo evaṃbhāvī etaṃ[597] *anatīto ti.*

iti ajjhattaṃ vā kāye kāyānupassī viharati, bahiddhā vā kāye kāyānupassī viharati, ajjhattabahiddhā vā kāye kāyānupassī viharati. samudayadhammānupassī vā kāyasmiṃ viharati, vayadhammānupassī vā kāyasmiṃ viharati, samudayavayadhammānupassī vā kāyasmiṃ viharati.

atthi kāyo ti vā pan' assa sati paccupaṭṭhitā hoti yāvad eva ñāṇamattāya paṭissatimattāya. anissito ca viharati, na ca kiñci loke upādiyati. evam pi...[598] *bhikkhave bhikkhu kāye kāyānupassī viharati.*

kathañ ca...[599] *bhikkhave bhikkhu vedanāsu vedanānupassī viharati?*

idha bhikkhave bhikkhu sukhaṃ...[600] *vedanaṃ vediyamāno:*[601] *sukhaṃ vedanaṃ vediyāmī*[602] *ti pajānāti. dukkhaṃ...*[603] *vedanaṃ vediyamāno:*[604] *dukkhaṃ vedanaṃ vediyāmī*[605] *ti pajānāti. adukkhamasukhaṃ...*[606] *vedanaṃ vediyamāno:*[607] *adukkhamasukhaṃ vedanaṃ vediyāmī*[608] *ti pajānāti.*

596. DN 22: 2–01.41. Be (abbreviated): *kho.*

597. DN 22: 2–02.36. Be and Se: *evaṃ.*

598. DN 22: 2–04.14. Be: *kho.*

599. DN 22: 2–04.26. Be: *pana.*

600. DN 22: 2–04.40. Be and Se: *vā.*

601. DN 22: 2–04.43. Be and Se: *vedayamāno.*

602. DN 22: 2–04.50. Be and Se: *vedayāmī.*

603. DN 22: 2–04.58. Be and Se: *vā.*

604. DN 22: 2–04.59. Be and Se: *vedayamāno.*

605. DN 22: 2–05.05. Be and Se: *vedayāmī.*

606. DN 22: 2–05.14. Be and Se: *vā.*

607. DN 22: 2–05.16. Be and Se: *vedayamāno.*

608. DN 22: 2–05.24. Be and Se: *vedayāmī.*

sāmisaṃ vā sukhaṃ vedanaṃ vediyamāno:[609] *sāmisaṃ sukhaṃ vedanaṃ vediyāmī*[610] *ti pajānāti, nirāmisaṃ vā sukhaṃ vedanaṃ vediyamāno:*[611] *nirāmisaṃ sukhaṃ vedanaṃ vediyāmī*[612] *ti pajānāti. sāmisaṃ vā dukkhaṃ vedanaṃ vediyamāno:*[613] *sāmisaṃ dukkhaṃ vedanaṃ vediyāmī*[614] *ti pajānāti, . . . ,*[615] *sāmisaṃ vā adukkhamasukhaṃ vedanaṃ vediyamāno:*[616] *sāmisaṃ adukkhamasukhaṃ vedanaṃ vediyāmī*[617] *ti pajānāti, nirāmisaṃ vā adukkhamasukhaṃ vedanaṃ vediyamāno:*[618] *nirāmisaṃ adukkhamasukhaṃ vedanaṃ vediyāmī*[619] *ti pajānāti.*

iti ajjhattaṃ vā vedanāsu vedanānupassī viharati, bahiddhā vā vedanāsu vedanānupassī viharati, ajjhattabahiddhā vā vedanāsu vedanānupassī viharati. samudayadhammānupassī vā vedanāsu vedanānupassī[620] *viharati, vayadhammānupassī vā vedanāsu vedanānupassī*[621] *viharati, samudayavayadhammānupassī vā vedanāsu vedanānupassī*[622] *viharati.*

atthi vedanā ti vā pan' assa sati paccupaṭṭhitā hoti yāvad eva ñāṇamattāya paṭissatimattāya. anissito ca viharati, na ca kiñci loke upādiyati. evam. . .[623] *kho bhikkhave bhikkhu vedanāsu vedanānupassī viharati.*

kathañ ca. . .[624] *bhikkhave bhikkhu citte cittānupassī viharati?*

609. DN 22: 2–05.36. B^e and S^e: *vedayamāno.*

610. DN 22: 2–05.45. B^e and S^e: *vedayāmī.*

611. DN 22: 2–05.56. B^e and S^e: *vedayamāno.*

612. DN 22: 2–06.04. B^e and S^e: *vedayāmī.*

613. DN 22: 2–06.16. B^e and S^e: *vedayamāno.*

614. DN 22: 2–06.25. B^e and S^e: *vedayāmī.*

615. DN 22: 2–06.31. B^e and S^e: *nirāmisaṃ vā dukkhaṃ vedanaṃ vedayamāno: nirāmisaṃ dukkhaṃ vedanaṃ vedayāmī ti pajānāti.* C^e and E^e: *nirāmisaṃ vā dukkhaṃ vedanaṃ vediyamāno: nirāmisaṃ dukkhaṃ vedanaṃ vediyāmī ti pajānāti.*

616. DN 22: 2–06.38. B^e and S^e: *vedayamāno.*

617. DN 22: 2–06.47. B^e and S^e: *vedayāmī.*

618. DN 22: 2–07.01. B^e and S^e: *vedayamāno.*

619. DN 22: 2–07.11. B^e and S^e: *vedayāmī.*

620. DN 22: 2–07.56. Not in B^e, C^e, E^e, or S^e.

621. DN 22: 2–08.08. Not in B^e, C^e, E^e, or S^e.

622. DN 22: 2–08.22. Not in B^e, C^e, E^e, or S^e.

623. DN 22: 2–09.01. B^e and C^e: *pi.*

624. DN 22: 2–09.14. B^e and C^e: *pana.*

idha bhikkhave bhikkhu sarāgaṃ vā cittaṃ: sarāgaṃ cittan ti pajānāti, vītarāgaṃ vā cittaṃ: vītarāgaṃ cittan ti pajānāti. sadosaṃ vā cittaṃ: sadosaṃ cittan ti pajānāti, vītadosaṃ vā cittaṃ: vītadosaṃ cittan ti pajānāti. samohaṃ vā cittaṃ: samohaṃ cittan ti pajānāti, vītamohaṃ vā cittaṃ: vītamohaṃ cittan ti pajānāti. saṅkhittaṃ vā[625] *cittaṃ: saṅkhittaṃ cittan ti pajānāti, vikkhittaṃ vā cittaṃ: vikkhittaṃ cittan ti pajānāti.*

mahaggataṃ vā cittaṃ: mahaggataṃ cittan ti pajānāti, amahaggataṃ vā cittaṃ: amahaggataṃ cittan ti pajānāti. sa-uttaraṃ vā cittaṃ: sa-uttaraṃ cittan ti pajānāti, anuttaraṃ vā cittaṃ: anuttaraṃ cittan ti pajānāti. samāhitaṃ vā cittaṃ: samāhitaṃ cittan ti pajānāti, asamāhitaṃ vā cittaṃ: asamāhitaṃ cittan ti pajānāti. vimuttaṃ vā cittaṃ: vimuttaṃ cittan ti pajānāti, avimuttaṃ vā cittaṃ: avimuttaṃ cittan ti pajānāti.

iti ajjhattaṃ vā citte cittānupassī viharati, bahiddhā vā citte cittānupassī viharati, ajjhattabahiddhā vā citte cittānupassī viharati. samudayadhammānupassī vā cittasmiṃ viharati, vayadhammānupassī vā cittasmiṃ viharati, samudayavayadhammānupassī vā cittasmiṃ viharati.

atthi cittan ti vā pan' assa sati paccupaṭṭhitā hoti yāvad eva ñāṇamattāya paṭissatimattāya. anissito ca viharati, na ca kiñci loke upādiyati. evam...[626] *kho bhikkhave bhikkhu citte cittānupassī viharati.*

kathañ[627] *ca...*[628] *bhikkhave bhikkhu dhammesu dhammānupassī viharati?*

idha bhikkhave bhikkhu dhammesu dhammānupassī viharati pañcasu nīvaraṇesu.

kathañ ca...[629] *bhikkhave bhikkhu dhammesu dhammānupassī viharati pañcasu nīvaraṇesu?*

idha bhikkhave bhikkhu santaṃ vā ajjhattaṃ kāmacchandaṃ: atthi me ajjhattaṃ kāmacchando ti pajānāti, asantaṃ vā ajjhattaṃ kāmacchandaṃ: n' atthi me ajjhattaṃ kāmacchando ti pajānāti. yathā ca anuppannassa kāmacchandassa uppādo hoti tañ ca pajānāti, yathā ca

625. DN 22: 2–10.36. Not in Cᵉ.

626. DN 22: 2–13.50. Bᵉ and Cᵉ: *pi.*

627. DN 22: 2–14.01. Cᵉ: *kahiñca.*

628. DN 22: 2–14.03. Bᵉ and Cᵉ: *pana.*

629. DN 22: 2–14.30. Bᵉ and Cᵉ: *pana.*

uppannassa kāmacchandassa pahānaṃ hoti tañ ca pajānāti, yathā ca pahīnassa kāmacchandassa āyatiṃ anuppādo hoti tañ ca pajānāti.

santaṃ vā ajjhattaṃ vyāpādaṃ: atthi me ajjhattaṃ vyāpādo ti pajānāti, asantaṃ vā ajjhattaṃ vyāpādaṃ: n' atthi me ajjhattaṃ vyāpādo ti pajānāti. yathā ca anuppannassa vyāpādassa uppādo hoti tañ ca pajānāti, yathā ca uppannassa vyāpādassa pahānaṃ hoti tañ ca pajānāti, yathā ca pahīnassa vyāpādassa āyatiṃ anuppādo hoti tañ ca pajānāti.

santaṃ vā ajjhattaṃ thīnamiddhaṃ: atthi me ajjhattaṃ thīnamiddhan ti pajānāti, asantaṃ vā ajjhattaṃ thīnamiddhaṃ: n' atthi me ajjhattaṃ thīnamiddhan ti pajānāti. yathā ca anuppannassa thīnamiddhassa uppādo hoti tañ ca pajānāti, yathā ca uppannassa thīnamiddhassa pahānaṃ hoti tañ ca pajānāti, yathā ca pahīnassa thīnamiddhassa āyatiṃ anuppādo hoti tañ ca pajānāti.

santaṃ vā ajjhattaṃ uddhaccakukkuccaṃ: atthi me ajjhattaṃ uddhaccakukkuccan ti pajānāti, asantaṃ vā ajjhattaṃ uddhaccakukkuccaṃ: n' atthi me ajjhattaṃ uddhaccakukkuccan ti pajānāti. yathā ca anuppannassa uddhaccakukkuccassa uppādo hoti tañ ca pajānāti, yathā ca uppannassa uddhaccakukkuccassa pahānaṃ hoti tañ ca pajānāti, yathā ca pahīnassa uddhaccakukkuccassa āyatiṃ anuppādo hoti tañ ca pajānāti.

santaṃ vā ajjhattaṃ vicikicchaṃ: atthi me ajjhattaṃ <u>vicikicchan</u>[630] *ti pajānāti, asantaṃ vā ajjhattaṃ vicikicchaṃ: n' atthi me ajjhattaṃ <u>vicikicchan</u>*[631] *ti pajānāti. yathā ca anuppannāya vicikicchāya uppādo hoti tañ ca pajānāti, yathā ca uppannāya vicikicchāya pahānaṃ hoti tañ ca pajānāti, yathā ca pahīnāya vicikicchāya āyatiṃ anuppādo hoti tañ ca pajānāti.*

iti ajjhattaṃ vā dhammesu dhammānupassī viharati, bahiddhā vā dhammesu dhammānupassī viharati, ajjhattabahiddhā vā dhammesu dhammānupassī viharati. samudayadhammānupassī vā dhammesu viharati, vayadhammānupassī vā dhammesu viharati, samudayavayadhammānupassī vā dhammesu viharati.

atthi dhammā ti vā pan' assa sati paccupaṭṭhitā hoti yāvad eva ñāṇamattāya paṭissatimattāya. anissito ca viharati, na ca kiñci loke

630. DN 22: 2–20.42. B^{e}, C^{e}, E^{e}, and S^{e}: *vicikicchā.*

631. DN 22: 2–20.57. B^{e}, C^{e}, E^{e}, and S^{e}: *vicikicchā.*

upādiyati. evaṃ...[632] *kho bhikkhave bhikkhu dhammesu dhammānupassī viharati...*[633]

puna ca paraṃ bhikkhave bhikkhu dhammesu dhammānupassī viharati pañcas' upādānakkhandhesu.[634]

kathañ ca...[635] *bhikkhave bhikkhu dhammesu dhammānupassī viharati pañcas' upādānakkhandhesu?*[636]

idha bhikkhave bhikkhu: iti rūpaṃ, iti rūpassa samudayo, iti rūpassa atthagamo;[637] *iti vedanā, iti vedanāya samudayo, iti vedanāya atthagamo;*[638] *iti saññā, iti saññāya samudayo, iti saññāya atthagamo;*[639] *iti saṅkhārā, iti saṅkhārānaṃ samudayo, iti saṅkhārānaṃ atthagamo;*[640] *iti viññāṇaṃ, iti viññāṇassa samudayo,*[641] *iti viññāṇassa atthagamo*[642] *ti.*

iti ajjhattaṃ vā dhammesu dhammānupassī viharati, bahiddhā vā dhammesu dhammānupassī viharati, ajjhattabahiddhā vā dhammesu dhammānupassī viharati. samudayadhammānupassī vā dhammesu viharati, vayadhammānupassī vā dhammesu viharati, samudayavayadhammānupassī vā dhammesu viharati.

atthi dhammā ti vā pan' assa sati paccupaṭṭhitā hoti yāvad eva ñāṇamattāya paṭissatimattāya. anissito ca viharati, na ca kiñci loke upādiyati. evaṃ...[643] *kho bhikkhave bhikkhu dhammesu dhammānupassī viharati pañcas' upādānakkhandhesu.*[644]

puna ca paraṃ bhikkhave bhikkhu dhammesu dhammānupassī viharati chasu ajjhattikabāhiresu āyatanesu.

632. DN 22: 2–23.10. Be and Ce: *pi.*

633. DN 22: 2–23.20. Be, Ce, Ee, and Se: *pañcasu nīvaraṇesu.*

634. DN 22: 2–23.33. Be, Ce, and Se: *pañcasu upādānakkhandhesu.*

635. DN 22: 2–23.41. Be and Ce: *pana.*

636. DN 22: 2–23.52. Be, Ce, and Se: *pañcasu upādānakkhandhesu.*

637. DN 22: 2–24.13. Be, Ce, and Se: *atthaṅgamo.*

638. DN 22: 2–24.25. Be, Ce, and Se: *atthaṅgamo.*

639. DN 22: 2–24.37. Be, Ce, and Se: *atthaṅgamo.*

640. DN 22: 2–24.52. Be, Ce, and Se: *atthaṅgamo.*

641. DN 22: 2–24.58. Not in Ce.

642. DN 22: 2–25.07. Be, Ce, and Se: *atthaṅgamo.*

643. DN 22: 2–26.41. Be and Ce: *pi.*

644. DN 22: 2–26.53. Be, Ce, and Se: *pañcasu upādānakkhandhesu.*

kathañ ca...[645] *bhikkhave bhikkhu dhammesu dhammānupassī viharati chasu ajjhattikabāhiresu āyatanesu?*

idha bhikkhave bhikkhu cakkhuñ ca pajānāti, rūpe ca pajānāti, yañ ca tad ubhayaṃ paṭicca uppajjati saṃyojanaṃ tañ ca pajānāti. yathā ca anuppannassa saṃyojanassa uppādo hoti tañ ca pajānāti, yathā ca uppannassa saṃyojanassa pahānaṃ hoti tañ ca pajānāti, yathā ca pahīnassa saṃyojanassa āyatiṃ anuppādo hoti tañ ca pajānāti.

sotañ ca pajānāti, sadde ca pajānāti, yaṃ...[646] *tad ubhayaṃ paṭicca uppajjati saṃyojanaṃ tañ ca pajānāti. yathā ca anuppannassa saṃyojanassa uppādo hoti tañ ca pajānāti, yathā ca uppannassa saṃyojanassa pahānaṃ hoti tañ ca pajānāṭi,*[647] *yathā ca pahīnassa saṃyojanassa āyatiṃ anuppādo hoti tañ ca pajānāti.*

ghānañ ca pajānāti, gandhe ca pajānāti, yañ ca tad ubhayaṃ paṭicca uppajjati saṃyojanaṃ tañ ca pajānāti. yaṭhā ca anuppannassa saṃyojanassa uppādo hoti tañ ca pajānāti, yathā ca uppannassa saṃyojanassa pahānaṃ hoti tañ ca pajānāti, yathā ca pahīnassa saṃyojanassa āyatiṃ anuppādo hoti tañ ca pajānāti.

jivhañ ca pajānāti, rase ca pajānāti, yañ ca tad ubhayaṃ paṭicca uppajjati saṃyojanaṃ tañ ca pajānāti. yathā ca anuppannassa saṃyojanassa uppādo hoti tañ ca pajānāti, yathā ca uppannassa saṃyojanassa pahānaṃ hoti tañ ca pajānāti, yathā ca pahīnassa saṃyojanassa āyatiṃ anuppādo hoti tañ ca pajānāti.

kāyañ ca pajānāti, phoṭṭhabbe ca pajānāti, yañ ca tad ubhayaṃ paṭicca uppajjati saṃyojanaṃ tañ ca pajānāti. yathā ca anuppannassa saṃyojanassa uppādo hoti tañ ca pajānāti, yathā ca uppannassa saṃyojanassa pahānaṃ hoti tañ ca pajānāti, yathā ca pahīnassa saṃyojanassa āyatiṃ anuppādo hoti tañ ca pajānāti.

manañ ca pajānāti, dhamme ca pajānāti, yañ ca tad ubhayaṃ paṭicca uppajjati saṃyojanaṃ tañ ca pajānāti. yathā ca anuppannassa saṃyojanassa uppādo hoti tañ ca pajānāti, yathā ca uppannassa saṃyojanassa pahānaṃ

645. DN 22: 2–27.23. B^e^ and C^e^: *pana.*

646. DN 22: 2–29.12. B^e^, C^e^, E^e^, and S^e^ (the last two editions abbreviate): *yañ ca.*

647. DN 22: 2–29.43. Not in C^e^.

hoti tañ ca pajānāti, yathā ca pahīnassa saṃyojanassa āyatiṃ anuppādo hoti tañ ca pajānāti.

iti ajjhattaṃ vā dhammesu dhammānupassī viharati, bahiddhā vā dhammesu dhammānupassī viharati, ajjhattabahiddhā vā dhammesu dhammānupassī viharati. samudayadhammānupassī vā dhammesu viharati, vayadhammānupassī vā dhammesu viharati, samudayavayadhammānupassī vā dhammesu viharati.

atthi dhammā ti vā pan' assa sati paccupaṭṭhitā hoti yāvad eva ñāṇamattāya paṭissatimattāya. anissito ca viharati, na ca kiñci loke upādiyati. evaṃ...[648] *kho bhikkhave bhikkhu dhammesu dhammānupassī viharati chasu ajjhattikabāhiresu āyatanesu.*[649]

puna ca paraṃ bhikkhave bhikkhu dhammesu dhammānupassī viharati sattasu bojjhaṅgesu.

kathañ ca...[650] *bhikkhave bhikkhu dhammesu dhammānupassī viharati sattasu bojjhaṅgesu?*

idha bhikkhave bhikkhu santaṃ vā ajjhattaṃ satisambojjhaṅgaṃ: atthi me ajjhattaṃ satisambojjhaṅgo ti pajānāti, asantaṃ vā ajjhattaṃ satisambojjhaṅgaṃ: n' atthi me ajjhattaṃ satisambojjhaṅgo ti pajānāti. yathā ca anuppannassa satisambojjhaṅgassa uppādo hoti tañ ca pajānāti, yathā ca uppannassa satisambojjhaṅgassa bhāvanāya[651] *pāripūrī hoti tañ ca pajānāti.*

santaṃ vā ajjhattaṃ dhammavicayasambojjhaṅgaṃ: atthi me ajjhattaṃ dhammavicayasambojjhaṅgo ti pajānāti, asantaṃ vā ajjhattaṃ dhammavicayasambojjhaṅgaṃ: n' atthi me ajjhattaṃ dhammavicayasambojjhaṅgo ti pajānāti. yathā ca anuppannassa dhammavicayasambojjhaṅgassa uppādo hoti tañ ca pajānāti, yathā ca uppannassa dhammavicayasambojjhaṅgassa bhāvanāya[652] *pāripūrī hoti tañ ca pajānāti.*

santaṃ vā ajjhattaṃ viriyasambojjhaṅgaṃ: atthi me ajjhattaṃ viriyasambojjhaṅgo ti pajānāti, asantaṃ vā ajjhattaṃ viriyasambojjhaṅgaṃ:

648. DN 22: 2–36.46. B^{e} and C^{e}: *pi.*

649. End of tape 2, beginning of tape 3.

650. DN 22: 3–00.21. B^{e} and C^{e}: *pana.*

651. DN 22: 3–01.54. S^{e}: *bhāvanā.*

652. DN 22: 3–03.20. S^{e} (abbreviated): *bhāvanā.*

n' atthi me ajjhattaṃ viriyasambojjhaṅgo ti pajānāti. yathā ca anuppannassa viriyasambojjhaṅgassa uppādo hoti tañ ca pajānāti, yathā ca uppannassa viriyasambojjhaṅgassa bhāvanāya[653] *pāripūrī hoti tañ ca pajānāti.*

santaṃ vā ajjhattaṃ pītisambojjhaṅgaṃ: atthi me ajjhattaṃ pītisambojjhaṅgo ti pajānāti, asantaṃ vā ajjhattaṃ pītisambojjhaṅgaṃ: n' atthi me ajjhattaṃ pītisambojjhaṅgo ti pajānāti. yathā ca anuppannassa pītisambojjhaṅgassa uppādo hoti tañ ca pajānāti, yathā ca uppannassa pītisambojjhaṅgassa bhāvanāya[654] *pāripūrī hoti tañ ca pajānāti.*

santaṃ vā ajjhattaṃ passaddhisambojjhaṅgaṃ: atthi me ajjhattaṃ passaddhisambojjhaṅgo ti pajānāti, asantaṃ vā ajjhattaṃ passaddhisambojjhaṅgaṃ: n' atthi me ajjhattaṃ passaddhisambojjhaṅgo ti pajānāti. yathā ca anuppannassa passaddhisambojjhaṅgassa uppādo hoti tañ ca pajānāti, yathā ca uppannassa passaddhisambojjhaṅgassa bhāvanāya[655] *pāripūrī hoti tañ ca pajānāti.*

santaṃ vā ajjhattaṃ samādhisambojjhaṅgaṃ: atthi me ajjhattaṃ samādhisambojjhaṅgo ti pajānāti, asantaṃ vā ajjhattaṃ samādhisambojjhaṅgaṃ: n' atthi me ajjhattaṃ samādhisambojjhaṅgo ti pajānāti. yathā ca anuppannassa samādhisambojjhaṅgassa uppādo hoti tañ ca pajānāti, yathā ca uppannassa samādhisambojjhaṅgassa bhāvanāya[656] *pāripūrī hoti tañ ca pajānāti.*

santaṃ vā ajjhattaṃ upekkhāsambojjhaṅgaṃ: atthi me ajjhattaṃ upekkhāsambojjhaṅgo ti pajānāti, asantaṃ vā ajjhattaṃ upekkhāsambojjhaṅgaṃ: n' atthi me ajjhattaṃ upekkhāsambojjhaṅgo ti pajānāti. yathā ca anuppannassa upekkhāsambojjhaṅgassa uppādo hoti tañ ca pajānāti, yathā ca uppannassa upekkhāsambojjhaṅgassa bhāvanāya[657] *pāripūrī hoti tañ ca pajānāti.*

iti ajjhattaṃ vā dhammesu dhammānupassī viharati, bahiddhā vā dhammesu dhammānupassī viharati, ajjhattabahiddhā vā dhammesu dhammānupassī viharati. samudayadhammānupassī vā dhammesu viha-

653. DN 22: 3–04.45. S^e (abbreviated): *bhāvanā.*

654. DN 22: 3–06.05. S^e (abbreviated): *bhāvanā.*

655. DN 22: 3–07.26. S^e (abbreviated): *bhāvanā.*

656. DN 22: 3–08.46. S^e (abbreviated): *bhāvanā.*

657. DN 22: 3–10.04. S^e: *bhāvanā.*

rati, vayadhammānupassī vā dhammesu viharati, samudayavayadhammānupassī vā dhammesu viharati.

atthi dhammā ti vā pan' assa sati paccupaṭṭhitā hoti yāvad eva ñāṇamattāya paṭissatimattāya. anissito ca viharati, na ca kiñci loke upādiyati. evaṃ...[658] *kho bhikkhave bhikkhu dhammesu dhammānupassī viharati sattasu bojjhaṅgesu.*

puna ca paraṃ bhikkhave bhikkhu dhammesu dhammānupassī viharati catusu ariyasaccesu.

kathañ ca...[659] *bhikkhave bhikkhu dhammesu dhammānupassī viharati catusu ariyasaccesu?*

idha bhikkhave bhikkhu idaṃ dukkhan ti yathābhūtaṃ pajānāti, ayaṃ dukkhasamudayo ti yathābhūtaṃ pajānāti, ayaṃ dukkhanirodho ti yathābhūtaṃ pajānāti, ayaṃ dukkhanirodhagāminī paṭipadā ti yathābhūtaṃ pajānāti.

katamañ ca bhikkhave dukkhaṃ ariyasaccaṃ?

jāti pi dukkhā, jarā pi dukkhā, vyādhi pi dukkho,[660] *maraṇam pi dukkhaṃ, sokaparidevadukkhadomanassupāyāsā pi dukkhā, ...,*[661] *yam p' icchaṃ na labhati tam pi dukkhaṃ, saṅkhittena pañcupādānakkhandhā...*[662] *dukkhā.*

katamā ca bhikkhave jāti?

yā tesaṃ tesaṃ sattānaṃ tamhi tamhi sattanikāye jāti sañjāti okkanti...[663] *abhinibbanti*[664] *khandhānaṃ pātubhāvo āyatanānaṃ paṭilābho, ayaṃ vuccati bhikkhave jāti.*

katamā ca bhikkhave jarā?

yā tesaṃ tesaṃ sattānaṃ tamhi tamhi sattanikāye jarā jīraṇatā

658. DN 22: 3–11.40. Be and Ce: *pi.*

659. DN 22: 3–12.14. Be and Ce: *pana.*

660. DN 22: 3–13.32. Not in Be, Ce, or Se; Ee has *dukkhā.*

661. DN 22: 3–13.48. Be and Se: *appiyehi sampayogo pi dukkho, piyehi vippayogo pi dukkho,* Ce: *appiyehi sampayogo dukkho, piyehi vippayogo dukkho* (the whole phrase is noted in Ee as a variant).

662. DN 22: 3–13.59. Ce: *pi.*

663. DN 22: 3–14.26. Se: *nibbatti.*

664. DN 22: 3–14.27. Be, Ee, and Se: *abhinibbatti.*

khaṇḍiccaṃ pāliccaṃ valittacatā āyuno saṃhāni indriyānaṃ paripāko, ayaṃ vuccati bhikkhave jarā.[665]

katamañ ca bhikkhave maraṇaṃ?

yā[666] *tesaṃ tesaṃ sattānaṃ tamhā tamhā sattanikāyā cuti cavanatā bhedo antaradhānaṃ maccu maraṇaṃ kālakiriyā khandhānaṃ bhedo kaḷebarassa nikkhepo. . .,*[667] *idaṃ vuccati bhikkhave maraṇaṃ.*

katamo ca bhikkhave soko?

yo kho bhikkhave aññataraññatarena vyasanena samannāgatassa aññataraññatarena dukkhadhammena phuṭṭhassa soko socanā socitattaṃ antosoko antoparisoko, ayaṃ vuccati bhikkhave soko.

katama[668] *ca bhikkhave paridevo?*

yo kho bhikkhave aññataraññatarena vyasanena samannāgatassa aññataraññatarena dukkhadhammena phuṭṭhassa ādevo paridevo ādevanā paridevanā ādevitattaṃ paridevitattaṃ, ayaṃ vuccati bhikkhave paridevo.

katamañ ca bhikkhave dukkhaṃ?

yaṃ kho bhikkhave kāyikaṃ dukkhaṃ kāyikaṃ asātaṃ kāyasamphassajaṃ dukkhaṃ asātaṃ vedayitaṃ, idaṃ vuccati bhikkhave dukkhaṃ.

katamañ ca bhikkhave domanassaṃ?

yaṃ kho bhikkhave cetasikaṃ dukkhaṃ cetasikaṃ asātaṃ manosamphassajaṃ dukkhaṃ asātaṃ vedayitaṃ, idaṃ vuccati bhikkhave domanassaṃ.

katamo ca bhikkhave upāyāso?

yo kho bhikkhave aññataraññatarena vyasanena samannāgatassa aññataraññatarena dukkhadhammena phuṭṭhassa āyāso upāyāso āyāsitattaṃ upāyāsitattaṃ, ayaṃ vuccati bhikkhave upāyāso.

. . .[669]

665. Tape 5 begins here.

666. DN 22: 3–15.39 (= 5–00.09). B^e^, C^e^, and E^e^: *yam* (with *yā* noted in E^e^ as a variant).

667. DN 22: 3–16.14 (= 5–00.39). B^e^ and C^e^: *jīvitindriyassupacchedo* (E^e^ notes the phrase as a variant), S^e^: *jīvitindriyassa upacchedo.*

668. DN 22: 3–17.10 (= 5–01.31). B^e^, C^e^, E^e^, and S^e^: *katamo.*

669. DN 22: 3–19.49 (= 5–04.09). B^e^: *katamo ca bhikkhave appiyehi sampayogo dukkho? idha yassa te honti aniṭṭhā akantā amanāpā rūpā saddā gandhā rasā phoṭṭhabbā dhammā, ye vā pan' assa te honti anatthakāmā ahitakāmā aphāsukakāmā ayogakkhemakāmā, yā*

katamañ ca bhikkhave yam p' iccham na labhati tam pi dukkhaṃ? jātidhammānaṃ bhikkhave sattānaṃ evaṃ icchā uppajjati: aho vata mayaṃ na jātidhammā assāma, na ca vata no jāti āgaccheyyā ti. na kho pan' etaṃ icchāya pattabbaṃ, idam pi yam p' icchaṃ na labhati tam pi dukkhaṃ.

jarādhammānaṃ bhikkhave sattānaṃ evaṃ icchā uppajjati: aho vata mayaṃ na jarādhammā assāma, na ca vata no jarā āgaccheyyā ti. na kho pan' etaṃ icchāya pattabbaṃ, idam pi yam p' icchaṃ na labhati tam pi dukkhaṃ.

vyādhidhammānaṃ bhikkhave sattānaṃ evaṃ icchā uppajjati: aho vata mayaṃ na vyādhidhammā assāma, na ca vata no vyādhi āgaccheyyā ti. na kho pan' etaṃ icchāya pattabbaṃ, idam pi yam p' icchaṃ na labhati tam pi dukkhaṃ.

maraṇadhammānaṃ bhikkhave sattānaṃ evaṃ icchā uppajjati: aho vata mayaṃ na maraṇadhammā assāma, na ca vata no maraṇaṃ āgaccheyyā ti. na kho pan' etaṃ icchāya pattabbaṃ, idam pi yam p' icchaṃ na labhati tam pi dukkhaṃ.

---

tehi saddhiṃ saṅgati samāgamo samodhānaṃ missībhāvo, ayaṃ vuccati bhikkhave appiyehi sampayogo dukkho. katamo ca bhikkhave piyehi vippayogo dukkho? idha yassa te honti iṭṭhā kantā manāpā rūpā saddā gandhā rasā phoṭṭhabbā dhammā, ye vā pan' assa te honti atthakāmā hitakāmā phāsukakāmā yogakkhemakāmā mātā vā pitā vā bhātā vā bhaginī vā mittā vā amaccā vā ñātisālohitā vā, yā tehi saddhiṃ asaṅgati asamāgamo asamodhānaṃ amissībhāvo, ayaṃ vuccati bhikkhave piyehi vippayogo dukkho. C^{e}: *katamo ca bhikkhave appiyehi sampayogo dukkho? idha yassa te honti aniṭṭhā akantā amanāpā rūpā saddā gandhā rasā phoṭṭhabbā dhammā, ye vā pan' assa te honti anatthakāmā ahitakāmā aphāsukakāmā ayogakkhemakāmā, yā tehi saddhiṃ saṅgati samāgamo samodhānaṃ missībhāvo, ayaṃ vuccati bhikkhave appiyehi sampayogo dukkho. katamo ca bhikkhave piyehi vippayogo dukkho? idha yassa te honti iṭṭhā kantā manāpā rūpā saddā gandhā rasā phoṭṭhabbā dhammā, ye vā pan' assa te honti atthakāmā hitakāmā phāsukakāmā yogakkhemakāmā mātā vā pitā vā bhātā vā bhaginī vā jeṭṭhā vā kaniṭṭhā vā mittā vā amaccā vā ñāti sālohitā vā, yā tehi saddhiṃ asaṅgati asamāgamo asamodhānaṃ amissībhāvo, ayaṃ vuccati bhikkhave piyehi vippayogo dukkho* (E^{e} notes the presence of the whole passage as a variant). S^{e}: *katamo ca bhikkhave appiyehi sampayogo dukkho? idha yassa te honti aniṭṭhā akantā amanāpā rūpā saddā gandhā rasā phoṭṭhabbā, ye vā pan' assa honti anatthakāmā ahitakāmā aphāsukakāmā ayogakkhemakāmā, tesaṃ saṅgati samāgamo samodhānaṃ missībhāvo, ayaṃ vuccati bhikkhave appiyehi sampayogo dukkho. katamo ca bhikkhave piyehi vippayogo dukkho? idha yassa te honti iṭṭhā kantā manāpā rūpā saddā gandhā rasā phoṭṭhabbā, ye vā pan' assa honti atthakāmā hitakāmā phāsukakāmā yogakkhemakāmā mātā vā pitā vā bhātā vā bhaginī vā mittā vā amaccā vā ñātisālohitā vā, tesaṃ asaṅgati asamāgamo asamodhānaṃ amissībhāvo, ayaṃ vuccati bhikkhave piyehi vippayogo dukkho* (the absence of the whole section is noted in S^{e} as a variant).

sokadhammānaṃ[670] *bhikkhave sattānaṃ evaṃ icchā uppajjati: aho vata mayaṃ na sokadhammā assāma, na ca vata no soko āgaccheyyā ti. na kho pan' etaṃ icchāya pattabbaṃ, idam pi yam p' icchaṃ na labhati tam pi dukkhaṃ.*

paridevadhammānaṃ[671] *bhikkhave sattānaṃ evaṃ icchā uppajjati: aho vata mayaṃ na paridevadhammā assāma, na ca vata no paridevo āgaccheyyā ti. na kho pan' etaṃ icchāya pattabbaṃ, idam pi yam p' icchaṃ na labhati tam pi dukkhaṃ.*

dukkhadhammānaṃ[672] *bhikkhave sattānaṃ evaṃ icchā uppajjati: aho vata mayaṃ na dukkhadhammā assāma, na ca vata no dukkhaṃ āgaccheyyā ti. na kho pan' etaṃ icchāya pattabbaṃ, idam pi yam p' icchaṃ na labhati tam pi dukkhaṃ.*

domanassadhammānaṃ[673] *bhikkhave sattānaṃ evaṃ icchā uppajjati: aho vata mayaṃ na domanassadhammā assāma, na ca vata no domanassaṃ āgaccheyyā ti. na kho pan' etaṃ icchāya pattabbaṃ, idam pi yam p' icchaṃ na labhati tam pi dukkhaṃ.*

upāyāsadhammānaṃ[674] *bhikkhave sattānaṃ evaṃ icchā uppajjati: aho vata mayaṃ na upāyāsadhammā assāma, na ca vata no upāyāso āgaccheyyā ti. na kho pan' etaṃ icchāya pattabbaṃ, idam pi yam p' icchaṃ na labhati tam pi dukkhaṃ.*

katame[675] *ca bhikkhave saṅkhittena pañc' upādānakkhandhā dukkhā?*

670. DN 22: 3–22.51 (= 5–07.04). Bᵉ: *sokaparidevadukkhadomanass' upāyāsadhammānaṃ bhikkhave sattānaṃ evaṃ icchā uppajjati: aho vata mayaṃ na sokaparidevadukkhadomanass' upāyāsā assāma, na ca vata no sokaparidevadukkhadomanass' upāyāsadhammā āgaccheyyun ti. na kho pan' etaṃ icchāya pattabbaṃ, idam pi yam p' icchaṃ na labhati tam pi dukkhaṃ.* Eᵉ and Sᵉ: *sokaparidevadukkhadomanass' upāyāsadhammānaṃ bhikkhave sattānaṃ evaṃ icchā uppajjati: aho vata mayaṃ na sokaparidevadukkhadomanass' upāyāsadhammā assāma, na ca vata no sokaparidevadukkhadomanass' upāyāsā āgaccheyyun ti. na kho pan' etaṃ icchāya pattabbaṃ, idam pi yam p' icchaṃ na labhati tam pi dukkhaṃ* (Eᵉ notes the application of the formula to each individual term as a variant).

671. See above comment on DN 22: 3–22.51.

672. See above comment on DN 22: 3–22.51.

673. See above comment on DN 22: 3–22.51.

674. See above comment on DN 22: 3–22.51.

675. DN 22: 3–26.09 has *katame*, but DN 22: 5–10.34 has the incorrect *katamo*.

seyyathi idaṃ[676] *rūpūpādānakkhandho vedanānūpādānakkhandho*[677] *saññūpādānakkhandho saṅkhārūpādānakkhandho viññāṇūpādānakkhandho. ime vuccanti*[678] *bhikkhave saṅkhittena pañc' upādānakkhandhā dukkhā.*

idaṃ vuccati bhikkhave dukkhaṃ ariyasaccaṃ.

katamañ ca bhikkhave dukkhasamudayaṃ[679] *ariyasaccaṃ?*

yāyaṃ taṇhā ponobhavikā nandirāgasahagatā tatra tatrābhinandinī, seyyathi idaṃ[680] *kāmataṇhā bhavataṇhā vibhavataṇhā.*

sā kho pan' esā bhikkhave taṇhā kattha uppajjamānā uppajjati, kattha nivisamānā nivisati? yaṃ loke piyarūpaṃ sātarūpaṃ, etth' esā taṇhā uppajjamānā uppajjati, ettha nivisamānā nivisati.

kiñci[681] *loke piyarūpaṃ sātarūpaṃ, etth' esā taṇhā uppajjamānā uppajjati, ettha nivisamānā nivisati?*[682]

cakkhuṃ[683] *loke piyarūpaṃ sātarūpaṃ, etth' esā taṇhā uppajjamānā uppajjati, ettha nivisamānā nivisati. sotaṃ loke piyarūpaṃ sātarūpaṃ, etth' esā taṇhā uppajjamānā uppajjati, ettha nivisamānā nivisati. ghānaṃ loke piyarūpaṃ sātarūpaṃ, etth' esā taṇhā uppajjamānā uppajjati, ettha nivisamānā nivisati. jivhā loke piyarūpaṃ sātarūpaṃ, etth' esā taṇhā uppajjamānā uppajjati, ettha nivisamānā nivisati. kāyo loke piyarūpaṃ sātarūpaṃ, etth' esā taṇhā uppajjamānā uppajjati, ettha nivisamānā nivisati. mano loke piyarūpaṃ sātarūpaṃ, etth' esā taṇhā uppajjamānā uppajjati, ettha nivisamānā nivisati.*

rūpaṃ[684] *loke piyarūpaṃ sātarūpaṃ, etth' esā taṇhā uppajjamānā*

676. DN 22: 3–26.19; see the comments above in relation to DN 15: 08.25.

677. DN 22: 3–26.27 (= 5–10.54). B^e^: *vedanupādānakkhandho*, C^e^, E^e^, and S^e^: *vedanūpādānakkhandho.*

678. DN 22: 3–26.52 has the incorrect *vuccati*, but DN 22: 5–11.14 the correct *vuccanti.*

679. DN 22: 3–27.15 (= 5–11.38). C^e^ and S^e^: *dukkhasamudayo* (with *dukkhasamudayaṃ* noted in S^e^ as a variant).

680. DN 22: 3–27.35; see the comments above in relation to DN 15: 08.25.

681. DN 22: 3–28.35 (= 5–12.49). B^e^ and S^e^: *kiñca.*

682. DN 22: 3–28.42 (= 5–12.57). Not in B^e^, C^e^, E^e^, or S^e^.

683. DN 22: 3–29.01 (= 5–13.12). B^e^: *cakkhu.*

684. DN 22: 3–31.35 (= 5–15.28). B^e^, C^e^, E^e^, and S^e^: *rūpā* (with *rūpaṃ* noted in E^e^ as a variant).

uppajjati, ettha nivisamānā nivisati. saddā loke piyarūpaṃ sātarūpaṃ, etth' esā taṇhā uppajjamānā uppajjati, ettha nivisamānā nivisati. gandhā loke piyarūpaṃ sātarūpaṃ, etth' esā taṇhā uppajjamānā uppajjati, ettha nivisamānā nivisati. rasā loke piyarūpaṃ sātarūpaṃ, etth' esā taṇhā uppajjamānā uppajjati, ettha nivisamānā nivisati. phoṭṭhabbā loke piyarūpaṃ sātarūpaṃ, etth' esā taṇhā uppajjamānā uppajjati, ettha nivisamānā nivisati. dhammā loke piyarūpaṃ sātarūpaṃ, etth' esā taṇhā uppajjamānā uppajjati, ettha nivisamānā nivisati.

cakkhuviññāṇaṃ loke piyarūpaṃ sātarūpaṃ, etth' esā taṇhā uppajjamānā uppajjati, ettha nivisamānā nivisati. sotaviññāṇaṃ loke piyarūpaṃ sātarūpaṃ, etth' esā taṇhā uppajjamānā uppajjati, ettha nivisamānā nivisati. ghānaviññāṇaṃ loke piyarūpaṃ sātarūpaṃ, etth' esā taṇhā uppajjamānā uppajjati, ettha nivisamānā nivisati. jivhāviññāṇaṃ loke piyarūpaṃ sātarūpaṃ, etth' esā taṇhā uppajjamānā uppajjati, ettha nivisamānā nivisati. kāyaviññāṇaṃ loke piyarūpaṃ sātarūpaṃ, etth' esā taṇhā uppajjamānā uppajjati, ettha nivisamānā nivisati. manoviññāṇaṃ loke piyarūpaṃ sātarūpaṃ, etth' esā taṇhā uppajjamānā uppajjati, ettha nivisamānā nivisati.

cakkhusamphasso loke piyarūpaṃ sātarūpaṃ, etth' esā taṇhā uppajjamānā uppajjati, ettha nivisamānā nivisati. sotasamphasso loke piyarūpaṃ sātarūpaṃ, etth' esā taṇhā uppajjamānā uppajjati, ettha nivisamānā nivisati. ghānasamphasso loke piyarūpaṃ sātarūpaṃ, etth' esā taṇhā uppajjamānā uppajjati, ettha nivisamānā nivisati. jivhāsamphasso loke piyarūpaṃ sātarūpaṃ, etth' esā taṇhā uppajjamānā uppajjati, ettha nivisamānā nivisati. kāyasamphasso loke piyarūpaṃ sātarūpaṃ, etth' esā taṇhā uppajjamānā uppajjati, ettha nivisamānā nivisati. manosamphasso loke piyarūpaṃ sātarūpaṃ, etth' esā taṇhā uppajjamānā uppajjati, ettha nivisamānā nivisati.

cakkhusamphassajā vedanā loke piyarūpaṃ sātarūpaṃ, etth' esā taṇhā uppajjamānā uppajjati, ettha nivisamānā nivisati. sotasamphassajā vedanā loke piyarūpaṃ sātarūpaṃ, etth' esā taṇhā uppajjamānā uppajjati, ettha nivisamānā nivisati. ghānasamphassajā vedanā loke piyarūpaṃ sātarūpaṃ, etth' esā taṇhā uppajjamānā uppajjati, ettha nivisamānā nivisati. jivhāsamphassajā vedanā loke piyarūpaṃ sātarūpaṃ, etth' esā taṇhā uppajjamānā uppajjati, ettha nivisamānā nivisati. kāyasamphassajā vedanā loke piyarūpaṃ sātarūpaṃ, etth' esā taṇhā uppajjamānā uppajjati, ettha nivisamānā nivisati. manosamphassajā vedanā loke piyarūpaṃ sātarūpaṃ, etth' esā taṇhā uppajjamānā uppajjati, ettha nivisamānā nivisati.[685]

rūpasaññā loke piyarūpaṃ sātarūpaṃ, etth' esā taṇhā uppajjamānā uppajjati, ettha nivisamānā nivisati. saddasaññā loke piyarūpaṃ sātarūpaṃ, etth' esā taṇhā uppajjamānā uppajjati, ettha nivisamānā nivisati. gandhasaññā loke piyarūpaṃ sātarūpaṃ, etth' esā taṇhā uppajjamānā uppajjati, ettha nivisamānā nivisati. rasasaññā loke piyarūpaṃ sātarūpaṃ, etth' esā taṇhā uppajjamānā uppajjati, ettha nivisamānā nivisati. phoṭṭhabbasaññā loke piyarūpaṃ sātarūpaṃ, etth' esā taṇhā uppajjamānā uppajjati, ettha nivisamānā nivisati. dhammasaññā loke piyarūpaṃ sātarūpaṃ, etth' esā taṇhā uppajjamānā uppajjati, ettha nivisamānā nivisati.

rūpasañcetanā loke piyarūpaṃ sātarūpaṃ, etth' esā taṇhā uppajjamānā uppajjati, ettha nivisamānā nivisati. saddasañcetanā loke piyarūpaṃ sātarūpaṃ, etth' esā taṇhā uppajjamānā uppajjati, ettha nivisamānā nivisati. gandhasañcetanā loke piyarūpaṃ sātarūpaṃ, etth' esā taṇhā uppajjamānā uppajjati, ettha nivisamānā nivisati. rasasañcetanā loke piyarūpaṃ sātarūpaṃ, etth' esā taṇhā uppajjamānā uppajjati, ettha nivisamānā nivisati. phoṭṭhabbasañcetanā loke piyarūpaṃ sātarūpaṃ, etth' esā taṇhā uppajjamānā uppajjati, ettha nivisamānā nivisati. dhammasañcetanā loke piyarūpaṃ sātarūpaṃ, etth' esā taṇhā uppajjamānā uppajjati, ettha nivisamānā nivisati.

rūpataṇhā loke piyarūpaṃ sātarūpaṃ, etth' esā taṇhā uppajjamānā uppajjati, ettha nivisamānā nivisati. saddataṇhā loke piyarūpaṃ sātarūpaṃ, etth' esā taṇhā uppajjamānā uppajjati, ettha nivisamānā nivisati. gandhataṇhā loke piyarūpaṃ sātarūpaṃ, etth' esā taṇhā uppajjamānā uppajjati, ettha nivisamānā nivisati. rasataṇhā loke piyarūpaṃ sātarūpaṃ, etth' esā taṇhā uppajjamānā uppajjati, ettha nivisamānā nivisati. phoṭṭhabbataṇhā loke piyarūpaṃ sātarūpaṃ, etth' esā taṇhā uppajjamānā uppajjati, ettha nivisamānā nivisati. dhammataṇhā loke piyarūpaṃ

685. End of tape 3, beginning of tape 4.

sātarūpaṃ, etth' esā taṇhā uppajjamānā uppajjati, ettha nivisamānā nivisati.

rūpavitakko loke piyarūpaṃ sātarūpaṃ, etth' esā taṇhā uppajjamānā uppajjati, ettha nivisamānā nivisati. saddavitakko loke piyarūpaṃ sātarūpaṃ, etth' esā taṇhā uppajjamānā uppajjati, ettha nivisamānā nivisati. gandhavitakko loke piyarūpaṃ sātarūpaṃ, etth' esā taṇhā uppajjamānā uppajjati, ettha nivisamānā nivisati. rasavitakko loke piyarūpaṃ sātarūpaṃ, etth' esā taṇhā uppajjamānā uppajjati, ettha nivisamānā nivisati. phoṭṭhabbavitakko loke piyarūpaṃ sātarūpaṃ, etth' esā taṇhā uppajjamānā uppajjati, ettha nivisamānā nivisati. dhammavitakko loke piyarūpaṃ sātarūpaṃ, etth' esā taṇhā uppajjamānā uppajjati, ettha nivisamānā nivisati.

rūpavicāro loke piyarūpaṃ sātarūpaṃ, etth' esā taṇhā uppajjamānā uppajjati, ettha nivisamānā nivisati. saddavicāro loke piyarūpaṃ sātarūpaṃ, etth' esā taṇhā uppajjamānā uppajjati, ettha nivisamānā nivisati. gandhavicāro loke piyarūpaṃ sātarūpaṃ, etth' esā taṇhā uppajjamānā uppajjati, ettha nivisamānā nivisati. rasavicāro loke piyarūpaṃ sātarūpaṃ, etth' esā taṇhā uppajjamānā uppajjati, ettha nivisamānā nivisati. phoṭṭhabbavicāro loke piyarūpaṃ sātarūpaṃ, etth' esā taṇhā uppajjamānā uppajjati, ettha nivisamānā nivisati. dhammavicāro loke piyarūpaṃ sātarūpaṃ, etth' esā taṇhā uppajjamānā uppajjati, ettha nivisamānā nivisati.

idaṃ vuccati bhikkhave dukkhasamudayaṃ[686] *ariyasaccaṃ.*

katamañ ca bhikkhave dukkhanirodhaṃ[687] *ariyasaccaṃ?*

yo tassā yeva taṇhāya asesavirāganirodho cāgo paṭinissaggo mutti anālayo.

sā kho pan' esā bhikkhave taṇhā kattha pahīyamānā pahīyati, kattha nirujjhamānā nirujjhati?

yaṃ loke piyarūpaṃ sātarūpaṃ, etth' esā taṇhā pahīyamānā pahīyati, ettha nirujjhamānā nirujjhati.

686. DN 22: 4–14.23 (= 5–38.50). C^e and S^e: *dukkhasamudayo.*

687. DN 22: 4–14.32 (= 5–39.00). C^e and S^e: *dukkhanirodho* (with *dukkhanirodhaṃ* noted in S^e as a variant).

kiñci[688] *loke piyarūpaṃ sātarūpaṃ, etth' esā taṇhā pahīyamānā pahīyati, ettha nirujjhamānā nirujjhati?*[689]

cakkhuṃ[690] *loke piyarūpaṃ sātarūpaṃ, etth' esā taṇhā pahīyamānā pahīyati, ettha nirujjhamānā nirujjhati. sotaṃ loke piyarūpaṃ sātarūpaṃ, etth' esā taṇhā pahīyamānā pahīyati, ettha nirujjhamānā nirujjhati. ghānaṃ loke piyarūpaṃ sātarūpaṃ, etth' esā taṇhā pahīyamānā pahīyati, ettha nirujjhamānā nirujjhati. jivhā loke piyarūpaṃ sātarūpaṃ, etth' esā taṇhā pahīyamānā pahīyati, ettha nirujjhamānā nirujjhati. kāyo loke piyarūpaṃ sātarūpaṃ, etth' esā taṇhā pahīyamānā pahīyati, ettha nirujjhamānā nirujjhati. mano loke piyarūpaṃ sātarūpaṃ, etth' esā taṇhā pahīyamānā pahīyati, ettha nirujjhamānā nirujjhati.*

rūpaṃ[691] *loke piyarūpaṃ sātạrūpaṃ, etth' esā taṇhā pahīyamānā pahīyati, ettha nirujjhamānā nirujjhati. saddā loke piyarūpaṃ sātarūpaṃ, etth' esā taṇhā pahīyamānā pahīyati, ettha nirujjhamānā nirujjhati. gandhā loke piyarūpaṃ sātarūpaṃ, etth' esā taṇhā pahīyamānā pahīyati, ettha nirujjhamānā nirujjhati. rasā loke piyarūpaṃ sātarūpaṃ, etth' esā taṇhā pahīyamānā pahīyati, ettha nirujjhamānā nirujjhati. phoṭṭhabbā loke piyarūpaṃ sātarūpaṃ, etth' esā taṇhā pahīyamānā pahīyati, ettha nirujjhamānā nirujjhati. dhammā loke piyarūpaṃ sātarūpaṃ, etth' esā taṇhā pahīyamānā pahīyati, ettha nirujjhamānā nirujjhati.*

cakkhuviññāṇaṃ loke piyarūpaṃ sātarūpaṃ, etth' esā taṇhā pahīyamānā pahīyati, ettha nirujjhamānā nirujjhati. sotaviññāṇaṃ loke piyarūpaṃ sātarūpaṃ, etth' esā taṇhā pahīyamānā pahīyati, ettha nirujjhamānā nirujjhati.[692] *ghānaviññāṇaṃ loke piyarūpaṃ sātarūpaṃ, etth' esā taṇhā pahīyamānā pahīyati, ettha nirujjhamānā nirujjhati. jivhāviññāṇaṃ loke piyarūpaṃ sātarūpaṃ, etth' esā taṇhā pahīyamānā pahīyati, ettha nirujjhamānā nirujjhati. kāyaviññāṇaṃ loke piyarūpaṃ sātarūpaṃ, etth' esā taṇhā pahīyamānā pahīyati, ettha nirujjhamānā*

688. DN 22: 4–15.51 (= 5–40.06). Bᵉ, Cᵉ, and Sᵉ: *kiñca*.

689. DN 22: 4–15.59 (= 5–40.12). Not in Bᵉ, Cᵉ, Eᵉ, or Sᵉ (but noted in Eᵉ as a variant).

690. DN 22: 4–16.18 (= 5–40.30). Bᵉ and Cᵉ: *cakkhu*.

691. DN 22: 4–19.03 (= 5–42.46). Bᵉ, Cᵉ, Eᵉ, and Sᵉ: *rūpā* (with *rūpaṃ* noted in Eᵉ as a variant).

692. End of tape 5; beginning of tape 6 with °*viññāṇaṃ* of *ghānaviññāṇaṃ*, thus *ghāna*° is lost with the change of tape; the full term is found in tape 4.

nirujjhati. manoviññāṇaṃ loke piyarūpaṃ sātarūpaṃ, etth' esā taṇhā pahīyamānā pahīyati, ettha nirujjhamānā nirujjhati.

cakkhusamphasso loke piyarūpaṃ sātarūpaṃ, etth' esā taṇhā pahīyamānā pahīyati, ettha nirujjhamānā nirujjhati. sotasamphasso loke piyarūpaṃ sātarūpaṃ, etth' esā taṇhā pahīyamānā pahīyati, ettha nirujjhamānā nirujjhati. ghānasamphasso loke piyarūpaṃ sātarūpaṃ, etth' esā taṇhā pahīyamānā pahīyati, ettha nirujjhamānā nirujjhati. jivhāsamphasso loke piyarūpaṃ sātarūpaṃ, etth' esā taṇhā pahīyamānā pahīyati, ettha nirujjhamānā nirujjhati. kāyasamphasso loke piyarūpaṃ sātarūpaṃ, etth' esā taṇhā pahīyamānā pahīyati, ettha nirujjhamānā nirujjhati. manosamphasso loke piyarūpaṃ sātarūpaṃ, etth' esā taṇhā pahīyamānā pahīyati, ettha nirujjhamānā nirujjhati.

cakkhusamphassajā vedanā loke piyarūpaṃ sātarūpaṃ, etth' esā taṇhā pahīyamānā pahīyati, ettha nirujjhamānā nirujjhati. sotasamphassajā vedanā loke piyarūpaṃ sātarūpaṃ, etth' esā taṇhā pahīyamānā pahīyati, ettha nirujjhamānā nirujjhati. ghānasamphassajā vedanā loke piyarūpaṃ sātarūpaṃ, etth' esā taṇhā pahīyamānā pahīyati, ettha nirujjhamānā nirujjhati. jivhāsamphassajā vedanā loke piyarūpaṃ sātarūpaṃ, etth' esā taṇhā pahīyamānā pahīyati, ettha nirujjhamānā nirujjhati. kāyasamphassajā vedanā loke piyarūpaṃ sātarūpaṃ, etth' esā taṇhā pahīyamānā pahīyati, ettha nirujjhamānā nirujjhati. manosamphassajā vedanā loke piyarūpaṃ sātarūpaṃ, etth' esā taṇhā pahīyamānā pahīyati, ettha nirujjhamānā nirujjhati.

rūpasaññā loke piyarūpaṃ sātarūpaṃ, etth' esā taṇhā pahīyamānā pahīyati, ettha nirujjhamānā nirujjhati. saddasaññā loke piyarūpaṃ sātarūpaṃ, etth' esā taṇhā pahīyamānā pahīyati, ettha nirujjhamānā nirujjhati. gandhasaññā loke piyarūpaṃ sātarūpaṃ, etth' esā taṇhā pahīyamānā pahīyati, ettha nirujjhamānā nirujjhati. rasasaññā loke piyarūpaṃ sātarūpaṃ, etth' esā taṇhā pahīyamānā pahīyati, ettha nirujjhamānā nirujjhati. phoṭṭhabbasaññā loke piyarūpaṃ sātarūpaṃ, etth' esā taṇhā pahīyamānā pahīyati, ettha nirujjhamānā nirujjhati. dhammasaññā loke piyarūpaṃ sātarūpaṃ, etth' esā taṇhā pahīyamānā pahīyati, ettha nirujjhamānā nirujjhati.

rūpasañcetanā loke piyarūpaṃ sātarūpaṃ, etth' esā taṇhā pahīyamānā pahīyati, ettha nirujjhamānā nirujjhati. saddasañcetanā loke piyarūpaṃ sātarūpaṃ, etth' esā taṇhā pahīyamānā pahīyati, ettha nirujjhamānā nirujjhati. gandhasañcetanā loke piyarūpaṃ sātarūpaṃ, etth' esā taṇhā pahīyamānā pahīyati, ettha nirujjhamānā nirujjhati. rasasañcetanā loke piyarūpaṃ sātarūpaṃ, etth' esā taṇhā pahīyamānā pahīyati, ettha nirujjhamānā nirujjhati. phoṭṭhabbasañcetanā loke piyarūpaṃ sātarūpaṃ, etth' esā taṇhā pahīyamānā pahīyati, ettha nirujjhamānā nirujjhati. dhammasañcetanā loke piyarūpaṃ sātarūpaṃ, etth' esā taṇhā pahīyamānā pahīyati, ettha nirujjhamānā nirujjhati.

rūpataṇhā loke piyarūpaṃ sātarūpaṃ, etth' esā taṇhā pahīyamānā pahīyati, ettha nirujjhamānā nirujjhati. saddataṇhā loke piyarūpaṃ sātarūpaṃ, etth' esā taṇhā pahīyamānā pahīyati, ettha nirujjhamānā nirujjhati. gandhataṇhā loke piyarūpaṃ sātarūpaṃ, etth' esā taṇhā pahīyamānā pahīyati, ettha nirujjhamānā nirujjhati. rasataṇhā loke piyarūpaṃ sātarūpaṃ, etth' esā taṇhā pahīyamānā pahīyati, ettha nirujjhamānā nirujjhati. phoṭṭhabbataṇhā loke piyarūpaṃ sātarūpaṃ, etth' esā taṇhā pahīyamānā pahīyati, ettha nirujjhamānā nirujjhati. dhammataṇhā loke piyarūpaṃ sātarūpaṃ, etth' esā taṇhā pahīyamānā pahīyati, ettha nirujjhamānā nirujjhati.

rūpavitakko loke piyarūpaṃ sātarūpaṃ, etth' esā taṇhā pahīyamānā pahīyati, ettha nirujjhamānā nirujjhati. saddavitakko loke piyarūpaṃ sātarūpaṃ, etth' esā taṇhā pahīyamānā pahīyati, ettha nirujjhamānā nirujjhati. gandhavitakko loke piyarūpaṃ sātarūpaṃ, etth' esā taṇhā pahīyamānā pahīyati, ettha nirujjhamānā nirujjhati. rasavitakko loke piyarūpaṃ sātarūpaṃ, etth' esā taṇhā pahīyamānā pahīyati, ettha nirujjhamānā nirujjhati. phoṭṭhabbavitakko loke piyarūpaṃ sātarūpaṃ, etth' esā taṇhā pahīyamānā pahīyati, ettha nirujjhamānā nirujjhati. dhammavitakko loke piyarūpaṃ sātarūpaṃ, etth' esā taṇhā pahīyamānā pahīyati, ettha nirujjhamānā nirujjhati.[693]

rūpavicāro loke piyarūpaṃ sātarūpaṃ, etth' esā taṇhā pahīyamānā pahīyati, ettha nirujjhamānā nirujjhati. saddavicāro loke piyarūpaṃ sātarūpaṃ, etth' esā taṇhā pahīyamānā pahīyati, ettha nirujjhamānā nirujjhati. gandhavicāro loke piyarūpaṃ sātarūpaṃ, etth' esā taṇhā pahīyamānā pahīyati, ettha nirujjhamānā nirujjhati. rasavicāro loke

693. End of tape 4.

piyarūpaṃ sātarūpaṃ, etth' esā taṇhā pahīyamānā pahīyati, ettha nirujjhamānā nirujjhati. phoṭṭhabbavicāro loke piyarūpaṃ sātarūpaṃ, etth' esā taṇhā pahīyamānā pahīyati, ettha nirujjhamānā nirujjhati. dhammavicāro loke piyarūpaṃ sātarūpaṃ, etth' esā taṇhā pahīyamānā pahīyati, ettha nirujjhamānā nirujjhati.

idaṃ vuccati bhikkhave dukkhanirodhaṃ[694] *ariyasaccaṃ.*

katamañ ca bhikkhave dukkhanirodhagāminī paṭipadā ariyasaccaṃ?

ayam eva ariyo aṭṭhaṅgiko maggo, seyyathi idaṃ[695] *sammādiṭṭhi sammāsaṅkappo sammāvācā sammākammanto sammā-ājīvo sammāvāyāmo sammāsati sammā sammādiṭṭhi.*[696]

katamo[697] *ca bhikkhave sammādiṭṭhi?*

yaṃ kho bhikkhave dukkhe ñāṇaṃ dukkhasamudaye ñāṇaṃ dukkhanirodhe ñāṇaṃ dukkhanirodhagāminiyā paṭipadāya ñāṇaṃ, ayaṃ vuccati bhikkhave sammādiṭṭhi.

katamo ca bhikkhave sammāsaṅkappo?

nekkhammasaṅkappo avyāpādasaṅkappo avihiṃsāsaṅkappo, ayaṃ vuccati bhikkhave sammāsaṅkappo.

katamo[698] *ca bhikkhave sammāvācā? musāvādā veramaṇī, pisuṇā vācā*[699] *veramaṇī, pharusā vācā*[700] *veramaṇī, samphappalāpā veramaṇī, ayaṃ vuccati bhikkhave sammāvācā.*

katamo ca bhikkhave sammākammanto?

pāṇātipātā veramaṇī, adinnādānā veramaṇī, kāmesu micchācārā veramaṇī, ayaṃ vuccati bhikkhave sammākammanto.

katamo ca bhikkhave sammā-ājīvo?

694. DN 22: 6–20.45. Ce and Se *dukkhanirodho.*

695. DN 22: 6–21.09; see the comments above in relation to DN 15: 08.25.

696. DN 22: 6–21.36. Be, Ce, Ee, and Se: *sammāsamādhi* (and without another *sammā* preceding the term).

697. DN 22: 6–21.41. Be, Ce, Ee, and Se: *katamā.*

698. DN 22: 6–22.46. Be, Ce, Ee, and Se: *katamā.*

699. DN 22: 6–22.56. Be, Ce, Ee, and Se: *pisuṇāya vācāya* (with *pisuṇā vācā* noted in Ee as a variant).

700. DN 22: 6–23.01. Be, Ce, Ee, and Se: *pharusāya vācāya* (with *pharusā vācā* noted in Ee as a variant).

idha bhikkhave ariyasāvako micchā-ājīvaṃ pahāya sammā-ājīvena jīvikaṃ[701] *kappeti, ayaṃ vuccati bhikkhave sammā-ājīvo.*

katamo ca bhikkhave sammāvāyāmo?

idha bhikkhave bhikkhu anuppannānaṃ pāpakānaṃ akusalānaṃ dhammānaṃ anuppādāya chandaṃ janeti vāyamati viriyaṃ ārabhati cittaṃ paggaṇhāti padahati. uppannānaṃ pāpakānaṃ akusalānaṃ dhammānaṃ pahānāya chandaṃ janeti vāyamati viriyaṃ ārabhati cittaṃ paggaṇhāti padahati. anuppannānaṃ kusalānaṃ dhammānaṃ uppādāya chandaṃ janeti vāyamati viriyaṃ ārabhati cittaṃ paggaṇhāti padahati. uppannānaṃ kusalānaṃ dhammānaṃ ṭhitiyā asammosāya bhiyyobhāvāya vepullāya bhāvanāya pāripūriyā chandaṃ janeti vāyamati viriyaṃ ārabhati cittaṃ paggaṇhāti padahati. ayaṃ vuccati bhikkhave sammāvāyāmo.

katamo[702] *ca bhikkhave sammāsati?*

idha bhikkhave bhikkhu kāye kāyānupassī viharati ātāpī sampajāno satimā vineyya loke abhijjhādomanassaṃ, vedanāsu vedanānupassī viharati ātāpī sampajāno satimā vineyya loke abhijjhādomanassaṃ, citte cittānupassī viharati ātāpī sampajāno satimā vineyya loke abhijjhādomanassaṃ, dhammesu dhammānupassī viharati ātāpī sampajāno satimā vineyya loke abhijjhādomanassaṃ. ayaṃ vuccati bhikkhave sammāsati.

katamo ca bhikkhave sammāsamādhi?

idha bhikkhave bhikkhu vivicc' eva kāmehi vivicca akusalehi dhammehi savitakkaṃ savicāraṃ vivekajaṃ pītisukhaṃ paṭhamajjhānaṃ[703] *upasampajja viharati. vitakkavicārānaṃ vūpasamā ajjhattaṃ sampasādanaṃ cetaso ekodibhāvaṃ avitakkaṃ avicāraṃ samādhijaṃ pītisukhaṃ dutiyajjhānaṃ*[704] *upasampajja viharati. pītiyā ca virāgā upekkhako ca viharati, sato ca sampajāno, sukhañca kāyena paṭisaṃvedeti, yaṃ taṃ*

701. DN 22: 6–24.14. B^{e}: *jīvitaṃ*.

702. DN 22: 6–26.44. B^{e}, C^{e}, E^{e}, and S^{e}: *katamā*.

703. DN 22: 6–29.06. B^{e}, C^{e}, and S^{e}: *paṭhamaṃ jhānaṃ*.

704. DN 22: 6–29.40. B^{e}, C^{e}, and S^{e}: *dutiyaṃ jhānaṃ*.

ariyā ācikkhanti: upekkho[705] *satimā sukhavihārī ti tatiyajjhānaṃ*[706] *upasampajja viharati. sukhassa ca pahānā dukkhassa ca pahānā pubb' eva somanassadomanassānaṃ atthagamā*[707] *adukkhamasukhaṃ upekkhāsatipārisuddhiṃ catutthajjhānaṃ*[708] *upasampajja viharati. ayaṃ vuccati bhikkhave sammāsamādhi.*

idaṃ vuccati bhikkhave dukkhanirodhagāminī paṭipadā ariyasaccaṃ.

iti ajjhattaṃ vā dhammesu dhammānupassī viharati, bahiddhā vā dhammesu dhammānupassī viharati, ajjhattabahiddhā vā dhammesu dhammānupassī viharati. samudayadhammānupassī vā dhammesu viharati, vayadhammānupassī vā dhammesu viharati, samudayavayadhammānupassī vā dhammesu viharati.

atthi dhammā ti vā pan' assa sati paccupaṭṭhitā hoti yāvad eva ñāṇamattāya paṭissatimattāya. anissito ca viharati, na ca kiñci loke upādiyati. evam...[709] *kho bhikkhave bhikkhu dhammesu dhammānupassī viharati catusu ariyasaccesu.*

yo hi koci bhikkhave ime cattāro satipaṭṭhāne evaṃ bhāveyya satta vassāni, tassa dvinnaṃ phalānaṃ aññataraṃ phalaṃ pāṭikaṅkhaṃ: diṭṭh' eva dhamme aññā, sati vā upādisese anāgāmitā...[710]

ekāyano ayaṃ bhikkhave maggo sattānaṃ visuddhiyā sokapariddavānaṃ[711] *samatikkamāya dukkhadomanassānaṃ atthagamāya*[712] *ñāyassa adhigamāya nibbānassa sacchikiriyāya, yad idaṃ cattāro satipaṭṭhānā ti. iti yaṃ taṃ vuttaṃ, idam etaṃ paṭicca vuttan ti.*

705. DN 22: 6–30.13. B^e and C^e: *upekkhako* (S^e abbreviates, but can safely be assumed to stand for the same, as elsewhere it employs *upekkhako* in descriptions of the third *jhāna*), E^e: *upekhako.*

706. DN 22: 6–30.20. B^e, C^e, and S^e: *tatiyaṃ jhānaṃ.*

707. DN 22: 6–30.42. B^e, C^e, and S^e: *atthaṅgamā.*

708. DN 22: 6–30.54. B^e, C^e, and S^e: *catutthaṃ jhānaṃ.*

709. DN 22: 6–32.53. B^e and C^e: *pi.*

710. DN 22: 6–33.52. B^e, C^e, E^e, and S^e continue by working through different time periods of *satipaṭṭhāna* practice with the potential to lead to full awakening or nonreturn (six years, five years, four years, three years, two years, one year, seven months, six months, five months, four months, three months, two months, one month, half a month, and seven days), corresponding to DN 22 from DN II 314,14 to 315,7.

711. DN 22: 6–34.06. B^e and S^e: *sokaparidevānaṃ.*

712. DN 22: 6–34.18. B^e, C^e, and S^e: *atthaṅgamāya.*

idaṃ avoca bhagavā. attamanā te bhikkhū bhagavato bhāsitaṃ abhinandun ti.

SN 22.59 *Anattalakkhaṇa-sutta*[713]

evaṃ me sutaṃ.[714] *ekaṃ samayaṃ bhagavā bārāṇasiyaṃ viharati isipatane migadāye.*[715] *tatra kho bhagavā pañcavaggiye bhikkhū āmantesi:*[716]

bhikkhavo ti.

bhadante ti te bhikkhū bhagavato paccassosuṃ.

bhagavā etad avoca:

rūpaṃ bhikkhave anattā. rūpañ ca h' idaṃ bhikkhave attā abhavissa, na yidaṃ rūpaṃ ābādhāya saṃvatteyya, labbhetha ca rūpe: evaṃ me rūpaṃ hotu, evaṃ me rūpaṃ mā ahosī ti. yasmā ca kho bhikkhave rūpaṃ anattā, tasmā rūpaṃ ābādhāya saṃvattati, na ca labbhatha[717] *rūpe: evaṃ me rūpaṃ hotu, evaṃ me rūpaṃ mā ahosī ti.*

vedanā. . .[718] *anattā. vedanā ca h' idaṃ bhikkhave attā abhavissa, na yidaṃ vedanā ābādhāya saṃvatteyya, labbhetha ca vedanāya: evaṃ me vedanā hotu, evaṃ me vedanā mā ahosī ti. yasmā ca kho bhikkhave vedanā anattā, tasmā vedanā ābādhāya saṃvattati, na ca labbhatha*[719] *vedanāya: evaṃ me vedanā hotu, evaṃ me vedanā mā ahosī ti.*

saññā. . .[720] *anattā. saññā ca h' idaṃ bhikkhave attā abhavissa, na*

713. The recording corresponds to SN 22.59 at SN III 66,23–68,23 and thus has preserved almost the complete discourse, which is also known as the *Pañca-sutta* or the *Pañcavaggiya-sutta*.

714. SN 22: 29.10. Not in Bᵉ, Cᵉ, Eᵉ, or Sᵉ.

715. Eᵉ gives the location in an abbreviated manner just as *bārāṇasiyaṃ nidānaṃ migadāye*, which during actual oral recitation would be expanded to become *ekaṃ samayaṃ bhagavā bārāṇasiyaṃ viharati isipatane migadāye.*

716. Eᵉ and Sᵉ abbreviate the introductory exchange between the Buddha and the monks by following āmantesi just with *la* or *pe* and then having *etad avoca*. Here, too, during actual oral recitation this would be expanded to become: *bhikkhavo ti. bhadante ti te bhikkhū bhagavato paccassosuṃ. bhagavā etad avoca.*

717. SN 22: 30.51. Bᵉ, Cᵉ, Eᵉ, and Sᵉ: *labbhati.*

718. SN 22: 31.09. Cᵉ and Sᵉ add *bhikkhave.*

719. SN 22: 32.03. Bᵉ, Cᵉ (abbreviated), Eᵉ, and Sᵉ: *labbhati.*

720. SN 22: 32.21. Cᵉ and Sᵉ add *bhikkhave.*

yidaṃ saññā ābādhāya saṃvatteyya, labbhetha ca saññā: evaṃ me saññā hotu, evaṃ me saññā mā ahosī ti. yasmā ca kho bhikkhave saññā anattā, tasmā saññā ābādhāya saṃvattati, na ca labbhatha[721] *saññā: evaṃ me saññā hotu, evaṃ me saññā mā ahosī ti.*

saṅkhārā. . .[722] *anattā. saṅkhārā ca h' idaṃ bhikkhave attā abhavissaṃsu, na yidaṃ saṅkhārā ābādhāya saṃvatteyyuṃ, labbhetha ca saṅkhāresu: evaṃ me saṅkhārā hontu, evaṃ me saṅkhārā mā ahesun ti. yasmā ca kho bhikkhave saṅkhārā anattā, tasmā saṅkhārā ābādhāya saṃvattanti, na ca labbhati saṅkhāresu: evaṃ me saṅkhārā hontu, evaṃ me saṅkhārā mā ahesun ti.*

viññāṇaṃ. . .[723] *anattā. viññāṇañ ca*[724] *h' idaṃ bhikkhave attā abhavissa, na yidaṃ viññāṇaṃ ābādhāya saṃvatteyya, labbhetha ca viññāṇe: evaṃ me viññāṇaṃ hotu, evaṃ me viññāṇaṃ mā ahosī ti. yasmā ca kho bhikkhave viññāṇaṃ anattā, tasmā viññāṇaṃ ābādhāya saṃvattati, na ca labbhatha*[725] *viññāṇe: evaṃ me viññāṇaṃ hotu, evaṃ me viññāṇaṃ mā ahosī ti.*

taṃ kiṃ maññatha bhikkhave rūpaṃ niccaṃ vā aniccaṃ vā ti?

aniccaṃ bhante.

yaṃ panāniccaṃ dukkhaṃ vā taṃ sukhaṃ vā ti?

dukkhaṃ bhante.

yaṃ panāniccaṃ dukkhaṃ vipariṇāmadhammaṃ, kallan nu taṃ samanupassituṃ: etaṃ mama, eso' ham asmi, eso me attā ti?

no h' etaṃ bhante.

vedanā niccaṃ vā aniccaṃ vā[726] *ti?*

aniccaṃ bhante.

yaṃ panāniccaṃ dukkhaṃ vā taṃ sukhaṃ vā ti?

721. SN 22: 33.12. B^e (abbreviated), C^e (abbreviated), E^e (abbreviated), and S^e (abbreviated): *labbhati.*

722. SN 22: 33.29. C^e and S^e add *bhikkhave.*

723. SN 22: 34.44. C^e and S^e add *bhikkhave.*

724. SN 22: 34.48. Not in E^e.

725. SN 22: 35.38. B^e, C^e, E^e, and S^e: *labbhati.*

726. SN 22: 36.52. Here and below for *saññā* and *saṅkhārā* the editions abbreviate, which on being filled out in oral recitation should rather be *niccā vā aniccā vā*, etc; this problem continues until 44.02. For a discussion of the grammatical errors, see pages 134–35 .

dukkhaṃ bhante.

yaṃ panāniccaṃ dukkhaṃ vipariṇāmadhammaṃ, kallan nu taṃ samanupassituṃ: etaṃ mama, eso' ham asmi, eso me attā ti?

no h' etaṃ bhante.

saññā niccaṃ vā aniccaṃ vā ti?

aniccaṃ bhante.

yaṃ panāniccaṃ dukkhaṃ vā taṃ sukhaṃ vā ti?

dukkhaṃ bhante.

yaṃ panāniccaṃ dukkhaṃ vipariṇāmadhammaṃ, kallan nu taṃ samanupassituṃ: etaṃ mama, eso' ham asmi, eso me attā ti?

no h' etaṃ bhante.

saṅkhārā niccaṃ vā aniccaṃ vā ti?

aniccaṃ bhante.

yaṃ panāniccaṃ dukkhaṃ vā taṃ sukhaṃ vā ti?

dukkhaṃ bhante.

yaṃ panāniccaṃ dukkhaṃ vipariṇāmadhammaṃ, kallan nu taṃ samanupassituṃ: etaṃ mama, eso' ham asmi, eso me attā ti?

no h' etaṃ bhante.

viññāṇaṃ niccaṃ vā aniccaṃ vā ti?

aniccaṃ bhante.

yaṃ panāniccaṃ dukkhaṃ vā taṃ sukhaṃ vā ti?

dukkhaṃ bhante.

yaṃ panāniccaṃ dukkhaṃ vipariṇāmadhammaṃ, kallan nu taṃ samanupassituṃ: etaṃ mama, eso' ham asmi, eso me attā ti?

no h' etaṃ bhante.

tasmātiha bhikkhave yaṃ kiñci rūpaṃ atītānāgatapaccuppannaṃ ajjhattaṃ vā bahiddhā vā oḷārikaṃ vā sukhumaṃ vā hīnaṃ vā paṇītaṃ vā yaṃ dūre santike vā, sabbaṃ rūpaṃ: n' etaṃ mama, n' eso 'ham asmi, na meso attā ti evam etaṃ yathābhūtaṃ sammappaññāya daṭṭhabbaṃ.

yaṃ kiñci[727] *vedanā atītānāgatapaccuppannaṃ*[728] *ajjhattaṃ*[729] *vā bahiddhā vā oḷārikaṃ vā sukhumaṃ vā hīnaṃ vā paṇītaṃ vā yaṃ*[730] *dūre santike vā, sabbaṃ*[731] *vedanā: n' etaṃ mama, n' eso 'ham asmi, na meso attā ti evam etaṃ yathābhūtaṃ sammappaññāya daṭṭhabbaṃ.*

yaṃ kiñci[732] *saññā atītānāgatapaccuppannaṃ ajjhattaṃ vā bahiddhā vā oḷārikaṃ vā sukhumaṃ vā hīnaṃ vā paṇītaṃ vā yaṃ dūre santike vā, sabbaṃ saññā: n' etaṃ mama, n' eso 'ham asmi, na meso attā ti evam etaṃ yathābhūtaṃ sammappaññāya daṭṭhabbaṃ.*

yaṃ kiñci[733] *saṅkhārā atītānāgatapaccuppannaṃ*[734] *ajjhattaṃ vā bahiddhā vā oḷārikaṃ vā sukhumaṃ vā hīnaṃ vā paṇītaṃ vā yaṃ*[735] *dūre santike vā, sabbaṃ*[736] *saṅkhārā: n' etaṃ mama, n' eso 'ham asmi asmi, na meso attā ti evam etaṃ yathābhūtaṃ sammappaññāya daṭṭhabbaṃ.*

yaṃ kiñci viññāṇaṃ atītānāgatapaccuppannaṃ ajjhattaṃ vā bahiddhā vā oḷārikaṃ vā sukhumaṃ vā hīnaṃ vā paṇītaṃ vā yaṃ dūre santike vā, sabbaṃ viññāṇaṃ: n' etaṃ mama, n' eso 'ham asmi, na meso attā ti evam etaṃ yathābhūtaṃ sammappaññāya daṭṭhabbaṃ.

evaṃ passaṃ bhikkhave sutavā ariyasāvako rūpasmim pi[737] *nibbindati,*

727. SN 22: 41.23. B^e, C^e, E^e, and S^e: *yā kāci* (after mentioning *vedanā* C^e and E^e abbreviate the rest of the exposition, thus in the present case several errors occur that I only note explicitly when they show up against written text that has not been affected by abbreviation).

728. SN 22: 41.26. B^e and S^e: *atītānāgatapaccuppannā* (S^e then abbreviates until *yā dūre*).

729. SN 22: 41.35. B^e: *ajjhattā* (B^e abbreviates from *bahiddhā vā* to *yā dūre*).

730. SN 22: 41.53. B^e and S^e: *yā.*

731. SN 22: 41.59. B^e and S^e: *sabbā.*

732. SN 22: 42.26. B^e, C^e, E^e, and S^e: *yā kāci* (after mentioning *saññā*, B^e, C^e, E^e, and S^e abbreviate the rest of the exposition).

733. SN 22: 43.27. B^e, C^e, E^e, and S^e: *ye keci* (after mentioning *saṅkhārā*, C^e and E^e abbreviate the rest of the exposition).

734. SN 22: 43.31. B^e and S^e: *atītānāgatapaccuppannā* (S^e abbreviates from here to *ye dūre*, B^e from *bahiddhā vā* to *ye dūre*).

735. SN 22: 43.57. B^e and S^e: *ye.*

736. SN 22: 44.02. B^e and S^e: *sabbe.*

737. SN 22: 45.45. Not in E^e.

vedanāya pi⁷³⁸ nibbindati, saññāya pi⁷³⁹ nibbindati, saṅkhāresu pi⁷⁴⁰ nibbindati, viññāṇasmim pi⁷⁴¹ nibbindati.

*nibbindaṃ virajjati, virāgā vimuccati, vimuttasmiṃ vimuttam iti ñāṇaṃ hoti.*⁷⁴²

SN 46.14 Gilāna-sutta (1)⁷⁴³

*evaṃ me sutaṃ.*⁷⁴⁴ *ekaṃ samayaṃ bhagavā rājagahe viharati (veḷuvane kalandakanivāpe).*⁷⁴⁵ *tena kho pana samayena āyasmā mahākassapo pipphaliguhāyaṃ viharati ābādhiko dukkhito bāḷhagilāno.*

atha kho bhagavā sāyaṇhasamayaṃ paṭisallānā vuṭṭhito yen' āyasmā mahākassapo ten' upasaṅkami. upasaṅkamitvā paññatte āsane nisīdi. nisajja kho bhagavā āyasmantaṃ mahākassapaṃ etad avoca:

kacci te kassapa khamanīyaṃ, kacci yāpanīyaṃ, kacci dukkhā vedanā paṭikkamanti, no abhikkamanti, paṭikkamosānaṃ paññāyati, no abhikkamo ti?

na me bhante khamanīyaṃ na yāpanīyaṃ. bāḷhā me dukkhā vedanā abhikkamanti, no paṭikkamanti, abhikkamosānaṃ paññāyati, no paṭikkamo ti.

*satt' ime kassapa bojjhaṅgā mayā sammadakkhātā bhāvitā bahulīkatā abhiññāya sambodhāya nibbānāya saṃvattati.*⁷⁴⁶ *katame satta?*

satisambojjhaṅgo kho kassapa mayā sammadakkhāto bhāvito bahulīkato

---

738. SN 22: 45.50. Not in Eᵉ.

739. SN 22: 45.55. Not in Eᵉ (abbreviated).

740. SN 22: 46.01. Not in Eᵉ (abbreviated).

741. SN 22: 46.07. Not in Eᵉ.

742. SN 22.59 at SN III 68,24 continues with the standard description of awakening, *khīṇā jāti, vusitaṃ brahmacariyaṃ, kataṃ karaṇīyaṃ, nāparaṃ itthattāyā ti pajānāti* (Eᵉ actually reads *khīnā* and *vusitam*, which I have corrected), then reports the delight of the five monks in regard to the exposition received and their attainment of full awakening.

743. The recording corresponds to three consecutive discourses, SN 46.14, SN 46.15, and SN 46.16 at SN V 79,17–81,24, all three of which are completely preserved.

744. SN 46: 00.00. Not in Bᵉ or Sᵉ.

745. The text in brackets is not clearly audible due to the poor quality of the tape.

746. SN 46: 02.58. Bᵉ, Cᵉ, Eᵉ, and Sᵉ: *saṃvattanti*.

abhiññāya sambodhāya nibbānāya saṃvattati. dhammavicayasambojjhaṅgo kho kassapa mayā sammadakkhāto bhāvito bahulīkato abhiññāya sambodhāya nibbānāya saṃvattati. viriyasambojjhaṅgo kho kassapa mayā sammadakkhāto bhāvito bahulīkato abhiññāya sambodhāya nibbānāya saṃvattati. pītisambojjhaṅgo kho kassapa mayā sammadakkhāto bhāvito bahulīkato abhiññāya sambodhāya nibbānāya saṃvattati. passaddhisambojjhaṅgo kho kassapa mayā sammadakkhāto bhāvito bahulīkato abhiññāya sambodhāya nibbānāya saṃvattati. samādhisambojjhaṅgo kho kassapa mayā sammadakkhāto bhāvito bahulīkato abhiññāya sambodhāya nibbānāya saṃvattati. upekkhāsambojjhaṅgo kho kassapa mayā sammadakkhāto bhāvito bahulīkato abhiññāya sambodhāya nibbānāya saṃvattati.

ime kho kassapa satta bojjhaṅgā mayā sammadakkhātā bhāvitā bahulīkatā abhiññāya sambodhāya nibbānāya saṃvattanti.[747]

taggha bhagava bojjhaṅgā, taggha sugata bojjhaṅgā ti.

idam avoca bhagavā. attamano āyasmā mahākassapo bhagavato bhāsitaṃ abhinandi. vuṭṭhāhi ca āyasmā mahākassapo tamhā ābādhā, tathā pahīno ca āyasmato mahākassapassa so ābādho ahosī ti.

SN 46.15 *Gilāna-sutta* (2)

evaṃ me sutaṃ.[748] *ekaṃ samayaṃ bhagavā rājagahe viharati veḷuvane kalandakanivāpe. tena kho pana samayena āyasmā mahāmoggallāno gijjhakūṭe pabbate viharati ābādhiko dukkhito bāḷhagilāno.*

atha kho bhagavā sāyaṇhasamayaṃ paṭisallānā vuṭṭhito yen' āyasmā mahāmoggallāno ten' upasaṅkami. upasaṅkamitvā paññatte āsane nisīdi. nisajja kho bhagavā āyasmantaṃ mahāmoggallānaṃ etad avoca:

kacci te moggallāna khamanīyaṃ, kacci yāpanīyaṃ, kacci dukkhā vedanā paṭikkamanti, no abhikkamanti, paṭikkamosānaṃ paññāyati, no abhikkamo ti?

na me bhante khamanīyaṃ, na yāpanīyaṃ. bāḷhā me dukkhā vedanā

747. SN 46: 07.00. B^e, C^e, E^e, and S^e: *saṃvattantī ti.*

748. SN 46: 08.01. Not in B^e or S^e.

abhikkamanti, no paṭikkamanti, abhikkamosānaṃ paññāyati, no paṭikkamo ti.

satt' ime moggallāna bojjhaṅgā mayā sammadakkhātā bhāvitā bahulīkatā abhiññāya sambodhāya nibbānāya saṃvattanti. katame satta? satisambojjhaṅgo kho moggallāna mayā sammadakkhāto bhāvito bahulīkato abhiññāya sambodhāya nibbānāya saṃvattati. dhammavicayasambojjhaṅgo kho moggallāna mayā sammadakkhāto bhāvito bahulīkato abhiññāya sambodhāya nibbānāya saṃvattati. viriyasambojjhaṅgo kho moggallāna mayā sammadakkhāto bhāvito bahulīkato abhiññāya sambodhāya nibbānāya saṃvattati. pītisambojjhaṅgo kho moggallāna mayā sammadakkhāto bhāvito bahulīkato abhiññāya sambodhāya nibbānāya saṃvattati. passaddhisambojjhaṅgo kho moggallāna mayā sammadakkhāto bhāvito bahulīkato abhiññāya sambodhāya nibbānāya saṃvattati. samādhisambojjhaṅgo kho moggallāna mayā sammadakkhāto bhāvito bahulīkato abhiññāya sambodhāya nibbānāya saṃvattati. upekkhāsambojjhaṅgo kho moggallāna mayā sammadakkhāto bhāvito bahulīkato abhiññāya sambodhāya nibbānāya saṃvattati.

ime kho moggallāna satta bojjhaṅgā mayā sammadakkhātā bhāvitā bahulīkatā abhiññāya sambodhāya nibbānāya saṃvattanti.[749]

taggha bhagava bojjhaṅgā, taggha sugata bojjhaṅgā ti.

idam avoca bhagavā. attamano āyasmā mahāmoggallāno bhagavato bhāsitaṃ abhinandi. vuṭṭhāhi ca āyasmā mahāmoggallāno tamhā ābādhā, tathā pahīno ca āyasmato mahāmoggallānassa so ābādho ahosī ti.

SN 46.16 *Gilāna-sutta* (3)

evaṃ me sutaṃ.[750] *ekaṃ samayaṃ bhagavā rājagahe viharati veḷuvane kalandakanivāpe. tena kho pana samayena bhagavā ābādhiko hoti dukkhito bāḷhagilāno.*

atha kho āyasmā mahācundo sāyaṇhasamayaṃ paṭisallānā vuṭṭhito[751] *yena bhagavā ten' upasaṅkami. upasaṅkamitvā bhagavantaṃ abhivādetvā*

749. SN 46: 15.55. B^{e}, C^{e}, E^{e} (abbreviated), and S^{e}: *saṃvattantī ti.*

750. SN 46: 17.00. Not in B^{e} or S^{e}.

751. SN 46: 17.53. Not in B^{e}, C^{e}, E^{e}, or S^{e}.

ekamantaṃ nisīdi. ekamantaṃ nisinnaṃ kho āyasmantaṃ mahācundaṃ bhagavā etad avoca:

paṭibhantu taṃ cunda bojjhaṅgā ti.

satt' ime bhante bojjhaṅgā bhagavatā sammadakkhātā bhāvitā bahulīkatā abhiññāya sambodhāya nibbānāya saṃvattati.[752] *katame satta?*

satisambojjhaṅgo kho bhante bhagavatā sammadakkhāto bhāvito bahulīkato abhiññāya sambodhāya nibbānāya saṃvattati. dhammavicayasambojjhaṅgo kho bhante bhagavatā sammadakkhāto bhāvito bahulīkato abhiññāya sambodhāya nibbānāya saṃvattati. viriyasambojjhaṅgo kho bhante bhagavatā sammadakkhāto bhāvito bahulīkato abhiññāya sambodhāya nibbānāya saṃvattati. pītisambojjhaṅgo kho bhante bhagavatā sammadakkhāto bhāvito bahulīkato abhiññāya sambodhāya nibbānāya saṃvattati. passaddhisambojjhaṅgo kho bhante bhagavatā sammadakkhāto bhāvito bahulīkato abhiññāya sambodhāya nibbānāya saṃvattati. samādhisambojjhaṅgo kho bhante bhagavatā sammadakkhāto bhāvito bahulīkato abhiññāya sambodhāya nibbānāya saṃvattati. upekkhāsambojjhaṅgo kho bhante bhagavatā sammadakkhāto bhāvito bahulīkato abhiññāya sambodhāya nibbānāya saṃvattati.

ime kho bhante satta bojjhaṅgā bhagavatā sammadakkhātā bhāvitā bahulīkatā abhiññāya sambodhāya nibbānāya saṃvattati.[753]

taggha cunda bojjhaṅgā, taggha cunda bojjhaṅgā ti.

idam avoca āyasmā mahācundo, samanuñño satthā ahosi. vuṭṭhāhi ca bhagavā tamhā ābādhā, tathā pahīno ca bhagavato so ābādho ahosī ti.

SN 56.11 *Dhammacakkappavattana-sutta*[754]

namo tassa bhagavato arahato sammāsambuddhassa.[755]

752. SN 46: 19.16. Be, Ce, Ee, and Se: *saṃvattanti.*

753. SN 46: 23.43. Be, Ce, Ee, and Se: *saṃvattantī ti.*

754. The recording corresponds to SN 56.11 at SN V 420,22–424,11 and thus has preserved the complete discourse.

755. SN 56: 00.00. This is a standard expression of respect usually employed at the outset of an oral recitation. Even though this is not mentioned in any of the editions consulted, this is of no further significance.

evaṃ me sutaṃ.[756] *ekaṃ samayaṃ bhagavā bārāṇasiyaṃ viharati isipatane migadāye. tatra kho bhagavā pañcavaggiye bhikkhū āmantesi:*

dve 'me bhikkhave antā pabbajitena na sevitabbā. . . .[757] *yo cāyaṃ kāmesu kāmasukhallikānuyogo*[758] *hīno gammo pothujjaniko*[759] *anariyo anatthasaṃhito, yo cāyaṃ attakilamathānuyogo dukkho anariyo anatthasaṃhito.*

ete te bhikkhave ubho ante anupagamma[760] *majjhimā paṭipadā tathāgatena abhisambuddhā cakkhukaraṇī ñāṇakaraṇī upasamāya abhiññāya sambodhāya nibbānāya saṃvattati.*

katamā ca sā bhikkhave majjhimā paṭipadā tathāgatena abhisambuddhā cakkhukaraṇī ñāṇakaraṇī upasamāya abhiññāya sambodhāya nibbānāya saṃvattati?

ayam eva ariyo aṭṭhaṅgiko maggo seyyathi idaṃ:[761] *sammādiṭṭhi sammāsaṅkappo sammāvācā sammākammanto sammā-ājīvo sammāvāyāmo sammāsati sammāsamādhi.*

ayaṃ kho sā bhikkhave majjhimā paṭipadā tathāgatena abhisambuddhā cakkhukaraṇī ñāṇakaraṇī upasamāya abhiññāya sambodhāya nibbānāya saṃvattati.

idaṃ kho pana bhikkhave dukkhaṃ ariyasaccaṃ: jāti pi dukkhā, jarā pi dukkhā, vyādhi pi dukkho,[762] *maraṇam pi dukkhaṃ, . . .*[763] *appiyehi sampayogo dukkho, piyehi vippayogo dukkho, yam p' icchaṃ na labhati tam pi dukkhaṃ, saṅkhittena pañc' upādānakkhandhā. . .*[764] *dukkhā.*

idaṃ kho pana bhikkhave dukkhasamudayaṃ[765] *ariyasaccaṃ: yā' yaṃ*

756. SN 56: 00.12. Not in B^e^.

757. SN 56: 00.53. B^e^, E^e^, and S^e^: *katame dve?* (with the absence of this query noted in S^e^ as a variant).

758. SN 56: 01.00. E^e^: *kāmesu khallikānuyogo.*

759. SN 56: 01.08. E^e^: *puthujjanīko* (with *pothujjaniko* noted as a variant).

760. SN 56: 01.39. E^e^: *anupakamma.*

761. SN 56: 02.56; see the comments above in relation to DN 15: 08.25.

762. SN 56: 04.21. E^e^ and S^e^: *dukkhā.*

763. SN 56: 04.26. E^e^: *sokaparidevadukkhadomanassupāyāsā pi dukkhā* (with the absence of this phrase noted in E^e^ as a variant); see also Skilling 1993, 104.

764. SN 56: 04.51. E^e^: *pi* (with its absence noted in E^e^ as a variant).

765. SN 56: 05.00. C^e^ and S^e^: *dukkhasamudayo* (with *dukkhasamudayaṃ* noted in both as *taṇhā ponobhavikā nandirāgasahagatā tatra tatrābhinandinī, seyyathi idaṃ:*[766] *kāmataṇhā bhavataṇhā vibhavataṇhā.*

idaṃ kho pana bhikkhave dukkhanirodhaṃ[767] *ariyasaccaṃ: yo tassā yeva taṇhāya asesavirāganirodho cāgo paṭinissaggo mutti anālayo.*

idaṃ kho pana bhikkhave dukkhanirodhagāminī paṭipadā ariyasaccaṃ: ayam eva ariyo aṭṭhaṅgiko maggo, seyyathi idaṃ:[768] *sammādiṭṭhi sammāsaṅkappo sammāvācā sammākammanto sammā-ājīvo sammāvāyāmo sammāsati sammāsamādhi.*

idaṃ dukkhaṃ ariyasaccan ti me bhikkhave pubbe ananussutesu dhammesu cakkhuṃ udapādi ñāṇaṃ udapādi paññā udapādi vijjā udapādi āloko udapādi. taṃ kho pan' idaṃ dukkhaṃ ariyasaccaṃ pariññeyyan ti me bhikkhave pubbe ananussutesu dhammesu cakkhuṃ udapādi ñāṇaṃ udapādi paññā udapādi vijjā udapādi āloko udapādi. taṃ kho pan' idaṃ dukkhaṃ ariyasaccaṃ pariññātan ti me bhikkhave pubbe ananussutesu dhammesu cakkhuṃ udapādi ñāṇaṃ udapādi paññā udapādi vijjā udapādi āloko udapādi.

idaṃ dukkhasamudayaṃ[769] *ariyasaccan ti me bhikkhave pubbe ananussutesu dhammesu cakkhuṃ udapādi ñāṇaṃ udapādi paññā udapādi vijjā udapādi āloko udapādi. taṃ kho pan' idaṃ dukkhasamudayaṃ*[770] *ariyasaccaṃ pahātabban ti me bhikkhave pubbe ananussutesu dhammesu cakkhuṃ udapādi ñāṇaṃ udapādi paññā udapādi vijjā udapādi āloko udapādi. taṃ kho pan' idaṃ dukkhasamudayaṃ*[771] *ariyasaccaṃ pahīnan ti me bhikkhave pubbe ananussutesu dhammesu cakkhuṃ udapādi ñāṇaṃ udapādi paññā udapādi vijjā udapādi āloko udapādi.*

idaṃ dukkhanirodhaṃ[772] *ariyasaccan ti me bhikkhave pubbe ananussutesu dhammesu cakkhuṃ udapādi ñāṇaṃ udapādi paññā udapādi vijjā*

---

a variant).

766. SN 56: 05.20; see the comments above in relation to DN 15: 08.25.

767. SN 56: 05.36. C^{e} and S^{e}: *dukkhanirodho* (with *dukkhanirodhaṃ* noted in both as a variant).

768. SN 56: 06.21; see the comments above in relation to DN 15: 08.25.

769. SN 56: 08.46. C^{e} and S^{e}: *dukkhasamudayo.*

770. SN 56: 09.22. C^{e} and S^{e}: *dukkhasamudayo.*

771. SN 56: 10.02. C^{e} and S^{e} (abbreviated): *dukkhasamudayo.*

772. SN 56: 10.39. C^{e} and S^{e}: *dukkhanirodho.*

udapādi āloko udapādi. taṃ kho pan' idaṃ dukkhanirodhaṃ[773] *ariyasaccaṃ sacchikātabban ti me bhikkhave pubbe ananussutesu dhammesu cakkhuṃ udapādi ñāṇaṃ udapādi paññā udapādi vijjā udapādi āloko udapādi. taṃ kho pan' idaṃ dukkhanirodhaṃ*[774] *ariyasaccaṃ sacchikatan ti me bhikkhave pubbe ananussutesu dhammesu cakkhuṃ udapādi ñāṇaṃ udapādi paññā udapādi vijjā udapādi āloko udapādi.*

idaṃ dukkhanirodhagāminī paṭipadā ariyasaccan ti me bhikkhave pubbe ananussutesu dhammesu cakkhuṃ udapādi ñāṇaṃ udapādi paññā udapādi vijjā udapādi āloko udapādi. taṃ kho pan' idaṃ dukkhanirodhagāminī paṭipadā ariyasaccaṃ bhāvetabban ti me bhikkhave pubbe ananussutesu dhammesu cakkhuṃ udapādi ñāṇaṃ udapādi paññā udapādi vijjā udapādi āloko udapādi. taṃ kho pan' idaṃ dukkhanirodhagāminī paṭipadā ariyasaccaṃ bhāvitan ti me bhikkhave pubbe ananussutesu dhammesu cakkhuṃ udapādi ñāṇaṃ udapādi paññā udapādi vijjā udapādi āloko udapādi.

yāva kīvañ ca me bhikkhave imesu catusu ariyasaccesu evaṃ tiparivaṭṭaṃ dvādas' ākāraṃ yathābhūtaṃ ñāṇadassanaṃ na suvisuddhaṃ ahosi, n' eva tāvāhaṃ bhikkhave sadevake loke samārake sabrahmake sassamaṇabrāhmaṇiyā pajāya sadevamanussāya anuttaraṃ sammāsambodhiṃ abhisambuddho. . .[775] *paccaññāsiṃ.*

yato ca kho me bhikkhave imesu catusu ariyasaccesu evaṃ tiparivaṭṭaṃ dvādas' ākāraṃ yathābhūtaṃ ñāṇadassanaṃ suvisuddhaṃ ahosi, athāhaṃ bhikkhave sadevake loke samārake sabrahmake sassamaṇabrāhmaṇiyā pajāya sadevamanussāya anuttaraṃ sammāsambodhiṃ abhisambuddho. . .[776] *paccaññāsiṃ. ñāṇañ ca pana me dassanaṃ udapādi: akuppā me cetovimutti,*[777] *ayam antimā jāti n' atthi dāni punabbhavo ti.*

idam avoca bhagavā. attamanā pañcavaggiyā bhikkhū bhagavato bhāsitaṃ abhinanduntī ti.[778]

773. SN 56: 11.16. C^e and S^e: *dukkhanirodho.*

774. SN 56: 11.56. C^e and S^e: *dukkhanirodho.*

775. SN 56: 15.40. B^e and E^e: *ti* (with its absence noted in both as a variant).

776. SN 56: 16.41. B^e and E^e: *ti* (with its absence noted in E^e as a variant).

777. SN 56: 16.53. B^e and S^e: *vimutti* (with *cetovimutti* noted in both as a variant).

778. SN 56: 17.22. B^e and S^e: *abhinandun ti,* E^e: *abhinanduṃ.*

imasmiñ ca pana veyyākaraṇasmiṃ bhaññamāne āyasmato koṇḍaññassa virajaṃ vītamalaṃ dhammacakkhuṃ udapādi: yaṃ kiñci samudayadhammaṃ sabban taṃ nirodhadhamman ti.

. . .[779] *pavattite ca pana*[780] *bhagavatā dhammacakke bhummā devā saddamanussāvesuṃ: etaṃ bhagavatā bārāṇasiyaṃ isipatane migadāye anuttaraṃ dhammacakkaṃ pavattitaṃ appativattiyaṃ samaṇena vā brāhmaṇena vā devena vā mārena vā brahmunā vā kenaci vā lokasmin ti.*

bhummānaṃ devānaṃ saddaṃ sutvā cātummahārājikā devā saddamanussāvesuṃ: etaṃ bhagavatā bārāṇasiyaṃ isipatane migadāye anuttaraṃ dhammacakkaṃ pavattitaṃ appativattiyaṃ samaṇena vā brāhmaṇena vā devena vā mārena vā brahmunā vā kenaci vā lokasmin ti.

cātummahārājikānaṃ devānaṃ saddaṃ sutvā tāvatiṃsā devā saddamanussāvesuṃ: etaṃ bhagavatā bārāṇasiyaṃ isipatane migadāye anuttaraṃ dhammacakkaṃ pavattitaṃ appativattiyaṃ samaṇena vā brāhmaṇena vā devena vā mārena vā brahmunā vā kenaci vā lokasmin ti.

tāvatiṃsānaṃ devānaṃ saddaṃ sutvā yāmā devā saddamanussāvesuṃ: etaṃ bhagavatā bārāṇasiyaṃ isipatane migadāye anuttaraṃ dhammacakkaṃ pavattitaṃ appativattiyaṃ samaṇena vā brāhmaṇena vā devena vā mārena vā brahmunā vā kenaci vā lokasmin ti.

yāmānaṃ devānaṃ saddaṃ sutvā tusitā devā saddamanussāvesuṃ. . .

tusitānaṃ devānaṃ saddaṃ sutvā nimmāṇaratī devā saddamanussāvesuṃ. . .

nimmāṇaratīnaṃ devānaṃ saddaṃ sutvā paranimmitavasavattino[781] *devā saddamanussāvesuṃ. . .*

paranimmitavasavattīnaṃ devānaṃ saddaṃ sutvā brahmapārisajjā[782] *devā saddamanussāvesuṃ. . .*

brahmapārisajjānaṃ devānaṃ saddaṃ sutvā brahmapurohitā devā saddamanussāvesuṃ. . .

779. SN 56: 17.57. E^{e}: *evaṃ* (with its absence noted in E^{e} as a variant).

780. SN 56: 18.02. Not in S^{e}.

781. SN 56: 22.30. B^{e}, C^{e}, and S^{e}: *paranimmittavasavattī.*

782. SN 56: 22.47. B^{e}, C^{e}, E^{e}, and S^{e} continue here just with the *brahmakāyikā devā* as the last type of *devas* mentioned, so that the ensuing *devas* in the chanting are not found in any edition.

brahmapurohitānaṃ devānaṃ saddaṃ sutvā mahābrahmā devā saddamanussāvesuṃ...

mahābrahmānaṃ devānaṃ saddaṃ sutvā parittābhā devā saddamanussāvesuṃ...

parittābhānaṃ devānaṃ saddaṃ sutvā appamāṇābhā devā saddamanussāvesuṃ...

appamāṇābhānaṃ devānaṃ saddaṃ sutvā ābhassarā devā saddamanussāvesuṃ...

ābhassarāṇaṃ devānaṃ saddaṃ sutvā parittasubhā devā saddamanussāvesuṃ...

parittasubhānaṃ devānaṃ saddaṃ sutvā appamāṇasubhā devā saddamanussāvesuṃ...

appamāṇasubhānaṃ devānaṃ saddaṃ sutvā subhakiṇhakā devā saddamanussāvesuṃ...

subhakiṇhakānaṃ devānaṃ saddaṃ sutvā vehapphalā devā saddamanussāvesuṃ...

vehapphalānaṃ devānaṃ saddaṃ sutvā avihā devā saddamanussāvesuṃ...

avihānaṃ devānaṃ saddaṃ sutvā atappā devā saddamanussāvesuṃ...

atappānaṃ devānaṃ saddaṃ sutvā sudassā devā saddamanussāvesuṃ...

sudassānaṃ devānaṃ saddaṃ sutvā sudassī devā saddamanussāvesuṃ...

sudassīnaṃ devānaṃ saddaṃ sutvā akaniṭṭhakā devā saddamanussāvesuṃ: etaṃ bhagavatā bārāṇasiyaṃ isipatane migadāye anuttaraṃ dhammacakkaṃ pavattitaṃ appativattiyaṃ samaṇena vā brāhmaṇena vā devena vā mārena vā brahmunā vā kenaci vā lokasmin ti.

iti ha tena khaṇena...[783] *tena muhuttena yāva brahmalokā saddo abbhuggañchi.*[784] *ayañ ca dasasahassa*[785] *lokadhātu saṅkampi sampakampi sampavedhi, appamāṇo ca uḷāro obhāso loke pāturahosi atikkamma*[786] *devānaṃ devānubhāvan ti.*

783. SN 56: 27.21. Be and Ee: *tena layena* (with its absence noted in both as a variant; in Be the expression is given in brackets).

784. SN 56: 27.28. Be, Ee, and Se: *abbhugacchi* (with *abbhugañchi* noted in Ee as a variant).

785. SN 56: 27.34. Be: *dasasahassi*, Ce, Ee, and Se: *dasasahassī*.

786. SN 56: 27.55. Se: *atikkamm' eva* (with *atikkamma* noted in Se as a variant).

atha kho bhagavā udānaṃ udānesi: aññāsi vata bho koṇḍañño, aññāsi vata bho koṇḍañño ti.

iti h' idaṃ āyasmato koṇḍaññassa aññākoṇḍañño[787] *tveva nāmaṃ ahosī ti.*

AN 10.60 *Girimānanda-sutta*[788]

evaṃ me sutaṃ.[789] *ekaṃ samayaṃ bhagavā sāvatthiyaṃ viharati jetavane anāthapiṇḍikassa ārāme. tena kho pana samayena āyasmā girimānando ābādhiko hoti dukkhito bāḷhagilāno.*

atha kho āyasmā ānando yena bhagavā ten' upasaṅkami. upasaṅkamitvā bhagavantaṃ abhivādetvā ekamantaṃ nisīdi. ekamantaṃ nisinno kho āyasmā ānando bhagavantaṃ etad avoca:

āyasmā bhante girimānando ābādhiko...[790] *dukkhito bāḷhagilāno. sādhu bhante bhagavā yen' āyasmā girimānando ten' upasaṅkamatu anukampaṃ upādāyā ti.*

sace kho tvaṃ ānanda girimānandassa bhikkhuno upasaṅkamitvā[791] *dasa saññā bhāseyyāsi, ṭhānaṃ kho pan' etaṃ vijjati yaṃ girimānandassa bhikkhuno dasa saññā sutvā so ābādho ṭhānaso paṭippassambheyya.*

katame[792] *dasa?*

aniccasaññā anattasaññā asubhasaññā ādīnavasaññā pahānasaññā virāgasaññā nirodhasaññā sabbaloke anabhiratasaññā sabbasaṅkhāresu aniccasaññā ānāpānasati.

katamā c' ānanda aniccasaññā?

idh' ānanda bhikkhu araññagato vā rukkhamūlagato vā suññāgāragato vā iti paṭisaṃcikkhati: rūpaṃ aniccaṃ vedanā aniccā saññā aniccā

787. SN 56: 28.34. B^e: *aññāsikoṇḍañño*, E^e: *aññātakoṇḍañño*.

788. The recording corresponds to AN 10.60 at AN V 108,17–112,18 and thus has preserved the complete discourse.

789. AN 10: 00.00. Not in B^e, C^e, E^e, or S^e.

790. AN 10: 01.20. B^e, C^e, E^e, and S^e: *hoti*.

791. AN 10: 01.49. Not in B^e.

792. AN 10: 02.19. B^e, C^e, E^e, and S^e: *katamā*.

saṅkhārā aniccā viññāṇaṃ aniccan ti. iti imesu pañcas' upādānakkhandhesu[793] *aniccānupassī viharati. ayaṃ vuccat' ānanda aniccasaññā.*

katamā c' ānanda anattasaññā?

idh' ānanda bhikkhu araññagato vā rukkhamūlagato vā suññāgāragato vā iti paṭisaṃcikkhati: cakkhuṃ[794] *anattā rūpaṃ*[795] *anattā sotaṃ anattā saddā anattā ghānaṃ anattā gandhā anattā jivhā anattā rasā anattā kāyo anattā phoṭṭhabbā anattā mano anattā dhammā anattā ti. iti imesu chasu ajjhattikabāhiresu āyatanesu anattānupassī viharati. ayaṃ vuccat' ānanda anattasaññā.*

katamā c' ānanda asubhasaññā?

idh' ānanda bhikkhu imam eva kāyaṃ uddhaṃ pādatalā adho kesamatthakā tacapariyantaṃ pūraṃ nānappakārassa[796] *asucino paccavekkhati: atthi imasmiṃ kāye kesā lomā nakhā dantā taco maṃsaṃ nahāru aṭṭhi aṭṭhimiñjā*[797] *vakkaṃ hadayaṃ yakanaṃ kilomakaṃ pihakaṃ papphāsaṃ antaṃ antaguṇaṃ udariyaṃ karīsaṃ matthaluṅgaṃ*[798] *pittaṃ semhaṃ pubbo lohitaṃ sedo medo assu vasā kheḷo siṅghāṇikā lasikā muttan ti. iti imasmiṃ kāye asubhānupassī viharati. ayaṃ vuccat' ānanda asubhasaññā.*

katamā c' ānanda ādīnavasaññā?

idh' ānanda bhikkhu araññagato vā rukkhamūlagato vā suññāgāragato vā iti paṭisañcikkhati: bahu dukkho kho ayaṃ kāyo bahu ādīnavo. . .:[799] *iti imasmiṃ kāye vividhā ābādhā uppajjanti, seyyathi idaṃ:*[800] *cakkhurogo sotarogo ghānarogo jivhārogo kāyarogo sīsarogo kaṇṇarogo mukharogo dantarogo kāso sāso pināso ḍaho jaro kucchirogo muñja*[801] *pakkhandikā sūlā*

793. AN 10: 03.36. Bᵉ, Eᵉ, and Sᵉ: *pañcasu upādānakkhandhesu* (with *pañcas' upādānakkhandhesu* noted in Eᵉ as a variant).

794. AN 10: 04.15. Bᵉ: *cakkhu.*

795. AN 10: 04.17. Bᵉ and Cᵉ: *rūpā* (with *rūpaṃ* noted in Cᵉ as a variant).

796. AN 10: 05.28. Sᵉ: *pūrannānappakārassa.*

797. AN 10: 05.49. Bᵉ, Eᵉ, and Sᵉ: *aṭṭhimiñjaṃ* (with *aṭṭhīmiñjā* noted in Eᵉ as a variant).

798. AN 10: 06.05. Not in Bᵉ, Cᵉ, Eᵉ, or Sᵉ.

799. AN 10: 07.08. Eᵉ and Sᵉ: *ti* (with the absence of *ti* noted in both as a variant).

800. AN 10: 07.17; see the comments above in relation to DN 15: 08.25.

801. AN 10: 07.49. Bᵉ, Cᵉ, Eᵉ, and Sᵉ: *mucchā.*

visūcikā kuṭṭhaṃ gaṇḍā[802] *kilāso soso apamādo*[803] *daddu kaṇḍu kacchu rakhasā*[804] *vitacchikā lohitapittaṃ*[805] *madhumeho aṃsā piḷakā bhagandalā pittasamuṭṭhānā ābādhā semhasamuṭṭhānā ābādhā vātasamuṭṭhānā ābādhā sannipātikā ābādhā utupariṇāmajā ābādhā visamaparihārajā ābādhā opakkamikā ābādhā kammavipākajā ābādhā sītaṃ uṇhaṃ jighañca*[806] *pipāsā uccāro passāvo ti. iti imasmiṃ kāye ādīnavānupassī viharati. ayaṃ vuccat' ānanda ādīnavasaññā.*

katamā c' ānanda pahānasaññā?

idh' ānanda bhikkhu uppannaṃ kāmavitakkaṃ nādhivāseti pajahati vinodeti vyantikaroti anabhāvaṃ gameti. uppannaṃ vyāpādavitakkaṃ nādhivāseti pajahati vinodeti vyantikaroti anabhāvaṃ gameti. uppannaṃ vihiṃsāvitakkaṃ nādhivāseti pajahati vinodeti vyantikaroti anabhāvaṃ gameti. uppann' uppanne pāpake akusale dhamme nādhivāseti pajahati vinodeti vyantīkaroti anabhāvaṃ gameti. ayaṃ vuccat' ānanda pahānasaññā.

katamā c' ānanda virāgasaññā?

idh' ānanda bhikkhu araññagato vā rukkhamūlagato vā suññāgāragato vā iti paṭisañcikkhati: etaṃ santaṃ etaṃ paṇītaṃ yad idaṃ sabbasaṅkhārasamatho sabbūpadhipaṭinissaggo taṇhakkhayo virāgo nibbānan ti. ayaṃ vuccat' ānanda virāgasaññā.

katamā c' ānanda nirodhasaññā?

idh' ānanda bhikkhu araññagato vā rukkhamūlagato vā suññāgāragato vā iti paṭisañcikkhati: etaṃ santaṃ etaṃ paṇītaṃ yad idaṃ sabbasaṅkhārasamatho sabbūpadhipaṭinissaggo taṇhakkhayo nirodho nibbānan ti. ayaṃ vuccat' ānanda nirodhasaññā.

katamā c' ānanda sabbaloke anabhiratasaññā?

idh' ānanda bhikkhu ye loke upāy' upādānā[807] *cetaso adhiṭṭhānābhini-*

802. AN 10: 07.53. Be, Ce, Ee, and Se: *gaṇḍo*.

803. AN 10: 07.58. Be, Ce, Ee, and Se: *apamāro*.

804. AN 10: 08.03. Be: *nakhasā*.

805. AN 10: 08.06. Be and Se: *lohitaṃ pittaṃ* (with *lohitapittaṃ* noted in both as a variant).

806. AN 10: 08.50. Be, Ce, Ee, and Se: *jighacchā*.

807. AN 10: 12.27. Be: *upādāna*.

vesānusayā, te pajahantā[808] *viramati*[809] *na upādiyanto.*[810] *ayaṃ vuccat' ānanda sabbaloke anabhiratasaññā.*

katamā c' ānanda sabbasaṅkhāresu aniccasaññā?

idh' ānanda bhikkhu sabbasaṅkhārehi[811] *aṭṭīyati harāyati jigucchati. ayaṃ vuccat' ānanda sabbasaṅkhāresu aniccasaññā.*

katamā c' ānanda ānāpānasati?

idh' ānanda bhikkhu araññagato vā rukkhamūlagato vā suññāgāragato vā nisīdati pallaṅkaṃ ābhujitvā ujuṃ kāyaṃ paṇidhāya parimukhaṃ satiṃ upaṭṭhapetvā. so sato va assasati, sato va[812] *passasati.*

dīghaṃ vā assasanto: dīghaṃ assasāmī ti pajānāti, dīghaṃ vā passasanto: dīghaṃ passasāmī ti pajānāti. rassaṃ vā assasanto: rassaṃ assasāmī ti pajānāti, rassaṃ vā passasanto: rassaṃ passasāmī ti pajānāti. sabbakāyapaṭisaṃvedī assasissāmī ti sikkhati, sabbakāyapaṭisaṃvedī passasissāmī ti sikkhati. passambhayaṃ kāyasaṅkhāraṃ assasissāmī ti sikkhati, passambhayaṃ kāyasaṅkhāraṃ passasissāmī ti sikkhati.

pītipaṭisaṃvedī assasissāmī ti sikkhati, pītipaṭisaṃvedī passasissāmī ti sikkhati. sukhapaṭisaṃvedī assasissāmī ti sikkhati, sukhapaṭisaṃvedī passasissāmī ti sikkhati. cittasaṅkhārapaṭisaṃvedī assasissāmī ti sikkhati, cittasaṅkhārapaṭisaṃvedī passasissāmī ti sikkhati. passambhayaṃ cittasaṅkhāraṃ assasissāmī ti sikkhati, passambhayaṃ cittasaṅkhāraṃ passasissāmī ti sikkhati.

cittapaṭisaṃvedī assasissāmī ti sikkhati, cittapaṭisaṃvedī passasissāmī ti sikkhati. abhippamodayaṃ cittaṃ assasissāmī ti sikkhati, abhippamodayaṃ cittaṃ passasissāmī ti sikkhati. samādahaṃ cittaṃ assasissāmī ti sikkhati, samādahaṃ cittaṃ passasissāmī ti sikkhati. vimocayaṃ cittaṃ assasissāmī ti sikkhati, vimocayaṃ cittaṃ passasissāmī ti sikkhati.

aniccānupassī assasissāmī ti sikkhati, aniccānupassī passasissāmī ti sikkhati. virāgānupassī assasissāmī ti sikkhati, virāgānupassī passasissāmī ti sikkhati. nirodhānupassī assasissāmī ti sikkhati, nirodhānupassī

808. AN 10: 12.39. Bᵉ, Cᵉ, Eᵉ, and Sᵉ: *pajahanto.*

809. AN 10: 12.40. Bᵉ: *viharati.*

810. AN 10: 12.42. Bᵉ: *anupādiyanto.*

811. AN 10: 13.06. Bᵉ: *sabbasaṅkhāresu.*

812. AN 10: 14.05. Not in Cᵉ, Eᵉ, or Sᵉ (but noted in Eᵉ and Sᵉ as a variant).

passasissāmī ti sikkhati. paṭinissaggānupassī[813] *assasissāmī ti sikkhati, paṭinissaggānupassī passasissāmī ti sikkhati.*

ayaṃ vuccat' ānanda ānāpānasati.

sace kho tvaṃ ānanda girimānandassa bhikkhuno upasaṅkamitvā imā dasa saññā bhāseyyāsi, ṭhānaṃ kho pan' etaṃ vijjati yaṃ girimānandassa bhikkhuno imā dasa saññā sutvā so ābādho ṭhānaso paṭippassambheyyā ti.

atha kho āyasmā ānando bhagavato santike imā dasa saññā uggahetvā yen' āyasmā girimānando ten' upasaṅkami. upasaṅkamitvā āyasmato girimānandassa imā dasa saññā abhāsi. atha kho āyasmato girimānandassa imā dasa saññā sutvā so ābādho ṭhānaso paṭippassambhi. vuṭṭhāhi[814] *c' āyasmā girimānando tamhā ābādhā, tathā pahīno ca pan' āyasmato girimānandassa so ābādho ahosī ti.*

Khp 5 / Sn 258–69 *(Mahā-)maṅgala-sutta*[815]

evaṃ me sutaṃ. ekaṃ samayaṃ bhagavā sāvatthiyaṃ viharati jetavane anāthapiṇḍikassa ārāme.

atha kho aññatarā devatā abhikkantāya rattiyā abhikkantavaṇṇā kevalakappaṃ jetavanaṃ obhāsetvā yena bhagavā ten' upasaṅkami. upasaṅkamitvā bhagavantaṃ abhivādetvā ekamantaṃ aṭṭhāsi. ekamantaṃ ṭhitā kho sā devatā bhagavantaṃ gāthāya ajjhabhāsi:

bahū devā manussā ca
maṅgalāni acintayuṃ
ākaṅkhamānā sotthānaṃ
brūhi maṅgalam uttamaṃ.

813. The recording reflects a very brief break, apparently to clear the throat, thus the recitation actually has a short *paṭi* and after that the full *paṭinissaggānupassī*; I do not consider this to be an actual variant and will not refer to it further.

814. AN 10: 20.59. E^e^: *uṭṭhāhi.*

815. The recording corresponds to three discourses, Khp 5 / Sn 258–69 (including the prose prologue), Khp 6 / Sn 222–38, and Khp 9 / Sn 143–52, which are completely preserved and are recited in the order usually employed for traditional *paritta* chanting. This is the order followed in the *Khuddakapāṭha* (although with two other discourses between the second and the third discourses that in the chanting occur one after the other), not the order in which they are found in the *Sutta-nipāta.*

asevanā ca bālānaṃ
paṇḍitānañ ca sevanā
pūjā ca pūjanīyānaṃ[816]
etaṃ maṅgalam uttamaṃ.

patirūpadesavāso ca
pubbe ca katapuññatā
attasammāpaṇidhi ca
etaṃ maṅgalam uttamaṃ.

bāhusaccañ ca sippañ ca
vinayo ca susikkhito
subhāsitā ca yā vācā
etaṃ maṅgalam uttamaṃ.

mātāpitu upaṭṭhānaṃ
puttadārassa saṅgaho
anākulā ca kammantā
etaṃ maṅgalam uttamaṃ.

dānañ ca dhammacariyā ca
ñātakānañ ca saṅgaho
anavajjāni kammāni
etaṃ maṅgalam uttamaṃ.

ārati virati pāpā
majjapānā ca saññamo
appamādo ca dhammesu
etaṃ maṅgalam uttamaṃ.

gāravo ca nivāto ca
santuṭṭhī ca kataññutā

816. Khp/Sn: 02.07. Khp/Sn-B^{e} and Khp-E^{e}: *pūjaneyyānaṃ* (with *pūjanīyānaṃ* noted as a variant in Khp/Sn-B^{e}).

kālena dhammasavaṇaṃ
etaṃ maṅgalam uttamaṃ.

khantī ca sovacassatā
samaṇānañ ca dassanaṃ
kālena dhammasākacchā
etaṃ maṅgalam uttamaṃ.

tapo ca brahmacariyā ca[817]
ariyasaccāna dassanaṃ
nibbānasacchikiriyā ca
etaṃ maṅgalam uttamaṃ.

phuṭṭhassa lokadhammehi
cittaṃ yassa na kampati
asokaṃ virajaṃ khemaṃ
etaṃ maṅgalam uttamaṃ.

etādisāni katvāna
sabbatthamaparājitā
sabbattha sotthiṃ gacchanti
taṃ tesaṃ maṅgalam uttaman...[818]

Khp 6 / Sn 222–38 *Ratana-sutta*

yānīdha bhūtāni samāgatāni
bhummāni vā yāni va antalikkhe
sabbe va bhūtā sumanā bhavantu
atho pi sakkacca suṇantu bhāsitaṃ.

tasmā hi bhūtā nisāmetha sabbe

817. Khp/Sn: 05.01. Khp/Sn-B^{e}, Khp-C^{e}, Khp-E^{e}, and Khp/Sn-S^{e}: *brahmacariyañ ca* (with *brahmacariyā ca* noted in S^{e} as a variant).

818. Khp/Sn: 06.09. Khp/Sn-B^{e}, Khp/Sn-C^{e}, Sn-E^{e}, and Khp/Sn-S^{e}: *ti*.

mettaṃ karotha mānusiyā pajāya
divā ca ratto ca haranti ye baliṃ
tasmā hi ne rakkhatha appamattā.

yaṃ kiñci vittaṃ idha vā huraṃ vā
saggesu vā yaṃ ratanaṃ paṇītaṃ
na no samaṃ atthi tathāgatena.
idam pi buddhe ratanaṃ paṇītaṃ
etena saccena suvatthi hotu.

khayaṃ virāgaṃ amataṃ paṇītaṃ
yad ajjhagā sakyamunī samāhito
na tena dhammena sam' atthi kiñcī.
idam pi dhamme ratanaṃ paṇītaṃ
etena saccena suvatthi hotu.

yaṃ buddhaseṭṭho parivaṇṇahī[819] *suciṃ*
samādhim ānantarikaññam āhu
samādhinā tena samo na vijjati.
idam pi dhamme ratanaṃ paṇītaṃ
etena saccena suvatthi hotu.

ye puggalā aṭṭha sataṃ pasatthā
cattāri etāni yugāni honti
te dakkhiṇeyyā sugatassa sāvakā
etesu dinnāni mahapphalāni.
idam pi saṅghe ratanaṃ paṇītaṃ
etena saccena suvatthi hotu.

ye suppayuttā manasā daḷhena
nikkāmino gotamasāsanamhi
te pattipattā amataṃ vigayha
laddhā mudhā nibbutiṃ bhuñjamānā.

819. Khp/Sn: 08.29. Khp/Sn-B^{e}, Khp/Sn-C^{e}, Khp/Sn-E^{e}, and Khp/Sn-S^{e}: *parivaṇṇayī.*

idam pi saṅghe ratanaṃ paṇītaṃ
etena saccena suvatthi hotu.

yath' indakhīlo paṭhaviṃ sito[820] *siyā*
catubbhi vātehi[821] *asampakampiyo*
tathūpamaṃ sappurisaṃ vadāmi
yo ariyasaccāni avecca passati.
idam pi saṅghe ratanaṃ paṇītaṃ
etena saccena suvatthi hotu.

ye ariyasaccāni[822] *vibhāvayanti*
gambhīrapaññena sudesitāni
kiñcāpi te honti bhusappamattā[823]
na te bhavaṃ aṭṭhamam ādiyanti.
idam pi saṅghe ratanaṃ paṇītaṃ
etena saccena suvatthi hotu.

sahā v' assa dassanasampadāya
tayassu dhammā jahitā bhavanti
sakkāyadiṭṭhi vicikicchitañ ca
sīlabbataṃ vā pi yad atthi kiñci
catūh' apāyehi ca vippamutto
cha cābhiṭhānāni abhabbo[824] *kātuṃ.*
idam pi saṅghe ratanaṃ paṇītaṃ
etena saccena suvatthi hotu.

kiñcāpi so kammaṃ[825] *karoti pāpakaṃ*

820. Khp/Sn: 10.40. Khp/Sn-B^e: *pathavissito* (with *paṭhaviṃ sito* noted as a variant).

821. Khp/Sn: 10.46. Khp-C^e, Khp/Sn-S^e: *vātebhi.*

822. Khp: 11.23. Khp-S^e: *yerīyasaccāni* (with *ye ariyasaccāni* noted as a variant).

823. Khp/Sn: 11.40. Khp/Sn-B^e: *bhusaṃ pamattā.*

824. Khp/Sn: 12.48. Khp/Sn-B^e: *abhabba* (with *abhabbo* noted as a variant).

825. Khp/Sn: 13.08. Khp/Sn-B^e: *kamma* (with *kammaṃ* noted as a variant).

kāyena vācā uda[826] *cetasā vā*
abhabbo[827] *so tassa paṭicchādāya*
abhabbatā diṭṭhapadassa vuttā.
idam pi saṅghe ratanaṃ paṇītaṃ
etena saccena suvatthi hotu.

vanappagumbe yathā phussitagge
gimhāna māse paṭhamasmiṃ gimhihe[828]
tathūpamaṃ dhammavaraṃ adesayi
nibbānagāmiṃ paramaṃ hitāya.
idam pi buddhe ratanaṃ paṇītaṃ
etena saccena suvatthi hotu.

varo varaññū varado varāharo
anuttaro dhammavaraṃ adesayī.
idam pi buddhe ratanaṃ paṇītaṃ
etena saccena suvatthi hotu.

khīṇaṃ purāṇaṃ navaṃ[829] *n' atthi sambhavaṃ*
virattacittā āyatike bhavasmiṃ
te khīṇabījā avirūḷhicchandā
nibbanti dhīrā yath' āyam padīpo.
idam pi saṅghe ratanaṃ paṇītaṃ
etena saccena suvatthi hotu.

yānīdha bhūtāni samāgatāni
bhummāni vā yāni va antalikkhe,
tathāgataṃ devamanussapūjitaṃ
buddhaṃ namassāma suvatthi hotu.

826. Khp/Sn: 13.16. Khp/Sn-S^{e}: *vācāyuda*.

827. Khp/Sn: 13.22. Khp/Sn-B^{e}: *abhabba* (with *abhabbo* noted as a variant).

828. Khp/Sn: 14.02. Khp/Sn-B^{e}, Khp/Sn-C^{e}, Khp/Sn-E^{e}, and Khp/Sn-S^{e}: gimhe; see page 132.

829. Khp/Sn: 15.05. Khp/Sn-B^{e}: *nava*.

yānīdha bhūtāni samāgatāni
bhummāni vā yāni va antalikkhe,
tathāgataṃ devamanussapūjitaṃ
dhammaṃ namassāma suvatthi hotu.

yānīdha bhūtāni samāgatāni
bhummāni vā yāni va antalikkhe,
tathāgataṃ devamanussapūjitaṃ
saṅghaṃ namassāma suvatthi hotu.

Khp 9 / Sn 143–52 *Metta-sutta*

karaṇīyam atthakusalena
yan taṃ santaṃ padaṃ abhisamecca:
sakko ujū ca suhujū[830] *ca*
suvaco c' assa mudu anatimānī.

santussako ca subharo ca
appakicco ca sallahukavutti
santindriyo ca nipako ca
appagabbho kulesu[831] *ananugiddho.*

na ca khuddaṃ samācare[832] *kiñci*
yena viññū pare upavadeyyuṃ
sukhino vā khemino hontu
sabbe[833] *sattā bhavantu sukhitattā.*

ye keci pāṇabhūt' atthi
tasā vā thāvarā vā anavasesā

830. Khp/Sn: 17.31. Khp/Sn-C^{e} and Khp/Sn-E^{e}: *sūjū* (with *suhujū* noted as a variant in Khp-C^{e}).

831. Khp/Sn: 18.03. Khp/Sn-B^{e}: *kulesv'*.

832. Khp/Sn: 18.09. Khp/Sn-B^{e}: *khuddamācare.*

833. Khp/Sn: 18.25. Khp/Sn-B^{e}: *sabba°* (with *sabbe* noted as a variant).

dīghā vā ye mahantā vā[834]
majjhimā rassakā aṇukathūlā

diṭṭhā vā ye vā[835] *addiṭṭhā*
ye ca[836] *dūre vasanti avidūre*
bhūtā vā sambhavesī vā
sabbe[837] *sattā bhavantu sukhitattā.*

na paro paraṃ nikubbetha
nātimaññetha katthaci naṃ[838] *kañci*[839]
vyārosanā paṭighasaññā
nāññamaññassa dukkham iccheyya.

mātā yathā niyaṃ puttaṃ
āyusā ekaputtam anurakkhe
evam pi sabbabhūtesu
mānasaṃ bhāvaye aparimānaṃ.

mettañ ca sabbalokasmiṃ
mānasaṃ bhāvaye aparimānaṃ
uddhaṃ adho ca tiriyañ ca
asambādhaṃ averaṃ asapattaṃ

tiṭṭhaṃ caraṃ nisinno vā
sayāno vā[840] *yāvat' assa vigatamiddho*[841]
etaṃ satiṃ adhiṭṭheyya

834. Khp/Sn: 18.52. Khp/Sn-B^e: *va mahantā.*

835. Khp: 19.04. Khp-S^e: *ca* (with *va* noted as a variant).

836. Khp/Sn: 19.08. Khp/Sn-B^e: *va* (with *ca* noted as a variant).

837. Khp/Sn: 19.20. Khp/Sn-B^e: *sabba°.*

838. Khp/Sn: 19.37. Khp/Sn-B^e: *na* (with *naṃ* noted as a variant).

839. Khp/Sn: 19.38. Khp/Sn-S^e: *kiñci.*

840. Khp/Sn: 20.49. Not in Khp/Sn-B^e.

841. Khp/Sn: 20.52. Khp/Sn-B^e: *vitamiddho* (with *vigatamiddho* noted as a variant).

brahmam etaṃ vihāraṃ idham āhu.

diṭṭhiñ ca anupagamma
sīlavā dassanena sampanno
kāmesu vineyya[842] *gedhaṃ*
na hi jātu gabbhaseyyaṃ[843] *punar etī ti.*[844]

Dhp *Dhammapada*[845]

manopubbaṅgamā dhammā
manoseṭṭhā manomayā,
manasā ce paduṭṭhena
bhāsati vā karoti vā
tato naṃ dukkham anveti
cakkaṃ va vahato padaṃ. (1)

manopubbaṅgamā dhammā
manoseṭṭhā manomayā,
manasā ce pasannena
bhāsati vā karoti vā
tato naṃ sukham anveti
chāyā va anapāyinī.[846] (2)

na hi verena verāni
sammant' idha kudācanaṃ,[847]
averena ca sammanti

842. Khp/Sn: 21.24. Khp/Sn-Bᵉ: *vinaya* (with *vineyya* noted as a variant).

843. Khp/Sn: 21.31. Khp/Sn-Bᵉ: *gabbhaseyya*.

844. Khp: 21.35. Not in Khp-Eᵉ.

845. The recording has selected verses from the *Dhammapada* as follows: Dhp 1, Dhp 2, Dhp 5, Dhp 18, Dhp 60, Dhp 62, Dhp 183, Dhp 212, Dhp 213, Dh 214, Dhp 215, Dhp 216, Dhp 277, Dhp 278, and Dhp 279. For ease of reference I add the verse number in brackets at the end of each stanza.

846. Dhp: 23.13. Sᵉ: *anupāyinī*.

847. Dhp: 23.26. Eᵉ: *kudācana*.

esa dhammo sanantano. (5)

idha nandati pecca nandati
katapuñño ubhayattha nandati,
puññaṃ me katan ti nandati
bhiyyo nandati suggatiṃ gato. (18)

dīghā jāgarato ratti
dīghaṃ santassa yojanaṃ
dīgho bālānaṃ saṃsāro
saddhammaṃ avijānataṃ. (60)

puttā m' atthi dhanam m' atthi
iti bālo vihaññati,
attā hi attano n' atthi
kuto puttā kuto dhanaṃ? (62)

sabbapāpassa akaraṇaṃ
kusalassa upasampadā[848]
sacittapariyodapanaṃ
etaṃ buddhāna sāsanaṃ. (183)

piyato jāyatī soko
piyato jāyatī bhayaṃ
piyato vippamuttassa
n' atthi soko kuto bhayaṃ? (212)

pemato jāyatī soko
pemato jāyatī bhayaṃ
pemato vippamuttassa
n' atthi soko kuto bhayaṃ? (213)

ratiyā jāyatī soko

848. Dhp: 25.09. S^{e}: *kusalassūpasampadā* (with *kusalassa upasampadā* noted as a variant).

ratiyā jāyatī bhayaṃ
ratiyā vippamuttassa
n' atthi soko kuto bhayaṃ? (214)

kāmato jāyatī soko
kāmato jāyatī bhayaṃ
kāmato vippamuttassa
n' atthi soko kuto bhayaṃ? (215)

taṇhāya jāyatī soko
taṇhāya jāyatī bhayaṃ
taṇhāya vippamuttassa
n' atthi soko kuto bhayaṃ. (216)

sabbe saṅkhārā aniccā ti
yadā paññāya passati
atha nibbindati dukkhe
esa maggo visuddhiyā. (277)

sabbe saṅkhārā dukkhā ti
yadā paññāya passati
atha nibbindati dukkhe
esa maggo visuddhiyā. (278)

sabbe dhammā anattā ti
yadā paññāya passati
atha nibbindati dukkhe
esa maggo visuddhiyā. (279)

References

Abeynayake, Oliver. 2016. "The Origin of the Concept of paritta." *Anveṣaṇā* 7: 1–11.

Adikaram, E. W. 1946/1994. *Early History of Buddhism in Ceylon, or "State of Buddhism in Ceylon as Revealed by the Pāli Commentaries of the 5th Century A.D."* Dehiwala, Sri Lanka: Buddhist Cultural Centre.

Agrillo, C. 2011. "Near-Death Experience: Out-of-Body and Out-of-Brain?" *Review of General Psychology* 15.1: 1–10.

Allon, Mark. 1997. *Style and Function: A Study of the Dominant Stylistic Features of the Prose Portions of Pāli Canonical Sutta Texts and Their Mnemonic Function.* Tokyo: International Institute for Buddhist Studies of the International College for Advanced Buddhist Studies.

Amoni, Leopoldo. 1880. *Vita Prima di S. Francesco d'Assisi del B. Tommaso da Celano, Terza Edizione.* Assisi: Tipografia Sensi.

Anālayo. 2003. *Satipaṭṭhāna: The Direct Path to Realization.* Birmingham: Windhorse Publications.

———. 2005. "Some Pāli Discourses in the Light of Their Chinese Parallels (2)." *Buddhist Studies Review* 22.2: 93–105.

———. 2006a. "The Ekottarika-āgama Parallel to the Saccavibhaṅga-sutta and the Four (Noble) Truths." *Buddhist Studies Review* 23.2: 145–53.

———. 2006b. "The Saṃyukta-āgama Parallel to the Sāleyyaka-sutta." *Journal of Buddhist Ethics* 13: 1–22.

———. 2008a. "The Conversion of Aṅgulimāla in the Saṃyukta-āgama." *Buddhist Studies Review* 25.2: 135–48.

———. 2008b. "Rebirth and the gandhabba." *Mahachulalongkorn Journal of Buddhist Studies* 1: 91–105.

———. 2008c. "The Sixfold Purity of an Arahant, according to the

Chabbisodhana-sutta and Its Parallel." *Journal of Buddhist Ethics* 15: 241–77.

———. 2009a. "Karma and Liberation: The Karajakāya-sutta (AN 10.208) in the Light of Its Parallels." In *Pāsādikadānaṃ, Festschrift für Bhikkhu Pāsādika*, edited by M. Straube, R. Steiner, J. Soni, M. Hahn, and M. Demoto, 1–24. Marburg: Indica et Tibetica.

———. 2009b. "Views and the Tathāgata—A Comparative Study and Translation of the Brahmajāla in the Chinese Dīrgha-āgama." In *Buddhist and Pali Studies in Honour of the Venerable Professor Kakkapalliye Anuruddha*, edited by K. L. Dhammajoti and Y. Karunadasa, 183–234. Hong Kong: Centre of Buddhist Studies, University of Hong Kong.

———. 2011a. *A Comparative Study of the Majjhima-nikāya*. Taipei: Dharma Drum Publishing Corporation.

———. 2011b. "Vakkali's Suicide in the Chinese Āgamas." *Buddhist Studies Review* 28.2: 155–70.

———. 2012a. "The Chinese Parallels to the Dhammacakkappavattana-sutta (1)." *Journal of the Oxford Centre for Buddhist Studies* 3: 12–46.

——— 2012b. "Debate with a Sceptic—The Dīrgha-āgama Parallel to the Pāyāsi-sutta (1)." *Indian International Journal of Buddhist Studies* 13: 1–26.

———. 2012c. "The Historical Value of the Pāli Discourses." *Indo-Iranian Journal* 55: 223–53.

———. 2013a. "The Chinese Parallels to the Dhammacakkappavattana-sutta (2)." *Journal of the Oxford Centre for Buddhist Studies* 5: 9–41.

———. 2013b. "Debate with a Sceptic—The Dīrgha-āgama Parallel to the Pāyāsi-sutta (2)." *Indian International Journal of Buddhist Studies* 14: 1–27.

———. 2014a. "The Brahmajāla and the Early Buddhist Oral Tradition." *Annual Report of the International Research Institute for Advanced Buddhology at Soka University* 17: 41–59.

———. 2014b. *The Dawn of Abhidharma*. Hamburg: Hamburg University Press.

———. 2014c. "Exploring Satipaṭṭhāna in Study and Practice." *Canadian Journal of Buddhist Studies* 10: 73–95.

———. 2014d. "Defying Māra—Bhikkhunīs in the Saṃyukta-āgama." In *Women in Early Indian Buddhism: Comparative Textual Studies*, edited by A. Collett, 116–39. New York: Oxford University Press.

———. 2015. "Āgama/Nikāya." In *Brill's Encyclopedia of Buddhism*, edited by J. Silk, O. von Hinüber, and V. Eltschinger, 1: 50–59. Leiden: Brill.

———. 2016a. "Levitation in Early Buddhist Discourse." *Journal of the Oxford Centre for Buddhist Studies* 12: 11–26.

———. 2016b. *Mindfully Facing Disease and Death: Compassionate Advice from Early Buddhist Texts*. Cambridge: Windhorse Publications.

———. 2017a. *Buddhapada and the Bodhisattva Path*. Bochum: Projekt Verlag.

———. 2017b. "Nāma-rūpa." In *Encyclopedia of Indian Religions*, edited by A. Sharma. Dordrecht: Springer.

———. 2017c. "Some Renditions of the Term Tathāgata in the Chinese Āgamas." *Annual Report of the International Research Institute for Advanced Buddhology at Soka University* 20: 11–21.

Ānandajoti, Bhikkhu. 2009. *Catubhāṇavārapāḷi, Additional Material and Indexes*. http://bit.ly/1TnSrzX.

Anderson, Richard C., and J. W. Pichert. 1978. "Recall of Previously Unrecallable Information Following a Shift in Perspective." *Journal of Verbal Learning and Verbal Behavior* 17.1: 1–12.

Arunasiri, K. 2002. "Milinda." In *Encyclopaedia of Buddhism*, edited by W. G. Weeraratne, 6.4: 683–88. Sri Lanka: Department of Buddhist Affairs.

Assandri, Friederike. 2013. "Examples of Buddho-Daoist Interaction: Concepts of the Afterlife in Early Medieval Epigraphic Sources." *The Electronic Journal of East and Central Asian Religions* 1: 1–38.

Assandri, Friederike, and Wang Ping. 2010. "Multiple Souls and Destinations: Early Medieval After-Life Conceptions in the Mirror of Six Dynasties' Stone Inscriptions." 韓國漢字研究 3: 113–85.

Athappilly, Geena K., B. Greyson, and I. Stevenson. 2006. "Do Prevailing Societal Models Influence Reports of Near-Death Experiences? A Comparison of Accounts Reported before and after 1975." *The Journal of Nervous and Mental Disease* 194.3: 218–22.

Atwater, P. M. H. 2003. *Children of the New Millennium: Children's Near-Death Experiences and the Evolution of Humankind.* New York: Three Rivers Press.

Augustine, Keith. 2007. "Does Paranormal Perception Occur in Near-Death Experiences?" and "'Does Paranormal Perception Occur in Near-Death Experiences?' Defended." *Journal of Near-Death Studies* 25.4: 203–36 and 261–83.

Aung Than, U. 1990. *Thirimangalaparittataw.* Rangoon: Directorate of Religious Affairs.

Bain, Brian A. 1999. "Near Death Experiences and Gnostic Christianity: Parallels in Antiquity." *Journal of Near-Death Studies* 17.3: 205–9.

Baker, Robert A. 1992. *Hidden Memories: Voices and Visions from Within.* New York: Prometheus Books.

Bapat, P. V. 1945 (part 1) and 1950 (part 2). "The Arthapada-sūtra Spoken by the Buddha." *Visva-Bharati Annals* 1: 135–227 and 3: 1–109.

———. 1948. "The Śrāmaṇyaphala-sūtra and Its Different Versions in Buddhist Literature." *Indian Culture* 15: 107–14.

Bareau, André. 1955. *Les sectes bouddhiques du Petit Véhicule.* Paris: Publications de l'École Française d'Extrême-Orient.

———. 1979. "Chūu." *Hōbōgirin, dictionnaire encyclopédique du bouddhisme d'après les sources chinoises et japonaises,* edited by J. May, 5: 558–63. Paris: Librairie d'Amérique et d'Orient.

Bartlett, Frederic C. 1932. *Remembering: A Study in Experimental and Social Psychology.* Cambridge: Cambridge University Press.

Batchelor, Stephen. 1997. *Buddhism without Beliefs: A Contemporary Guide to Awakening.* New York: Riverhead Books.

———. 2010/2011. *Confession of a Buddhist Atheist.* New York: Spiegel & Grau.

———. 2015. *After Buddhism: Rethinking the Dharma for a Secular Age.* New Haven, CT: Yale University Press.

Beauregard, Mario, E. L. St-Pierre, G. Rayburn, and P. Demers. 2012. "Conscious Mental Activity during a Deep Hypothermic Cardiocirculatory Arrest?" *Resuscitation* 83 e19. http://dx.doi.org/10.1016/j.resuscitation.2011.09.027.

Bechert, Heinz. 1992. "The Writing Down of the Tripiṭaka in Pāli." *Wiener Zeitschrift für die Kunde Südasiens* 36: 45–53.

Bechert, Heinz, and K. Wille. 1989. *Sanskrithandschriften aus den Turfanfunden, Teil 6.* Stuttgart: Franz Steiner.

———. 1996. *Sanskrithandschriften aus den Turfanfunden, Teil 7.* Stuttgart: Franz Steiner.

———. 2004. *Sanskrithandschriften aus den Turfanfunden, Teil 9.* Stuttgart: Franz Steiner.

Becker, Carl B. 1993. *Breaking the Circle: Death and the Afterlife in Buddhism.* Carbondale: Southern Illinois University Press.

Beckh, Hermann. 1919. *Buddhismus (Der Buddha und seine Lehre), I Einleitung, Der Buddha.* Berlin: Göschen.

Belanti, John, M. Perera, and K. Jagadheesan. 2008. "Phenomenology of Near-Death Experiences: A Cross-Cultural Perspective." *Transcultural Psychiatry* 45.1: 121–33.

Bernhard, Franz. 1965 (vol. 1). *Udānavarga.* Göttingen: Vandenhoeck & Ruprecht.

Blackmore, Susan. 1993. *Dying to Live: Near-Death Experiences.* New York: Prometheus Books.

Blezer, Henk. 1997. *Kar gliṅ Źi khro: A Tantric Buddhist Concept.* Leiden: Research School CNWS.

Blum, Mark L. 2004. "Death." In *Encyclopedia of Buddhism*, edited by R. E. Buswell, 1: 203–10. New York: Macmillan.

Bodhi, Bhikkhu. 1978/1992. *The All-Embracing Net of Views: The Brahmajāla Sutta and Its Commentaries, Translated from the Pali.* Kandy: Buddhist Publication Society.

———. 2000. *The Connected Discourses of the Buddha: A New Translation of the Saṃyutta Nikāya.* Boston: Wisdom Publications.

———. 2012. *The Numerical Discourses of the Buddha: A Translation of the Aṅguttara Nikāya.* Boston: Wisdom Publications.

———. 2015. *Dhamma Reflections.* Kandy: Buddhist Publication Society.

———. 2017. *The Suttanipāta: An Ancient Collection of the Buddha's Discourses Together with Its Commentaries.* Boston: Wisdom Publications.

Bokenkamp, Stephen R. 2007. *Ancestors and Anxiety: Daoism and the Birth of Rebirth in China.* Berkeley: University of California Press.

Bollée, Willem B. 2002. *The Story of Paesi (Paesi-kahāṇayaṃ): Soul and Body in Ancient India, A Dialogue on Materialism, Text, Translation, Notes and Commentary*. Wiesbaden: Otto Harrassowitz.

Bradley, William L. 1966. "Prince Mongkut and Jesse Caswell." *Journal of the Siam Society* 54.1: 29–41.

Bransford, John D., and M. K. Johnson. 1973. "Considerations of Some Problems of Comprehension." In *Visual Information Processing*, edited by W. G. Chase, 383–438. New York: Academic Press.

Braude, S. E. 1992. "Survival or Super-Psi?" *Journal of Scientific Exploration* 6: 127–44.

Bremmer, Jan N. 2002. *The Rise and Fall of the Afterlife: The 1995 Read-Tuckwell Lectures at the University of Bristol*. London: Routledge.

Brody, E. B. 1979. Review of *Cases of the Reincarnation Type, Volume II: Ten Cases in Sri Lanka* by I. Stevenson. *Journal of Nervous and Mental Disease* 167: 769–74.

Bronkhorst, Johannes. 2016. *How the Brahmins Won: From Alexander to the Guptas*. Leiden: Brill.

Brough, John. 1962/2001. *The Gāndhārī Dharmapada: Edited with an Introduction and Commentary*. Delhi: Motilal Banarsidass.

Bruhn, Klaus. 1983. "Repetition in Jaina Narrative Literature." *Indologica Taurinensia* 11: 27–75.

Bucknell, Roderick S., and M. Stuart-Fox. 1983. "The 'Three Knowledges' of Buddhism: Implications of Buddhadasa's Interpretation of Rebirth." *Religion* 13: 99–112.

Buddhadatta, A. P. 1944. "Who Was Buddhaghosa?" *University of Ceylon Review* 2.1/2: 77–85.

Burford, Grace G. 1991. *Desire, Death and Goodness: The Conflict of Ultimate Values in Theravāda Buddhism*. New York: Peter Lang.

Bush, Nancy Evans. 2002. "Afterward: Making Meaning after a Frightening Near-Death Experience." *Journal of Near-Death Studies* 21.2: 99–133.

———. 2009. "Distressing Western Near-Death Experiences: Finding a Way through the Abyss." In *The Handbook of Near-Death Experiences: Thirty Years of Investigation*, edited by J. M. Holden, B. Greyson, and D. James, 63–86. Santa Barbara, CA: Praeger.

Caillies, Stéphanie, G. Denhière, and W. Kintsch. 2002. "The Effect of Prior Knowledge on Understanding from Text: Evidence from Primed Recognition." *European Journal of Cognitive Psychology* 14: 267–86.

Campany, Robert Ford. 1990. "Return-from-Death Narratives in Early Medieval China." *Journal of Chinese Religions* 18: 91–125.

Carrithers, Michael. 1983. *The Buddha*. Oxford: Oxford University Press.

Carter, Chris. 2012. *Science and the Afterlife Experience: Evidence for the Immortality of Consciousness*. Rochester, VT: Inner Traditions.

Cedzich, Ursula-Angelika. 2001. "Corpse Deliverance, Substitute Bodies, Name Change, and Feigned Death: Aspects of Metamorphosis and Immortality in Early Medieval China." *Journal of Chinese Religions* 29: 1–68.

Childers, Robert Caesar. 1875/1993. *A Dictionary of the Pali Language*. New Delhi: Asian Educational Services.

Clark, Kimberly. 1984. "Clinical Interventions with Near-Death Experiencers." In *The Near-Death Experience: Problems, Prospects, Perspectives*, edited by B. Greyson and C. P. Flynn, 242–55. Springfield, IL: Charles C. Thomas.

———. 2007. "The Other Shoe Drops: Comments on 'Does Paranormal Perception Occur in Near-Death Experiences?" *Journal of Near-Death Studies* 25.4: 245–50.

Collins, Steven. 1982. *Selfless Persons: Imagery and Thought in Theravāda Buddhism*. Cambridge: Cambridge University Press.

Cone, Margaret. 1989. "Patna Dharmapada." *Journal of the Pali Text Society*, 13: 101–217.

Cook, Emily Williams, B. Greyson, and I. Stevenson. 1998. "Do Any Near-Death Experiences Provide Evidence for the Survival of Human Personality after Death? Relevant Features and Illustrative Case Reports." *Journal of Scientific Exploration* 12.3: 377–406.

Cook, Emily Williams, S. Pasricha, G. Samararatne, U Win Maung, and I. Stevenson. 1983. "A Review and Analysis of 'Unsolved' Cases of the Reincarnation Type. II. Comparison of Features of Solved and Unsolved Cases." *Journal of the American Society for Psychical Research* 77: 115–35.

Cooper-Rompato, Christine. 2010. *The Gift of Tongues: Women's Xenoglossia in the Later Middle Ages*. University Park: Pennsylvania State University Press.

Cousins, L. S. 2015. "The Sutta on Mindfulness with In and Out Breathing." In *Buddhist Meditative Praxis: Traditional Teachings & Modern Applications*, edited by K. L. Dhammajoti, 1–24. University of Hong Kong: Centre of Buddhist Studies.

Cox, Collett. 1995. *Disputed Dharmas: Early Buddhist Theories on Existence, An Annotated Translation of the Section on Factors Dissociated from Thought from Saṅghabhadra's Nyāyānusāra*. Tokyo: International Institute for Buddhist Studies.

Cuevas, Bryan Jaré. 1996. "Predecessors and Prototypes: Towards a Conceptual History of the Buddhist Antarābhava." *Numen* 43: 263–302.

———. 2003. *The Hidden History of the Tibetan Book of the Dead*. New York: Oxford University Press.

de Jong, Jan Willem. 1974/1979. "À propos du Nidānasaṃyukta." In *Buddhist Studies (by J. W. de Jong)*, edited by G. Schopen, 237–49. Berkeley, CA: Asian Humanities Press.

de La Vallée Poussin, Louis. 1913. "Documents sanscrits de la seconde collection M. A. Stein." *Journal of the Royal Asiatic Society* 569–80.

———. 1926/1971 (vol. 2). *L'Abhidharmakośa de Vasubandhu, traduction et annotations*, edited by É. Lamotte. Brussels: Institut Belge des Hautes Études Chinoises.

———. 1928. "Agnosticism (Buddhist)." In *Encyclopedia of Religion and Ethics*, edited by J. Hastings, 1: 220–25. New York: Charles Scribner's Sons.

Dell'Olio, Andrew J. 2010. "Do Near-Death Experiences Provide a Rational Basis for Belief in Life after Death?" *Sophia* 49: 113–28.

Demiéville, Paul. 1924. "Les versions chinoises du Milindapañha." *Bulletin de l'École Française d'Extrême-Orient* 24: 1–258.

de Silva, Lily. 1981. *Paritta: A Historical and Religious Study of the Buddhist Ceremony for Peace and Prosperity in Sri Lanka*. Spolia Zeylanica 36.1. Colombo: National Museums of Sri Lanka.

———. 1991. "Freedom." In *Encyclopaedia of Buddhism*, edited by W. G. Weeraratne, 5.2: 272–77. Sri Lanka: Department of Buddhist Affairs.

———. 1991/2001. "The paritta Ceremony of Sri Lanka: Its Antiquity and Symbolism." In *Buddhist Thought and Ritual*, edited by D. J. Kalupahana, 139–50. Delhi: Motilal Banarsidass.

———. 2004. "The Antarābhava." *Bukkyō Kenkyū* 32: 55–58.

Dhammadinnā, Sāmaṇerī. 2014. "Semantics of Wholesomeness: Purification of Intention and the Soteriological Function of the Immeasurables (appamāṇas) in Early Buddhist Thought." In *Buddhist Meditative Traditions: Their Origin and Development*, edited by Chuang Kuo-pin, 51–129. Taipei: Shin Wen Feng Print.

Dinzelbacher, P., M. P. Ciccarese, Y. Christe, and W. Berschin. 1990. *Le 'visiones' nella cultura medievale, Testi della VI settimana residenziale di studie medievali*. Palermo: Officina di Studi Medievali.

Ducasse, C. J. 1960. "How the Case of 'The Search for Bridey Murphy' Stands Today." *Journal of the American Society for Psychical Research* 60.1: 3–22.

Dutt, Nalinaksha. 1984. *Gilgit Manuscripts: Mūlasarvāstivāda Vinaya-vastu, Vol. III Part 1*. Delhi: Sri Satguru.

Duyvendak, J. J. L. 1952. "A Chinese 'Divina Commedia.'" *T'oung Pao* 41.4/5: 255–316.

Ebbern, H., S. Mulligan, and B. L. Beyerstein. 1996. "Maria's Near-Death Experience: Waiting for the Other Shoe to Drop." *The Skeptical Inquirer* 20.4: 27–33.

Edwards, Paul. 1996. *Reincarnation: A Critical Examination*. Amherst, NY: Prometheus Books.

Eimer, H. 1976. *Skizzen des Erlösungsweges in buddhistischen Begriffsreihen*. Bonn: Religionswissenschaftliches Seminar der Universität Bonn.

Enomoto, Fumio. 1994. *A Comprehensive Study of the Chinese Saṃyuktāgama, Indic Texts Corresponding to the Chinese Saṃyuktāgama as Found in the Sarvāstivāda-Mūlasarvāstivāda Literature, Part 1: *Saṃgītanipāta*. Kyoto: Kacho Junior College.

Evans-Wentz, W. Y. 1927/2000. *The Tibetan Book of the Dead or The After-Death Experiences on the Bardo Plane, according to Lāma Kazi Dawa-Samdup's English Rendering*. New York: Oxford University Press.

Facco, Enrico, and C. Agrillo. 2012. "Near-Death Experiences between Science and Prejudice." *Frontiers in Human Neuroscience* 6.209: 1–7.

Feer, Léon. 1883. *Fragments extraits du Kandjour, traduits du tibétain*. Paris: Ernest Leroux.

Feng, Zhi-ying, and Jian-xun Liu. 1992. "Near-Death Experiences among Survivors of the 1976 Tangshan Earthquake." *Journal of Near-Death Studies* 11.1: 39–48.

Fiore, Edith. 1979/1986. *You Have Been Here Before: A Psychologist Looks at Past Lives*. New York: Ballantine Books.

Fox, Mark. 2003. *Religion, Spirituality and the Near-Death Experience*. London: Routledge.

Frauwallner, Erich. 1956/2003a: *Geschichte der indischen Philosophie, I. Band, Die Philosophie des Veda and des Epos, Der Buddha und der Jina, Das Sāṃkhya und das klassische Yoga-System*. Aachen: Shaker Verlag.

———. 1956/2003b: *Geschichte der Indischen Philosophie, II. Band, Die naturphilosophischen Schulen und das Vaiśeṣika-System, das System der Jaina, der Materialismus*. Aachen: Shaker Verlag.

Fronsdal, Gil. 2016. *The Buddha before Buddhism: Wisdom from the Early Teachings*. Boulder, CO: Shambhala.

Freedman, Thelma B. 2002. *Soul Echoes: The Healing Power of Past-Life Therapy*. New York: Citadel Press.

Fujita, Kotatsu. 1982. "The Doctrinal Characteristics of Karman in Early Buddhism." In *Indological and Buddhist Studies, Volume in Honour of Professor J. W. de Jong on His Sixtieth Birthday*, edited by L. A. Hercus, F. B. J. Kuiper, T. Rajapatirana, and E. R. Skrzypczak, 149–59. Canberra: Faculty of Asian Studies.

Fuller, Paul. 2005. *The Notion of diṭṭhi in Theravāda Buddhism: The Point of View*. London: Curzon.

Fung, Yu-lan. 1953. *A History of Chinese Philosophy, Volume II: The Period of Classical Learning (from the Second Century B.C. to the Twentieth Century A.D.)*, translated by D. Bodde. Princeton, NJ: Princeton University Press.

Gabaude, Louis. 1990. "Thai Society and Buddhadasa: Structural Difficulties." In *Radical Conservatism, Buddhism in the Contemporary*

World: Articles in Honour of Bhikkhu Buddhadasa's 84th Birthday Anniversary, edited by S. Sivaraksa, 211–29. Bangkok: Thai Inter-Religious Commission for Development and International Network of Engaged Buddhists.

Ganeri, Jonardon. 2014. "Experiment, Imagination, and the Self: The Story of Payāsi." In *Buddhist and Jaina Studies: Proceedings of the Conference in Lumbini, February 2013*, edited by J. Soni, M. Pahlke, and C. Cueppers, 367–76. Lumbini: Lumbini International Research Institute.

Gethin, Rupert. 1996. "The Resurrection and Buddhism." In *Resurrection Reconsidered*, edited by G. D'Costa, 201–16. Oxford: Oneworld.

———. 1997. "Cosmology and Meditation: From the Aggañña-sutta to the Mahāyāna." *History of Religions* 36: 183–217.

Gjertson, Donald E. 1980. "Rebirth as an Animal in Medieval Chinese Buddhism." *Society for the Study of Chinese Religions Bulletin* 8: 56–69.

———. 1981. "The Early Chinese Buddhist Miracle Tale." *Journal of the American Oriental Society* 101.3: 287–301.

Glass, Andrew. 2007. *Four Gāndhārī Saṃyuktāgama Sūtras: Senior Kharoṣṭhī Fragment 5*. Seattle: University of Washington Press.

Gnanarama, P. 1997. "Tathāgata: A Study of the Canonical and Commentarial Definitions." In *Recent Researches in Buddhist Studies, Essays in Honour of Professor Y. Karunadasa*, edited by K. L. Dhammajoti, A. Tilakaratne, and K. Abhayawansa, 230–41. Colombo: Y. Karunadasa Felicitation Committee.

Gnoli, Raniero. 1977 (part 1) and 1978 (part 2). *The Gilgit Manuscript of the Saṅghabhedavastu, Being the 17th and Last Section of the Vinaya of the Mūlasarvāstivādin*. Rome: Istituto Italiano per il Medio ed Estremo Oriente.

Goff, Lyn M., and H. L. Roediger. 1998. "Imagination Inflation for Action Events: Repeated Imaginings Lead to Illusory Recollections." *Memory & Cognition* 26.1: 20–33.

Gombrich, Richard F. 1990. "How the Mahāyāna Began." *The Buddhist Forum* 1: 21–30.

———. 2003. "Obsession with Origins." In *Approaching the Dhamma:*

Buddhist Texts and Practice in South and Southeast Asia, edited by A. M. Blackburn and J. Samuels, 3–15. Seattle: Pariyatti Editions.

———. 2009. *What the Buddha Thought*. London: Equinox.

Gómez, Luis O. 1975. "Some Aspects of the Free-Will Question in the Nikāyas." *Philosophy East and West* 25.1: 81–90.

———. 1976. "Proto-Mādhyamika in the Pāli Canon." *Philosophy East and West* 26.2: 137–65.

Greenhoot, Andrea F., G. Semb, J. Colombo, and T. Schreiber. 2004. "Prior Beliefs and Methodological Concepts in Scientific Reasoning." *Applied Cognitive Reasoning* 18: 203–21.

Greyson, Bruce. 2007. "Comments on 'Does Paranormal Perception Occur in Near-Death Experiences?" *Journal of Near-Death Studies* 25.4: 237–44.

———. 2010. "Implications of Near-Death Experiences for a Postmaterialist Psychology." *Psychology of Religion and Spirituality* 2.1: 37–45.

———. 2014. "Near-Death Experiences." In *Varieties of Anomalous Experience: Examining the Scientific Evidence, Second Edition*, edited by E. Cardeña, S. J. Lynn, and S. Krippner, 333–67. Washington, DC: American Psychological Association.

Greyson, Bruce, and N. E. Bush. 1992. "Distressing Near-Death Experiences." *Psychiatry* 55: 95–110.

Greyson, Bruce, E. W. Kelly, and E. F. Kelly. 2009. "Explanatory Models for Near-Death Experience." In *The Handbook of Near-Death Experiences: Thirty Years of Investigation*, edited by J. M. Holden, B. Greyson, and D. James, 213–34. Santa Barbara, CA: Praeger.

Griffiths, Paul J. 1982. "Notes towards a Critique of Buddhist Karma Theory." *Religious Studies* 18: 277–91.

Guang Xing. 2007. "Nāgasena Bhikṣu Sūtra." *Journal of the Centre for Buddhist Studies, Sri Lanka* 5: 117–216.

Halbfass, Wilhelm. 2000. *Karma und Wiedergeburt im Indischen Denken*. Kreuzlingen: Hugendubel.

Hamilton, Sue. 1996. *Identity and Experience: The Constitution of the Human Being according to Early Buddhism*. London: Luzac Oriental.

Hara, Minoru. 2009. "Divine Procreation." *Indo-Iranian Journal* 52: 217–49.

Haraldsson, Erlendur. 1991. "Children Claiming Past-Life Memories: Four Cases in Sri Lanka." *Journal of Scientific Exploration* 5: 233–61.

———. 2000/2006. "Birthmarks and Claims of Previous-Life Memories: The Case of Purnima Ekanayake." In *The Survival of Human Consciousness: Essays on the Possibility of Life after Death*, edited by L. Storm and M. A. Thalbourne, 194–205. Jefferson, NC: McFarland.

Haraldsson, Erlendur, and G. Samararatne. 1999. "Children Who Speak of Memories of a Previous Life as a Buddhist Monk: Three New Cases." *Journal of the Society for Psychical Research* 63.857: 268–91.

Harper, Donald. 1994. "Resurrection in Warring States Popular Religion." *Taoist Resources* 5.2: 13–29.

Hart, William, D. Albarracín, A. H. Eagly, I. Brechan, M. J. Lindberg, and L. Merrill. 2009. "Feeling Validated versus Being Correct: A Meta-Analysis of Selective Exposure to Information." *Psychological Bulletin* 135.4: 555–88.

Harvey, Peter. 1993a. "The Dynamics of paritta Chanting in Southern Buddhism." In *Love Divine: Studies in Bhakti and Devotional Mysticism*, edited by K. Werner, 53–84. Richmond: Curzon.

———. 1993b. "The Mind–Body Relationship in Pāli Buddhism: A Philosophical Investigation." *Asian Philosophy*, 3.1: 29–41.

———. 1995. *The Selfless Mind: Personality, Consciousness and Nirvāṇa in Early Buddhism*. Richmond: Curzon.

———. 2000/2005. *An Introduction to Buddhist Ethics: Foundations, Values and Issues*. Cambridge: Cambridge University Press.

———. 2007. "'Freedom of the Will' in the Light of Theravāda Buddhist Teachings." *Journal of Buddhist Ethics* 14: 35–98.

———. 2009. "The Four ariya-saccas as 'True Realities for the Spiritually Ennobled'—The Painful, Its Origin, Its Cessation, and the Way Going to This—Rather Than 'Noble Truths' concerning These." *Buddhist Studies Review* 26.2: 197–227.

———. 2013. "The Conditioned Co-Arising of Mental and Bodily Processes within Life and between Lives." In *A Companion to Buddhist Philosophy*, edited by S. M. Emmanuel, 46–68. Chichester, UK: Wiley-Blackwell.

Hershock, Peter D. 2005. "Valuing Karma: A Critical Concept for Orienting Interdependence toward Personal and Public Good." *Journal of Buddhist Ethics*, online conference on "Revisioning Karma." http://blogs.dickinson.edu/buddhistethics/files/2011/01/hershock01.pdf.

Hoffman, Frank J. 1987. *Rationality and Mind in Early Buddhism*. Delhi: Motilal Banarsidass.

Holden, Janice Miner. 2009. "Veridical Perception in Near-Death Experience." In *The Handbook of Near-Death Experiences: Thirty Years of Investigation*, edited by J. M. Holden, B. Greyson, and D. James, 185–211. Santa Barbara, CA: Praeger.

Holden, Janice Miner, B. Greyson, and D. James. 2009. "The Field of Near-Death Studies: Past, Present, and Future." In *The Handbook of Near-Death Experiences: Thirty Years of Investigation*, edited by J. M. Holden, B. Greyson, and D. James, 1–16. Santa Barbara, CA: Praeger.

Huntington, John. 1986. "Sowing the Seeds of the Lotus: A Journey to the Great Pilgrimage Sites of Buddhism, Part II, The Ṛṣipatana Mṛgadāva ('Deer Park') near Vārāṇasī." *Orientations* 17: 28–43.

Jayatilleke, K. N. 1963/1980. *Early Buddhist Theory of Knowledge*. Delhi: Motilal Banarsidass.

———. 1968. "The Buddhist Doctrine of Karma." *The Mahābodhi* 76: 314–20.

———. 1969. *Survival and Karma in Buddhist Perspective*. Kandy: Buddhist Publication Society.

Jayawardhana, Bandula. 1988. "Determinism and Indeterminism." In *Encyclopaedia of Buddhism*, edited by W. G. Weeraratne, 4.3: 392–412. Sri Lanka: Department of Buddhist Affairs.

Jayawickrama, N. A. 1948/1978. "A Critical Analysis of the Sutta Nipāta." *Pāli Buddhist Review* 3: 45–64.

Johansson, Rune E. A. 1973/1998. *Pali Buddhist Texts, Explained to the Beginner*. Richmond: Curzon.

———. 1979/1985. *The Dynamic Psychology of Early Buddhism*. London: Curzon.

Johnston, Edward Hamilton. 1936/1995. *Aśvagoṣa's Buddhacarita or Acts of the Buddha: Sanskrit Text with English Translation, Cantos I to XIV Translated from the Original Sanskrit and Cantos XV to XXVIII*

Translated from the Tibetan and Chinese Versions Together with an Introduction and Notes. Delhi: Munshiram Manoharlal.

Jones, Dhivan Thomas. 2009. "New Light on the Twelve nidānas." *Contemporary Buddhism* 10.2: 241–59.

Jurewicz, J. 2000. "Playing with Fire: The pratītyasamutpāda from the Perspective of Vedic Thought." *Journal of the Pali Text Society* 26: 77–103.

Kalupahana, D. J. 1975. *Causality: The Central Philosophy of Buddhism*. Honolulu: University of Hawai'i Press.

Kalupahana, D. J., and K. Tamura. 1965. "Antarābhava." In *Encyclopaedia of Buddhism*, edited by G. P. Malalasekera, 1.4: 730–33. Sri Lanka: Department of Buddhist Affairs.

Kampman, Reima, and R. Hirvenoja. 1978. "Dynamic Relation of the Secondary Personality Induced by Hypnosis to the Present Personality." In *Hypnosis at Its Bicentennial*, edited by F. H. Frankel and H. S. Zamansky, 183–88. New York: Plenum Press.

Kao, Karl S. Y. 1985. *Classical Chinese Tales of the Supernatural and the Fantastic: Selections from the Third to the Tenth Century*. Bloomington: Indiana University Press.

Karunadasa, Y. 2007. "The Unanswered Questions: Why Were They Unanswered? A Re-Examination of the Textual Data." *Pacific World, Third Series* 9: 3–31.

———. 2013. *Early Buddhist Teachings: The Middle Position in Theory and Practice*. Hong Kong: Centre of Buddhist Studies, University of Hong Kong.

Karunaratne, U. 1977. "Catubhāṇavāra." In *Encyclopaedia of Buddhism*, edited by G. P. Malalasekera, 3.4: 694–95. Sri Lanka: Department of Buddhist Affairs.

———. 1991. "Gandhabba." In *Encyclopaedia of Buddhism*, edited by G. P. Malalasekera, 5.2: 293–95. Sri Lanka: Department of Buddhist Affairs.

Kastenbaum, Robert. 1979. "Happily Ever After." In *Between Life and Death*, edited by R. Kastenbaum, 15–28. New York: Springer.

Katz, Nathan. 1982/1989. *Buddhist Images of Human Perfection: The*

Arahant of the Sutta Piṭaka Compared with the Bodhisattva and the Mahāsiddha. Delhi: Motilal Banarsidass.

Keil, H. H. J., and J. Tucker. 2005. "Children Who Claim to Remember Previous Lives: Cases with Written Records Made before the Previous Personality Was Identified." *Journal of Scientific Exploration* 19.1: 91–101.

Keith, A. Berriedale. 1923/1979. *Buddhist Philosophy in India and Ceylon*. Delhi: Oriental Books Reprint Corporation.

Kellehear, Allan. 2009. "Census of Non-Western Near-Death Experiences to 2005: Observations and Critical Reflections." In *The Handbook of Near-Death Experiences: Thirty Years of Investigation*, edited by J. M. Holden, B. Greyson, and D. James, 135–58. Santa Barbara, CA: Praeger.

Kellehear, Allan, P. Heaven, and Jia Gao. 1990. "Community Attitudes towards Near-Death Experiences, A Chinese Study." *Journal of Near-Death Studies* 8.3: 163–73.

Kelly, Emily Williams, B. Greyson, and I. Stevenson. 1999/2000. "Can Experiences Near Death Furnish Evidence of Life after Death?" *Omega* 40.4: 513–19.

Keown, Damien. 1996. "Karma, Character, and Consequentialism." *Journal of Religious Ethics* 24: 329–50.

Knaster, Mirka. 2010. *Living This Life Fully: Stories and Teachings of Munindra*. Boston: Shambhala.

Kritzer, Robert. 1997. "Antarābhava in the Vibhāṣā." *Maranatha* 5: 11–33.

———. 1998. "Semen, Blood, and the Intermediate Existence." *Indogaku Bukkyōgaku Kenkyū* 46.2: 30–36.

———. 2000a: "The Four Ways of Entering the Womb (garbhāvakrānti)." *Bukkyō Bunka* 10: 1–41.

———. 2000b: "Rūpa and the antarābhava." *Journal of Indian Philosophy* 28: 235–72.

———. 2008. "Life in the Womb: Conception and Gestation in Buddhist Scripture and Classical Indian Medical Literature." In *Imagining the Fetus: The Unborn in Myth, Religion and Culture*, edited by V. R. Sasson and J. M. Law, 73–89. New York: Oxford University Press.

———. 2013. "Garbhāvakrāntau ('In the garbhāvakrānti'), Quotations from the Garbhāvakrāntisūtra in Abhidharma Literature and the Yogācārabhūmi." In *The Foundation for Yoga Practitioners: The Buddhist Yogācārabhūmi Treatise and Its Adaptation in India, East Asia, and Tibet*, edited by U. T. Kragh, 738–71. Cambridge, MA: Harvard University Press.

———. 2014. *Garbhāvakrāntisūtra: The Sūtra on Entry into the Womb*. Tokyo: The International Institute for Buddhist Studies.

Kudo, Noriyuki. 2004. *The Karmavibhaṅga: Transliterations and Annotations of the Original Sanskrit Manuscript from Nepal*. Tokyo: Soka University.

———. 2007. "One More Manuscript of the Karmavibhaṅga in the National Archives of Nepal, Kathmandu: Transliteration of Manuscript E (2)." *Annual Report of the International Research Institute for Advanced Buddhology at Soka University* 10: 93–116.

Lamotte, Étienne. 1976 (vol. 4). *Le traité de la Grande Vertu de Sagesse de Nāgārjuna (Mahāprajñāpāramitāśāstra)*. Louvain-la-Neuve: Institut Orientaliste.

Langer, Rita. 2000. *Das Bewusstsein als Träger des Lebens, einige weniger beachtete Aspekte des viññāṇa im Pālikanon*. Vienna: Arbeitskreis für tibetische und buddhistische Studien, Universität Wien.

———. 2007. *Rituals of Death and Rebirth: Contemporary Sri Lankan Practice and Its Origins*. London: Routledge.

———. 2012. "Chanting as 'Bricolage Technique': A Comparison of South and Southeast Asian Funeral Recitation." In *Buddhist Funeral Cultures of Southeast Asia and China*, edited by P. Williams and P. Ladwig, 21–58. Cambridge: Cambridge University Press.

Law, Bimala Charan. 1923. *The Life and Work of Buddhaghosa*. Calcutta: Thacker, Spink & Co.

Lee, Sumi. 2014. "The Meaning of 'Mind-Made Body' (S. manomaya-kāya, C. yisheng shen 意生身) in Buddhist Cosmological and Soteriological Systems." *Buddhist Studies Review* 31.1: 65–90.

Lefmann, S. 1902. *Lalita Vistara, Leben und Lehre des Çâkya-Buddha, Textausgabe mit Varianten-, Metren- und Wörterverzeichnis*. Halle: Verlag der Buchhandlung des Waisenhauses.

Leumann, Ernst. 1885. "Beziehungen der Jaina-Literatur zu anderen Literaturkreisen Indiens." *Actes du Sixième Congrès International des Orientalistes Tenu en 1883 à Leyde, Troisième Partie, Section 2, Aryenne* 3.2: 467–564.

Lévi, Sylvain. 1915. "Sur la récitation primitive des textes bouddhiques." *Journal Asiatique* 11.5: 401–47.

———. 1932. *Mahākarmavibhaṅga (la Grande Classification des Actes) et Karmavibhaṅgopadeśa (Discussion sur le Mahā Karmavibhaṅga), textes sanscrits rapportés du Népal, édités et traduits avec les textes parallèles en sanscrit, en pali, en tibétain, en chinois et en koutchéen.* Paris: Ernest Leroux.

Liebenthal, Walter. 1952. "The Immortality of the Soul in Chinese Thought." *Monumenta Nipponica* 8.1/2: 327–97.

Lin, Li-Kouang. 1949. *L'aide-mémoire de la Vraie Loi (Saddharma-Smṛtyupasthāna Sūtra).* Paris: Adrien-Maisonneuve.

Lin, Qian. 2011/2012. "The antarābhava Dispute among Abhidharma Traditions and the List of anāgāmins." *Journal of the International Association of Buddhist Studies* 34.1/2: 149–86.

Long, Jeffrey, and P. Perry. 2010. *Evidence of the Afterlife: The Science of Near-Death Experiences.* New York: HarperOne.

Lönnerstrand, Sture. 1998. *I Have Lived Before: The True Story of the Reincarnation of Shanti Devi.* Huntsville, AR: Ozark Mountain Publishers.

Lord, Charles G., L. Ross, and M. R. Lepper. 1979. "Biased Assimilation and Attitude Polarization: The Effects of Prior Theories on Subsequently Considered Evidence." *Journal of Personality and Social Psychology* 37.11: 2098–109.

Lucas, Winafred Blake. 1993. *Regression Therapy: A Handbook for Professionals, Volume 1: Past-Life Therapy.* Crest Park, CA: Deep Forest Press.

MacQueen, Graeme. 1988. *A Study of the Śrāmaṇyaphala-sūtra.* Wiesbaden: Otto Harrassowitz.

Malalasekera, G. P. 1928/1994. *The Pāli Literature of Ceylon.* Kandy: Buddhist Publication Society.

———. 1937/1995 (vol. 1). *Dictionary of Pāli Proper Names.* Delhi: Munshiram Manoharlal.

Manda, Michitoshi. 2005. "The Meaning of Tathāgata in the Avyākata Questions." In *Buddhism and Jainism: Essays in Honour of Dr. Hojun Nagasaki on His Seventieth Birthday*, 724–13. Kyoto: Committee for the Felicitation of Dr. Hojun Nagasaki's Seventieth Birthday.

Marasinghe, M. M. J. 1974. *Gods in Early Buddhism: A Study in Their Social and Mythological Milieu as Depicted in the Nikāyas of the Pāli Canon*. Kelaniya: University of Sri Lanka, Vidyalankara Campus Press.

Masefield, Peter. 1983. "Mind/Cosmos Maps in the Pāli Nikāyas." In *Buddhist and Western Psychology*, edited by N. Katz, 69–93. Boulder, CO: Prajñā Press.

Masson, Joseph, S.J. 1942. *La religion populaire dans le canon bouddhique Pâli*. Leuven: Bureaux du Muséon.

Matlock, James G. 1990. "Past Life Memory Case Studies." In *Advances in Parapsychological Research 6*, edited by S. Krippner, 184–267. Jefferson, NC: McFarland.

McClenon, James. 1991. "Near-Death Folklore in Medieval China and Japan, A Comparative Analysis." *Asian Folklore Studies* 50: 319–42.

McDermott, James Paul. 1980. "Karma and Rebirth in Early Buddhism." In *Karma and Rebirth in Classical Indian Traditions*, edited by W. D. O'Flaherty, 165–92. Berkeley: University of California Press.

Meisig, Konrad. 1987. *Das Śrāmaṇyaphala-sūtra, synoptische Übersetzung und Glossar der chinesischen Fassungen verglichen mit dem Sanskrit und Pāli*. Wiesbaden: Otto Harrassowitz.

Meyersburg, Cynthia A., R. Bogdan, D. A. Gallo, and R. J. McNally. 2009. "False Memory Propensity in People Reporting Recovered Memories of Past Lives." *Journal of Abnormal Psychology* 118.2: 399–404.

Mills, Antonia. 1989. "A Replication Study: Three Cases of Children in Northern India Who Are Said to Remember a Previous Life." *Journal of Scientific Exploration* 3.2: 133–84.

———. 1990. "Moslem Cases of the Reincarnation Type in Northern India: A Test of the Hypothesis of Imposed Identification Part I: Analysis of 26 Cases" and "Moslem Cases of the Reincarnation Type in Northern India: A Test of the Hypothesis of Imposed Identification Part II: Reports of Three Cases." *Journal of Scientific Exploration* 4: 171–202.

———. 1994. "Introduction." In *Amerindian Rebirth: Reincarnation Belief among North American Indians and Inuit*, edited by A. Mills and R. Slobodin, 3–14. Toronto: University of Toronto Press.

———. 2004. "Inferences from the Case of Ajendra Singh Chauhan, The Effect of Parental Questioning, of Meeting the 'Previous Life' Family, an Aborted Attempt to Quantify Probabilities, and the Impact on His Life as a Young Adult." *Journal of Scientific Exploration* 18.4: 609–41.

———. 2006. "Back from Death: Young Adults in Northern India Who as Children Were Said to Remember a Previous Life, with or without a Shift in Religion (Hindu to Moslem or Vice Versa)." *Anthropology and Humanism Quarterly* 31.2: 141–56.

Mills, Antonia, and S. J. Lynn. 2000. "Past Life Experiences." In *Varieties of Anomalous Experience: Examining the Scientific Evidence*, edited by E. Cardeña, S. J. Lynn, and S. Krippner, 283–313. Washington, DC: American Psychological Association.

Minh Chau, Thich. 1964/1991. *The Chinese Madhyama Āgama and the Pāli Majjhima Nikāya*. Delhi: Motilal Banarsidass.

Moody, Raymond A. 1975/1986. *Life after Life*. New York: Bantam Books.

Moricca, Umberto. 1924. *Gregorii Magni Dialogi, Libri IV*. Rome: Tipografia del Senato.

Morse, Melvin, P. Castillo, D. Venecia, J. Milstein, and D. C. Tyler. 1986. "Childhood Near-Death Experiences." *The American Journal of Diseases of Children* 140: 1110–14.

Murti, T. R. V. 1955/2008. *The Central Philosophy of Buddhism: A Study of the Mādhyamika System*. Abingdon: Routledge.

Nagao, G. M. 1955/1992. "The Silence of the Buddha and Its Madhyamic Interpretation." In *Mādhyamika and Yogācāra: A Study of Mahāyāna Philosophies, Collected Papers of G. M. Nagao*, edited by L. S. Kawamura, 35–49. Delhi: Sri Satguru.

Nagashima, Jundo. 2009. "The Sanskrit Fragments Or. 15009/51–90 in the Hoernle Collection." In *Buddhist Manuscripts from Central*

Asia: The British Library Sanskrit Fragments, edited by S. Karashima and K. Wille, 2: 128–59. Tokyo: International Research Institute for Advanced Buddhology, Soka University.

Ñāṇamoli, Bhikkhu. 1956/1991. *The Path of Purification (Visuddhimagga) by Bhadantācariya Buddhaghosa.* Kandy: Buddhist Publication Society.

———. 1994. *A Pali–English Glossary of Buddhist Technical Terms.* Kandy: Buddhist Publication Society.

Ñāṇananda, Bhikkhu. 2003 (vol. 1). *Nibbāna: The Mind Stilled.* Sri Lanka: Dharma Grantha Mudrana Bhāraya.

Ñāṇaponika, Thera. 1975. "Reflections on Kamma and Its Fruit." In *Kamma and Its Fruit: Selected Essays*, edited by Ñāṇaponika, 86–95. Kandy: Buddhist Publication Society.

Ñāṇavīra, Thera. 1987/2001. *Clearing the Path: Writings of Ñānavīra Thera (1960–1965), Volume I, Notes on Dhamma.* Sri Lanka: Buddhist Cultural Centre.

Negi, J. S. 1993 (vol. 1). *Tibetan–Sanskrit Dictionary.* Sarnath: Dictionary Unit, Central Institute of Higher Tibetan Studies.

Nelson, Eric Sean. 2005. "Questioning Karma: Buddhism and the Phenomenology of the Ethical." *Journal of Buddhist Ethics*, online conference on "Revisioning Karma." http://blogs.dickinson.edu /buddhistethics/files/2011/01/nelson01.pdf.

Nickerson, Raymond S. 1998. "Confirmation Bias: A Ubiquitous Phenomenon in Many Guises." *Review of General Psychology* 2.2: 175–220.

Nicol, J. Fraser. 1976. Review of *Cases of the Reincarnation Type, Volume I* by I. Stevenson. *Parapsychological Review* 12–15.

Norman, K. R. 1984. "The Four Noble Truths: A Problem of Pāli Syntax." In *Indological and Buddhist Studies: Volume in Honour of Professor J. W. de Jong on His Sixtieth Birthday*, edited by L. A. Hercus, 2nd ed., 377–91. Delhi: Sri Satguru.

———. 1991/1993. "Death and the Tathāgata." In *Collected Papers*, edited by K. R. Norman, 4: 251–63. Oxford: Pali Text Society.

———. 2003. "The Aṭṭhakavagga and Early Buddhism." In *Jainism and Early Buddhism: Essays in Honor of Padmanabh S. Jaini*, edited by O. Qvarnström, 511–22. Fremont, CA: Asian Humanities Press.

Oberlies, Thomas. 2005. "Der Gandharva und die drei Tage währende 'Quarantäne.'" *Indo-Iranian Journal* 48: 97–109.

Obeyesekere, Ganath. 2002. *Imagining Karma: Ethical Transformation in Amerindian, Buddhist, and Greek Rebirth.* Berkeley: University of California Press.

Oldenberg, Hermann. 1881/1961. *Buddha, Sein Leben, Seine Lehre, Seine Gemeinde.* Munich: Wilhelm Goldmann Verlag.

———. 1894. *Die Religion des Veda.* Berlin: Wilhelm Hertz.

Organ, Troy Wilson. 1954. "The Silence of the Buddha." *Philosophy East and West* 4.2: 125–40.

Osis, Karlis, and E. Haraldsson. 1977/1986. *At the Hour of Death, Revised Edition.* New York: Hastings House.

Pannikar, Raimundo. 1989/1990. *The Silence of God: The Answer of the Buddha.* New York: Orbis Books.

Park, Jungnok. 2012. *How Buddhism Acquired a Soul on the Way to China.* Oxford Centre for Buddhist Studies Monograph. Sheffield: Equinox.

Parnia, Sam, and P. Fenwick. 2002. "Near Death Experiences in Cardiac Arrest: Visions of a Dying Brain or Visions of a New Science of Consciousness." *Resuscitation* 52: 5–11.

Pāsādika, Bhikkhu. 1989. *Nāgārjuna's Sūtrasamuccaya: A Critical Edition of the mDo kun las btus pa.* Copenhagen: Akademisk Forlag.

Pasricha, Satwant K. 1990/2005. *Claims of Reincarnation: An Empirical Study of Cases in India.* Delhi: Harman Publishing House.

———. 1993/2008. "A Systematic Survey of Near-Death Experiences in South India." In *Can the Mind Survive beyond Death? In Pursuit of Scientific Evidence, Volume 2: Reincarnation and Other Anomalous Experiences,* edited by S. K. Pasricha, 415–30. New Delhi: Harman Publishing House.

———. 1995/2008. "Near-Death Experiences in South India: A Systematic Survey." In *Can the Mind Survive beyond Death? In Pursuit of Scientific Evidence, Volume 2: Reincarnation and Other Anomalous Experiences,* edited by S. K. Pasricha, 431–45. New Delhi: Harman Publishing House.

Pasricha, Satwant K., and I. Stevenson. 1986/2008. "Near-Death Experiences in India, A Preliminary Report." In *Can the Mind Survive beyond Death? In Pursuit of Scientific Evidence, Volume 2: Reincarnation and Other Anomalous Experiences*, edited by S. K. Pasricha, 399–414. New Delhi: Harman Publishing House.

Pirazzoli-t'Serstevens, Michèle. 2009. "Death and the Dead: Practices and Images in the Qin and Han." In *Early Chinese Religion, Part One: Shang through Han (1250 BC–220 AD)*, edited by J. Lagerwey and M. Kalinowski, 949–1026. Leiden: Brill.

Pischel, Richard, and K. F. Geldner. 1889 (vol. 1). *Vedische Studien*. Stuttgart: Kohlhammer.

Platthy, Jeno. 1992. *Near-Death Experiences in Antiquity*. Santa Claus, IN: Federation of International Poetry Associations of UNESCO.

Poo, Mu-chou. 1990. "Ideas concerning Death and Burial in Pre-Han and Han China." *Asia Major, Third Series* 3.2: 25–62.

Pradhan, P. 1967. *Abhidharmakośabhāṣya of Vasubandhu*. Patna: K. P. Jayaswal Research Institute.

Premasiri, P. D. 1972. *The Philosophy of the Aṭṭhakavagga*. Kandy: Buddhist Publication Society.

———. 1996. "The Theravada Buddhist Doctrine of Survival after Death." In *Concepts of Transmigration: Perspectives on Reincarnation*, edited by S. J. Kaplan, 133–87. New York: Edwin Mellen Press.

———. 2001/2006. "Buddhist Philosophy on Rebirth." In *Studies in Buddhist Philosophy and Religion: Collected Papers of Professor P. D. Premasiri*, edited by G. A. Somaratne, S. Pemaratana, and R. Padmasiri, 209–19. Singapore: Buddha Dhamma Mandala Society.

———. 2005. "Rebirth." In *Encyclopaedia of Buddhism*, edited by W. G. Weeraratne, 7.3: 521–32. Sri Lanka: Department of Buddhist Affairs.

Radich, Michael David. 2007. *The Somatics of Liberation: Ideas about Embodiment in Buddhism from Its Origins to the Fifth Century C.E.* PhD diss., Harvard University.

Ramster, Peter. 1994. "Past Lives and Hypnosis." *Australian Journal of Clinical Hypnotherapy and Hypnosis* 15.2: 67–91.

Rawat, Kirti Swaroop, and T. Rivas. 2007. *Reincarnation: The Scientific Evidence Is Building*. Vancouver: Writers Publisher.

Rawlings, Maurice. 1978/1980. *Beyond Death's Door*. London: Sheldon.

Reat, Noble Ross. 1996/1998. "The Historical Buddha and His Teachings." In *Encyclopaedia of Indian Philosophies, Vol. VII: Abhidharma Buddhism to 150 AD*, edited by K. H. Potter, 3–57. Delhi: Motilal Banarsidass.

Renou, Louis, and J. Filliozat. 1953/2001. *L'Inde classique, manuel des études indiennes, Tome II*. Paris: Publications de l'École Française d'Extrême-Orient.

Reynolds, Craig J. 1976. "Buddhist Cosmography in Thai History, with Special Reference to Nineteenth-Century Cultural Change." *Journal of Asian Studies* 35.2: 203–20.

Ring, Kenneth, and S. Cooper. 1997. "Near-Death and Out-of-Body Experiences in the Blind: A Study of Apparent Eyeless Vision." *Journal of Near-Death Studies* 16.2: 101–47.

———. 1999/2008. *Mindsight: Near-Death and Out-of-Body Experiences in the Blind*, 2nd ed. New York: iUniverse.

Ring, Kenneth, and M. Lawrence. 1993. "Further Evidence for Veridical Perception during Near-Death Experiences." *Journal of Near-Death Studies* 11.4: 223–29.

Ring, Kenneth, and E. E. Valarino. 1998. *Lessons from the Light: What We Can Learn from the Near-Death Experience*. Portsmouth, NH: Moment Point Press.

Roediger, Henry L. 1996. "Memory Illusions." *Journal of Memory and Language* 35: 76–100.

Rogo, D. Scott. 1985/2005. *The Search for Yesterday: A Critical Examination of the Evidence for Reincarnation*. San Antonio, NY: Anomalist Books.

Roll, William G. 1982. "The Changing Perspective on Life after Death." In *Advances in Parapsychological Research, Volume 3*, edited by S. Krippner, 147–291. New York: Plenum Press.

Rommer, B. R. 2000. *Blessing in Disguise: Another Side of the Near Death Experience*. Woodbury, MN: Lewellyn Publications.

Ross, Barbara. 1979. "The Same Old Story: A Historical Perspective." In *Between Life and Death*, edited by R. Kastenbaum, 29–44. New York: Springer.

Ruben, Walter. 1935. "Materialismus im Leben des alten Indiens." *Acta Orientalia* 13: 128–62.

Sabom, Michael. 1982. *Recollections of Death: A Medical Investigation*. London: Corgi Books.

———. 1998. *Light & Death: One Doctor's Fascinating Account of Near-Death Experiences*. Grand Rapids, MI: Zondervan.

———. 2007. "Commentary on 'Does Paranormal Perception Occur in Near-Death Experiences?'" *Journal of Near-Death Studies* 25.4: 257–60.

Saddhatissa, Hammalawa. 1991/2001. "The Significance of paritta and Its Application in the Theravāda Tradition." In *Buddhist Thought and Ritual*, edited by D. J. Kalupahana, 125–37. Delhi: Motilal Banarsidass.

Sakaki, Ryōzaburō. 1916/1962. 飜譯名義大集. Tokyo: Suzuki Research Foundation.

Samarin, William J. 1976. [Review of Stevenson 1974b]. *Language* 52.1: 270–74.

Samuel, Geoffrey. 1993/1995. *Civilized Shamans: Buddhism in Tibetan Society*. Kathmandu: Nepal Lithographing Co.

Sander, Lore. 1991. "The Earliest Manuscripts from Central Asia and the Sarvāstivāda Mission." In *Corolla Iranica: Papers in Honour of Prof. Dr. David Neil MacKenzie on the Occasion of His 65th Birthday on April 8th, 1991*, edited by R. E. Emmerick and D. Weber, 133–50. Frankfurt: Peter Lang.

Sander, Lore, and E. Waldschmidt. 1980. *Sanskrithandschriften aus den Turfanfunden, Teil IV.* Wiesbaden: Franz Steiner.

———. 1985. *Sanskrithandschriften aus den Turfanfunden, Teil 5*. Stuttgart: Franz Steiner.

Sartori, Penny. 2008. *The Near-Death Experiences of Hospitalized Intensive Care Patients: A Five Year Clinical Study*. Lewiston, ME: Edwin Mellen Press.

Sartori, Penny, P. Badham, and P. Fenwick. 2006. "A Prospectively Studied Near-Death Experience with Corroborated Out-of-Body Perceptions and Unexplained Healing." *Journal of Near-Death Studies* 25.2: 69–84.

Schacter, Daniel L. 1999. "The Seven Sins of Memory: Insights from Psychology and Cognitive Neuroscience." *American Psychologist* 54.3: 182–203.

Schmithausen, Lambert. 1987. "Beiträge zur Schulzugehörigkeit und Textgeschichte kanonischer und postkanonischer buddhistischer Materialien." In *Zur Schulzugehörigkeit von Werken der Hīnayāna-Literatur, Zweiter Teil*, edited by H. Bechert, 304–403. Göttingen: Vandenhoeck & Ruprecht.

Schopen, Gregory. 1978. *The Bhaiṣajyaguru-sūtra and the Buddhism of Gilgit*. PhD diss., Australian National University.

———. 1983. "The Generalization of an Old Yogic Attainment in Medieval Mahāyāna Sūtra Literature: Some Notes on Jātismara." *Journal of the International Association of Buddhist Studies* 6.1: 109–47.

Schrader, Otto F. 1904/1905. "On the Problem of Nirvāṇa." *Journal of the Pali Text Society* 157–70.

Schumann, Ruth Antelme, and S. Rossini. 1995/1998. *Becoming Osiris: The Ancient Egyptian Death Experience*. Rochester, VT: Inner Traditions.

Schwieger, Peter. 2015. *The Dalai Lama and the Emperor of China: A Political History of the Tibetan Institution of Reincarnation*. New York: Columbia University Press.

Seeger, Martin. 2005. "How Long Is a Lifetime? Buddhadāsa and Phra Payutto's Interpretations of paṭiccasamuppāda in Comparison." *Buddhist Studies Review* 22: 107–30.

Seidel, Anna. 1987. "Post-Mortem Immortality or the Taoist Resurrection of the Body." In *Gilgul: Essays on Transformation, Revolution and Permanence in the History of Religions, Dedicated to R. J. Zwi Werblowsky*, edited by S. Shaked, D. Shulman, and G. G. Stroumsa, 223–37. Leiden: Brill.

Senart, Émile. 1890 (vol. 2). *Le Mahāvastu, texte sanscrit publié pour la première fois et accompagné d'introductions et d'un commentaire*. Paris: Imprimerie Nationale.

Sharma, Poonam, and J. B. Tucker. 2005. "Cases of the Reincarnation Type with Memories from the Intermission between Lives." *Journal of Near-Death Studies* 23.2: 101–18.

Shulman, Eviatar. 2012/2013. "Early Buddhist Imagination: The Aṭṭhakavagga as Buddhist Poetry." *Journal of the International Association of Buddhist Studies* 35.1/2: 363–411.

Siderits, Mark. 1987. "Beyond Compatibilism: A Buddhist Approach to Freedom and Determinism." *American Philosophical Quarterly* 24.2: 149–59.

Siegel, Ronald K. 1981. "Life after Death." In *Science and the Paranormal: Probing the Existence of the Supernatural*, edited by G. O. Abell and B. Singer, 159–84. New York: Charles Scribner's Sons.

Silk, Jonathan A. 2007. "Good and Evil in Indian Buddhism: The Five Sins of Immediate Retribution." *Journal of Indian Philosophy* 35: 253–86.

Skilling, Peter. 1992. "The rakṣā Literature of the Śrāvakayāna." *Journal of the Pali Text Society* 16: 109–82.

———. 1993. "Theravādin Literature in Tibetan Translation." *Journal of the Pali Text Society* 19: 69–201.

———. 1998. "A Note on Dhammapada 60 and the Length of the yojana." *Journal of the Pali Text Society* 24: 149–70.

Skjærvø, Pros Oktor. 2013. "Afterlife in Zoroastrianism." In *Jenseitsvorstellungen im Orient, Kongreßakten der 2. Tagung der RVO (3./4. Juni 2011, Tübingen)*, edited by P. Bukovec and B. Kolkmann-Klamt, 311–49. Hamburg: Verlag Dr. Kovač.

Smart, Ninian. 1964/1976. *Doctrine and Argument in Indian Philosophy*. Atlantic Highlands, NJ: Humanities Press.

Snellgrove, David L. 1987. *Indo-Tibetan Buddhism: Indian Buddhists and Their Tibetan Successors*. London: Serindia Publications.

Somaratne, G. A. 1998. *The Saṃyuttanikāya of the Suttapiṭaka: Volume I, The Sagāthavagga*. Oxford: Pali Text Society.

———. 1999. "Intermediate Existence and the Higher Fetters in the Pāli Nikāyas." *Journal of the Pali Text Society* 25: 121–54.

———. 2005. "Citta, manas & viññāṇa: Aspects of Mind as Presented in Early Buddhist Pali Discourses." In *Dhamma-Vinaya: Essays in Honour of Venerable Professor Dhammavihari (Jotiya Dhirasekera)*, edited by A. Tilakaratne, T. Endo, G. A. Somaratne, and S. Nānāyakkāra, 169–202. Colombo: Sri Lanka Association for Buddhist Studies.

Spanos, Nicholas P. 1994. "Multiple Identity Enactments and Multiple Personality Disorder: A Sociocognitive Perspective." *Psychological Bulletin* 116.1: 143–65.

———. 1996. *Multiple Identities & False Memories: A Sociocognitive Perspective.* Washington, DC: American Psychological Association.

Spanos, Nicholas P., E. Menary, N. J. Gabora, S. C. DuBreuil, and B. Dewhirst. 1991. "Secondary Identity Enactments during Hypnotic Past-Life Regression: A Sociocognitive Perspective." *Journal of Personality and Social Psychology* 61.2: 308–20.

Speyer, J. S. 1909/1970 (vol. 2). *Avadānaçataka: A Century of Edifying Tales Belonging to the Hīnayāna.* Osnabrück: Biblio Verlag.

Stache-Rosen, Valentina. 1968 (vol. 1). *Dogmatische Begriffsreihen im älteren Buddhismus II; Das Saṅgītisūtra und sein Kommentar Saṅgītiparyāya.* Berlin: Akademie Verlag.

Stanovich, Keith E., R. F. West, and M. E. Toplak. 2013. "Myside Bias, Rational Thinking, and Intelligence." *Current Directions in Psychological Science* 22.4: 259–64.

Stevenson, Ian. 1960. "The Evidence for Survival from Claimed Memories of Former Incarnations: The Winning Essay of the Contest in Honor of William James." *Journal of the American Society for Psychical Research* 54.2: 51–71.

———. 1966/1974. *Twenty Cases Suggestive of Reincarnation, Second Edition, Revised and Enlarged.* Charlottesville: University of Virginia Press.

———. 1974a. "Some Questions Related to Cases of the Reincarnation Type." *Journal of the American Society for Psychical Research*, 395–416.

———. 1974b. *Xenoglossy: A Review and Report of a Case.* Charlottesville: University of Virginia Press.

———. 1975. *Cases of the Reincarnation Type, Volume I: Ten Cases in India.* Charlottesville: University of Virginia Press.

———. 1977. *Cases of the Reincarnation Type, Volume II: Ten Cases in Sri Lanka.* Charlottesville: University of Virginia Press.

———. 1980. *Cases of the Reincarnation Type, Volume III: Twelve Cases in Lebanon and Turkey.* Charlottesville: University of Virginia Press.

———. 1983a. "American Children Who Claim to Remember Previous Lives." *The Journal of Nervous and Mental Disease* 171.12: 742–48.

———. 1983b. *Cases of the Reincarnation Type, Volume IV: Twelve Cases in Thailand and Burma.* Charlottesville: University of Virginia Press.

———. 1984. *Unlearned Language: New Studies in Xenoglossy.* Charlottesville: University of Virginia Press.

———. 1986. "Comments by Ian Stevenson." *Journal of the Society for Psychical Research* 53.802: 232–39.

———. 1987/2001. *Children Who Remember Previous Lives: A Question of Reincarnation, Revised Edition.* Jefferson, NC: McFarland.

———. 1994. "A Case of the Psychotherapist's Fallacy: Hypnotic Regression to 'Previous Lives.'" *American Journal of Critical Hypnosis* 36.3: 188–93.

———. 1997a: *Reincarnation and Biology: A Contribution to the Etiology of Birthmarks and Birth Defects.* Westport, CT: Praeger.

———. 1997b: *Where Reincarnation and Biology Intersect.* Westport, CT: Praeger.

———. 2003/2008. *European Cases of the Reincarnation Type.* Jefferson, NC: McFarland.

Stevenson, Ian, and S. Pasricha. 1980. "A Preliminary Report on an Unusual Case of the Reincarnation Type with Xenoglossy." *Journal of the American Society for Psychical Research* 74: 331–48.

Stevenson, Ian, and Godwin Samararatne. 1988. "Three New Cases of the Reincarnation Type with Written Records Made Before Verification." *Journal of Scientific Exploration* 2.2: 217–38.

Story, Francis. 1975. "Karma and Freedom." In *Kamma and Its Fruit: Selected Essays*, edited by Ñāṇaponika, 74–80. Kandy: Buddhist Publication Society.

———. 1975/2010. *Rebirth as Doctrine and Experience.* Kandy: Buddhist Publication Society.

Sudduth, Michael. 2016. *A Philosophical Critique of Empirical Arguments for Postmortem Survival.* New York: Palgrave Macmillan.

Sutherland, Cherie. 2009. "'Trailing Clouds of Glory': The Near-Death Experiences of Western Children and Teens." In *The Handbook of Near-Death Experiences: Thirty Years of Investigation*, edited by J. M. Holden, B. Greyson, and D. James, 87–107. Santa Barbara, CA: Praeger.

Tamai, Tatsushi. 2017. "The Tocharian Mūgapakkha-Jātaka." *Annual*

Report of the International Research Institute for Advanced Buddhology at Soka University 20: 251–75.

Tarazi, Linda. 1990. "An Unusual Case of Hypnotic Regression with Some Unexplained Contents." *The Journal of the American Society for Psychical Research* 84.4: 309–44.

Tart, Charles T. 2007. "Comments on 'Does Paranormal Perception Occur in Near-Death Experiences?" *Journal of Near-Death Studies* 25.4: 251–56.

Teiser, Stephen F. 1988. "'Having Once Died and Returned to Life': Representations of Hell in Medieval China." *Journal of Asiatic Studies* 48.2: 433–64.

———. 1996. *The Ghost Festival in Medieval China*. Princeton, NJ: Princeton University Press.

Thomas, E. J. 1927/2003. *The Life of Buddha as Legend and History*. Delhi: Munshiram Manoharlal.

Thomason, Sarah Grey. 1984. "Do You Remember Your Previous Life's Language in Your Present Incarnation?" *American Speech* 59.4: 340–50.

———. 1987. "Past Tongues Remembered?" *The Skeptical Inquirer* 11.4: 367–75.

———. 1988. "Reply to 'Response to "Past Tongues Remembered."'" *The Skeptical Inquirer* 12.3: 323–24.

———. 1996. "Xenoglossy." In *The Encyclopedia of the Paranormal*, edited by Gordon Stein, 835–44. Amherst, NY: Prometheus Books.

Thompson, Evan. 2015. *Waking, Dreaming, Being: Self and Consciousness in Neuroscience, Meditation, and Philosophy*. New York: Columbia University Press.

Thondup, Tulku. 2011. *Incarnation: The History and Mysticism of the Tulku Tradition of Tibet*. Boston: Shambhala.

Tilakaratne, Asaṅga. 1993. *Nirvana and Ineffability: A Study of the Buddhist Theory of Reality and Language*. Sri Lanka: University of Kelaniya, Postgraduate Institute of Pali and Buddhist Studies.

Trenckner, V. 1888/1993. *The Majjhima-nikāya, Vol. I*. Oxford: Pali Text Society.

Trenckner, V., D. Andersen, and H. Smith. 1924 (vol. 1). *A Critical Pāli Dictionary*. Copenhagen: The Royal Danish Academy.

Tripāṭhī, Chandrabhāl. 1962. *Fünfundzwanzig sūtras des Nidānasaṃyukta*. Berlin: Akademie Verlag.

Tucker, Jim B. 2005/2014. *Life before Life: A Scientific Investigation of Children's Memories of Previous Lives*. London: Piatkus.

———. 2013. *Return to Life: Extraordinary Cases of Children Who Remember Past Lives*. New York: St. Martin's Griffin.

Tucker, Jim B., and F. D. Nidiffer. 2014. "Psychological Evaluation of American Children Who Report Memories of Previous Lives." *Journal of Scientific Exploration* 28.4: 583–94.

Uebach, Helga. 2005. *Wörterbuch der tibetischen Schriftsprache, im Auftrag der Kommission für zentral- und ostasiatische Studien der Bayerischen Akademie der Wissenschaften herausgegeben von Herbert Franke, 1. Lieferung ka—kun chub par byed pa*. Munich: Verlag der Bayerischen Akademie der Wissenschaften in Kommission beim Verlag C. H. Beck.

Upadhyaya, K. N. 1971. *Early Buddhism and the Bhagavadgītā*. Delhi: Motilal Banarsidass.

van der Sluijs, M. A. 2009. "Three Ancient Reports of Near-Death Experiences: Bremmer Revisited." *Journal of Near-Death Experiences* 27.4: 223–53.

van Lommel, P. 2010. *Consciousness beyond Life: The Science of the Near-Death Experience*. New York: HarperOne.

van Zeyst, H. G. A. 1971. "Bkaḥ-ḥgyur." In *Encyclopaedia of Buddhism*, edited by G. P. Malalasekera, 3.1: 152–54. Sri Lanka: Department of Buddhist Affairs.

Vélez de Cea, Abraham. 2004. "The Silence of the Buddha and the Questions about the Tathāgata after Death." *Indian International Journal of Buddhist Studies* 5: 119–41.

Venn, Jonathan. 1986. "Hypnosis and the Reincarnation Hypothesis: A Critical Review and Intensive Case Study." *Journal of the American Society for Psychical Research* 80: 409–25.

Vetter, Tilmann. 1990. "Some Remarks on Older Parts of the Suttanipāta."

In *Earliest Buddhism and Madhyamaka*, edited by D. S. Ruegg, 36–56. Leiden: Brill.

Visoni, Vitor Moura. 2010. "How to Improve the Study and Documentation of Cases of the Reincarnation Type? A Reappraisal of the Case of Kemal Atasoy." *Journal of Scientific Exploration* 24: 95–102.

Vogel, Claus. 1970. *The Teachings of the Six Heretics, according to the Pravrajyāvastu of the Tibetan Mūlasarvāstivāda Vinaya, Edited and Rendered into English, with an Appendix Containing an English Translation of the Pertinent Sections in the Chinese Mūlasarvāstivāda Vinaya*. Wiesbaden: Franz Steiner.

von Hinüber, Oskar. 1989. *Der Beginn der Schrift und frühe Schriftlichkeit in Indien*. Wiesbaden: Franz Steiner.

———. 1991. "Das buddhistische Recht und die Phonetik des Pāli, Ein Abschnitt aus der Samantapāsādikā über die Vermeidung von Aussprachefehlern in kammavācās." *Studien zur Indologie und Iranistik* 13/14: 101–27.

———. 1994. *Untersuchungen zur Mündlichkeit früher mittelindischer Texte der Buddhisten*. Stuttgart: Franz Steiner.

———. 2015. "Building the Theravāda Commentaries: Buddhaghosa and Dhammapāla as Authors, Compilers, Redactors, Editors and Critics." *Journal of the International Association of Buddhist Studies* 36/37: 353–87.

———. 2016. "Manuscripts and Printing: South, Southeast, and Central Asia." In *Brill's Encyclopedia of Buddhism*, edited by J. Silk, O. von Hinüber, and V. Eltschinger, 1: 943–58. Leiden: Brill.

von Rospatt, Alexander. 1995. *The Buddhist Doctrine of Momentariness: A Survey of the Origins and Early Phase of This Doctrine up to Vasubandhu*. Stuttgart: Franz Steiner.

Waldschmidt, Ernst. 1951 (vol. 2). *Das Mahāparinirvāṇasūtra, Text in Sanskrit und Tibetisch, verglichen mit dem Pāli nebst einer Übersetzung der chinesischen Entsprechung im Vinaya der Mūlasarvāstivādins, auf Grund von Turfan-Handschriften herausgegeben und bearbeitet*. Berlin: Akademie Verlag.

———. 1956 (vol. 2). *Das Mahāvadānasūtra, ein kanonischer Text über die sieben letzten Buddhas, Sanskrit, verglichen mit dem Pāli nebst einer*

Analyse der in chinesischer Übersetzung überlieferten Parallelversion, auf Grund von Turfan-Handschriften herausgegeben. Berlin: Akademie Verlag.

———. 1957 (vol. 2). *Das Catuṣpariṣatsūtra, eine kanonische Lehrschrift über die Begründung der buddhistischen Gemeinde*. Berlin: Akademie Verlag.

———. 1958. "Ein Zweites Daśabalasūtra." *Mitteilungen des Institutes für Orientforschung, Berlin, Deutsche Akademie der Wissenschaft* 6: 382–405.

Waldschmidt, Ernst, W. Clawiter, and L. Holzmann. 1965. *Sanskrithandschriften aus den Turfanfunden, Teil I*. Wiesbaden: Franz Steiner.

Waldschmidt, Ernst, W. Clawiter, and L. Sander-Holzmann. 1971. *Sanskrithandschriften aus den Turfanfunden, Teil 3*. Wiesbaden: Franz Steiner.

Walker, Barbara A., and W. J. Serdahely. 1990. "Historical Perspectives on Near-Death Phenomena." *Journal of Near-Death Studies* 9.2: 105–21.

Wambach, Helen. 1978. *Reliving Past Lives: The Evidence under Hypnosis*. London: Hutchinson.

Warder, A. K. 1982. "Introduction." In *The Path of Discrimination (Paṭisambhidāmagga)*, translated by Ñāṇamoli Thera, v–lxiv. London: Pali Text Society.

Wayman, Alex. 1974. "The Intermediate-State Dispute in Buddhism." In *Buddhist Studies in Honour of I. B. Horner*, edited by L. S. Cousins, A. Kunst, and K. R. Norman, 227–39. Dordrecht: D. Reidel.

Weller, Friedrich. 1934. *Brahmajālasūtra, Tibetischer und Mongolischer Text*. Leipzig: Otto Harrassowitz.

———. 1940. "Über die Formel der vier edlen Wahrheiten." *Orientalistische Literaturzeitung* 43.3/4: 73–79.

Werner, Karel. 2008. "Death, Rebirth and Personal Identity in Buddhism." *International Journal of Buddhist Thought & Culture* 10: 19–39.

West, Richard F., R. J. Meserve, K. E. Stanovich. 2012. "Cognitive Sophistication Does Not Attenuate the Bias Blind Spot." *Journal of Personal and Social Psychology* 103.3: 506–19.

Wijesekera, O. H. de A. 1945/1994. "Vedic Gandharva and Pali Gandhabba."

In *Buddhist and Vedic Studies, A Miscellany*, edited by M. H. F. Jayasuriya, 175–212. Delhi: Motilal Banarsidass.

Wille, Klaus. 2008. *Sanskrithandschriften aus den Turfanfunden, Teil 10*. Stuttgart: Franz Steiner.

Willson, Martin. 1984/1987. *Rebirth and the Western Buddhist*. London: Wisdom Publications.

Wilson, Ian. 1981. *Mind Out of Time? Reincarnation Claims Investigated*. London: Gollancz.

Windisch, Ernst. 1908. *Buddha's Geburt und die Lehre von der Seelenwanderung*. Leipzig: B. G. Teubner.

Woerlee, G. M. 2005a. "An Anaesthesiologist Examines the Pam Reynolds Story, Part 1: Background Considerations." *The Skeptic* 18.1: 14–17.

———. 2005b. "An Anaesthesiologist Examines the Pam Reynolds Story, Part 2: The Experience." *The Skeptic* 18.2: 16–20.

———. 2011. "Could Pam Reynolds Hear? A New Investigation into the Possibility of Hearing during This Famous Near-Death Experience." *Journal of Near-Death Studies* 30.1: 3–25.

Wogihara, Unrai. 1936. *Sphuṭārthā Abhidharmakośavyākhyā by Yaśomitra, Part II*. Tokyo: The Publishing Association of Abhidharmakośavyākhyā.

Woods, Kellye, and I. Barušs. 2004. "Experimental Test of Possible Psychological Benefits of Past-Life Regression." *Journal of Scientific Exploration* 18.4: 597–608.

Woodward, F. L. 1930/1979 (vol. 5). *The Book of the Kindred Sayings (Saṃyutta-nikāya) or Grouped Suttas*. London: Pali Text Society.

Wujastyk, Dominik. 2011. "The Path to Liberation through Yogic Mindfulness in Early Āyurveda." In *Yoga in Practice*, edited by D. G. White, 31–42. Princeton, NJ: Princeton University Press.

Young, R. F., and G. P. V. Somaratna. 1996. *Vain Debates: The Buddhist–Christian Controversies of Nineteenth-Century Ceylon*. Vienna: Institut für Indologie der Universität Wien.

Yü, Ying-shih. 1987. "'O Soul, Come Back!' A Study in the Changing Conceptions of the Soul and Afterlife in Pre-Buddhist China." *Harvard Journal of Asiatic Studies* 47.2: 363–95.

Yün-Hua, Jan. 1986. "The Chinese Understanding and Assimilation of Karma Doctrine." In *Karma and Rebirth: Post Classical Developments*, edited by R. W. Neufeldt, 145–68. Albany: State University of New York Press.

Zaleski, Carol. 1987. *Otherworld Journeys: Accounts of Near-Death Experience in Medieval and Modern Times*. New York: Oxford University Press.

Zhang, Lixiang. 2004. *Das Śaṃkarasūtra: Eine Übersetzung des Sanskrit-Textes im Vergleich mit der Pāli Fassung.* MA thesis, Ludwig-Maximilians-Universität München.

Zürcher, Erik. 1959/1972. *The Buddhist Conquest of China: The Spread and Adaptation of Buddhism in Early Medieval China*. Leiden: Brill.

———. 1980. "Buddhist Influence on Early Taoism: A Survey of Scriptural Evidence." *T'oung Pao, Second Series* 66.1/3: 84–147.

Zysk, Kenneth G. 1982. "Studies in Traditional Indian Medicine in the Pāli Canon: Jīvaka and Āyurveda." *Journal of the International Association of Buddhist Studies* 5.1: 70–86.

Index

A

abhiññā (higher knowledge), 33
absent-mindedness, 81–82
Acts of the Apostles, 113
anattā. *See* notself
Andary, Suleyman, 92n232
Aṅgulimāla, 25
Aṅguttara-nikāya, 21, 22, 167n452
antarāparinibbāyī, 21n41
Apaṇṇaka-sutta, 31, 32
Assandri, Friederike, 53n116
attention, 11
Aṭṭhaka-vagga, 37–39
Augustine, Keith, 72n172
awakening
  destiny of an awakened one after death, 42–44
  See also Buddha: awakening of

B

Badham, P., 76n189
Baker, Robert A., 86n215
Barušs, I., 84n208
Batchelor, Stephen, 58n134, 59n136, 60n142
Bechert, Heinz, 126n325
Bhaiṣajyaguru, 68
Bhayabherava-sutta, 18–20
birth
  definition and use of the term, 8
  dependent arising and, 7–9
birthmarks, birth defects, and past-life memories, 93n237, 105, 106, 108–12
blind persons, near-death experiences of, 77–78
blocking (memory), 81
Bodhi, Bhikkhu, 21n41, 38n81, 39n85, 57n132
Bokenkamp, Stephen R., 53n115
Brahmā, 155–58
Brahmajāla-sutta, 26, 28, 39
Brahmin, 15, 52, 53, 94, 102, 103, 122
Bransford, John D., 83n206
Braude, S. E., 96n244
Brody, E. B., 91n229
Buddha, 32, 39, 41, 97, 127
  awakening of, 20, 29n62, 43n91; night of the, 18, 19, 33, 35, 81
  birthmarks, 108
  disciples, 32, 40, 42, 44, 67, 128
  encounters with celestial beings, 67
  expressing respect toward, 130
  first sermon, 128, 154–62
  householders and, 31, 32n69
  karma and, 20, 57n132, 60n141
  liberating teachings, 29
  liberation and, 32
  preawakening recollection of past lives, 18–19, 91
  preawakening witnessing of the rebirth of others, 19–20
  rebirth and, 19, 20, 28–31, 33, 57n132, 60nn140–42; claims that Buddha did not teach rebirth, 59, 60, 163; claims that Buddha did teach rebirth, 33, 35, 59n139, 60, 163
  setting into motion the wheel of Dhamma, 154–56
  undeclared questions: destiny of an awakened one after death, 42–44;

the poisoned arrow of speculative views, 39–40; reason for setting aside speculative views, 41–42; refusal to answer questions about past and future (lives), 39–40, 60nn141–42, 62; right view and speculative views, 37–39
xenoglossy and, 113
Buddhadatta, 42n89, 122–23, 123n322
Buddhism, ultimate goal of, 34n78

C

Carter, Chris, 116n309
Catubhāṇavārapāḷi, 158–61
Cedzich, Ursula-Angelika, 55n127
Chandra, Jagdish, 102–3
children
near-death experiences (NDEs), 77–78
See also past-life memories
China
discussions on rebirth during early imperial period, 50–56
near-death experiences in ancient, 55–56
Choomalaiwong, Chanai, 110
Christianity, 68–69, 71
clinging, 7, 39, 150
collective guilt and karma, 52–53
Collins, Steven, 30n65
conditionality, 3, 7–10, 34, 44, 127, 133. *See also* dependent arising
confirmation bias, 1–2, 60–62
consciousness, 12, 14–16, 46
continuity of, 12, 16, 49
in early Buddhist thought, 10
external, 15n31
and name-and-form, 13
rebirth and, 12–16
reciprocal conditioning of name-and-form and, 9–14, 17, 22–23, 34, 58, 127
residing outside of the body, 13, 14, 46, 47, 73n176
as self-conditioning, 10
terminology, 12
at the time of conception, 17
transfer of, 14n27
transition from one life to another, 14, 35, 44, 47 (*see also* transition from one life to another)
contact, 7, 10, 11, 150
continuity
behavioral continuities (between lives), 91–103
during life, 13, 34–35
of memory, 17, 35
from one life to another, 34–35, 58
of a sense of identity, 19
See also under unchanging agent
Cook, Emily Williams, 107n277
Corinthians, Second Epistle to the, 69
craving, 22, 38, 39, 150
crucifixion of Jesus. *See* stigmata
cryptomnesia, 87–89, 95–96, 98n250, 99
Cūḷakammavibhaṅga-sutta, 24
Cūḷamāluṅkya-sutta, 40, 42

D

Dalai Lama, Fourteenth (Tenzin Gyatso), 90n228
death, dependent arising and, 7, 9, 16, 150
Dell'Olio, Andrew J., 116n309
dependent arising (*paṭicca samuppāda*), 6, 7, 9, 33–34, 44, 58–59
Buddha and, 9
Mahānidāna-sutta and, 150
rebirth and, 9, 12–15
twelve links, 7–9 (*see also* consciousness; name-and-form)
See also conditionality
Devi, Shanti, 91n230
Dhammacakkappavattana-sutta, 121, 128, 146, 148, 154–58, 161–62, 164
Dhammaruwan, 126, 129
Bhikkhu Anālayo's personal contact with, 119–22, 129
chanting, 120, 121, 129, 158, 159n441, 161–62, 167n453
Pāli chants by, 122, 167–236
past-life story and verification of the recordings, 122–25
present-life story, 120–22
See also Pāli xenoglossy
direct realization, 34, 37

Dīrgha-āgama, 9–10, 12–13, 19, 28–29, 45–46
dukkha, 7

E

Edwards, Paul, 56n130, 58n135
Egyptian Book of the Dead, 68
Ekanyake, Purnima, 111
Ekottarika-āgama, 10, 18–20
Elawar, Rabih, 93–94

F

fatalism, 57
feeling, 7, 10, 11
Fenwick, P., 73–74, 76n189
form, 10. *See also* name-and-form
four noble truths, 30, 38, 39, 128
Frañcis of Assisi, St., 108
Fronsdal, Gil, 38n80

G

gandhabba, 3n3, 15
Girimānanda-sutta, 128, 151–54, 158, 161, 164
Gnanarama, P., 42n89
Gregory the Great (Pope Saint Gregory I), 69
Greyson, Bruce, 78n194, 79n196
Griffiths, Paul J., 12n23, 27n54
Gunasekera, Subashini, 101–2
Gupta, Gopal, 94–95

H

Haidar, Mounzer, 93
Hancharoen, Som Pit, 110
Harper, Donald, 55n126
hell, 69, 90, 107n278
Hettiaratchi, Sivanthie and Sheromie, 112

I

identity
  continuity of a sense of, 19
  motif of mistaken, 70–71
ignorance, 7, 8, 22, 35
intention, 11
intermediate existence, 20–22, 35
Inthanu, Pratomwan, 81
Ishwara, Indika, 92

J

Jayakody, Iranga, 101
Jayaratne, Sujith Lakmal, 100–101
Jayasena, Gamini, 91–92
Jayatilleke, K. N., 24n47, 29nn61–62, 59n138, 60n141
Jayewardena, J. R., 121, 123
Jesus, 71, 108
  resurrection, 68–69
  See also stigmata
Johnson, M. K., 83n206

K

Kālāma-sutta, 31, 32
Kapoor, Bishen Chand, 103–4
karma, 26
  arguments against, 51–53
  attempt to verify the workings of, 58
  Buddha and, 20, 57n132, 60n141
  China and, 50–53, 50n107
  early Buddhist notion of, 35, 56–58, 60n141, 128
  fruition and results of, 23–27, 30, 35, 44, 58, 107, 163; collective guilt and, 52–53
  inability to empirically prove or disprove, 35, 58, 59
  meaning of the term, 23
  misinterpretations of, 56–59, 60n141; blaming the one who suffers, 56–57; identifying karma as volition, 57
  monocausality and, 23–25, 35, 57
  nature of, 57–58, 57n130
  as nondeterministic, 24, 27, 35, 107, 128, 163
  notself and, 44
  rebirth and, 35, 57, 107
  right view and, 27, 30
  suffering and, 24n47, 53n115, 56–57, 60n141
  volition and, 9, 11, 22–24, 35, 37, 57
Kassapa, 46–47, 158n440
Katz, Bob, 124–25

Khuddakapāṭha, 37, 129n331, 137, 139–41, 152, 167n452, 226n815
Kılıc, Erkan, 94
Kose, Yusuf, 109
Kumārakassapa, 45, 47–48

L

Langer, Rita, 162n447
Lazarus, resurrection of, 68–69
Leininger, James, 104
liberating teachings, Buddha's, 29
liberation (*vimutti*), 32, 34, 34n78
life after death, 60nn141–42
Long, Jeffrey, 73n176
Lucas, Winafred Blake, 86n216

M

Madhyama-āgama, 14, 16–17, 21, 32, 40, 149, 151n412, 157
Mahākammavibhaṅga-sutta, 25, 27, 58
Mahānidāna-sutta, 9, 12, 58, 127, 133, 150
Mahāsatipaṭṭhāna-sutta, 128, 131, 132, 148–50, 157
  Dīgha-nikāya and, 137
  instructions for contemplating the hindrance of "doubt" in, 134
  instructions for contemplation of feeling in, 148–50
  loss of text (omissions), 148–50
  reference to "brain" in listings of anatomical parts of body, 151–52, 154
  Mahātaṇhāsaṅkhaya-sutta, 33, 44
  Majjhima-nikāya, 67
  materialist position, 30, 59n139, 62
  in Chinese circles, 51
  experiments to prove the, 45–48
  rebirth and, 28–30, 47, 59n139
Matlock, James G., 92n234
McClenon, James, 55n122
memory
  continuity of, 17, 35
  the workings and shortcomings of, 81–83 (*see also under* Pāli xenoglossy)
Meserve, R. J., 61n144
Milindapañha, 48–49, 50n106
Mills, Antonia, 105n269, 105n273
mind and body, 60n142
mind-made body, 15, 67
misattribution, 81
Mishra, Swarnlata, 113–14, 121
mistaken identity, motif of, 70–71
momentariness, 12
monocausality and karma, 23–25, 35, 57
Moody, Raymond A., 71n169
Murphey, Bridey, 85
my-side bias, 1–2, 60–62
Myo, Ma Tin Aung, 98, 111n292, 120
Myth of Er, 68

N

Nāgasena, 48–50, 53–54
name, 10–11, 22
name-and-form, 13–14
  reciprocal conditioning of consciousness and, 9–13, 17, 22–23, 34, 58, 127
near-death experiences (NDEs), 66, 164
  from ancient to contemporary reports of, 67–71
  the case of Pam Reynolds, 72–74
  of children and the blind, 77–80
  contrasting with person's expectations and beliefs, 71
  verified information apparently obtained during, 74–77
New Testament, 68–69, 113
Nibbāna (nirvana), 21n41
Nimi, King, 67
nonreturners, 19n37, 20–22, 34
Norman, K. R., 38n81, 44n94
notself (*anattā*)
  definition and nature of, 128
  early Buddhist doctrine of, 11–12, 49, 50, 128
  rebirth and, 12n23, 18, 50, 58

O

old age, 7, 9, 16, 150
out-of-body experiences (OBEs) during near-death experiences, 78n194, 79n196. *See also* near-death experiences: verified information apparently obtained during

P

Pāli xenoglossy, case study in, 119
the case history, 119; past-life story and verification of recordings, 122–25; personal contacts, 119–20; present-life story, 120–22
the chanted texts, 127–29
errors and variants, 129–30; major variants, 144–48, 160–61; memory errors, 130–36; minor variants, 136–44, 160
omissions and additions: the brain in the listing of anatomical parts, 151–54; the *devas'* acclaim of Buddha's first sermon, 154–62; loss of text, 148–51
textual memory, 126–27
transmission of the Pāli canon, 125–26
See also Dhammaruwan
paramnesia, 99–100
Parnia, Sam, 73–74
Pasricha, Satwant K., 96n245
past-life memories, children's, 89–91
birthmarks and birth defects, 93n237, 105, 106, 108–12
cases documented before verification attempts, 99–107
parents' negative reactions to, 105–6
specific information recalled and behavioral continuities, 91–99 (*see also under* continuity)
superstitions related to, 106n274
past-life regression, 80–81
therapeutic benefits, 83–84
verified information apparently obtained from, 85–89
and the workings of memory, 81–83
past lives, 80
recollection of, 18–19
paṭicca samuppāda. *See* dependent arising
Paul the Apostle, 69
Pāyāsi, 45, 47–48, 51
Pāyāsi-sutta, 28n2, 45–47
perception, 10–11
Perry, P., 73n176
Plato, 68
possession, 115–16
Prema, Shamlinie, 97–98
Premasiri, P. D., 29n62, 34n78
Promsin, Bongkuch, 96
Pure Abodes, 19, 21, 21n41, 34, 157n435

R

Ramster, Peter, 88n225
Rawat, Kirti Swaroop, 106n274
realization, direct, 34, 37
rebirth, 19, 31, 50, 163
consequences of believing vs. not believing in, 31
underlying tendencies and, 15–17
rebirth doctrine
arguments against, in Early Imperial China, 51–53
Buddhist, 37, 54, 60n140, 62; dependent arising and, 9; doctrine of not-self and, 12n23; early, 5, 9, 12n23, 27, 29, 34, 35, 44, 60n141, 163; rejection of, 54
Chinese and, 50, 53
debates on, in modern times, 56–62
debating, in ancient India, 44–50
defending the, 45, 53–54
denial of, 28–30
misinterpretations of, 56–60
misunderstandings of ancient Indian teaching on, 44–45
Thai monks who rejected, 3n4
reciprocal conditioning of consciousness and name-and-form, 9–14, 17, 22–23, 34, 58, 127
regression therapy. *See* past-life regression
reincarnation. *See* rebirth
religious doctrine, experimental testing of, 47
responsibility, karma and, 57
Reynolds, Pam, 72–73
right view, 35, 38, 134
definitions, 30
karma and, 25–27
significance of, 27–34
speculative views and, 37–39
types of, 30–32, 30n65

Rivas, T., 106n274
Rogo, D. Scott, 114n300

S

Sabbāsava-sutta, 32–33
Sabom, Michael, 72–73nn174–175
Saddhatissa, Hammalawa, 158n439
Samādhikusala, Bhikkhu. *See* Dhammaruwan
Samarasinghe, Disna, 92
Samioğlu, Mehmet, 110
saṃsāra, 16, 30n65, 84
Samuel, Geoffrey, 90n228
Saṃyukta-āgama, 7–8, 15–16, 39, 43, 157
Saṃyutta-nikāya, 8, 10, 14–16, 23, 42, 43
Sartori, Penny, 76n189
Seidel, Anna, 56n127
self. *See* identity
Shah, Nasruddin, 105
Silva, Ruby Kusuma, 98
Silva, Thusitha, 101
Singh, Toran, 111
Sint, Ma Than Than, 93
Skilling, Peter, 152n421, 158n440, 159n441
soul, 41
Spanos, Nicholas P., 85n214
speculation and direct knowledge, 32–34
speculative views. *See under* Buddha: undeclared questions
spirit possession, 115–16
Stanovich, K. E., 61n144
Stevenson, Ian, 117, 121
  on beliefs about rebirth and reactions to hearing past-life memories, 106
  on birthmarks and defects, 108, 112n294
  cases reported by, 81, 90–105, 108–17, 124, 164n448
  on past-life memories, 64n209
  on past lives, 107n279
  on reincarnation, 57n131, 164n448
  on spirit possession, 115–16
  on stigmata, 108n283, 112n294
  on suicide, 107n278
  on suppression of reincarnation cases, 105, 105n270, 106n274
stigmata, 108, 112
Story, Francis, 32n70, 59–60nn139–140
suffering, 7
  causes of, 24n47, 57
  dukkha and, 7
  karma and, 24n47, 53n115, 56–57, 60n141
suggestibility, 81
Sutta-nipāta, 37, 137, 139–41, 167n452, 226n815

T

Tarazi, Linda, 87–88nn220–222, 88
Tathāgata, 40–44
Teiser, Stephen F., 50n107, 53n116
textual memory, 126–27
Thein, Maung Myo Min, 111–12
Thompson, Evan, 73n175
Tibetan Book of the Dead, 68
Tibetan Buddhism, 90
Toplak, M. E., 61n144
transience (memory), 81
transition from one life to another, 14, 19, 20, 22, 23, 26, 35, 44, 47
twelve-link model, 7–9

U

unchanging agent
  continuity without an, 11, 18, 45, 48–50
  rebirth without an, 37
underlying tendencies, rebirth and, 15–17

V

Verma, Kumkum, 102
Vibhaṅga, 8–9, 156
volition, 7, 22–23
  karma and, 9, 11, 22–24, 35, 37, 57

W

Wambach, Helen, 86–87nn218–219
West, Richard F., 61n144
Wilson, Ian, 85n211
Wilsson, Martin, 58n136, 105n270
Woerlee, G. M., 72n175
Wongsombat, Ratana, 96–97, 121
Woods, Kellye, 84n208

X

xenoglossy, 113
  defined, 113
  recitative, 113–14
  responsive, 114–16
  See also Pāli xenoglossy

Y

Yü, Ying-shih, 50n107
Yün-Hua, Jan, 53n116

Z

Zaleski, Carol, 71n168
Zeytun, Süleyman, 95
Zürcher, Erik, 50n108, 52n115

About the Author

BORN IN 1962 in Germany, Bhikkhu Anālayo was ordained in 1995 in Sri Lanka, where he completed a PhD on the *Satipaṭṭhāna-sutta* in 2000. He next completed a habilitation research in Germany in 2007, in which he compared the *Majjhima-nikāya* discourses with their Chinese, Buddhist Hybrid Sanskrit and Tibetan counterparts. Bhikkhu Anālayo's main research area is early Buddhism, with a particular focus on the topics of the Chinese *Āgama*s, Buddhist meditation, and women in Buddhism. Besides his academic pursuits, he regularly teaches meditation. He presently resides at the Barre Center for Buddhist Studies in Massachusetts, where he spends most of his time in silent meditation retreat.

What to Read Next by Bhikkhu Anālayo from Wisdom Publications

Superiority Conceit in Buddhist Traditions
A Historical Perspective

"This book is a courageous call for integrity and self-reflection. Bhikkhu Anālayo argues that if Buddhism is to engage the modern world with any enduring success, it must abandon its own conceit and reckon with its internal prejudices. This book is a much-needed contribution that will help reshape the direction of the field." —Vanessa Sasson, professor, Marianopolis College

Early Buddhist Oral Tradition
Textual Formation and Transmission

In-depth but still accessible, *Early Buddhist Oral Tradition* is an engrossing and enlightening inquiry into the early Buddhist oral tradition.

Daughters of the Buddha
Teachings by Ancient Indian Women

"Beyond merely recounting their life stories here, this group of translations gives testimony to these early women's abilities, agency, and important—and even singular—contributions to what we know of today as Buddhist Dharma." —Jan Willis, PhD, author of *Dreaming Me: Black, Baptist, and Buddhist*

The Signless and the Deathless
On the Realization of Nirvana

"Venerable Anālayo skillfully illuminates how some of the earliest Buddhist texts provide a systematic path for engaging with and experiencing the world in its pure essence, free from the defilements that cause so much suffering. He then takes us one step further to show how this clear perception, once applied and stable, recognizes Nirvana for what it truly is: empty or deathless. An essential read for students of the Buddhadharma." —Yongey Mingyur Rinpoche

Abiding in Emptiness
A Guide for Meditative Practice

"The venerable Bhikkhu Anālayo brings his meticulous scholarship and his deep meditative experience to bear in this beautiful volume that explains how emptiness is understood in early Buddhist traditions, and how to use this understanding in one's meditative practice. The union of exposition and meditative advice is powerful and is presented with perfect clarity." —Jay Garfield, Doris Silbert Professor in the Humanities and Professor of Philosophy and Buddhist Studies, Smith College and the Harvard Divinity School

About Wisdom Publications

Wisdom Publications is the leading publisher of classic and contemporary Buddhist books and practical works on mindfulness. To learn more about us or to explore our other books, please visit our website at wisdom.org or contact us at the address below.

Wisdom Publications
132 Perry Street
New York, NY 10014 USA

We are a 501(c)(3) organization, and donations in support of our mission are tax deductible.

Wisdom Publications is affiliated with the Foundation for the Preservation of the Mahayana Tradition (FPMT).